INTERNATIONAL CONFERENCE ON RHEOLOGY AND SOIL MECHANICS

Proceedings of the International Conference on Rheology and Soil Mechanics—held in Coventry, UK, 12–16 September 1988

INTERNATIONAL CONFERENCE ON RHEOLOGY AND SOIL MECHANICS

Edited by

M. J. KEEDWELL

Coventry Polytechnic,
Coventry, UK

ELSEVIER APPLIED SCIENCE
LONDON and NEW YORK

ELSEVIER APPLIED SCIENCE PUBLISHERS LTD
Crown House, Linton Road, Barking, Essex IG11 8JU, England

Sole Distributor in the USA and Canada
ELSEVIER SCIENCE PUBLISHING CO., INC.
52 Vanderbilt Avenue, New York, NY 10017, USA

WITH 26 TABLES AND 215 ILLUSTRATIONS

British Library Cataloguing in Publication Data

International Conference on Rheology and Soil Mechanics
(*1988: Coventry, England*). International conference on
rheology and soil mechanics.
1. Soil Mechanics
I. Title II. Keedwell, M. J.
624.1′5136

Library of Congress Cataloging in Publication Data

International Conference on Rheology and Soil Mechanics
(1988: Coventry, England)
International Conference on Rheology and Soil
Mechanics.

Proceedings of the International Conference on
Rheology and Soil Mechanics, held at Coventry, England,
12–16 September 1988.
Bibliography: p.
1. Soil mechanics—Congresses. 2. Rheology—
Congresses. I. Keedwell, M. J. II. Title.
TA710.A1I477 1988 624.1′5136 88-21356

ISBN 1-85166-273-1

Printed in Great Britain by Galliard (Printers) Ltd, Great Yarmouth

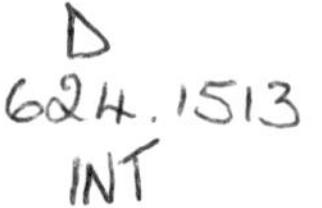

PREFACE

The last major International Conference on Rheology and Soil Mechanics took place in 1964. Since then considerable progress has been made in defining time-independent rheological models for soil following the pioneering work of Professor Roscoe and his colleagues and disciples. Many rheological problems, however, require a time-dependent rheological model for their understanding and solution. Consequently a conference was planned at Coventry Polytechnic, Coventry, England, from 12–16 September 1988 to provide a forum for discussion and exchange of views between researchers and designers on topics related to the rheology of soils; rheology being defined at the conference as 'the study of the time-dependent deformation and flow of matter'. More than twenty-four contributions were offered from thirteen countries. These papers are published in this volume of Proceedings. In addition experts in the field were invited to deliver review papers and some authors offered software for the computer session. Unfortunately a few contributions did not arrive in time and have not been included.

I would like to thank all the authors for their contributions and all those who have worked hard to organise and promote the conference. In the latter category I wish particularly to thank Chris Browne of the Coventry Consortium and the following members of the Organising and Technical Committees.

Professor T. Adachi
Kyoto University
Kyoto
Japan

Dr J. B. Carter
University of Sydney
Sydney
Australia

Mr K. Davis
Coventry Polytechnic
Coventry
UK

Mr P. R. Dimmer
Coventry Polytechnic
Coventry
UK

Dr E. Juarez-Badillo
Tepanco 32
04030—Mexico D F
Mexico

Professor W. D. Liam Finn
University of British Columbia
Vancouver
Canada

Dr R. Y. K. Liang
University of Akron
Akron
USA

Dr G. N. Pande
University of Wales
Swansea
UK

Dr D. J. Petty
University of Warwick
Coventry
UK

Professor S. S. Vyalov
USSR Academy of Science
Moscow
USSR

M. J. KEEDWELL

CONTENTS

LIST OF CONTRIBUTORS

T. Adachi
Department of Transportation Engineering, Kyoto University, Sakyo-ku, Yoshida, 601 Kyoto, Japan

D. M. Akhpatelov
Moscow Institute of Civil Engineering (MICE), Moscow, USSR

W. F. Anderson
Department of Civil and Structural Engineering, The University, Mappin Street, Sheffield S1 3JD, UK

G. Austin
Johnson, Poole & Bloomer, Consulting Engineers, West Midlands, UK

A. A. Bartolomey
Perm Polytechnic Institute, Komsomolsky Prospekt 22-a, Perm 614000, USSR

S. F. Brown
Department of Civil Engineering, University of Nottingham, Nottingham, UK

N. S. Chetyrkin
Research Institute of Bases and Underground Structures, Gosstroy USSR, Pushkinskaya Str. 26, 103828 Moscow, USSR

N. N. Fotiyeva
Tula Polytechnical Institute, Pr Lenina 92, 300600 Tula, USSR

T. Germanov
University of Architecture and Civil Engineering, 1421 Sofia, Bulgaria

S. G. Hairoyan
Institute 'Gidroproyekt', Yerevan, USSR

F. Haji-Ali
Department of Civil and Structural Engineering, University of Malaya, Kuala Lumpur 22-11, Malaysia

P-Y. Hicher
Laboratoire de Mécanique des Sols-Structures, CNRS, UA 850, 92290 Chatenay-Malabry, France

K. HIRAO
Department of Civil Engineering, Nishinippon Institute of Technology, Kanda 1633, Fukuoka-ken 800-03, Japan

H-S. HSIEH
Moh and Associates, Taipei, Taiwan

P. JAŘVENMÄKI
Helsinki University of Technology, Rakentajanaukio 4A, 02150 Espoo, Finland

V. N. KALIAKIN
Solid Mechanics Division, Sandi National Laboratory, Livermore, CA 94550, USA

E. KAVAZANJIAN, JR
Parsons Brinckerhoff Quade & Douglas Inc., One Penn Plaza, New York, NY 10119, USA

M. J. KEEDWELL
Department of Civil Engineering and Building, Coventry Polytechnic, Priory Street, Coventry CV1 5FB, UK

L. N. KHRUSTALYOV
The USSR NCSMFE, Gosstroy USSR, Pushkinskaya Str. 26, Moscow 103828, USSR

K-H. KORHONEN
Helsinki University of Technology, Rakentajanaukio 4A, 02150 Espoo, Finland

M. LOJANDER
Helsinki University of Technology, Rakentajanaukio 4A, 02150 Espoo, Finland

C. A. MEJIA
Department of Civil Engineering, University of British Columbia, 2324 Main Mall, Vancouver, British Columbia, Canada V6T 1W5

S. R. MESCHYAN
Academy of Sciences of the Armenian SSR, Yerevan, USSR

M. MIMURA
Disaster Prevention Research Institute, Kyoto University, Gokasho, Uji, Kyoto 611, Japan

U. S. MIRENBURG
The USSR NCSMFE, Gosstroy USSR, Pushkinskaya Str. 26, Moscow 103828, USSR

G. MURTAZA
Department of Civil Engineering, AMU, Aligarh, India

A. A. Mustafayev
Department of Civil Engineering, Azerbaidjan Civil Engineering Institute, Krivola St 13, Baku 370073, USSR

D. Negussey
Golder Associates, 224 West 8th Avenue, Vancouver, British Columbia, Canada V5Y 1N5

F. Oka
Department of Civil Engineering, Gifu University, Yanagido 1-1, Gifu 501-11, Japan

I. M. Omelchak
Perm Polytechnic Institute, Komsomolsky Prospekt 29-a, Perm 614000, USSR

M. P. O'Reilly
Arup Geotechnics, 13 Fitzroy Street, London W1P 6BQ, UK

L. S. Pang
Scott Wilson Kirkpatrick and Partners, Bayheath House, Rosehill West, Chesterfield, Derbyshire S40 1JF, UK

T. B. Permyakova
Perm Polytechnic Institute, Komsomolsky Prospekt 29-a, Perm 614000, USSR

D. A. Ponniah
Department of Civil Engineering and Building Science, University of Edinburgh, Edinburgh EH9 3JL, UK

S. Prakash
Department of Civil Engineering, University of Missouri Rolla, Rolla, Missouri 65401, USA

I. C. Pyrah
Department of Civil and Structural Engineering, The University, Mappin Street, Sheffield S1 3JD, UK

G. Ranjan
Department of Civil Engineering, University of Roorkee, Roorkee, India

E. Rojas
Instituto de Ingeniería, UNAM, Apdo Postal 70-472, Coyoacán, 04510 Mexico DF, Mexico

A. S. Sammal
Tula Polytechnical Institute, Pr Lenina 92, 300600 Tula, USSR

H. SEKIGUCHI
Disaster Prevention Research Institute, Kyoto University, Gokasho, Uji, Kyoto 611, Japan

T. SHIBATA
Disaster Prevention Research Institute, Kyoto University, Gokasho, Uji, Kyoto 611, Japan

M. E. SLEPAK
Research Institute of Bases and Underground Structures, Gosstroy USSR, Pushkinskaya Str. 26, 103828 Moscow, USSR

Y. TANAKA
Department of Civil Engineering, Kobe University, Nada, Kobe, Japan

K. TANIMOTO
Department of Civil Engineering, Kobe University, Nada, Kobe, Japan

V. K. TSVETKOV
Volgograd Institute of Civil Engineering, Volgograd, USSR

S. UE
Department of Civil Engineering and Architecture, Tokuyama College of Technology, 3538 Takajo, Kume, Tokuyama 745, Japan

Y. P. VAID
Department of Civil Engineering, University of British Columbia, 2324 Main Mall, Vancouver, British Columbia, Canada V6T 1W5

S. P. S. VIRDI
Bilston Community College, Westfield Road, Bilston, UK

S. S. VYALOV
Moscow Civil Engineering Institute, Yaroslavskoye Road 26, 129337 Moscow, USSR

K. YASUHARA
Department of Civil Engineering, Nishinippon Institute of Technology, Kanda 1633, Fukuoka-ken 800-03, Japan

PLATE ANCHOR BEHAVIOUR UNDER LONG TERM LOADING

Dr.D.A.Ponniah
Department of Civil Engineering and Building Science
University of Edinburgh
Edinburgh EH9 3JL
Scotland

ABSTRACT

The paper presents the results of a series of model tests on plate anchors in normally consolidated kaolin, and subjected to long term static and cyclic loading. The tests showed that while there was an increase in anchor capacity from the 'undrained' to the 'drained' states, with further increases in test time to failure a small reduction in capacity was observed. The anchors when subjected to a sustained load were observed to creep with significant movements at loads above about 60 % of the ultimate capacity. Under cyclic loading there were additional displacements associated with pore pressure changes.

INTRODUCTION

As a part of a broader investigation into the behaviour of anchors for the tethering of offshore structures, a series of model tests were conducted on plate anchors in a cohesive soil, in order to examine the time dependent behaviour of the anchors. This was considered necessary because in comparison to anchors used on-shore, on which information is available, the offshore anchors would be expected to be serviceable for longer periods of time in harsher environments and without economically feasible remedial measures.

The three particular aspects of time dependency of the plate anchors investigated were;
i. the effect of the failure load or the ultimate capacity of the anchor,
ii. the effect on the displacement of the anchor subjected to a sustained load,
iii. the effect on the displacement of the anchor subjected to a cyclic load.

SOIL AND ITS PREPARATION

The series of tests on the 50 mm diameter plate anchors were conducted in kaolin which had been anisotropically reconsolidated to 690 kN/m^2 . The choice of the Speswhite kaolin was governed by the availability of the soil in a suitable form for remoulding and with a relatively high permeability had an added advantage of being able to reduce consolidation time.

The naturally occurring Speswhite kaolin used was obtained from Cornwall, and its physical properties were;

specific gravity	2.62	% finer than 2μ	60
activity	0.45	plastic limit	36 %
		liquid limit	63 %

The kaolin, obtained in a powder form, was slurried in a 0.17 cu.m pan mixer with measured quantities of water, with the resultant slurry having a moisture content of 1.75 times the liquid limit, details given in reference 1. The subsequent one-dimensional consolidation of the kaolin slurry to the specified pressure of 690 kN/m^2 was carried out in a cylindrical container, 300 mm in diameter and 600 mm high.

The pressure was applied through bellows at the base of the tank with a thin plate above the bellows to support the weight of the slurry before consolidation was initiated, and to minimise dishing later during the consolidation.

During the consolidation of the slurry, drainage was permitted at the top and bottom, through porous plastic sheets and then to the atmosphere. The consolidation pressures were applied in icrements starting at 20 kN/m^2 and increasing to 86, 172,345 and finally to 690 kN/m^2. Each increment of pressure was maintained till 90% consolidation was achieved.

The in-situ undrained strength of the consolidated kaolin was measured with a 12.7 mm diameter, 19.0 mm high hand operated Pilcon vane. Plugs were provided, at 37.5 mm, 75 mm and 115 mm, from the axis of the anchor, through which the vane tests were conducted. Measurements were made over the entire depth of the samples and in steps of 50 mm with the final measured average shear strength of 180 kN/m^2.

A series of triaxial tests were carried out on 38 mm diameter,76 mm long cylindrical samples, trimmed from the blocks of clay in which the anchors were tested and these relatively simple tests were conducted in order to identify any significant changes in strength as a function of time.

The 38 mm samples were saturated with a back pressure and then consolidated to two different states of stress. In the first state with anisotropic consolidation, the vertical and lateral stresses in the tanks were represented by the axial stress and cell pressure respectively. The lateral stress or cell pressure was estimated with a coefficient of at-rest earth pressure as (1 - Sin ϕ) with ϕ of 23°. The anisotrpy was obtained with an additional load hanger as shown on figure 1. In the second state the sample was isotropically consolidated under a cell pressure equal to the mean normal stress in the tank .

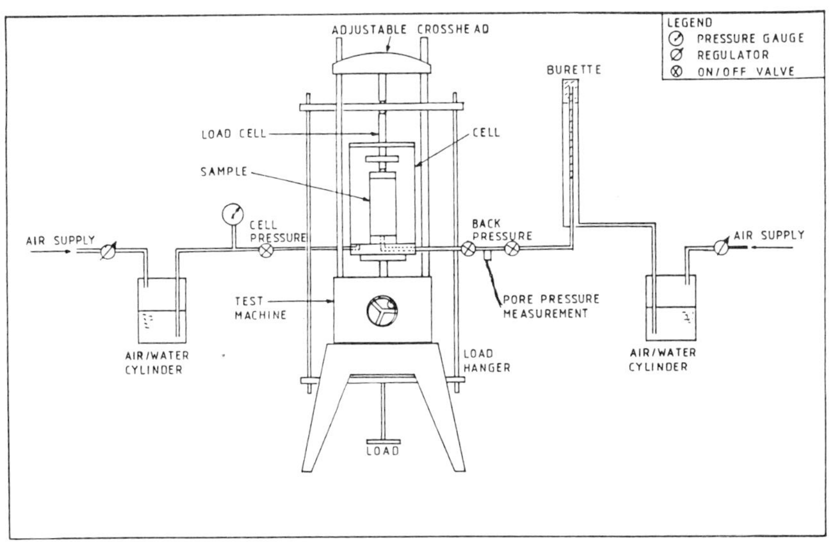

Figure 1. Schematic layout for triaxial test

The duration of the loading to failure was varied between 17 minutes and 19 days and the effect of this duration on the failure deviator stress in the various types is shown on figure 2. Similar percentage decreases in strength were observed by Bjerrum et al [2] and Bishop and Henkel [3]. These changes in strength were not considered to be sufficiently significant for further consideration in the anchor investigation.

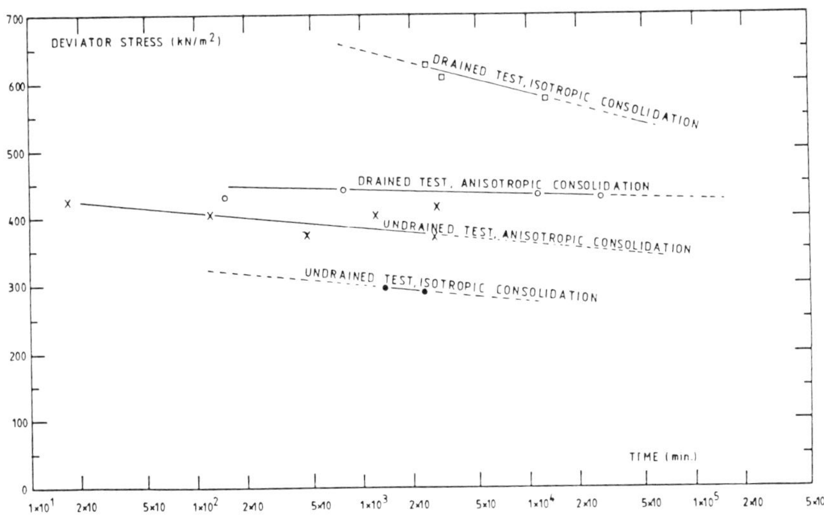

Figure 2. Effect of time on the failure deviator stress

The effective friction angles estimated from all the triaxial tests are summarised on figure 3. Despite the many parameters incorporated in the tests, the friction angles compare well with the failure line corresponding to an angle of 21°.

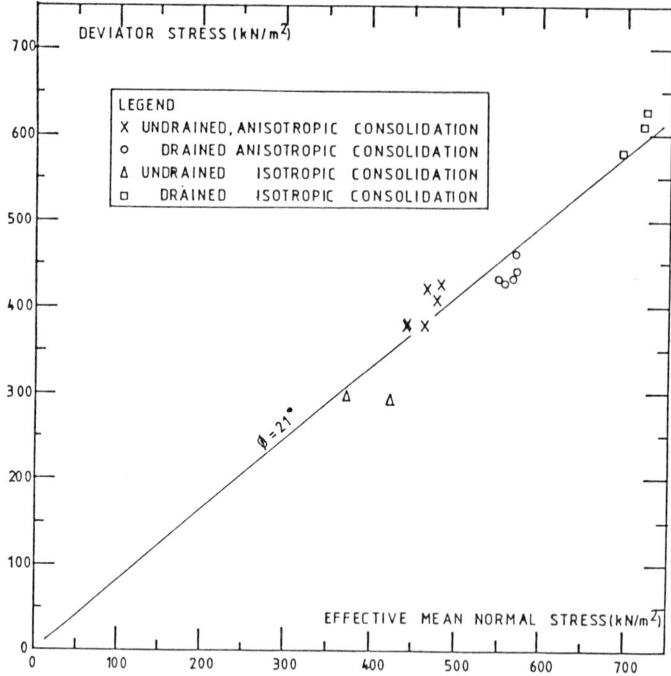

Figure 3. Summary of effective friction angles.

ANCHOR TESTS

The anchors embedded in the consolidated kaolin were subjected to four types of tensile loading, illustrated in figure 4, and were;

(i) displacement controlled
(ii) load controlled
(iii) incremental
(iv) cyclic.

The displacement controlled test, similar to the constant rate of penetration tests on piles, has been widely used to measure the undrained ultimate load capacity of plate anchors, and were conducted at rates, of upto about 0.00081 mm/min.

The increase of load and displacement with time is different for the displacement controlled and load controlled types of loading, and additional load controlled tests were conducted to identify any effect this difference in behaviour may have on the ultimate capacity of the anchor.

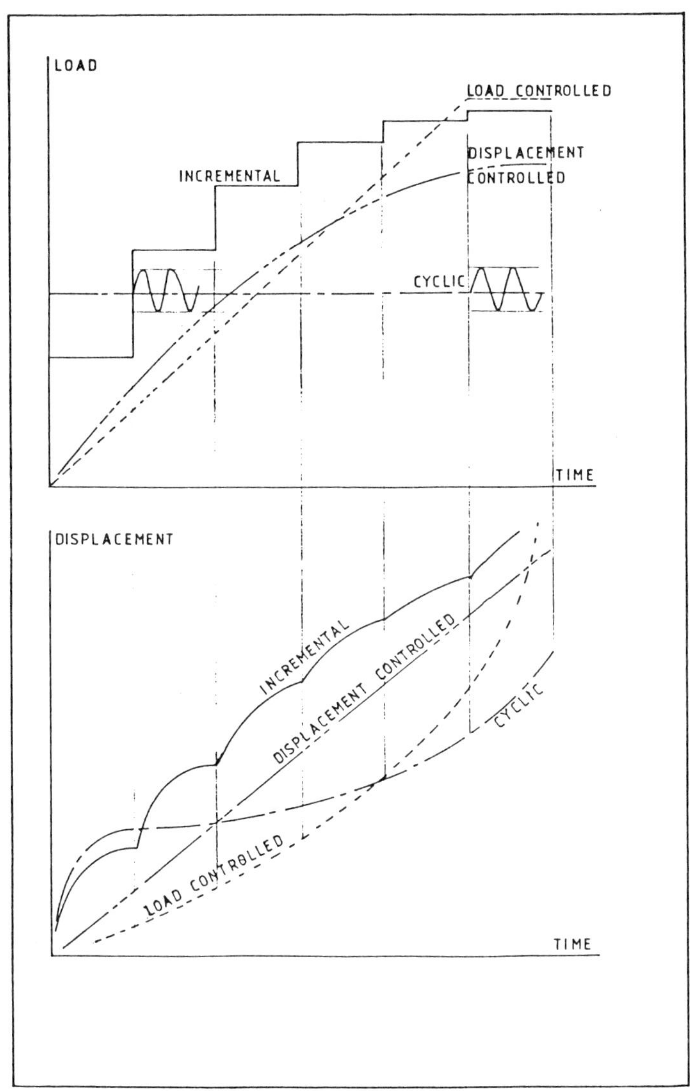

Figure 4. Types of anchor tests.

The third type of loading was included to obtain the drained ultimate capacity under load control. Pore pressure dissipation was permitted by applying increments of loading, with each increment maintained for 24 hours.

The fourth type of loading was included to examine the effect of cycling on the displacements of an anchor in tension.

For the displacement controlled tests, the base of a triaxial testing machine was mounted onto the top of the reaction frame which was made up of three lengths of 100 x 100 mm box sections, and the load was applied to the anchor by an adjustable saddle arrangement consisting of two cross beams connected by two threaded steel rods. The possible range of rates of displacement was 0.00081 to 1.52 mm/min.

The arrangement for the other two static tests, and the cyclic test was different. A pneumatic 150 mm diameter piston, was controlled by a signal generator through a electro-pneumatic converter. The electrical signal generator was capable of four functions, namely, a ramp for a constantly increasing load, and sine, square and triangular waves for cyclic loading.

The electrical signal in turn controlled a electro-pneumatic, e - p, converter which, as the name implies, converts an incoming current change into a proportional pressure change, which in turn caused corresponding changes in the load applied through the pneumatic piston.

The tank, with the anchors in the consolidated soil, was positioned below the reaction frame. Two adjustable props were placed between the tank and the frame and tightened. With the adjustable saddle, the bottom and top cross beams of the load frame were levelled and connected to the anchor shaft through the load cell. The displacement transducers were then fitted to the shaft. After taking a set of zero readings the test was initiated.

During the static and cyclic loading of the anchors, the vertical loads and deflections at the top of the anchor shaft, were measured at two diametrically opposite points on the shaft.

The majority of the load and displacement controlled static tests were completed within four hours, the exact duration depending on the rate of loading. The load controlled tests were terminated when there was a load drop and/or the movements became excessive. The displacement controlled tests were terminated after a displacement of 25 mm, 50 % of the diameter of the anchor.

The drained load controlled tests were conducted with incremental loading, each increment applied for 24 hours.

The cyclic loads were made up of a sinusoidal load superimposed on a mean static load. The mean static load was applied for 24 hours and then followed by the cyclic load.

EFFECT OF TIME ON ULTIMATE CAPACITY

The time to reach failure as affected by the rate of load increase was investigated and was shown to increase initially , upto about 50 minute duration of test, and with further increase in time, these failure pressures decreased, as shown on figure 5.

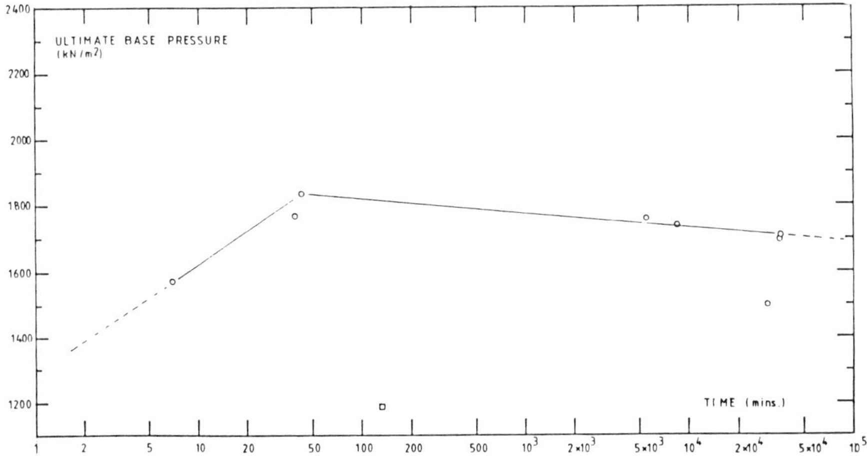

Figure 5. Effect of time on ultimate capacity

The anchors tested to failure in a short time allowed little excess pore pressure dissipation, but with increasing duration to failure the excess pore pressure dissipation would be greater with the resulting stiffening of the soil, giving higher failure base pressures. A maximum of the failure base pressure is reached when most of the excess pore pressures are dissipated. Increasing the failure time further has resulted in a decrease in the failure base pressure, a decrease of about 5 % for a 1000 fold increase in time.

In summary, the effect of the rate of loading was important and increasing the time to failure of upto 50 mins., increased the failure base pressures, and are due to the dissipation of pore pressures. Further increases in time resulted in small reductions in the failure base pressures, and these reductions were not considered to be significant.

DISPLACEMENTS UNDER SUSTAINED LOADING

The anchor creep rates were required to later differentiate between the movements due to creep and those due to cycling of the anchors. These creep rates were estimated from the incremental load control tests.

During the incremental load controlled tests the anchor displacements were monitored as a function of time, for each increment of loading. A plot of these movements with time are shown on figure 6 with two discernible parts, to each load increment.

These two parts are similar to those observed in a laboratory consolidation test, with the anchor displacement in the anchor test being similar to the sample compression in the consolidation test. The first, upto about 30 minutes in the anchor test, is non linear and is associated with primary consolidation. The second part is linear and increasing with log of time, and is due to secondary consolidation or creep of the soil.

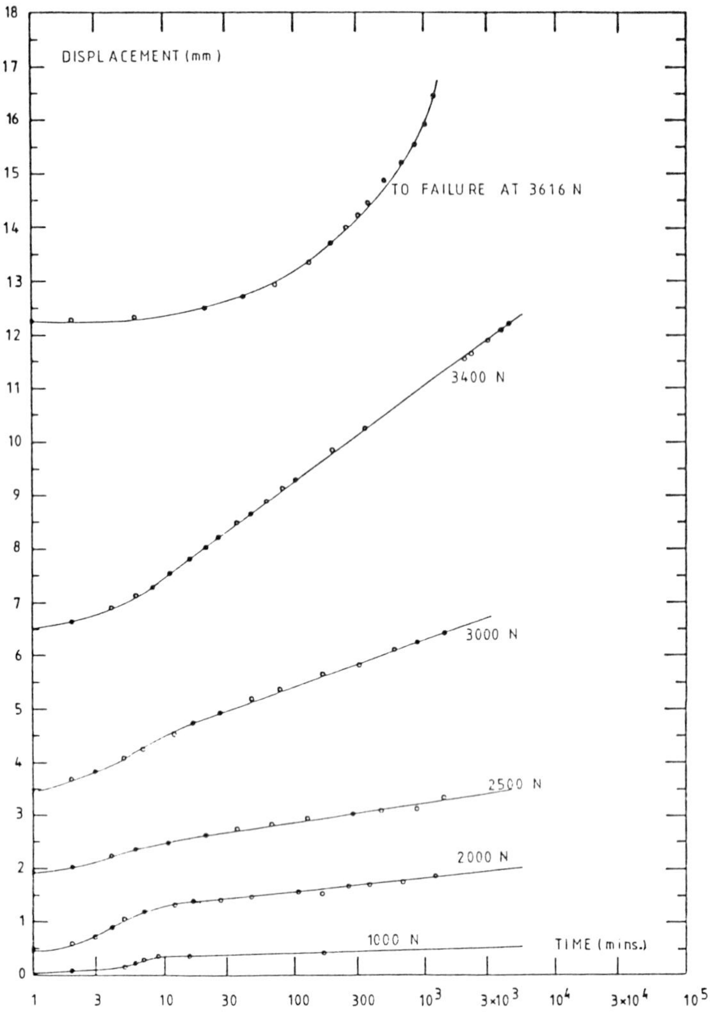

Figure 6. Displacements under sustained loads

From the above, the creep rates are estimated for each increment of loading, expressed as a percentage of the drained capacity of the anchor, and graphically shown on figure 7 for the tests. The creep rate increases with increasing load, and becomes significant above about 60% of the failure load.

CYCLIC ANCHOR TESTS

The effect of the load amplitude, ranging between 5 and 20% of the drained capacity, on the displacements was examined for two mean loads, namely 30% and 50% of the drained capacity of the anchor, and are shown on figure 8 and 9, respectively. The creep displacements corresponding to the peak cyclic stresses are also shown. It would seem that in this figure that the displacements are made up of cyclic and creep components.

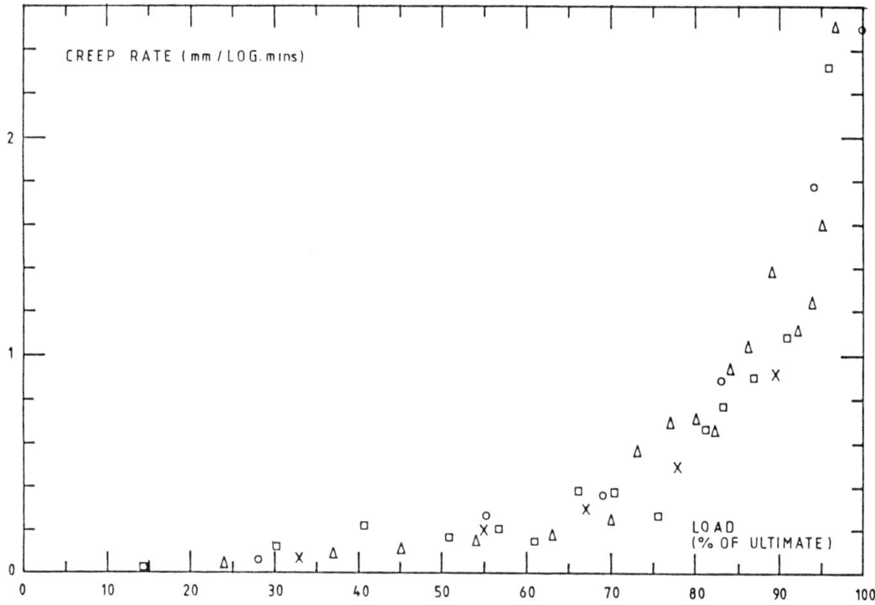

Figure 7. Effect of load on creep rate

There appears to be three parts to this cyclic displacement, and in the absence of other information, the following explanation is proposed for these tests. In the first part upto about a 1000 cycles, the displacements are due to the consolidation of the surrounding soil caused by the extra loading of the amplitude. As such the magnitude of this displacement is governed by the amplitude, and seen on figures 8 and 9.

In the second part, equilibrium is reached between the build up of excess pore pressure caused by external loads and the dissipation of this pore pressure into the sorrounding soil, within each cycle of loading. Associated with this dissipation per cycle, are small consolidation displacements which over a period of time add up to give the displacement-time relationship. These part two displacements seem less dependent on the mean load, than on the amplitude.

The third part to the displacement occurs only when failure is reached , where the build up of excess pore pressure in a cycle of load is greater than the dissipation, and hence with each application of load cycle the excess pore pressures are increased and the effective stresses decreased till failure occurs. In figure 9 , the level of loading to failure was 50 + 20% with failure occurring after 40,000 cycles.

In summary, the displacements during the cyclic loading of an anchor are due to the build-up and dissipation of pore pressures, and anchor failure occurs if the build-up of pore pressure is greater than the dissipation, within each load cycle.

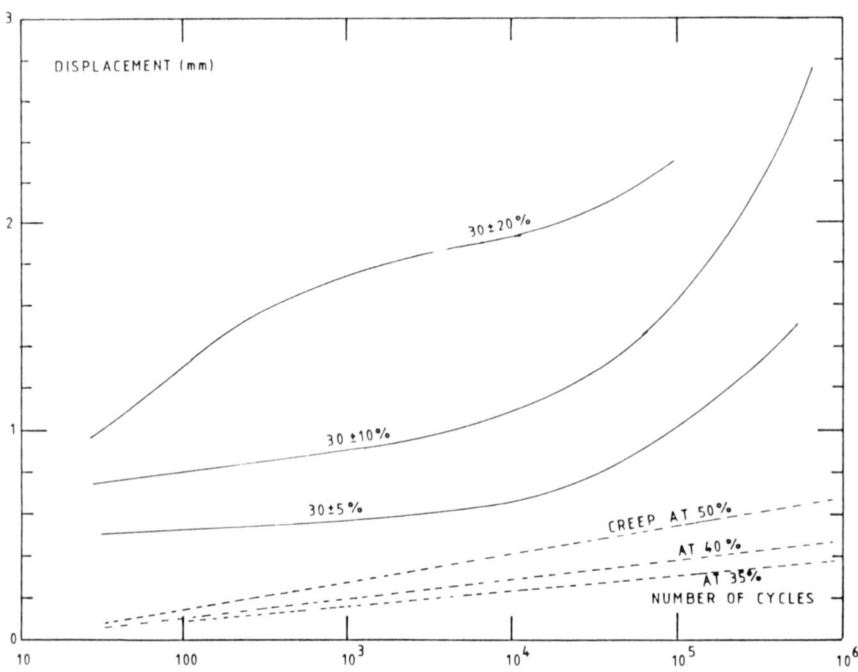

Figure 8. Effect of cycling at 30 % mean load.

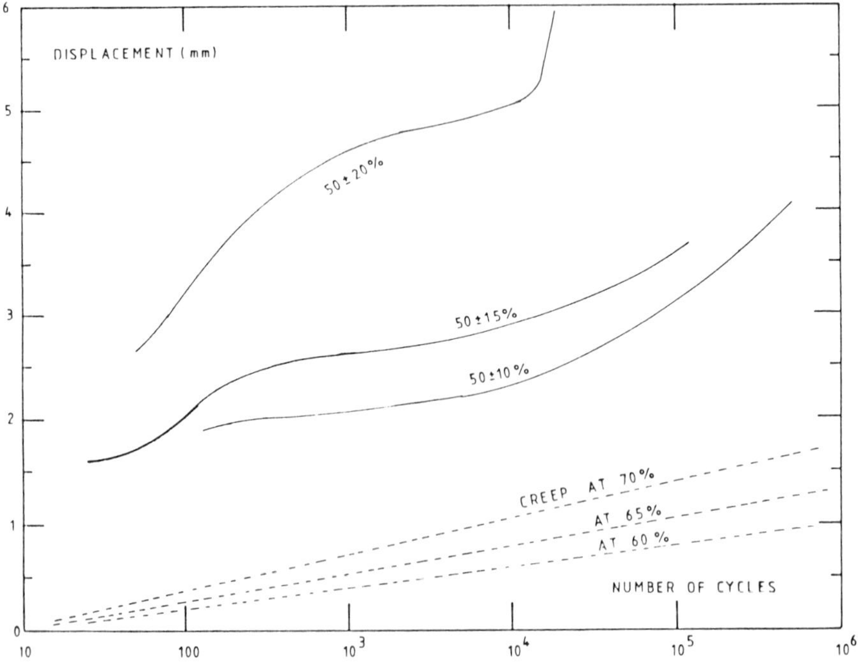

Figure 9. Effect of cycling at 50 % mean load.

ACKNOWLEDGEMENTS

This work was carried out in the Department of Civil Engineering of the University of Glasgow, as a part of a research programme financed by the Marine Technology Directorate of the SERC.

REFERENCES

1. Ponniah.D.A., Behaviour of plate anchors in cohesive soils under static and cyclic loads. Ph.D. Thesis, University of Glasgow, 1984.

2. Bjerrum.L., Simons.N.,Tarblaa.I., The effect of time on the shear strength of a soft marine clay. Proceedings of the Brussels Conference on Earth Pressure Problems, Vol. 1, 1958, pp 148 - 158.

3. Bishop.A.W., Henkel.D.J., The measurement of soil properties in triaxial test. Arnold, London, 1964.

ELASTO-VISCOPLASTIC CONSTITUTIVE MODELS FOR CLAYS

F.OKA
Associate Professor, Department of Civil Engng.
Gifu University,Yanagido 1-1 Gifu 501-11,Japan

T.Adachi
Professor, Department of Transportation Engng.
Kyoto University,Sakyo-ku Yoshida 601 Kyoto Japan

M.Mimura
Research Associate, Disaster Prevention Research
Institute of Kyoto University,Uji 611 Kyoto Japan

ABSTRACT

This paper is concerned with elasto-viscoplastic constitutive models for normally- and over-consolidated clays. For normally consolidated clay, the elasto-viscoplastic constituive model was developed based on the Cam-clay model and generalized Perzyna's type elasto-viscoplasticity theory. As for overconsolidated clay, an elasto-viscoplastic model was derived using the non-associated flow rule and Perzyna's type viscoplasticity theory.

INTRODUCTION

It is widely accepted that clay shows rate sensitive properties during the deformation process. Many constitutive models have been developed for describing time-dependent and rate-sensitive behaviors of saturated normally consolidated clay. A large number of studies on time-dependent behavior of clay are reported in the state of the art report by (Sekiguchi (1)). As for the viscoplastic constitutive model, overstress model based on the Perzyna's viscoplasticity theory(2)(Adachi and Okano (3),Oka (4),Adachi and Oka(5),Dafalias(6),Kantona(7),Adachi,Oka and Mimura(8)) and non-stationary flow surface model(Sekiguchi (9),Nova (10), Matsui and Abe(11)) are representative. Adachi and Okano(3) was the first to try to develop a constitutive model of clay based on Perzyna's viscoplastic theory and Cam-clay model(12). Based on the experimental findings of strain rate effects on the deformation behaviour of normally consolidated clay, Adachi and Oka(5) extended the first model such that the constitutive model was able to describe not only such time-dependent behaviour as creep, strain rate effect but also secondary compression, and they confirmed the effectiveness of the proposed model.

It has been found that the overstress model is applicable for normally consolidated clays, however, this model has a defect. Overstress model cannot describe the accelerating creep behaviour except in the case that the static stress-strain curve is a strain hardening-softening one(Oka(13)). On the other hand, non-stationary flow surafce theory can effective for simulating the acceleration creep phenomena(Sekiguchi(9)). Adachi et al. (8) pointed out that this problem can be solved by considering a stress-ratio dependency of the viscoplastic parameter and proposed a modified model considering a variation of viscoplastic parameter. Aubry et al.(14) proposed the modified overstress model introducing the damage creep law to explain the creep failure of normally consolidated clay. Perzyna(15) modified his original viscoplasticity theory to take into account a strain rate effect on the instability of plastic flow using the new material function.

In this paper, in order to overcome this defect concerened with the acceleration creep behavior, introducing a new material function and an internal variable we have modified the overstress model proposed by Adachi and Oka(5). We used a new material function which is a variant of Perzyna's one to develop an elastic-viscoplastic constitutive model for describing the failure of clays within the framework of the theory of internal variables. The proposed model includes Aubry's model(14) and was numerically and experimentally confirmed for undrained triaxial tests. The part of the modified theory for isotropically consolidated clay was first presented by authors (Adachi,Oka,Mimura (16)). The present paper deals with both isotropically and anisotropically consolidated clays.

Recently, it has been emphasized on the effect of overconsolidation of clay deposits due to several reasons. For overconsolidated clay, we have also proposed an elasto-viscoplastic consitutive model based on the non-associated flow rule and Perzyna's type viscoplasticity theory.

CONSTITUTIVE EQUATION FOR NORMALLY CONSOLIDATED CLAY

According to the Adachi and Oka(5)and Oka(4), static stress strain relation is assumed to be given by Original cam-clay model(Roscoe et al.(12)).Static yield function is expressed by

$$F=\frac{f-\kappa_s}{\kappa_s}=0 \tag{1}$$

where κ_s is a strain hardening parameter and f is a dynamic yield function.

hardening equation are expressed by

$$f_s=\sqrt{2J_2}/(M^* \sigma'_m)+\ln(\sigma'_m/\sigma'_{m0})=\kappa_s \tag{2}$$

$$\kappa_s=\ln(\sigma'_m/\sigma'_{m0}) \tag{3}$$

$$v^p=\frac{\lambda-\kappa}{1+e}\ln(\sigma'_{my}/\sigma'_{myi}) \tag{4}$$

in which, v^p is the volumetric plastic strain, σ'_{my} is the static hardening prameter, J_2 is the second invariant of deviatoric stress tensor, σ'_m is the mean effective stress, M^* is the value of $\sqrt{2J_2}/\sigma'_m$ at critical state, σ'_{m0} is the unit value of σ'_m, e is the void ratio, λ is the consolidation index and κ is the swelling index.

We postulate a following flow rule for viscoplastic strain rate tensor.

$$\dot{\varepsilon}_{ij}^{vp}=\Phi_2(\xi)\langle\Phi_1(F)\rangle\frac{\partial f}{\partial\sigma_{ij}} \tag{5}$$

In which, σ_{ij} is the stress tensor, ξ is an internal variable and Φ_1 and Φ_2 are the first and the second material functions respectively.

In Eq.(5), the symbol is defined as,

$$\langle\Phi_1(F)\rangle=\Phi_1(F) \quad ; \quad F>0 \tag{6}$$
$$= 0 \quad ; \quad F<0$$

The reason why we introduce the second material function and a scaler internal variable ξ in the flow rule is that they control the failure phenomena during the deformation process.

From Eq.(5), we have

$$f(\sigma_{ij},\varepsilon_{ij}^{vp}) \tag{7}$$
$$=\kappa_s(\varepsilon_{ij}^{vp})(1+\langle\Phi_1^{-1}[\frac{\sqrt{I_2}}{\Phi_2(\xi)}(\frac{\partial f}{\partial\sigma_{ij}}\frac{\partial f}{\partial\sigma_{ij}})^{1/2}]\rangle)$$

where I_2 is the second invariant of viscoplastic strain rate tensor as expressed by

$$I_2=\dot{\varepsilon}_{ij}^{vp}\dot{\varepsilon}_{ij}^{vp} \tag{8}$$

In Eq.(7), we assumed

$$\langle\Phi_1^{-1}(X)\rangle=\Phi_1^{-1}(X) \quad ;X>0 \tag{9}$$
$$= 0 \quad ;X=0$$

As pointed out by Aubry et al.(14), strain rate has little effect on the stress ratio at the critical state. In other words, failure condition does not depend on the strain rate. Considering this experimental findings, we can postulate an evolution equation of ξ and a general form of second material function as follows:

$$\dot{\xi}=f_0(\xi,\sigma_{ij},\varepsilon_{ij}{}^{vp})+f_{1kl}(\xi,\sigma_{ij},\varepsilon_{ij}{}^{vp})\dot{\sigma}_{kl}$$
$$+f_{2kl}(\xi,\sigma_{ij},\varepsilon_{ij}{}^{vp})\dot{\varepsilon}_{kl}{}^{vp} \qquad (10)$$

About the second material function Φ_2, it is required that Φ_2 becomes infinite in the limit of $\xi\to\infty$ and ξ is positive , because strain rate dependency vanishes when the stress state reaches the failure state or critical state.

The evolution equation Eq.(10) includes the damage law that has been used by Aubry at al.(14) for explaining the acceleration creep rupture of normally consolidated clay.

Let's discuss about the form of the second material function Φ_2. From the previous work(Adachi et al. (16)), it can be seen that the second material function increases rapidly around the state where creep rate is minimum.

Considering the previous work(Adachi et al.(16)), for normally consolidated clay, we have used the following paticular evolution equation and the form of second material function with zero initial conditions $(\xi(0),X(0))=0$.

$$\dot{\xi}=\frac{M^{*2}}{C_2(M^*-X)^2}\dot{X} \qquad (11)$$

where X is a stress invariant ratio $(=\sqrt{2J_2}/\sigma'_m)$ and C_2 is the viscoplastic material parameters.

As for the form of first material function, we have used a same form of function by Adachi and Oka's model(5). Taking into consideration the elastic component of strain rate tensor, we obtain the constitutive equation of normally consolidated clay that can describe both strain rate effect on straining process and accelerating creep failure as:

$$\dot{\varepsilon}_{ij}=\frac{1}{2G}\dot{s}_{ij}+\frac{\kappa}{3(1+e)}\dot{\sigma}'_m\delta_{ij}+\Phi_2(\xi)\langle\Phi_1(F)\rangle\frac{\partial f}{\partial\sigma_{ij}} \qquad (12)$$

$$\Phi_1(F)=\exp[m'(\frac{\sqrt{2J_2}}{M^*\sigma'_m}+\ln(\sigma'_m/\sigma'_{me})-\frac{1+e}{\lambda-\kappa}v^p)] \qquad (13)$$

$$\Phi_2=C_0(1+\xi) \qquad (14)$$

where G is a elastic shear modulus, s_{ij} is the deviatoric stress tensor, δ_{ij} is the Kronecker's delta, σ'_{me} denotes a initial mean effective stress, m'and C_0 are viscoplastic parameters.

CONSTITUTIVE MODEL FOR ANISOTROPICALLY CONSOLIDATED CLAY

We have used the relative stress parameter, $\bar{\eta}^*_{(0)}$, which was first proposed by Sekiguchi and Ohta(17) in order to describe the behavior of anisotropically consolidated clay. We replace $\sqrt{2J_2}/\sigma'_m$ in Eq.(2) with the relative stress parameter, and the dynamic yield function becomes

$$f=\bar{\eta}^*_{(0)}/M^*+\ln(\sigma_m'/\sigma'_{m0})=\ln(\sigma_m'^{(d)}/\sigma'_{m0}) \tag{15}$$

in which σ'_{m0} is a unit mean effective stress.

In Eq.(15), is defined by

$$\bar{\eta}_{(0)}^*=[(\eta_{ij}^*-\eta_{ij(0)}^*)(\eta_{ij}^*-\eta_{ij(0)}^*)]^{1/2} \tag{16}$$

in which $\eta^*_{ij}=s_{ij}/\sigma'_m$ and subscript (0) denotes the value at the end of anisotropically consolidation.

As for the second material function in the flow rule, we have introduced the concept of failure stress components. We have defined the failure stress components(σ_{1f}, σ_{2f},σ_{3f}) on the

plane, which corresponds to the current direction of stress vector. In Fig.1 , the failure stress components corresponding to stress vector AB can be obtained as the values of stress at the intersection of line AB and Mohr-Coulomb's failure envelope on π plane. Using this failure stress components, the relative failure stress ratio is given by

$$\bar{\eta}_{(f)}=[(\eta^*_{ij(n)}-\eta_{ij(f)})(\eta^*_{ij(n)}-\eta_{ij(f)})]^{1/2} \tag{17}$$

$$\eta_{ij(f)}=s_{ij(f)}/\sigma'_{m(f)} \tag{18}$$

where $s_{ij(f)}$ and $\sigma'_{m(f)}$ are the values of s_{ij} and σ'_m derived from the failure stress components.

We also introduced a relative stress parameter defined as:

$$\bar{\eta}^*_{(n)}=[(\eta^*_{ij}-\eta_{ij(n)})(\eta^*_{ij}-\eta_{ij(n)})]^{1/2} \tag{19}$$

$$\eta^*_{ij}=s_{ij}/\sigma'_m \tag{20}$$

in which $\eta^*_{ij(n)}$ denotes the value of η^*_{ij} at the nth times turning over state of loading direction. $\eta^*_{ij(n)}$ will be updatd when loading direction on the plane is changed.

By use of the relative stress components, the second material function proposed previously is extended as follows:

$$\Phi_2(\xi)=1+\xi \tag{21}$$

$$\xi=\frac{\bar{\eta}^*_{(n)}\ \bar{\eta}_{(f)}}{C_2(\bar{\eta}_{(f)}-\bar{\eta}^*_{(n)})} \tag{22}$$

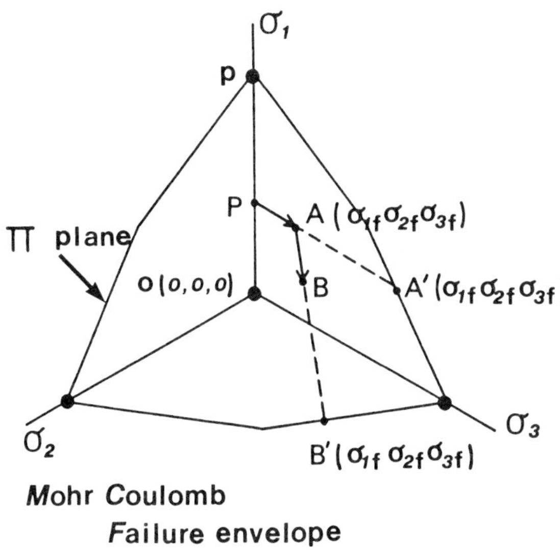

Figure 1. Failure stress components

PERFORMANCE OF THE PROPOSED MODEL

The proposed model was applied to the undrained triaxial compression tests with different constatnt strain rates and the undrained traiaxial creep tests. The material parameters are listed in Table I(18),II(19). Firstly, the performance of the model for undrained triaxial compression test are tried. Figs.2 and 3 present the comparison between the numeraial results and experimental rsults for Osaka alluvial clay.

Throughout of the numerical calculations, elastic shear modulus G was assumed to linearly vary with the square root of mean effective stress. Figs 2 and 3 show that the result by the newly proposed model agree well with expermental results, especially, around the critical state. The value of deviator stress slightly decreases after it reached the peak stress. With the old model, this phenomena was not able to be explained. As can be seen in Fig.3, material parameter C_2 governs the amount of strain softening.

Let's discuss about undarined creep behaviors. Figs.4-5 present the computed results for undrained triaxial creep test for natural Osaka alluvial clay. From these figures, the proposed model can simulate an acceleration creep failure. Exterimental results tested by Murayama et al.(19) are shown in Figs.4-5. In Fig.4, as shown by broken line, we can see that $\dot{\varepsilon}_m t_m$ is constant; $\dot{\varepsilon}_m$(minimum creep rate), t_m(time at the minimum creep rate). This fact has been experimentally found for the creep failure(Saito & Uezawa(20), Singh & Mitchell(21), Ting(22),Sekiguchi(23). The relationship between creep deviator stress q and minimum creep rate is plotted in Fig.5. This result also shows good agreement with experimental results.

Table I
Material parameters(Adachi et al.(18))

λ	κ	M^*	e_0	m'
0.372	0.054	1.05	1.28	21.5
C_0(1/sec)	σ'_{me}(Kgf/cm^2)		G(Kgf/cm^2)	
4.5x10^{-8}	6.0		132.1	

Table II
Material parameters(Murayama et al.(19))

λ	κ	M^*	e_0	m'	C_2
0.343	0.105	0.98	1.303	17.4	1600
C_0(1/sec)	σ'_{me}(Kgf/cm^2)		G(kgf/cm^2)		
8.0x10^{-9}	3.0		128		

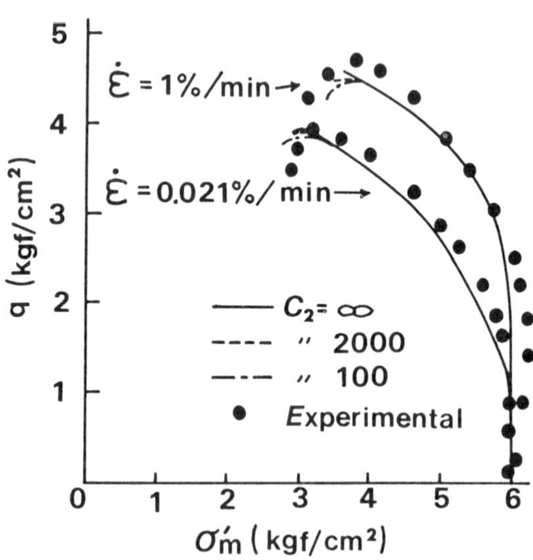

Figure 2. Stress paths for clay

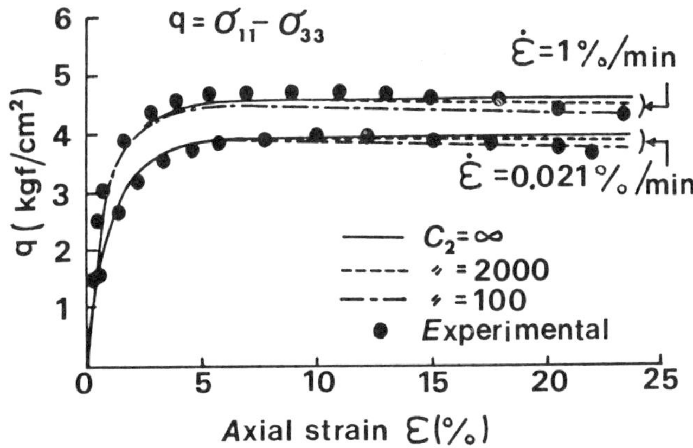

Figure 3. Stress-strain curves for clay

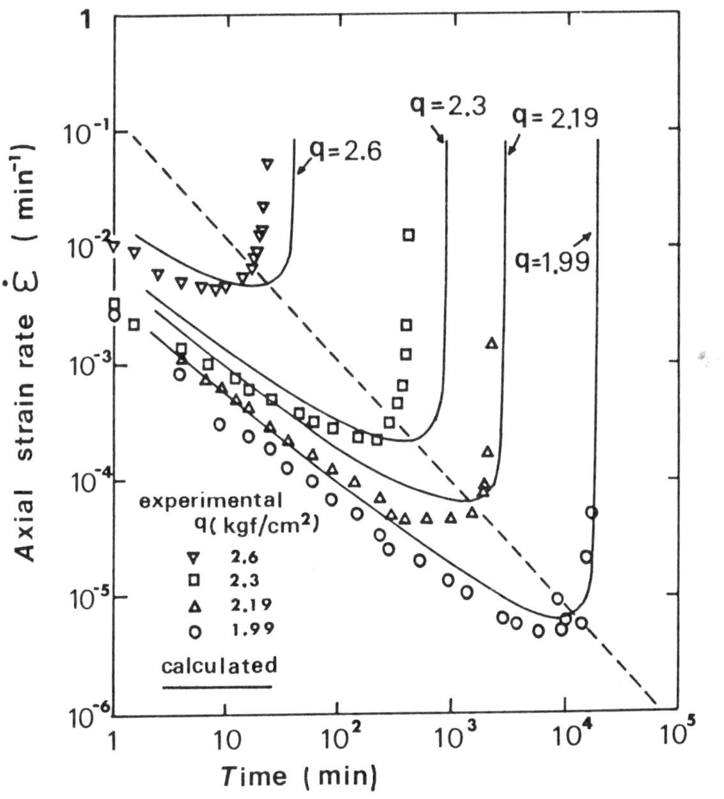

Figure 4. Variation in the axial strain rate with time

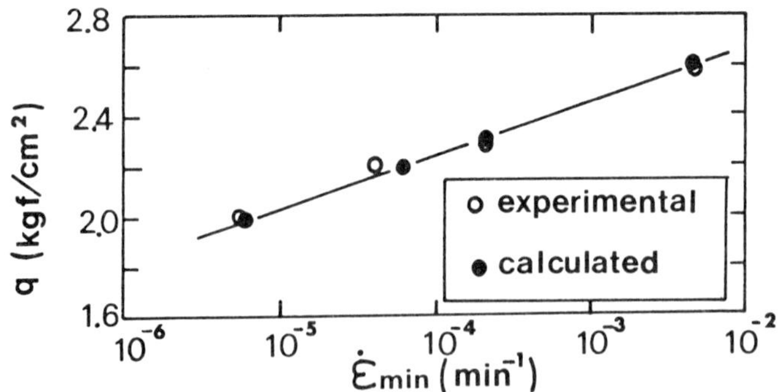

Figure 5. Creep deviator stress versus the minimum axial strain rate

CONSTITUTIVE MODEL FOR OVERCONSOLIDATED CLAY

In the present paper, an elasto-viscoplastic model for overconsolidated clay is developed based on the overstress type viscoplasticity theory and the elasto-plastic constitutive model for overconsolidated clay proposed by Adachi and Oka(24). The present work is the extention of the previous paper(25) concerned with the constittuive model for overconsolidated clay. Using the proposed model, the triaxial compression test results for soft clays which have been overconsolidated clay are simulated. The effect of strain rate is discussed. Comparison of predicted and experimental results shows that the proposed model is effective for simulating the behavior of overconsolidated clay.

O.C. Boundary surface

The O.C. boundary surface is introduced to define the boundary between the normally consolidated region($f_b>0$) and the overconcolidated region($f_b\leq 0$).

$$f_b=\bar{\eta}^*_{(0)}+M_m^*(\theta)\ln(\sigma'_m/\sigma'_{mb})=0 \tag{23}$$

in which σ'_m is the mean effective stress, θ is a Lode's angle and $\bar{\eta}_{(0)}^*$ is a stress parameter defined as follows:

$$\bar{\eta}_{(0)}^*=[(\eta_{ij}^*-\eta_{ij(0)}^*)(\eta_{ij}^*-\eta_{ij(0)}^*)]^{1/2} \tag{24}$$

$$\text{where } \eta_{ij}^*=s_{ij}/\sigma'_m \tag{25}$$

In Eq.(24), subscript (0) denotes the value at the end of anisotropic consolidation, and s_{ij} is a deviatoric stress tensor.

Outside the boundary surface(in the normally consolidated region), it is assumed that the behavior of saturated clay is described by the elasto-viscoplastic constitutive equation by Adachi and Oka(5). The constitutive model in the overcosolidated region is derived in the followings.

Plastic yield function

The plastic yield function is given by

$$\bar{\eta}_{(n)}^{*} - \kappa_s = 0 \tag{26}$$

where $\bar{\eta}_{(n)}^{*}$ is a relative stress parameter defined by Eq.(19).

Strain-hardening parameter

In the present paper, the strain-hardening function are generalized for explaining the behavior under the random cyclic loading condition. Using the relative failure stress ratio and relative stress ratio, which have been defined in the previous section, the strain-hardening function proposed before(Adachi and Oka(24)) is extended as

$$\gamma^{p*} = \frac{\bar{\eta}_{(n)}^{*}\ \bar{\eta}_{(f)}}{G'(\bar{\eta}_{(f)} - \bar{\eta}^{*}_{(n)})} \tag{27}$$

where γ^{p*} is the relative deviatoric strain given as:

$$\gamma^{p*} = [(e_{ij}^{p} - e_{ij(n)}^{p})(e_{ij}^{p} - e_{ij(n)}^{p})]^{1/2} \tag{28}$$

where $e_{ij(n)}^{p}$ is the value of plastic deviatoric strain tensor at the nth times reversion of loading direction.

Plastic potential function

The plastic potential function f_p is assumed to be given by

$$f_p = \bar{\eta}^{*}_{(n)} + \tilde{M}^{*} \ln(\sigma'_m / \sigma'_{ma(n)}) = 0 \tag{29}$$

where the parameter $\tilde{M}^{*}$ is given by

$$\tilde{M}^{*} = -\frac{\eta^{*}}{\ln(\sigma'_m / \sigma'_{mc})} \tag{30}$$

where η^{*} is a stress parameter defined by

$$\eta^{*} = (\eta^{*}_{ij}\ \eta^{*}_{ij})^{1/2} \tag{31}$$

$$\eta_{ij}^{*} = s_{ij}/\sigma'_m \qquad (32)$$

The rate independent plasticity model for overconsolidated clay can be formulated by use of non-associated flow rule, thc yield function Eq.(24), the hardening function Eq.(27) and the plastic potential function Eq.(29).

Viscoplastic constitutive equations

In this section, an elasto-viscoplastic constitutive model for clay are derived based on the Perzyna's type visco-plasticity theory and the rate independent plasticity theory in the previous section.

The viscoplastic strain rate tensor $\varepsilon_{ij}{}^{vp}$ is given by Oka(24)

$$\dot{\varepsilon}_{ij}{}^{vp} = \Phi_2(\xi)\langle\Phi_{ijkl}(F)\rangle \frac{\partial f_p}{\partial \sigma_{kl}} \qquad (33)$$

$$F = (f - \kappa_s)/\ \kappa_s \qquad (34)$$

$$\langle\Phi_{ijkl}(F)\rangle = 0 \quad (F<0) \qquad (35)$$

$$= \Phi_{ijkl}(F) \quad (F>0)$$

In Eq.(33), $\Phi_2(\xi)$ is the same function as that of Eq.(11).

Since F=0 expresses the statical yield function, the dynamic yield function f takes the same form of Eq.(26).

In the present theory, $\Phi_{ijkl}(F)$ is assumed to be 4th order isotropic tensor expressed by

$$\Phi_{ijkl}(F) = C_{ijkl}\Phi'(F) \qquad (36)$$

$$C_{ijkl} = A\delta_{ij} + B(\delta_{ik}\delta_{jl} + \delta_{il}\delta_{jk}) \qquad (37)$$

where δ_{ij} is Kronecker's delta.

Considering the elastic strain rate tensor, the total strain rate is obtained by the addition of viscoplastic and elastic strain rates.

$$\dot{\varepsilon}_{ij}{}^{e} = \dot{s}_{ij}/(2G) + (\lambda - \kappa)/(3(1+e))\delta_{ij}\dot{\sigma}'_m \qquad (38)$$

As for the shape of the funtion $\Phi'(F)$ in Eq.(36), we have adopted the following form Oka(26).

$$\Phi'(F) = \sigma'_m \exp(m'_o(\eta_{(n)}{}^{*} - \kappa_s)) \qquad (39)$$

VERIFICATION OF THE MODEL

In this section, the proposed elasto-viscoplastic model for

overconsolidated clay is verified for the triaxial compression test results of over-consolidated natural clay. In the experiemnt, the Osaka Senboku Clay are used. The clay specimen was sampled near Osaka. The material parameters and the test conditions are listed on Tables III and IV. Tests were carried out under the two constant strain rate. The boundary surface, which is similar to the limit state surface(Tavenas & Leroueil(26)), was experimentally determined as Fig.6. From this figure, it is seen that the clay specimen which were reconsoildated up to 2.0kgf/cm^2 is inside the boundary surface and assumed to be overconsolidated. Figs.7 and 8 show the experimental stress-strain relations and stress paths.Figs.9 and 10 are calculated stress-strain relations and stress paths. Comparison between predicted and experimental results shows that the proposed model can describe the rate-dependent behavior of overconsolidated clay.

Table III
Material Parameters of Osaka Senboku clay

λ	κ	M_m^*	M_f^*	m_o'	C_2	G'
0.230	0.054	1.33	1.33	31.6	80.0	240.0

C_{o1}(1/sec)	C_{o2}(1/sec)	σ'_{mb}(Kgf/cm^2)	G(kgf/cm^2)
$0.6\text{x}10^{-8}$	$1.0\text{X}10^{-9}$	4.0	133

Table IV Test condition for Osaka Senboku clay

Test No.	Initial mean effective stress(kgf/cm^2) σ'_{me}	Initial void Ratio e_0	Axial strain rate(%/min) $\dot{\varepsilon}_{11}$
NS3-3	2.0	1.667	$2.85\text{x}10^{-3}$
NS3-5	2.0	1.681	$5.88\text{x}10^{-4}$

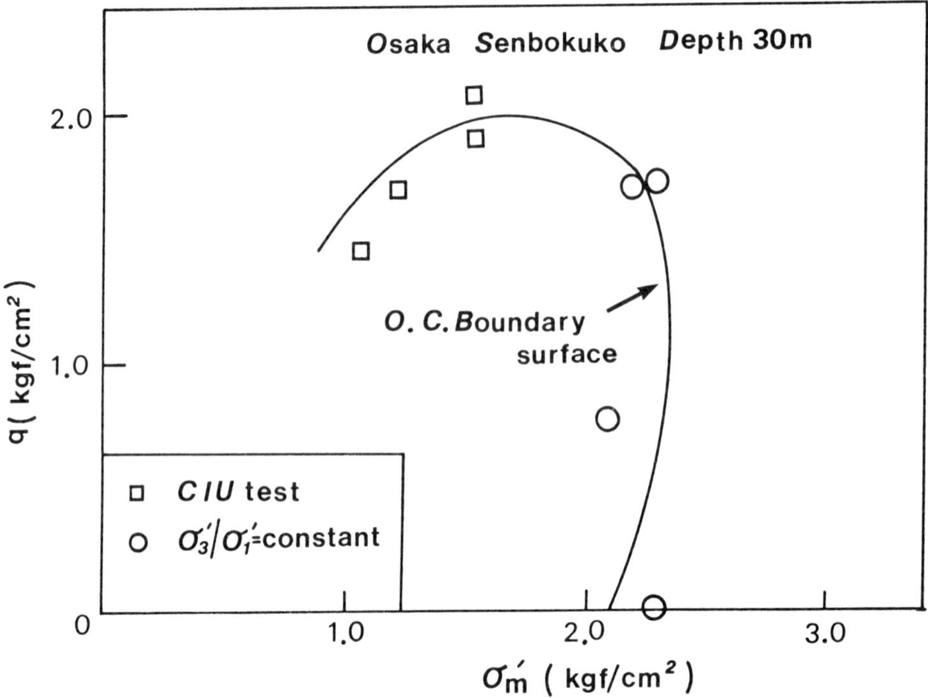

Figure 6. Overconsolidation boundary surface

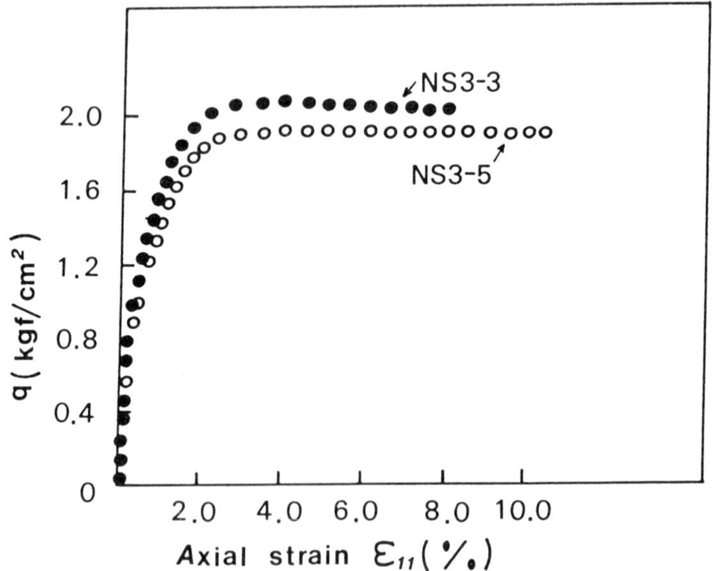

Figure 7. Stress-strain curves(Experimental results)

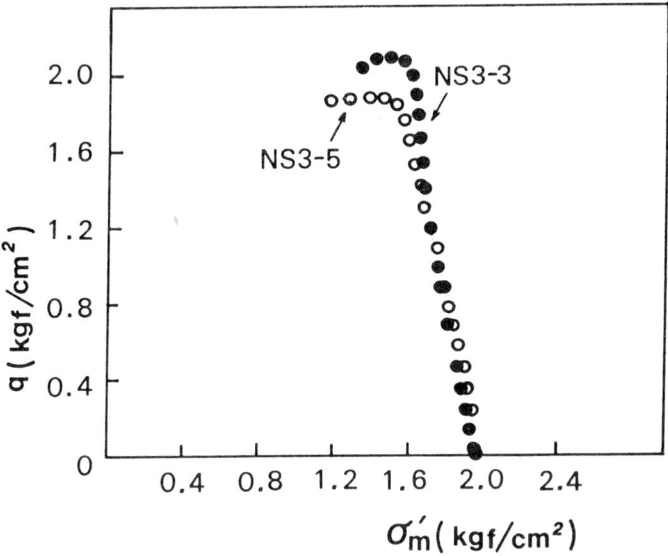

Figure 8. Stress Paths(Experimental results)

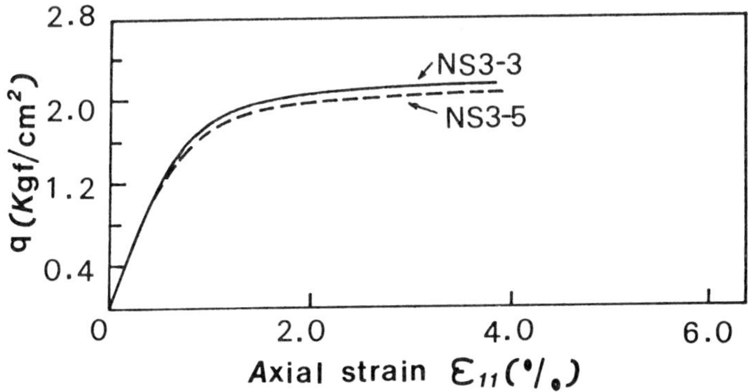

Figure 9. Stress-strain curves(Calculated results)

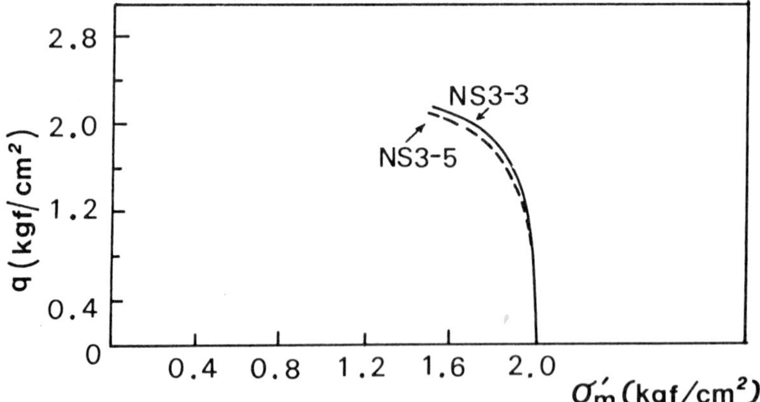

Figure 10. Stress paths(calculated results)

CONCLUSIONS

For normally consolidated clay

Introducing new material function and internal variable into the viscoplastic flow rule, we have modified the viscoplastic constitutive model of normally consolidated clay. The proposed model can describe the time-dependent bihaviors such as both strain-rate effect and creep phenomena with acceleration creep.

For overconsolidated clay

The present work is the extention of the previous elasto-plastic constitutive model for overconsolidated clay by considering the general hardening rule which is effective under random loadings. It is found that the proposed theory can estimate the viscoplastic effect of overconsolidated clay.

REFERENCES

1. Sekiguchi,H.,Constitutive laws of soils,Report of ISSMFE subcommittee on constitutive laws of soils,1985,Chap.III, 82-90.

2. Perzyna,P.,The constitutive equations for workhardening and rate sensitive plastic materials, Proc. of Vibrational problems, Warsaw,1963,Vol.4,No.3,281-290.

3. Adachi,T.and M.Okano,A Constitutive equation for normally consolidated clay,Soils and Foundations,1974,Vol14,No.4,53-73.

4. Oka,F.,Prediction of time dependent behavior of clay,Proc. 10th ICSMFE,1981,Vol.1,215-218.

5. Adachi,T. and F.Oka,Constitutive equations for normally consolidated clay based on elasto-viscoplasticity,Soils and foundations,1982,Vol.22,No.4,57-70.

6. Dafalias,Y.,Bounding surface elasto-plasticity-viscoplasticity,Proc. IUTAM Conf. on Deformation and Failure of Granular materials,1982,97-107.

7. Kantona,M.G., Evaluation of viscoplastic cap model, J. Geotech. Engng.,ASCE,1984, Vol.110, No.8,1106-1125.

8. Adachi,T.,F.Oka and M.Mimura,Mathematical structure of overstress type elasto-viscoplastic model for clay,Soils and Foundations,1987,31-42

9. Sekiguchi,H.,Rheological characteristics of clays, Proc. 9th ICSMFE,1977,Vol.1,289-292.

10 Nova,R.,A viscoplastic constitutive model for normally consolidated clay,1982,Proc. IUTAM Conf. on Deformation and Failure of Granular Materials,1982,287-295.

11. Matsui,T. and N.Abe,Elasto/viscoplastic constitutive equation of normally consolidated clays based on flow surface theory, Proc. 5th ICONMG,1985,Vol.1,407-413.

12. Roscoe,K.H.,A.N.Schofield and A.Thurairajah,Yielding of clays in states wetter than critical, Geotechnique,1963, Vol.13,No.3, 211-240.

13. Oka,F.,Elasto/viscoplastic constitutive equations with memory and internal variables,Computers & Geotechnics, 1985,Vol.1,59-69.

14. Aubry,D.,E.Kodaissi and E.Meimon,A viscoplastic constitutive equation for clays including damage law, Proc. 5th ICONMG,1985,Vol.1,421-428.

15. Perzyna,P.,Modified theory of viscoplasticity Application to advanced flow and instability phenomena, Arch. Mech.,1980, Vol.32,No.3,403-420.

16. Adachi,T.,F.Oka and M.Mimura,An elasto-viscoplastic theory for clay failure,Proc. 8th Asian regional conf. on SMFE, 1987,Vol.1,5-8.

17. Sekiguchi,H. and H.Ohta,Induced anisotropy and time dependency in clays,Proc. Speciality Session 9,9th ICSMFE, 1977,pp.229-238.

18. Adachi,T.,F.Oka,M.Mimura,Descriptive accuracy of several existing constitutive models for normally consolidated clays,Proc. 5th ICONMG,1985,Vol.1,259-266.

19. Murayama,S.,N.Kurihara and H.Sekiguchi,On creep rupture of normally consolidated clays, Annuals of Disaster Prevention Research Institute of Kyoto University,1970,No.13,525-541(in Japanese).

20. Saito,M. and H.Uezawa,Failure of soil due to creep,Proc. 5th ICSMFE,1961,Paris,Vol.1,315-318.

21. Singh,A. and J.K.Mitchell,Creep potential and creep rupture of soils,Proc.7th ICSMFE,1969,Vol.1,379-384.

22. Ting,J.M.,On the nature of the minimum creep rate-time correlation for soil,ice and frozen soil,Canadian.Geotech. J.,1983,Vo.20,176-182.

23. Sekiguchi,H.,Theory of undrained creep rupture of normally consolidated clay based on elasto-viscoplasticity,Soils & Foundations,1984, Vol.24,No.1,129-147.

24. T.Adachi and F.Oka,Constitutive equations for sands and overconsolidated clays, and assigned works for sand, Results of the Int. workshop on Constitutive Relations for soils,Grenoble, edt. by G.Gudehus et al.,1986,141-157.

25. F.Oka,Elasto-viscoplastic constitutive equation for overconsolidated clay,Proc. of Int.Symposium on Numerical models in Geomechanics, Zurich,1982,147-156.

26. Tavenas,F. and S.Leroueil,Effects of stresses and time on yielding of clays,Proc. 9th ICSMFE,Tokyo,1977,Vol.1,319-326.

A CREEP-INCLUSIVE NON-ASSOCIATIVE CAM-CLAY PLASTICITY MODEL

Edward Kavazanjian, Jr.
Supervising Geotechnical Engineer/Professional Associate
Parsons Brinckerhoff Quade & Douglas, Inc.
One Penn Plaza, New York 10119, USA

and

Hsii-Sheng Hsieh
Geotechnical Engineer
Moh and Associates
Taipei, Taiwan

ABSTRACT

A creep-inclusive non-associative plasticity model is developed within the framework of modified Cam-Clay theory. A second, horizontal yield surface is introduced within the modified Cam-Clay yield ellipse. Both yield surfaces isotropically harden during yield and expand with time as creep strains accumulate. The resulting plastic flow may not be associative with respect to either yield surface. This dual yield surface elasto-plastic constitutive model conforms closely to a unified phenomenological model for the stress-strain-time behavior of normally to lightly over-consolidated soft clay of low to intermediate sensitivity. The constitutive model is implemented within a large strain finite element consolidation program with a void ratio dependent permeability. The numerical model is shown to reproduce a variety of important facets of the time-dependent behavior of soft clays.

INTRODUCTION

The time-dependent behavior of soft clay is an important consideration in a variety of geotechnical problems. Time-dependent effects include consolidation, or hydro-dynamic lag, and creep, or deformation under constant effective stress. Historically, models for time-dependent behavior were initially developed to account for one or the other of these effects under restricted boundary conditions, e.g., one-dimensional consolidation, undrained triaxial creep. In the case of one-dimensional compression, separate models for consolidation and drained creep have been merged to create a model for combined consolidation and creep deformation that has proved very useful and gained wide acceptance in practice. Only recently has the state of the profession progressed to the point where comprehensive numerical models for the time dependent behavior of clay soils can be developed.

In this paper, the development of a comprehensive numerical model for the time-dependent behavior of normally to lightly over-consolidated soft clays of low to intermediate sensitivity is described. An elasto-plastic constitutive equation is developed to conform to a unified phenomenological model for the time-dependent behavior of soft clay. The constitutive equation is implemented in a large strain finite element consolidation program with a void ratio dependent permeability. The resulting numerical model is shown to reproduce a number of important facets of the one-dimensional compression behavior of soft clays observed in laboratory tests and field studies.

The model described in this paper is the product of a research program initiated at the University of California at Berkeley over 12 years ago to develop a general numerical model for the stress-time behavior of soft clays. Development of the model was guided by the philosophy that model components and parameters be familiar to geotechnical engineers and be readily evaluated from standard laboratory and/or field tests. Initially, a unified phenomenological model for stress-strain-time behavior under triaxial stress conditions was created. Soil deformation behavior was decomposed into four separable components: immediate, time-independent, and delayed, time-dependent, volumetric and deviatoric strains. Compatible model components were developed from existing, generally accepted phenomenological relationships. Subsequent model development included consideration of plane strain and general three-dimensional stress states and introduction of stress-strain and strength anisotropy.

Development of formal constitutive equations to describe model behavior has centered around Cam-Clay plasticity theory. Modified

Cam-Clay theory conforms closely to the volumetric phenomenological model component and reproduces the characteristic patterns of behavior of the time-independent deviatoric component. Initially, Cam-Clay plasticity theory was extended to include time-dependent creep deformations. The concept of the equivalent yield surface was introduced to define the direction of delayed, time-dependent strains. The time-dependent Cam-Clay constitutive model was implemented in a large strain finite element consolidation program. The resulting numerical model can conform closely to the phenomenological model components for immediate volumetric deformation and for either delayed volumetric or delayed deviatoric deformation. Both delayed components cannot be satisfied simultaneously. Furthermore, immediate deviatoric strains cannot be arbitrarily scaled to conform to the phenomenological model, though the characteristic patterns of immediate deviatoric behavior can be reproduced.

To allow the constitutive model to conform to the unified phenomenological immediate deviatoric stress-strain relationship, and to allow for simultaneous satisfaction of phenomenological volumetric and deviatoric delayed deformation relationships, a second, horizontal yield surface has been introduced beneath the ellipsoidal modified Cam-Clay yield ellipse. Both yield surfaces isotropically harden due to yielding under both immediate, time-independent strains and delayed, time-dependent strains. Flow with respect to each individual yield surface is associative. The resulting combined plastic deformation may not however be associative with respect to either individual yield surface. By appropriate choice of model parameters, this new constitutive model can be shown to conform closely to all components of the unified phenomenological model. The parameters used in the model are all readily attainable from standard laboratory tests, are familiar to most geotechnical engineers, and in many cases may be obtained from correlations with index properties of the soil.

The new constitutive equations have been emplaced within a quasi-static large strain finite element consolidation program to solve general boundary value problems. A void ratio-dependent anisotropic permeability has been introduced to more accurately model consolidation behavior. The program is capable of modeling important facets of time-dependent soil behavior, including quasi-preconsolidation due to ageing, pore pressure stagnation, the influence of load-increment ratio on the shape of the compression curve, and the time-dependence of the "at-rest" lateral earth pressure coefficient.

UNIFIED PHENOMENOLOGICAL MODEL

The constitutive model described in this paper was developed to conform to a unified phenomenological model for the stress-strain-time behavior of soft clays originally developed by Kavazanjian and Mitchell (1,2,3) and later modified with Bonaparte (4,5). Kavazanjian and Mitchel restricted the model to normally consolidated to slightly overconsolidated cohesive soils of low to intermediate sensitivity subjected to triaxial stress states. Soil deformation was conceptually decomposed into four separable but interdependent immediate and delayed volumetric and deviatoric components. As suggested by Bjerrum (6) for one-dimensional compression, immediate deformations were defined as time-independent deformations which occur instantly upon application of effective stress and delayed deformations were defined as time-dependent deformations which occur under sustained constant-stress loading. Existing, widely accepted phenomonological models for soil behavior were unified in a consistent manner within this framework to create a general stress-strain-time model.

Immediate Deformations

Immediate volumetric deformations during primary (virgin) loading at a constant deviatoric stress level are characterized by the conventional assumption of a linear relationship between void ratio and log stress. Hence virgin immediate volumetric compression can be represented by a series of parallel lines on a void ratio-log stress plot with a slope equal to C_c, the virgin compression index. Included in this family of parallel lines are the isotropic compression, one-dimensional compression, and undrained shear strength lines. Immediate volumetric deformations in the unloading and reloading range can be characterized by another series of parallel lines on the void ratio-log stress plot with a slope equal to C_r, the recompression index.

Immediate deviatoric deformations during primary loading for normally consolidated soils are characterized by a stress-strain curve normalized with respect to confining pressure. The normalized curve is assumed to follow a hyperbolic form. A normalized hyperbolic pore pressure curve is used to describe pore pressure induced by deviatoric loading. Unloading and reloading behavior is assumed to be linearly elastic, with the initial tangent modulus of the hyperbolic stress-strain curve used as the elastic modulus. Slight overconsolidation is accounted for using the equivalent consolidation pressure with the normalized stress-strain and pore pressure-strain curves.

The resulting immediate deformation model for primary loading can be represented as shown in Figure 1: by parallel contours of constant stress ratio with slope C_c on a void ratio-log stress plot, spaced horizontally according to the hyperbolic pore pressure curve, with each contour assigned a unique value of immediate deviatoric strain based on the hyperbolic stress-strain curve. Other characteristic behavior patterns of this portion of the model include the similar effective paths and radial lines of constant deviatoric strain passing through the origin of the p-q stress plot shown in Figure 2, and constant ratios of both undrained shear strength and shear modulus to effective confining pressure for a given overconsolidation ratio.

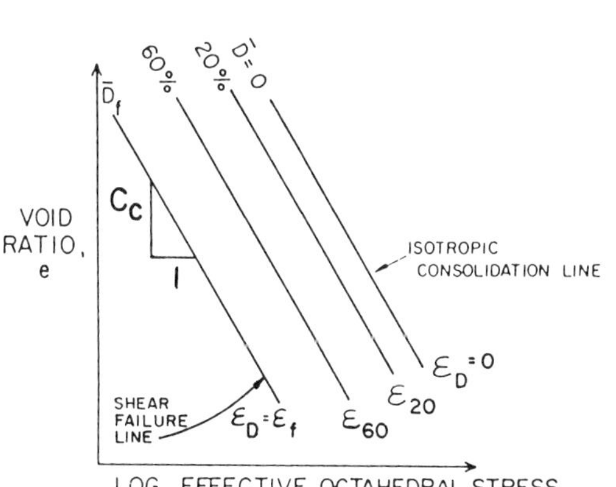

Figure 1. Immediate Compression Model

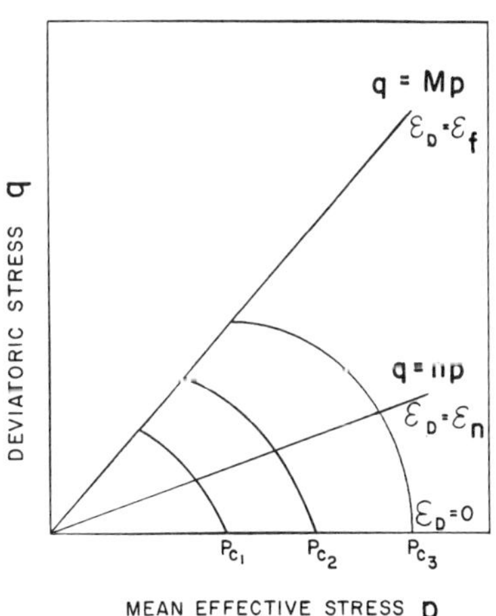

Figure 2. Similar Effective Stress Paths

Delayed Deformations

Delayed volumetric deformations are described using Taylor's secondary compression model. The coefficient of secondary compression, the slope of the void ratio-log time curve for sustained loading under constant volumetric stress, is assumed constant, independent of stress magnitude or stress level. Delayed volumetric deformation results in quasi-, or apparent, preconsolidation: upon loading after delayed volumetric deformation, the soil state moves along the unload/reload curve until encountering the virgin curve.

Delayed deviatoric strains are described by the Singh-Mitchell creep equation. Rules for deformation after sustained deviatoric loading are similar to the corresponding rules for volumetric deformation: the soil exhibits an apparent stiffening and moves along the elastic unload/reload line until encountering the hyperbolic curve for primary loading.

General Model

Figure 3 illustrates the general model. Each parallel plane in the void ratio-log stress-log time space represents deformation at a constant deviatoric stress level, e.g., isotropic compression, one-dimensional compression, or shear failure. Each plane is assigned a unique value of immediate deviatoric strain. For isotropic soils, the model is defined by the 14 parameters. All fourteen parameters are "conventional" parameters, familiar to engineers and readily obtainable from standard laboratory tests.

Kavazanjian, Mitchell, and Bonaparte (4) and Bonaparte (5) introduced refinements to improve the performance of the original model and to extend the model to general three-dimensional stress-states. The resulting model for primary loading is illustrated in Figure 4, where the nested conical surfaces represent surfaces of constant deviatoric stress level and immediate deviatoric strain. The shapes of these surfaces are defined by a three-dimensional failure criterion. The characteristic similar effective stress paths also revolve around these surfaces about the isotropic compression line to describe surfaces of constant void ratio.

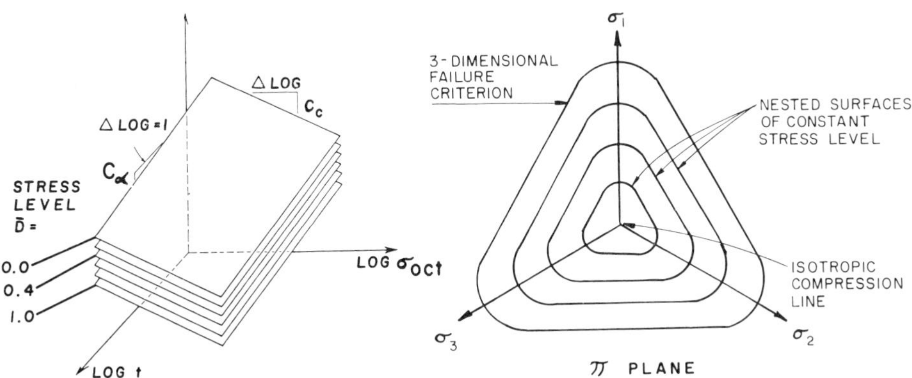

Figure 3. General Volumetric Model Figure 4. Three Dimensional Model

Bonaparte (5) refined the model component for delayed deformations using concepts from Cam-Clay plasticity theory. Bonaparte demonstrated that strain vectors during drained delayed deformation could reasonably be considered as normal to the modified Cam-Clay yield ellipse. Bonaparte also improved the predictive ability of the model for anisotropically consolidated soil and showed that the coefficient of secondary compression was not independent of stress, but instead appeared to be linearly related to deviatoric stress level.

TIME-DEPENDENT CAM-CLAY PLASTICITY

Borja and Kavazanjian (7, 8) developed a time-dependent elasto-plastic constitutive model based upon modified Cam-Clay plasticity theory (9) that conformed to a large extent to the unified phenomenological model. Cam-Clay theory was chosen because of Bonaparte's work and because of compatibility. The modified Cam-Clay model will conform precisely to the immediate volumetric phenomenological model at the two stress levels to which the yield ellipse is fit, typically one-dimensional compression and failure. Conformance at other stress levels depends on the accuracy of the shape of the yield surface. The Cam-Clay model results in a normalized stress-strain curve for undrained shear. However, the shape of this curve is prescribed by the shape of the Cam-Clay yield ellipse and cannot be fit to an arbitrary phenomenological relationship. The size of the yield ellipse, shear strength, and shear stiffness depend upon the equivalent consolidation pressure.

Modified Cam-Clay plasticity theory was extended to incorporate time-dependent strains using the concept of the equivalent yield surface. The equivalent yield surface is defined as the Cam-Clay ellipse passing through the current stress point, as shown in Figure 5. The direction of the delayed deformation strain rate is assumed normal to the equivalent yield surface. Similar results would be obtained if a bounding surface plasticity algorithm was used. The magnitude of the delayed strain rate is determined from either the secondary compression law or the Singh-Mitchell equation. Both phenomenological relationship cannot be satisfied simultaneously. The time-dependent yield surface expands with time according to the accumulation of plastic volumetric strain to account for quasi-preconsolidation effects, as depicted in Figure 5 for a stress relaxation test.

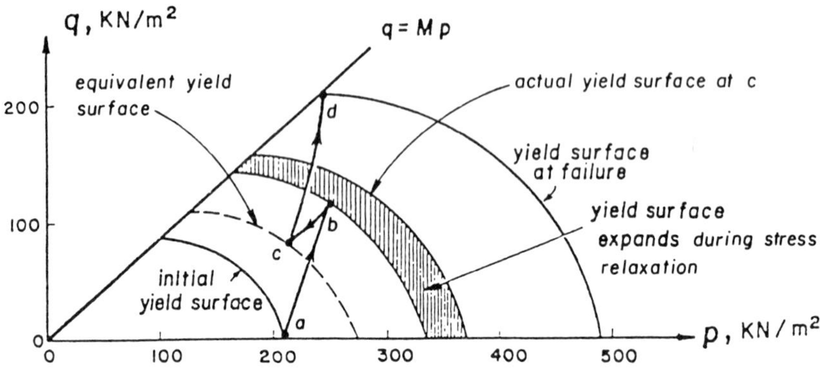

Figure 5. Time-Dependent Plasticity Model

The time-dependent Cam-Clay plasticity model was implemented in SPIN2D, a quasi-static finite element program with a large strain capacity and a coupled elasto-plastic consolidation scheme. The resulting numerical model was applied to laboratory tests and field case studies of time-dependent cohesive soil behavior (7, 8, 10, 11). Comparison of observed and predicted results showed the model to suffer from the same shortcoming as the conventional modified Cam-Clay model; under-prediction of deviatoric strain during primary loading.

NON-ASSOCIATIVE CAM-CLAY PLASTICITY

Recognizing the tendency of the modified Cam-Clay model to under predict deviatoric strain, Roscoe and Burland (9) hypothesized the existence of a second, horizontal yield surface within the modified Cam-Clay yield ellipse. As suggested by Borja and Kavazanjian, this hypothesis has now been incorporated in the time-dependent plasticity model to allow for simultaneous satisfaction of phenomenological relationships for both volumetric and deviatoric deformations. Both yield surfaces expand isotropically during primary loading and during delayed deformation. Equivalent yield surfaces are used to define the direction of time-dependent strains. Plastic flow components are calculated assuming normality with respect to each yield surface or equivalent yield surface, hence when both yield surfaces are engaged the resulting plastic flow is non-associative with respect to either yield surface.

The plastic potential associated with the horizontal yield surface is a function of the effective deviatoric stress level, n*, defined as the deviatoric stress level associated with the intersection of the two yield surfaces, as shown in Figure 6. A normalized hyperbolic curve is used for the n* - plastic shear distortion relationship. The horizontal deviatoric yield surface is coupled to the volumetric yield ellipse. The horizontal yield surface expands along the n* line as the yield ellipse expands without additional plastic shear strain.

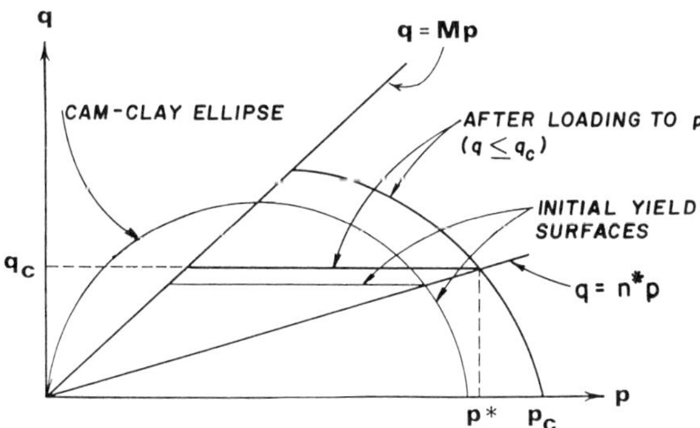

Figure 6. Dual Inter-dependent Yield Surface Model

The hyperbolic parameters which define the normalized n* - plastic strain relationship are not the same as those which describe undrained triaxial test results, as test results include elastic deformations. The hyperbolic values required for use in the plasticity model are most easily calculated by fitting numerical results to laboratory test results. Note that the elastic modulus is not related to the initial tangent modulus of this hyperbolic curve. Derivation of the governing constitutive equations for the model are presented by Hsieh and Kavazanjian (12). The equations have been coded into the finite element program CLAY2D, a modification of Borja and Kavazanjian's program, SPIN2D. A major difference between the two programs is the occurrence of a non-symmetric stiffness matrix in CLAY2D. One additional improvement in CLAY2D is the inclusion of a void ratio-dependent permeability.

The parameters required for input to CLAY2D, presented in Table 1, are are essentially the parameters of the unified phenomenological model, except that pore pressure parameters are not required. The hyperbolic parameters, as mentioned previously, are not the conventional stress-strain parameters but may be back calculated. The immediate void ratio should also be back calculated to eliminate any influence of creep during consolidation. However, a primary consolidation curve from standard laboratory tests is adequate for most purposes.

TABLE 1

Parameters of the Non-Associative Time-Dependent Plasticity Model

Parameters	Notation
Compression Indices	C_c, C_r
Immediate Void Ratio at $P_c = 1.0$	e_o
Coefficient of Secondary Compression	C_a
Hyperbolic Stress-Strain Parameters	a, b, R_f
Slope of Critical State Line (Friction Angle)	M
Singh-Mitchell Creep Paramters	A, $\bar{a}$, m
Vertical Permeability at C_o	k_o
Ratio of Horizontal to Vertical Permeability	K_{hv}
Permeability Exponent	(Assumed equal to 0.5)

NUMERICAL ANALAYSES

Numerical analyses performed by Hsieh and Kavazanjian with CLAY2D show the non-associative model to yield significantly better agreement with laboratory test results and field data than associative Cam-Clay plasticity theory (12). Numerical analyses of one-dimensional compression behavior serve to demonstrate the potential of the model for reproducing important aspects of time-dependent behavior and illustrate the importance of finite deformaton effects and a variable permeability on calculations of consolidation behavior.

Hsieh and Kavazanjian (13) have reported on the results of a one-dimensional consolidation test on undistrubed San Francisco Bay Mud (UBM) performed in a triaxial cell by isotropically consolidating the specimen, loading it at a constant axial strain rate while maintaining zero average radial strain up to a vertical pressure of 700 KPa, and then holding the vertical pressure constant while maintaining zero average radial strain. Figure 7 compares results of the strain controlled axial loading phase to predictions made using the associative model (SPIN2D) and the non-associative model (CLAY2D). Note the improved accuracy of the CLAY2D predictions compared to SPIN2D.

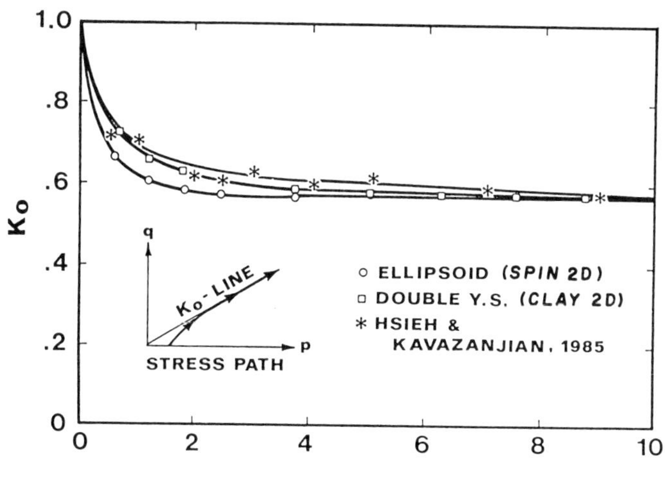

Figure 7. Strain-Controlled One-Dimensional Loading of UBM

Figure 8 compares numerical results during the constant vertical pressure phase of the test for two different elements to the test data. The CLAY2D-predicted lateral pressure coefficient varies with location within the consolidating layer, drops off sharply at the end of primary consolidation, increases at the beginning of secondary compression, and approaches an asymptotic value at longer times.

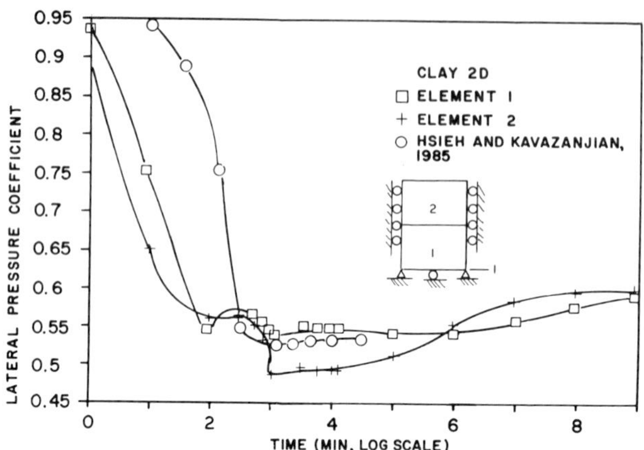

Figure 8. Time-Dependence of Lateral Earth Pressure Coefficient

Figure 9 compares pore pressure response for UBM predicted using a constant void ratio and neglecting creep to response predicted using a variable void ratio and including creep. Only with creep and a variable void ratio did the analysis show the characteristic pore pressure stagnation observed in laboratory tests and field studies (14).

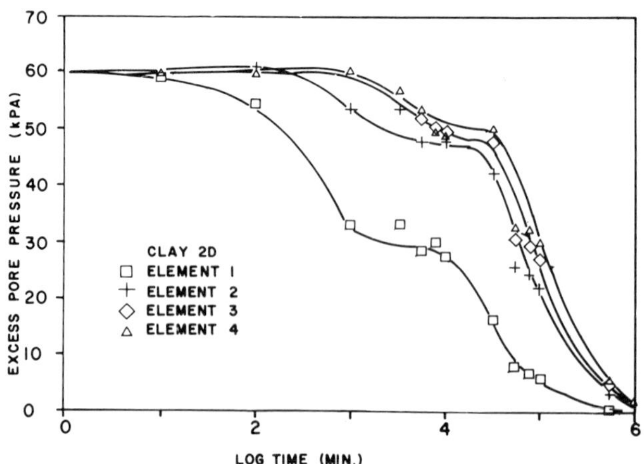

Figure 9. Pore Pressure Stagnation In UBM

Numerical analyses of stress-controlled consolidation show that response predicted using infinitesimal-strain theory and a void ratio-dependent permeability agrees closely with results using finite strain theory and a variable void ratio. Results using a constant void ratio deviate from the large strain-variable void ratio case regardless of whether finite or infinitesimal strain theory is used.

Figure 10 illustrates the influence of load increment ratio on a conventional consolidation test increment. Compression curves are plotted for a normally consoldiated soil, an overconsolidated soil, and a soil which makes a transition from a normally consolidated to an overconsolidated state during the load increment. The shapes of these curves correspond to the Type I, II, and III consolidation curves identified by Leonards and Girault (15).

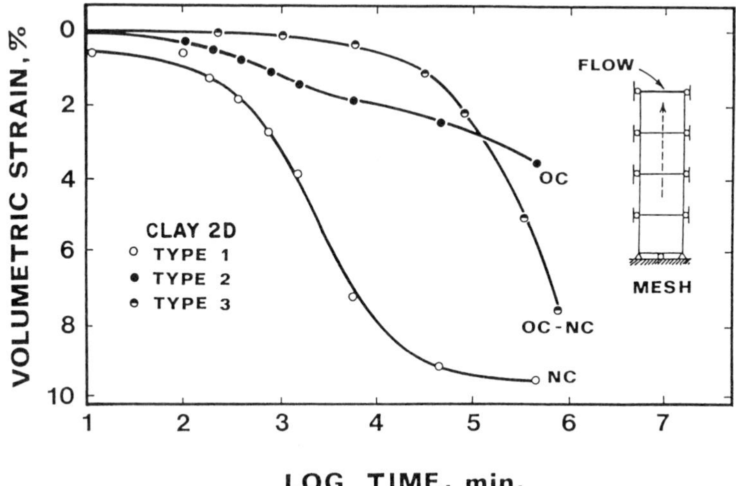

Figure 10. Influence of Load Increment Ratio on Consolidation

Figure 11 shows numerical results for consolidation of three UBM specimens of different thickness. These results indicate that the magnitude of primary consolidation and the average void ratio at the end of consolidation depend upon the length of the drainage path. Additional analyses indicates that as sample thickness increases, the influence of the length of drainage path diminishes and that the results of standard laboratory tests may be used for practical engineering purposes.

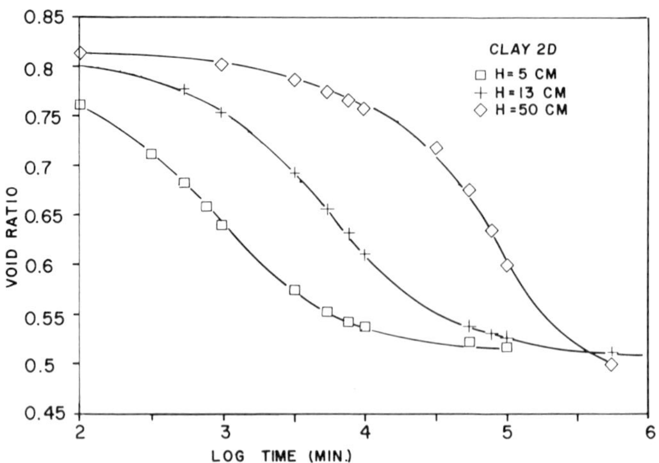

Figure 11. Influence of Specimen Size on Consolidation

CONCLUSION

A non-associative dual yield surface elasto-plastic constitutive model for the time-dependent behavior of soft clay has been developed within the framework of modified Cam-Clay plasticity theory. The constitutive equations conform closely to a previously developed unified phenomenological model. The equations are implemented in a quasi-static large strain finite element program that uses a void ratio dependent permeability during consolidation. Numerical analyses of one-dimensional compression demonstrate the improved predictive capacity of the dual yield surface model compared to the single yield surface associative Cam-Clay model. These analyses show the ability of the model to reproduce important facets of time-dependent behavior and illustrate the importance of a variable void ratio to accurate predictions of consolidation behavior. The constitutive equations and numerical model are applicable to a variety of important geotechnical problems.

REFERENCES

1. Kavazanjian, E., Jr., and Mitchell, J.K., A General Stress-Strain-Time Formulation for Soils, In Proc. Specialty Session 9, 9th ICSMFE, Tokyo, 1977, pp. 113-120.

2. Kavazanjian, E., Jr., A General Stress-Strain-Time Formulation for Soils, Ph.D. Dissertation, U. Cal., Berkeley, 1978.

3. Kavazanjian, E., Jr. and Mitchell, J.K., Time-Dependent Deformation of Clays, J. Geo. Eng., ASCE, 106, GT-6, June 1980, pp. 611-630.

4. Kavazanjian, E., Jr., Mitchell, J.K. and Bonaparte, R., Stress-Deformation Predictions Using a General Phenomenological Model, In Proc. Workshop on Limit Equilibrium, Plasticity, and Generalized Stress-Strain in Geo. Eng., ed. R.K. Yong and H-Y. Ko, ASCE, New York, 1981, pp. 461-491.

5. Bonaparte, R., A Time-Dependent Constitutive Model for Cohesive Soils, Ph.D. Dissertation, U. Cal., Berkeley, 1981.

6. Bjerrum, L., Engineering Geology of Normally Consolidated Marine Clays as Related to Settlements of Buildings, Seventh Rankine Lecture, Geotechnique, 17, No. 2, April 1967, pp. 82-118.

7. Borja, R.I. and Kavazanjian, E., Jr., Finite Element Analysis of the Time-Dependent Behavior of Soft Clays, Geo. Eng. Report GT1, Dept. Civil Eng., Stanford U., August 1984.

8. Borja, R.I. and Kavazanjian, E., Jr., A Constitutive Model for the Stress-Strain-Time Behavior of "Wet" Clays, Geotechnique, 35, No. 3, July 1985, pp. 283-298.

9. Roscoe, K.H., and Burland, J.B., On the Generalized Stress-Strain Behavior of "Wet" Clays, In Engineering Plasticity, Cambridge Univ. Press, 1968, pp. 535-609.

10. Kavazanjian, E., Jr., Borja, R.I., and Jong, H.L., Time-Dependent Deformation in Clay Soils, In Proc. 11th ICSMFE, San Francisco, August 1985, Vol. 2, pp. 535-538.

11. Liang, R.Y.K. and Mitchell, J.K., Centrifuge Evaluation of Numerical Model for Clay, J. Geo. Eng., ASCE, 114, GT-3, March 1988, pp. 265-283.

12. Hsieh, H.S. and Kavazanjian, E., Jr., A Non-Associative Cam-Clay Plasticity Model for the Stress-Strain-Time Behavior of Soft Clays, Geo. Eng. Report GT4, Dept. of Civil Eng., Stanford U., May 1987.

13. Hsieh, H. and Kavazanjian, E., Jr., An Automated Triaxial Device For Measuring the At-Rest Earth Pressure Coefficient, Geo. Eng. Report GT3, Dept. Civil Eng., Stanford U., April 1985.

14. Tse, E. C-C, Influence of Structure Change on Pore Pressure and Deformation Behavior of Soft Clays Under Surface Loadings, Ph.D. Dissertation, U. Cal., Berkeley, 1985.

15. Leonards, G.A. and Girault, P., A Study of the One-Dimensional Consolidation Test, In Proc. 5th ICSMFE, Paris, Vol. 1, 1961, pp. 213-218.

SOME OBSERVATIONS ON THE CREEP BEHAVIOUR OF A SILTY CLAY

M.P.O'Reilly, Arup Geotechnics
S.F. Brown, University of Nottingham
G. Austin, Johnson, Poole & Bloomer

SYNOPSIS

A large number of carefully controlled creep tests were carried out on reconstituted Keuper Marl, a silty clay. These were performed undrained in the triaxial apparatus, both on normally consolidated and lightly overconsolidated specimens and at a range of moisture contents. Data is presented showing the relationship between stress level, time, pore pressure development and the accumulation of shear strain.

It will be shown that for this soil under a constant deviator stress, the concept of a threshold stress level (above which creep strains will induce failure) is a useful one.

It will also be shown that whilst pore pressures change with time, they are also found to bear a direct relationship with the accumulated shear strain.

INTRODUCTION

The creep of soils is an important factor in the design of many engineering structures. One of the problems facing the engineer who wishes to design against creep deformations is the uncertainty concerning the applicability of the various models available. This is caused partly by the paucity of good quality laboratory and site observations on the creep behaviour of soil. The primary object of the research reported in this paper was to obtain good quality laboratory data in order to advance the understanding of the mechanisms involved in creep. Attention was concentrated on behaviour at relatively high levels of stress (close to, and in excess of the undrained strength as measured in slow deformation controlled tests).

Singh and Mitchell (1968) have described a simple model for the creep behaviour of clays under a constant deviator stress in undrained tests. They suggested that their model was applicable for deviator stress levels in the range 30% to 90% of the undrained strength. At stress levels which approach and exceed 100% of the undrained strength (as determined in a slow deformation controlled triaxial test), however, the creep behaviour is seen to depart significantly from the predictions of such simple models. Attempts have been made to deal with this empirically. For example Mesri et al (1981) made use of a "hyperbolic model" to provide a better fit with experimental observations over a wider range. They concluded however, that "in the absence of extensive reliable shear stress-strain-time observations on a variety of natural soils and under a wide range of loading conditions, the existing creep models for soils should be viewed as ad hoc generalisations necessitated by the immediate need for analysis of engineering problems.". The Authors generally agree with the sentiments of Mesri et al (1981), although it is submitted that there is much merit in using laboratory reconstituted clays since their stress history and homogeneity can be well-controlled. This paper, then, is concerned mainly with the presentation and discussion of creep data rather than with providing a detailed model.

The soil used in this study was reconstituted Keuper Marl, a silty clay (Plasticity Index = 17%), which is readily available in the English Midlands. Keuper Marl has been used extensively for research purposes at the University of Nottingham and elsewhere. A new constant stress creep loading rig was developed for this programme. This allowed dead weight loading to be used but was designed so that it automatically compensated for changes in stress caused by an increase in cross-sectional area of a specimen during undrained deformation.

EXPERIMENTAL PROCEDURES

Preparation of Soil Slurry

The Keuper Marl was obtained in the form of unfired bricks from a local brickworks. The soil was crushed, dried and powdered. Particles passing a BS52 (150 micron) sieve were added to water to form a slurry with a moisture content of 55% which was 1.8 times the liquid limit.

Initial Consolidation

The slurry was consolidated one dimensionally in perspex tubes with an internal diameter of 76 mm. Porous platens were provided at the top and bottom to allow drainage. An axial stress of 150 kPa was applied for four days which reduced the moisture content to a level such that the soil could be handled for making into test specimens.

Transfer of the Specimen into the Triaxial Apparatus

At the end of the initial consolidation phase the partly consolidated specimen was carefully transferred onto the base of a triaxial cell. A system of filter paper radial drains were assembled to facilitate further consolidation. A latex membrane was then fitted and a base-mounted pore pressure measuring device was installed. Careful precautions were taken at all stages to ensure that air did not enter the system either in the vicinity of the pore pressure probe or between the specimen and its membrane. The experimental specimen arrangement is shown in Fig.1.

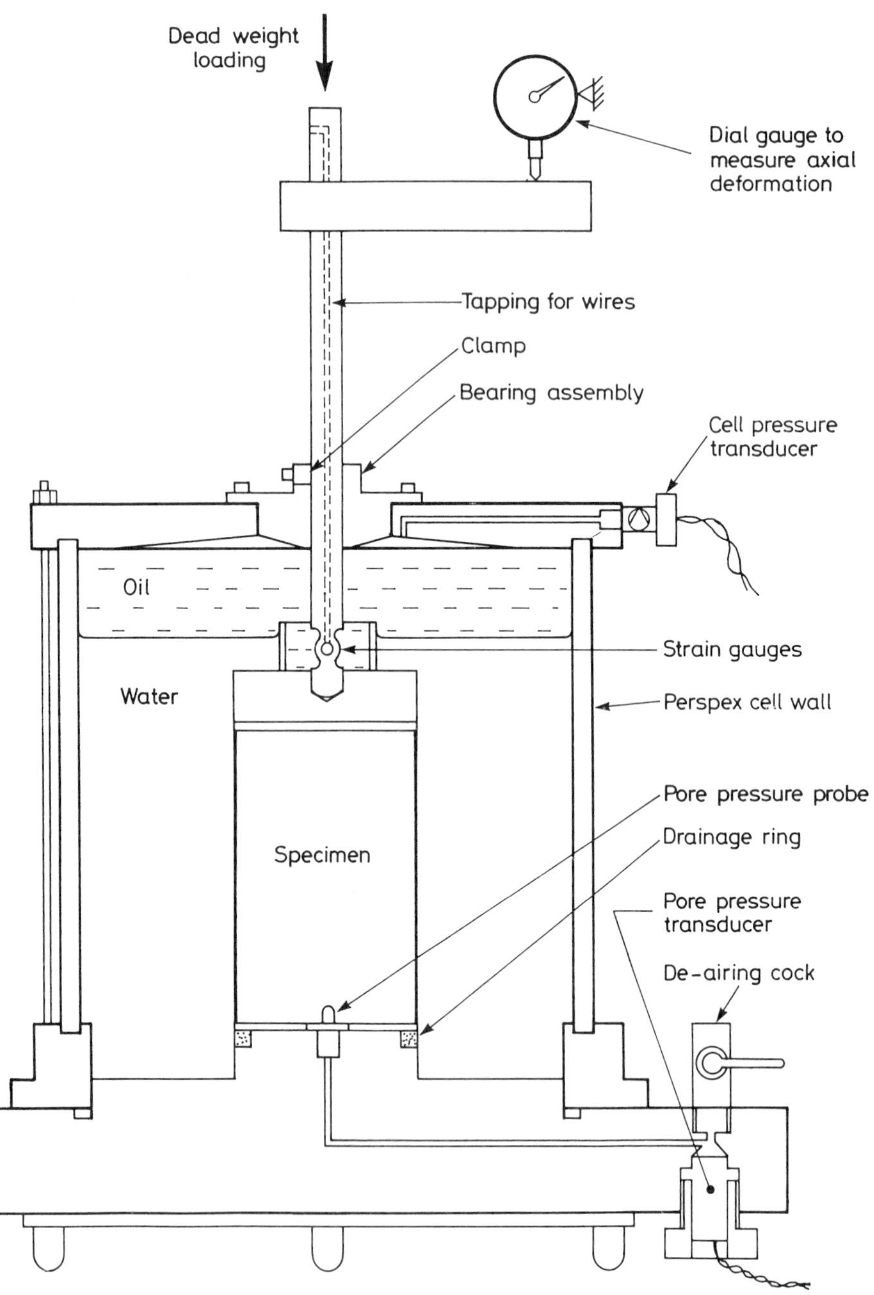

Fig. 1 General arrangement of specimen in the triaxial cell.

Consolidation was effected by sealing the top of the triaxial cell into position over the specimen, raising the confining pressure and allowing radial and vertical drainage to occur simultaneously. Consolidation regimes involving radial drainage have been reported to produce a degree of heterogeneity in the specimen (see eg. Atkinson et al, 1985). The effects of this lack of uniformity were considered to be small and all values of moisture content etc. quoted are average values.

Constant Stress Creep Rig

It was considered that in order to increase the stability of loading it would be useful to use a "dead loading" system. An arrangement was devised whereby changes in specimen diameter could automatically be compensated for by increasing the applied load in order that the applied stress would be constant. The principle of this arrangement is shown in Fig. 2.

A vertical specimen deflection caused a displacement of the lever system so that the fulcrum experienced a lateral translation δ '. By choosing a suitable lever dimension, this geometric transformation was utilised to provide a constant deviator stress during an undrained test (for which the volume was assumed to remain constant).

Temperature Control

The effect of temperature variation on the creep behaviour of soils is well-known. All tests were, therefore, performed in a temperature controlled environment. The air temperature was maintained at a constant level by a system of heating and cooling units all of which employed fans to ensure rapid circulation. A thermograph was produced during all tests. It was found that temperature fluctuations had an amplitude of less than 1°C. The mean temperature varied by approximately $\pm$ 0.25°C over a week which was the approximate duration of a creep test.

PRELIMINARY TEST RESULTS

Consolidation Results

Fig. 3 shows a typical graph of moisture content (w) against mean effective pressure ($p'=1/3\sigma'_a+2/3\sigma'_r$ where σ'_a and σ'_r are the effective axial and radial stresses) obtained during isotropic consolidation and swell-back. As can be seen, both compression and swelling phases yield approximately linear relationships in w, log p' space. Fig 4 shows that all specimens were brought to a final moisture content of either 21% or 25% and were either normally consolidated or had an overconsolidation ratio (OCR) of 2 where:

$$OCR = \frac{\text{Maximum } p' \text{ Experienced}}{\text{Current } p'}$$

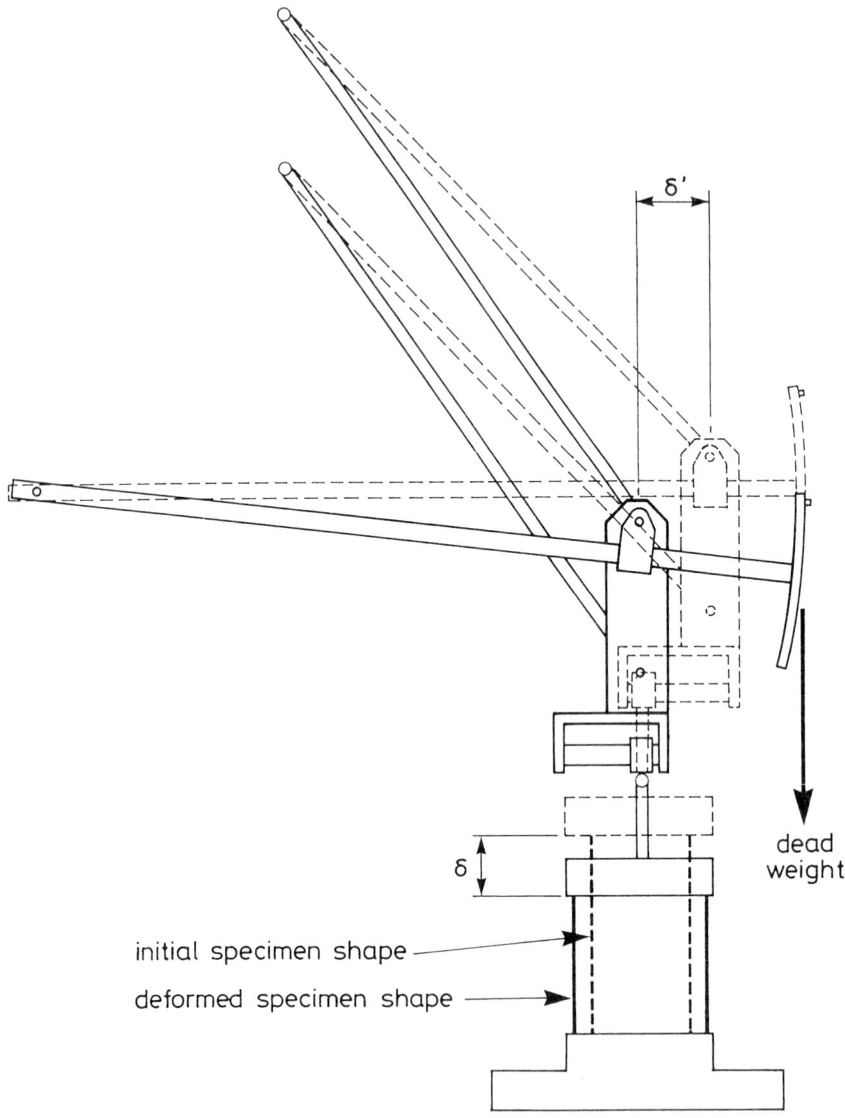

Fig. 2 Diagram showing the action of the stress compensation mechanism of the Creep testing apparatus.

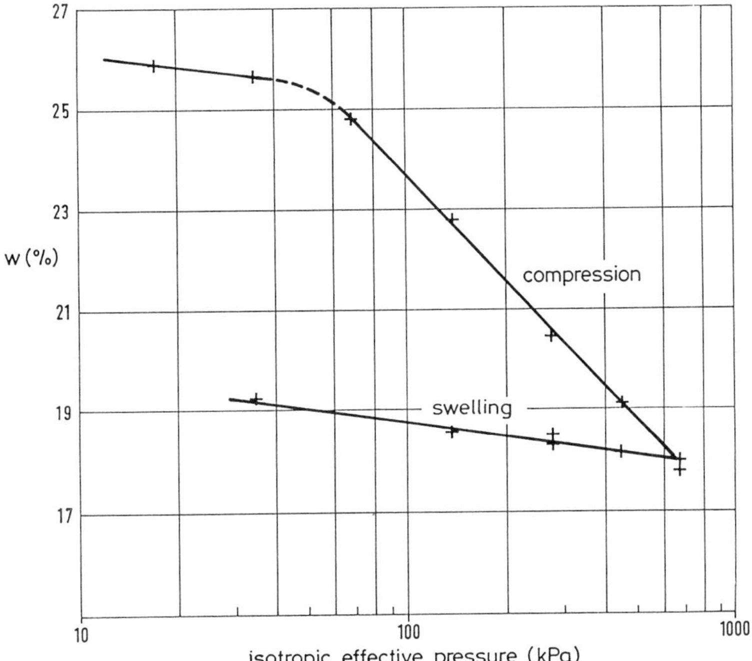

Fig. 3 Typical water content - Isotropic effective pressure plot.

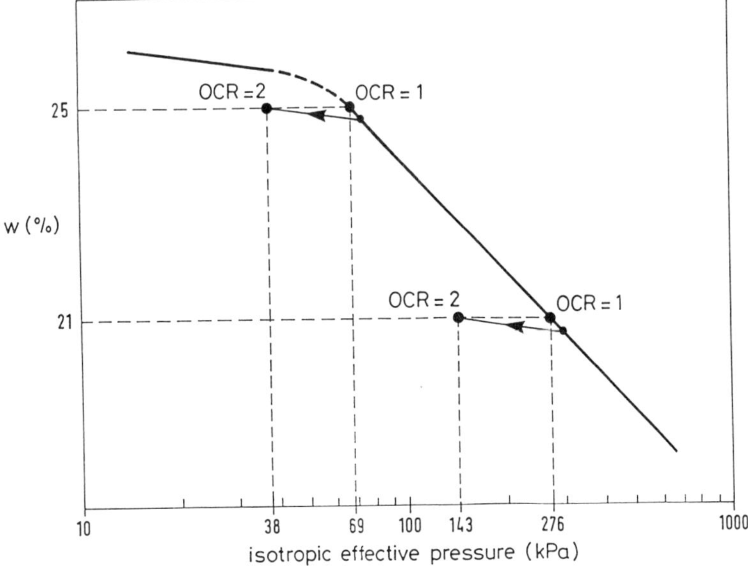

Fig. 4 Consolidation histories of specimens used in the present investigation.

Preliminary Strain Controlled Tests

A preliminary series of strain controlled tests was carried out both on normally consolidated specimens and at an OCR of 2 at a shear strain rate of 0.02% per minute. The results of these are shown in Fig. 5. As the consolidation pressure increased the shape of the graph for specimens with an OCR of 1 is seen to resemble more and more closely the "classical shape" of stress path for normally consolidated specimens. The shape of paths at low values of consolidation pressure indicates that the soil behaviour was still heavily influenced by its anisotropic primary consolidation in the perspex tubes. Anisotropically normally consolidated specimens generally tend to experience a lower pore pressure rise during the initial phase of loading than isotropically consolidated samples and to exhibit a peak strength. Both of these phenomena were observed for tests in which the maximum consolidation pressure was relatively low compared with the value at the end of primary consolidation.

CREEP TEST RESULTS

The Rate of Accumulation of Shear Strain

Fig. 6. shows a conceptual model in which three idealised constant deviator stress creep tests are portrayed. Line 1 shows a stable system in which the rate of shear strain continues to decrease at a increasing rate with respect to time. Line 3 shows an unstable system, while Line 2 shows the intermediate case, the ultimate fate of which is not known. Failure of a specimen may be considered to occur at the point marked by an "F" on Line 3.

The form of model suggested by line 2 has been advocated by a number of researchers (eg., Singh and Mitchell, 1968). It is generally accepted, as stated earlier, however, that such a model is limited in its application and cannot deal with the experimentally observed phenomena such as the stabilising and "runaway" systems portrayed in Fig 6 by lines 1 and 3 respectively.

Fig. 7 shows the experimental shear strain data collected during this research programme. In this figure the logarithm of shear strain rate is plotted against the logarithm of time for specimens at w = 21% and 25% and at overconsolidation ratios of 1 and 2. Each test is characterised by a deviator stress ratio, R_q defined as: the applied deviator stress (q) divided by the value of q at failure during slow strain controlled tests.

As can be seen, failure (as defined in Fig. 6) occurred in a number of tests. These points are indicated by the letter "F" on the relevant plots. Analysis of these results indicated that failure only occured when R_q was greater than a certain value. This lends support to the 'threshold stress level' hypothesis.

This hypothesis (which may be due to Murayama and Shibata, 1961) suggests that there is a level of stress which forms a boundary between loading conditions which cause failure and those which result in eventual

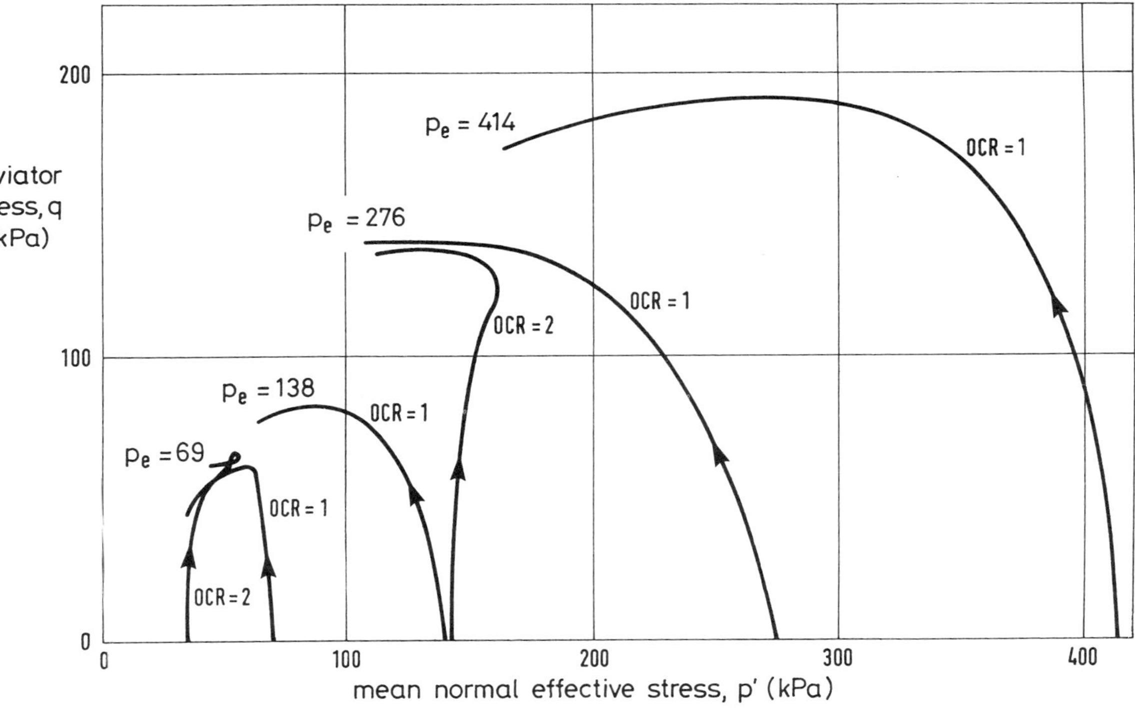

Fig. 5. Effective stress paths recorded during preliminary strain - controlled undrained triaxial tests.

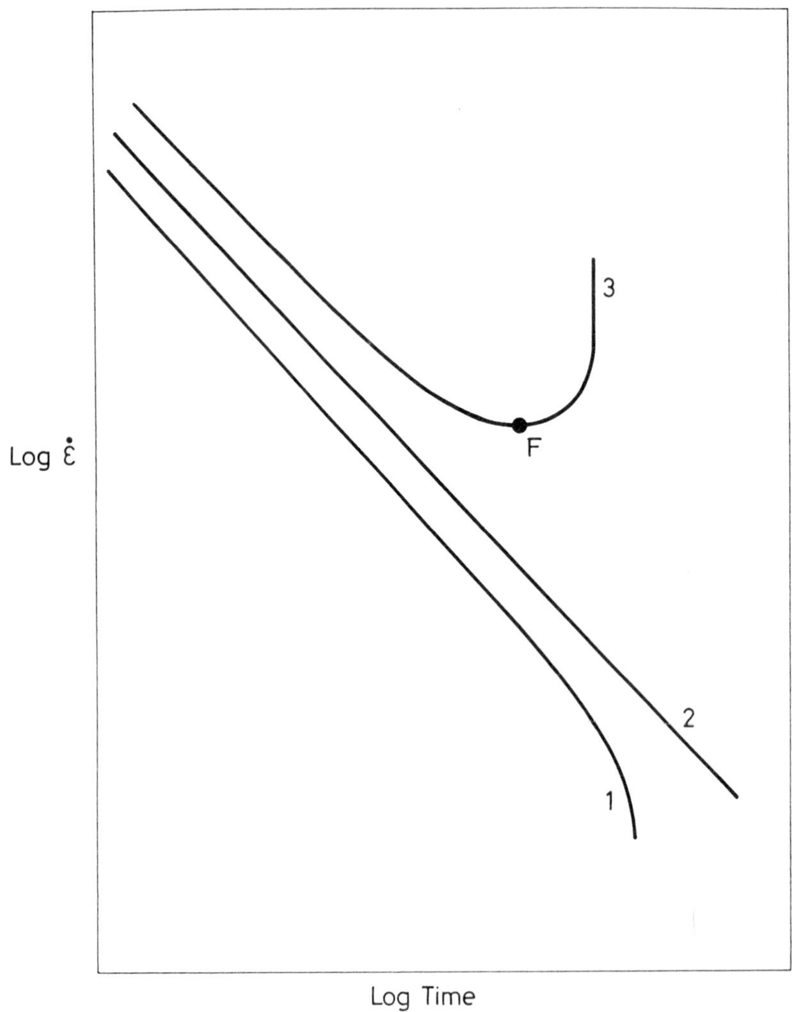

Fig. 6. Conceptual model of creep behaviour showing three idealised patterns of response.

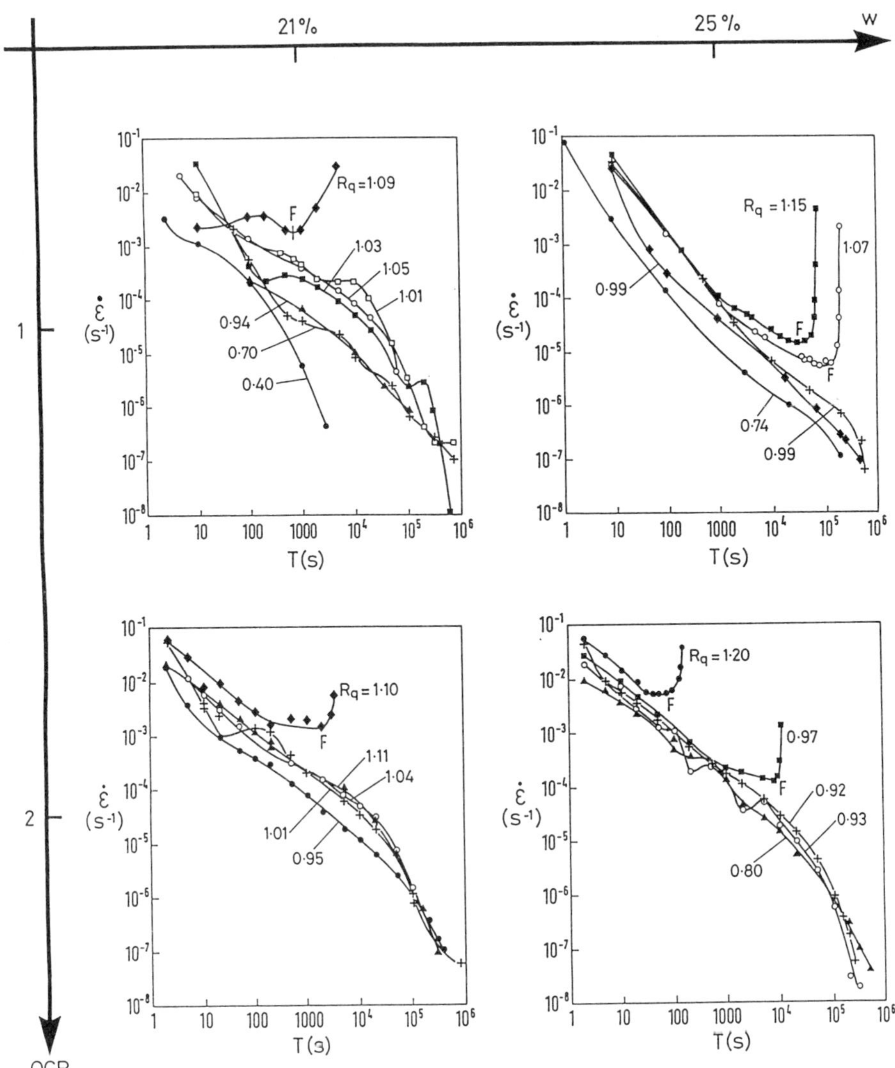

Fig. 7 Shear strain rates recorded during creep tests.

stabilisation of strains. A soil loaded at its threshold level will thus experience a build-up of shear strain characterised by Line 2 in Figure 6.

In Fig. 8 the observed threshold values are indicated using data from all tests. This figure shows, firstly, the highest values of R_q for which failure did not occur (i.e. a possible lower bound for the threshold value R_q) and the lowest values of R_q which caused failure (i.e. a possible upper bound for R_q). As can be seen, the threshold stress level in terms of R_q appears to be fairly well-defined for the normally and lightly over consolidated Keuper Marl tested in this research programme and has an approximate value of R_q = 1.03 for the soil with a water content of 25% and R_q = 1.07 for the soil with a water content of 21%. These threshold stress levels appear to be independent of the over consolidation ratio.

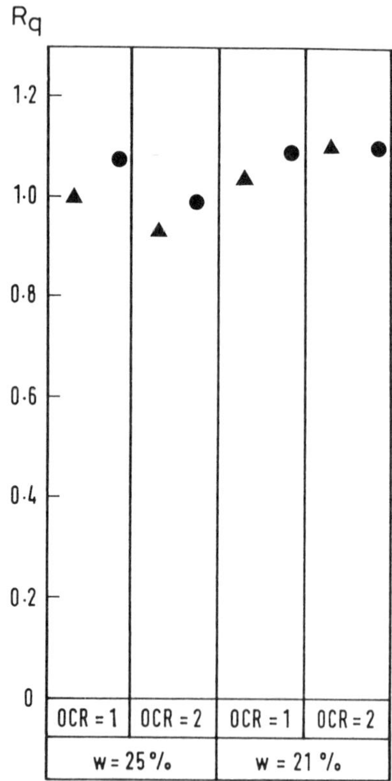

▲ HIGHEST Deviator Stress NOT CAUSING FAILURE
● LOWEST Deviator Stress WHICH CAUSED FAILURE

Fig. 8 Estimation of threshold stress levels.

Pore Pressure Development During Creep Testing

Fig. 9 shows the total stress path experienced by a specimen during a triaxial creep test. This figure also shows the effective stress path of a typical strain controlled triaxial shear test. The horizontal (abscissa) difference between the two is equal to the pore pressure which has developed.

As the deformation of clays has a time-dependent component the increase in pore pressure is not instantaneous. The effective stress path during the fast initial loading (which occurs in a finite time) and subsequent straining in the creep test is illustrated schemetically in Fig.9. The increase in pore pressure with time at constant deviator stress is represented by the horizontal dashed line.

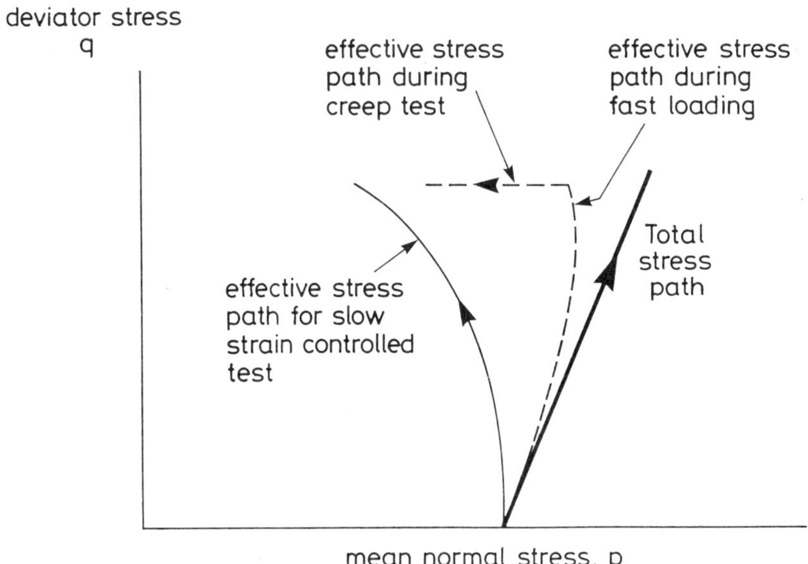

Fig. 9 Total and effective stress paths for slow strain controlled and creep tests.

The rate of accumulation of permanent pore pressure is important, since it controls the proximity of the soil state to the failure condition as a function of time. It was thus decided to investigate the way in which pore pressure accumulated. The idea of pore pressure being linked directly with strain was advanced by Lo (1969) and Walker (1969). Holzer et al (1972) found that applying a stress caused an instantaneous pore pressure increase followed by a steady rise in pore pressure which was directly related to the creep shear strain. Lacerda and Houston (1973) concluded that the magnitude of the pore water pressure depended, for all practical purposes, on the amount of shear strain only. The results of this test programme indicate this to be the case.

Fig. 10 shows the recorded relationships between pore pressure and shear strain for specimens at w = 21% and 25% and at overconsolidation ratios of 1 and 2. Included on each graph, as dashed lines, are the results from a standard strain controlled test. As can be seen, the results from each type of test are quite comparable indicating that the above hypothesis is approximately correct.

In Fig. 9 it was assumed that the time dependent component of change in pore pressure would result in a reduction of effective stress so the path would move horizontally towards the Critical State Line (see Schofield and Wroth, 1968). In the overconsolidated soils, however, the creep pore pressure changes were initially negative so that the effective stress increased in magnitude. This trend did appear to change at approximately 0.5 to 1.0% shear strain, so that an effective stress reversal occured. As the pore pressure decreases one might expect the rate of creep strain to decrease. In a number of tests, however, it was observed that failure occured at an early stage in the test despite this increase in effective stress. This suggests that failure during undrained creep is not determined exclusively by proximity to the Critical State.

CONCLUSIONS

1. A series of undrained creep tests was performed on a silty clay (Keuper Marl) using a dead loading system in which the vertical load was automatically corrected so that a constant deviator stress was applied.

2. It was found that a threshold stress level existed which had a value slightly greater than the undrained strength as measured in triaxial tests with a shear strain ratio of 0.02% per minute. Loading a specimen to a higher stress than this threshold invariably caused creep failure. Specimens subjected to stresses below the threshold level did not fail, i.e. their rate of accumulation of shear strain continued to decrease with time.

3. The build-up in pore pressure was shown to be related primarily to the shear strain which accumulated. The pore pressures built up during creep correlated well with those induced in standard deformation-controlled triaxial tests at the same value of shear strain.

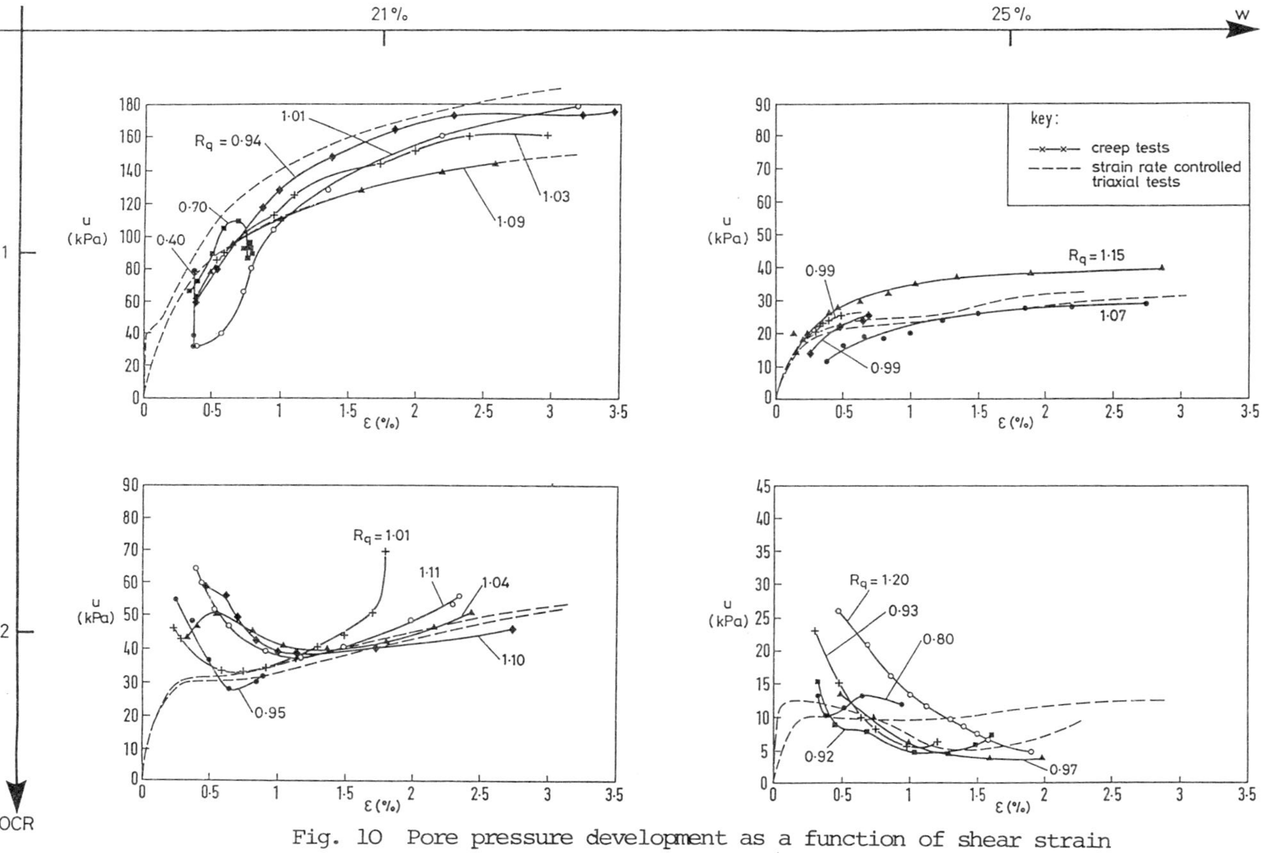

Fig. 10 Pore pressure development as a function of shear strain

ACKNOWLEDGMENTS

The Authors would like to acknowledge receipt of a Science Research Council Studentship for this work and to thank Dr. G.B. Parr for his assistance. The facilities of the Civil Engineering Department Laboratories at the University of Nottingham were made available by Professor R C Coates, Head of Department at the time.

REFERENCES

1. ATKINSON, J.H., EVANS, J.S. and HO, E.W.L. (1985), "Non-uniformity of triaxial samples due to consolidation with radial drainage", Geotechnique, Vol. 35, No.3 pp 353 - 356.

2. HOLZER, T.L., HOEG, K. and ARULANDAN, K. (1972), "Excess pore pressures during undrained clay creep", Canadian Geot. Journ., Vol. 10, No. 1, pp 12-24.

3. LACERDA, W.A. and HOUSTON, W.N. (1973), "Stress relaxation in soils", Proc. 8th Int. Conf. on Soil Mechs and Found. Eng., Moscow, Vol. 1, pp221-226.

4. LO, K.Y. (1961), "Stress-strain relationships and pore water pressure characteristics of a normally consolidated clay", Proc. 5th Int. Conf. on Soil Mechs and Found. Eng., Paris, Vol. 1, pp 219-224.

5. MESRI, G., FEBRES-CORDERO, E., SHIELDS, D.R. and CASTRO, A. (1981) "Shear Stress-Strain-Time behaviour of clays", Geotechnique, Vol. 31, No 4 pp 537-552.

6. MURAYAMA, S. and SHIBATA, T. (1961), "Rheological properties of clays", Proc. 5th Int. Conf. on Soil Mechs. and Found. Eng., Paris, Vol. 1, pp 269-273.

7. SCHOFIELD, A.N. and WROTH, C.P. (1968), "Critical State Soil Mechanics", McGraw-Hill, London.

8. SINGH, A. and MITCHELL, J.K. (1968), "General stress-strain-time function for soils", Proc. ASCE, Vol. 94 SM1, pp 21-36.

9. WALKER L.K.(1969), "Undrained creep in a sensitive clay", Geotechnique Vol. 19, No. 4 pp 515-529.

THE TEACHING OF RHEOLOGY AND SOIL MECHANICS ON AN UNDERGRADUATE COURSE

M J KEEDWELL

Senior Lecturer, Department of Civil Engineering and Building, Coventry Polytechnic, Priory Street, Coventry CV1 5FB

SYNOPSIS

In order to find reasonable solutions to practical problems, 'traditional' soil mechancis has generally assumed that soil is a perfectly plastic material when stability problems are considered and pseudo-elastic when estimates of deformation under working loads are required. While this elastic-plastic model has often proved quite adequate for design purposes, it creates a problem of credibility since the data from a typical axial loading test on a sample of soil produce a curved stress-strain graph, the slope of which, at any particular stress level, is dependent on the rate of stress increase.

With the objective of closing this credibility gap students in the third year of the MEng course in Civil Engineering are introduced to the visco-elastic rheological model for soil described in the author's book 'Rheology and Soil Mechanics'. This approach is a logical extension of the teaching in the materials module in the second year where simple rheological models are introduced to explain the behaviour of bituminous materials and concrete when subjected to static and dynamic loading.

The paper describes the coursework carried out by the students which includes creep and conventional triaxial tests to determine rheological parameters and the use of these parameters in an analysis of a foundation design by means of a non-linear finite element program. The results of the coursework exercises will be presented, analysed and discussed.

INTRODUCTION

The traditional elastic plastic model for soil behaviour creates a problem of credibility for students who observe, for example, that the data from a typical axial loading test produces a curved stress-strain graph; the slope of which at any particular stress level is dependent on the rate of stress increase. To explain similar behaviour in other materials, for example concrete and bituminous materials it is common practice to use visco-elastic or elastico-viscous models which are capable of predicting the observed time dependent behaviour. It seems logical, therefore, and helpful to the students to extend this type of model to soils. The author, Keedwell [1] has demonstrated the capabilities of this approach and has since introduced it into the teaching of soil mechanics to undergraduate students.

The purpose of this paper is to demonstrate one way of introducing rheological concepts into the teaching of soil mechanics.

THE STUDENTS

The author chose to introduce the rheological concepts outlined below to students in the third academic year of a four year MEng course in Civil Engineering. The normal British undergraduate course is of three years duration and the MEng students are a peer group selected after the second year of the normal BEng course to proceed to an enhanced course of four years leading to the MEng degree. As part of the enhancement of engineering education these students receive an extra 15 hours of tuition in each of the mechanics subjects including soil mechanics. In the latter subject the extra 15 hours were used to achieve the objectives described below.

THE TEACHING OBJECTIVES

The objectives of the teaching programme were as follows:

1. To use rheological concepts to help explain the observed behaviour of soils.

2. To estimate the values of rheological parameters from triaxial test data obtained in the laboratory by the students themselves.

3. To carry out a non-linear finite element analysis of a strip footing founded on the same soil using the above rheological parameters as input data.

4. To compare the results of the non-linear analysis with the behaviour predicted by conventional methods.

THE LABORATORY TESTS

These consisted of consolidated-undrained triaxial tests with pore pressure measurements carried out on nominally identical compacted samples of clay. The class was sub-divided into sixteen groups and each group was responsible for one sample of soil. Three of the groups consisted of MEng students. The following stages of testing were carried out.

All Students	M Eng only
1.Consolidation	Consolidation
2.Undrained hydrostatic compression	----
3.Axial loading to failure	Creep Test

The cell pressures used were as follows

TABLE 1 TEST PRESSURES

Sample No	Consolidation pressure bars	Cell Pressure during axial loading bars	Cell Pressure during Creep bars
1A,1B	1.0	2.0	
2A	1.1	2.1	
2B	1.1	---	1.1
3A	1.3	2.3	---
3B	1.1	---	1.1
4A	1.6	2.6	---
4B	1.1	---	1.1
5A,5B	2.0	3.0	---
6A,6B	2.5	3.5	---
7A,7B	3.1	4.1	---
8A,8B	3.8	4.8	---

Undrained hydrostatic compression was achieved by raising the cell pressure by 1 bar in all cases.

THE SOIL

The triaxial samples consisted of a local coal measures clay similar to Keuper Marl. The Clay was compacted at a nominal water content of 18% in a Procter mould and then extruded into 38 mm dia sample tubes.

THE TEACHING NOTES

The reference book for this part of the course is Keedwell [1] and in addition lectures were supplemented by the following notes intended to summarize the visco-elastic approach to the modelling of soil behaviour.

MENG REPORT

DETERMINATION OF RHEOLOGICAL PARAMETERS

1.THEORY

1.1. Introduction

The contact zones in a typical soil occupy only a minute proportion of the total soil volume. (See Fig.1.) Consequently the material in the contact zones is subjected to stresses orders of magnitude higher than the stresses typically applied at the boundaries of a soil element. The effect of these very high contact zone stresses is tocause viscous or thixotropic rather than elastic behaviour of a soil element. For a soil element under 5 m of overburden the contact zone shear stresses are typically in the range 10^6 - 10^8 kN/m^2.

1.2 Newtonian Viscosity

In this case strain rate is proportional to the stress level, i.e.:

$$d\varepsilon/dt = \sigma/\text{const.}$$

1.3 Non-linear Viscosity

Strain rate is proportional to a function of stress level, e.g:

$$d\varepsilon/dt = \sigma^k/\text{const.} \qquad \text{(power law)}$$

or

$$d\varepsilon/dt = \exp(\sigma)/\text{const.}$$

1.4 The Hyperbolic Sine Function of Stress

An equation of the type

$$d\varepsilon/dt = B.\sinh(a\sigma)$$

where B and a are constants, indicates Newtonian viscosity at low stress levels and non-linear viscosity at high stress levels.

1.5 Thixotropy

In this case the constant of porportionality appears to be dependent on the rate of stress change, i.e.:

$$d\varepsilon/dt = B.f(d\sigma/dt).\sinh(a\sigma)$$

For example a bentonite slurry is a liquid when agitated and becomes a gel when at rest.

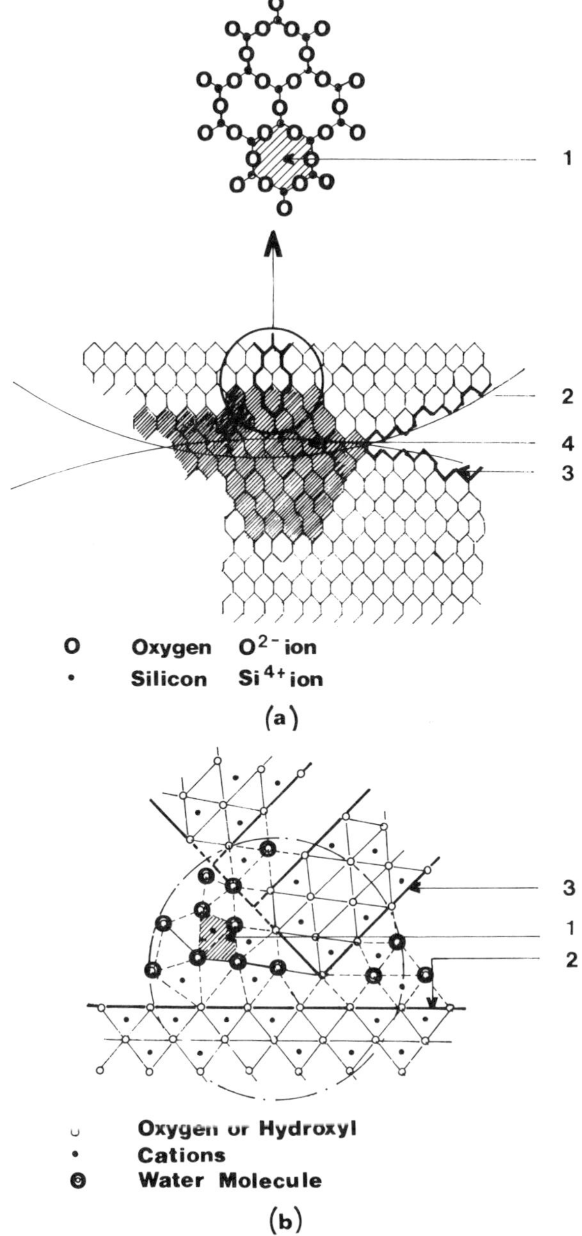

Fig 1 Two dimensional aralogs of contact zones

(a) Contact zone formed between two quartz particles: 1 - flow unit, 2 and 3 surfaces of particles, 4 contact zone.

(b) Contact zone formed between two montmorillonite clay particles (after Arnold, 1967): 1 - flow unit, 2 and 3 surfaces of particles.

1.6 General Equation for Viscous and Thixotropic Materials

Introducing a parameter m we may write:

$$d\varepsilon/dt = B.(d\sigma/dt)^{m}.\sinh(a\sigma)$$

where m = 0 for a viscous material,
m > 0 for a thixotropic material,
and m = 1 for a non-linear elastic material
$(d\sigma/d\varepsilon=(B.\sinh(a\sigma))^{-1})$

This equation applies only when $d\sigma/dt > 0$, e.g, the axial loading stage of a triaxial test. The stress level σ needs to be carefully defined (see paras 1.13 and 1.14)

1.7 Creep

Now the stress level is constant, i.e, $d\sigma/dt = 0$.

1.8 Creep of a Viscous Material

In this case the strain rate remains constant throughout the period of creep, i.e.:

$$(d\varepsilon/dt)_{t>t_1} = (d\varepsilon/dt)_{t = t_1}$$

where t_1 is the time during which the stress level is raised from zero to the constant stress level σ.

1.9 Creep of a Thixotropic Material

In this case the strain rate decreases with the lapse of time, i.e.:

$$(d\varepsilon/dt)_{t>t_1} < (d\varepsilon/dt)_{t = t_1}$$

The loading period represents agitation followed by a period in which gelling progessively reduces the strain rate.

1.10 General Equation for Creep

Using the parameter m again, we may write:

$$(d\varepsilon/dt)_{t>t_1} = (d\varepsilon/dt)_{t = t_1} .(t/t_1)^{-m}$$

where m = 0 for a viscous material,
m > 0 for a thixotropic material,

and $(d\varepsilon/dt)_{t=t_1} = B.(d\sigma/dt)^{m}_{t = t_1} .\sinh(a(\sigma)_{t = t_1})$

The strain rate during creep depends, therefore, on:

(1) the length of time the stress level has been kept constant $(t - t_1)$,

(2) the stress level $(\sigma)_{t > t_1}$,

(3) the rate of change of stress level just prior to the period of creep $(d\sigma/dt)_{t = t_1}$.

1.11 Typical Values of Parameter m

For cohesionless soils m = 0. (mineral to mineral type contact zones, Fig 1a)

For pure (fat) clays m = 1. (Absorbed water layer type contact zones, Fig 1b)

For sandy clays, boulder clays, clayey sands etc. $0 < m < 1$.
(a mixture of contact zone types or hybrid types or both)

1.12 Modes of Deformation

The modes of deformation differ at different stages of a triaxial test. During consolidation the mode may be described as compression without shear distortion (Fig 2b) and during axial loading the main effect of the axial load is to produce symmetrical shear distortion (Fig.2a) with a small amount of compression.

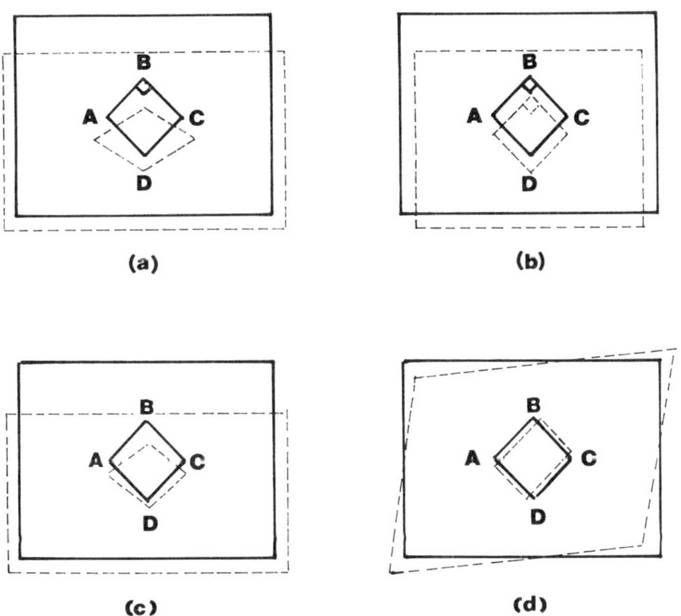

Fig 2 Two dimensional analog of various modes of deformation.

(a) symmetrical shear distortion without volume change.
(b) Compression without shear distortion
(c) Symmetrical shear distortion and volume change combined
(d) Asymetric shear distortion.

1.13 Rheological Equations for Compression without Shear Distortion

Compression without shear distortion is caused by a change in mean effective pressure p' (= $(\sigma'_1 + \sigma'_2 + \sigma'_3)$). However strain rate is insensitive to the magnitude of p'. For example, the coefficient of secondary consolidation is typically insensitive to the effective stress level.

Let $\sigma = (p')^n$ where n is small (say < 0.01)

then $d\sigma/dt = n.\ (dp'/dt).(p')^{n-1}$

$= n.\ (dp'/dt)/p'$ approx.

Hence when $dp'/dt > 0$ (i.e. the primary consolidation stage), the equation of para.1.6 becomes:

$$d\varepsilon_z/dt = B.n.((dp'dt)/p')^m.\sinh(a(p')^n)$$

but $(p')^n = 1$ approx., therefore:

$$d\varepsilon_z/dt = B_v.((dp'/dt)/p')^m \quad \text{where } B_v = n.\ \text{sinh}a.$$

Note that when m = 1 this equation becomes $d\varepsilon_z/dp' = \text{const.}/p'$
i.e. $\varepsilon_z = \text{const} + \text{const}_1 \ln p'$
which is consistent with the well known relationship for normally consolidated clay from which the compression index C_c is calculated

For $dp'/dt = 0$ (i.e. secondary consolidation)

$$(d\varepsilon/dt)_{t > t_1} = (d\varepsilon/dt)_{t = t_1}.(t/t_1)^{-m}$$

where $(d\varepsilon/dt)_{t=t_1} = B.((dp'/dt)/p')^m_{t=t_1}$

Note that when m = 1 this equation predicts the well-known linear relationship between secondary consolidation and the logarithm of time

1.14 Stress Level for Symmetrical Shear Distortion

In this case the vertical strain rate $d\varepsilon_z/dt$ is known to be very sensistive to the value of the vertical effective stress σ_z'. Also, for a given value of σ'_z the strain rate decreases as p' increases.

Hence we might choose the stress ratio

$$s'_z = \sigma'_z/p' \qquad \text{as stress level.}$$

However, a soil element can be at rest (i.e.$d\varepsilon/dt = 0$) when the stress ratio has some non-zero value $s'_{z,0}$. (e.g. after isotropic consolidation $s'_{z,0} = 1$).

Therefore let $\sigma = s'_{z,t} - s'_{z,0}$

where s'_z is the current value of stress ratio and $s'_{z,0}$ is the stress ratio when the soil element was last at rest.

1.15 Rheological Equations for Symmetrical Shear Distortion

Putting $\sigma = s'_{z,t} - s'_{z,0}$ then

for $ds'/dt > 0$, (e.g. the axial loading stage),

$$d\varepsilon_z/dt = B.(abs(ds'_z/dt))^m.\sinh(a(s'_z - s'_{z,0}))$$

(abs(ds'_z/dt) because the agitation affect is independent of the sign of the rate of stress change).

for $ds'_z/dt = 0$ (i.e. the drained creep test)

$$(d\varepsilon_z/dt)_{t>t_1} = (d\varepsilon_z/dt)_{t=t_1}.(t/t_1)^{-m}$$

where $(d\varepsilon_z/dt)_{t=t_1} = B.(abs(ds'_z/dt)^m_{t=t_1}.\sinh(a(s'_{z,t} - s'_{z,0})_{t=t_1})$.

1.16. Symmetrical Shear Distortion and Compression Combined

In this case:

$$(d\varepsilon_z/dt)_{a+b} = (d\varepsilon_z/dt)_a + (d\varepsilon_z/dt)_b$$

where subscript a refers to the equations in para.1.15
and subscript b refers to the equations in para.1.13.

1.17 Volumetric Strain Rate

According to stress-dilatancy theory;
for symmetrical shear distortion in triaxial conditions:

$$(d\varepsilon_v/dt)_{t,a} = (1 - \tan\beta\tan\eta)(d\varepsilon_z/dt)_{t,a} \quad \text{(Rowe [2])}$$

where β and η are angles describing the soil structure (see Fig 3)

For compression without shear distortion, assume:

$$(d\varepsilon_z/dt)_{t,b} = (1 + \tan\beta\tan\eta)(d\varepsilon_z/dt)_{t,b} \quad \text{(Keedwell [1])}$$

where symmetrical shear distortion and compression occur simultaneously:

$$(d\varepsilon_v/dt)_{a+b} = (d\varepsilon_v/dt)_a + (d\varepsilon_v/dt)_b$$

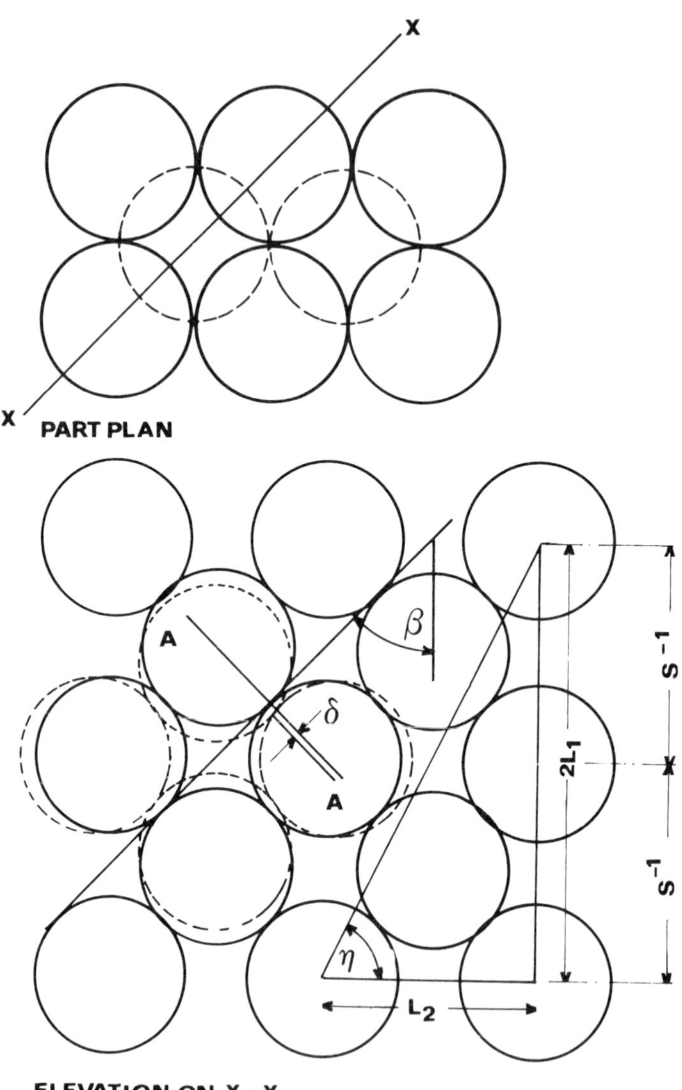

Fig 3 Real Soil Modelled as Consisting of Perfect Spheres (After Rowe [2]

1.18 Pore Water Pressures

For the undrained case, if soil is saturated then:

$$\delta u = K_s . \delta \varepsilon_v$$

where K_s is the bulk modulus of water corrected to take into account the compressibility of the soil particles.

Generally:

$$\delta u = B_s . K_s . \delta \varepsilon$$

where B_s is Skempton's pore pressure parameter.

Dividing both sides by δt and letting $\delta t \rightarrow 0$ yields:

$$du/dt = B_s . K_s .(d\varepsilon_v/dt)$$

2. ANALYSIS OF RESULTS

2.1 Creep Tests

(a) Plot ε_z versus lnt. If this plot is a straight line then m=1.

(b) Plot $\ln(d\varepsilon_z/dt)$ v lnt. The slope of this plot is -m.

(c) Using the data from several creep tests plot $(d\varepsilon_z/dt)_t$ at a specific time t versus $s'_{z,t} - s'_{z,0}$. If plot is linear determine the product B. (abs(ds'/dt)m.a.

(d) Plot $\ln(d\varepsilon_z/dt)$ v $s'_{z,t} - s'_{z,0}$ If plot is linear determine a.

2.2. Axial Loading Stage

(a) Select one set of data.

(b) Determine the average value of $B_s . K_s$.

Taking the average value of δu as $u_f - u_0$

and the average value of $\delta \varepsilon_v$ as $\varepsilon_{vf} - \varepsilon_{v0}$,

then $B_s . K_s = (u_f - u_0)/(\varepsilon_{vf} - \varepsilon_{v0})$.

where subscript 0 indicates values at commencement of axial loading,
subscript f indicates failure values.

(c) Estimate the value of B_v.

When m=1 $B_v \doteq 0.5 m_v . \sigma'_3$ (See Keedwell [1] page 161)

where σ'_3 = cell pressure during consolidation.

(d) Plot a curve of $s'_{z,t}$ versus $\varepsilon_{z,t}$ using experimental data.

(e) Plot a predicted curve of $s'_{z,t}$ versus $\varepsilon_{z,t}$. A program will be needed for this using the appropriate rheological equations in finite difference form, i.e.:

$$\delta\varepsilon_{z} = \delta\varepsilon_{z,a} + \delta\varepsilon_{z,b}$$

where $$\delta\varepsilon_{z,a} = B.(\mathrm{abs}\,\delta s')^{m}.\delta t^{1-m}.\sinh(a(s'_{z,t} - s'_{z,0}))$$

and $$\delta\varepsilon_{z,b} = B_{v}.(\mathrm{abs}\,\delta p')^{m}.\delta t^{1-m}.(p')^{-m}$$

If at time t the axial strain is $\varepsilon_{z,t}$ then the axial strain at t + δt is given by:

$$\varepsilon_{z,t+t} = \varepsilon_{z,t} + \delta\varepsilon_{z,t}$$

Use the m value determined in the creep test and B_v as estimated at c above. For the trial run try B_v = 0.05 min. $^{m-1}$ and a = 6, and use the values of u determined by experiment. For our data δt=1min.

(f) Compare the predicted and experimental curves and adjust the values of the parameters until good agreement is obtained.

(g) Plot a curve of $\varepsilon_{v,t}$ versus $\varepsilon_{z,t}$ using experimental data.

(h) Plot a predicted curve of $\varepsilon_{v,t}$ versus $\varepsilon_{z,t}$. For this modify the program used at e above.

In this case: $$\delta\varepsilon_{v} = \delta\varepsilon_{v,a} + \delta\varepsilon_{v,b}$$

where $$\delta\varepsilon_{v,a} = (1 - \tan\beta\tan\eta).\ \delta\varepsilon_{z,a}$$

and $$\delta\varepsilon_{v,b} = (1 + \tan\beta\tan\eta).\ \delta\varepsilon_{z,b}$$

If at the time t the volumetric strain is $\varepsilon_{v,t}$ then the volumetric strain at time t +δt is given by:

$$\varepsilon_{v,t+t} = \varepsilon_{v,t} + \delta\varepsilon_{v,t}$$

For the trial run try $\tan\beta\tan\eta$ = 1.02.

(i) Compare the predicted and experimental curves and adjust the value of $\tan\beta\tan\eta$ until good agreement is obtained.

(j) Modify the program so that it uses predicted instead of experimental values of u.

For this use: $$\delta u = B_{s}.K_{s}.\ \delta\varepsilon_{v}.$$

If at the time t the pore pressure is u_t then the pore pressure at time t + δt is given by:

$$u_{t+\delta t} = u_t + \delta u$$

(k) Using the final version of the program plot predicted and experimental curves of $\sigma_1 - \sigma_3$, u and ε_v versus ε_z .

(l) List the values of the rheological parameters obtained by all MEng groups. Comment on any variations.

VALUES OF RHEOLOGICAL PARAMETERS

The table below lists the values of the rheological parameters obtained by the MEng students. Since the triaxial samples were nominally indentical the values of the parameters obtained by all students should have been the same. This was approximately true in the case of parameters B_V, B, m, a and $\tan\beta\tan\eta$ but there was considerable variation in the value of the product $B_S K_S$. Both Bs and K_S are dependent on measurements of pore-water pressure and K_S is also dependent on measurements of volume change during axial loading. Both of these measurements are, of course, the most difficult to achieve with a high degree of accuracy. Fig 4 shows comparisons of predicted and observed soil behaviour for sample 3A.

TABLE 2 VALUES OF RHEOLOGICAL PARAMETERS

Sample No	Student	B_V	B	m	a	$B_S K_S$ (kN/m^2)	$\tan\beta\tan\eta$	n
	CD	0.0154	0.004	1.0	4.0	1457	0.96	0.41
2A	JF	0.0154	0.0009	1.0	5.0	2100	0.97	0.23
	MB	0.019	0.001	1.0	7.75	800	1.0	0.01
3A	JH	0.019	0.001	1.0	9.00	800	1.0	0.005
	NK	0.019	0.00095	1.0	7.15	800	1.0	0.017
4A	SN	0.021	0.0015	1.0	6.00	3000	1.02	0.07

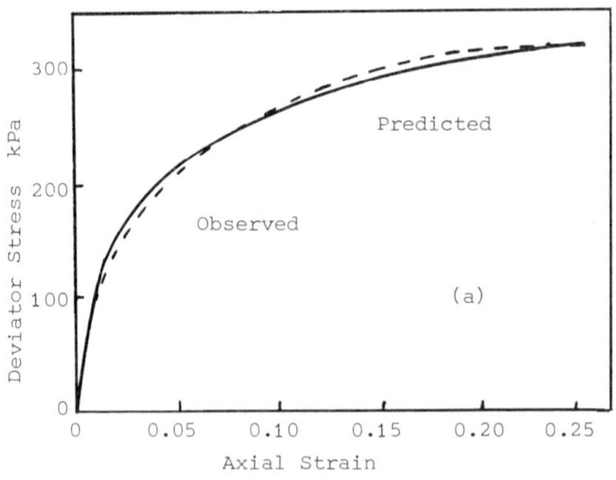

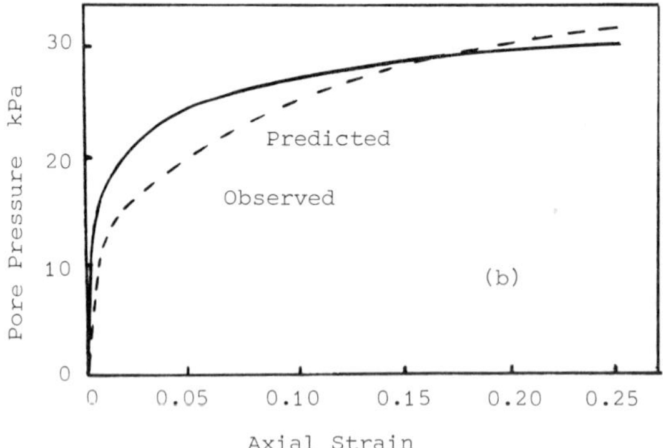

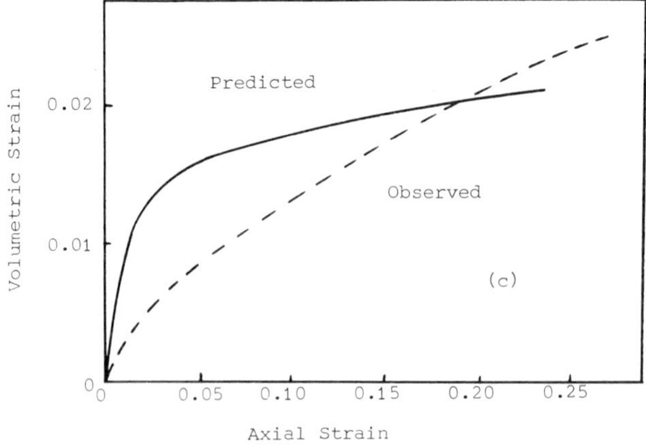

Fig 4 Comparison between predicted and observed behaviour of laboratory samples. (a) Deviator stress versus strain (b) Pore water pressure versus axial strain. (c) Volumetric strain versus Axial strain

ANALASIS OF STRIP FOOTING BY THE FINITE ELEMENT METHOD

At the time of writing it is proposed to use a finite element analysis program CCNONLIN to predict the behaviour of a strip footing founded on the clay soil tested in the laboratory. The following analyses will be carried out:

(a) An elastic analysis, ie. assuming the soil behaves as a linear elastic continuum.

(b) A non-linear analysis using the average values of the rheological parameters listed in Table 2.

In both cases undrained and drained conditions will be analysed.

The capabilities of CCNONLIN will be demonstrated during the interactive computer session of the conference.

CONCLUSIONS

1. A reasonably satisfactory prediction of the observed stress strain behaviour of triaxial test samples has been obtained using a comparitively simple viscous/thixotopic model for soil behaviour.

2. The agreement between predicted and observed volumetric strain was the least satisfactory feature of the results. It is not certain whether this is due to inadequacies in the experimental measurements of volume change or deficiencies in the theoretical model.

REFERENCES

1. Keedwell, M J, "Rheology and Soil Mechanics" Elsevier Applied Science Publishers, London, 1984.

2. Rowe, P W, "The Stress-Dilatancy Relation for Static Equilibrium of an Assembly of Particles in Contact" Proc. Royal Society, A269 pp 500-527, 1962.

RHEOLOGICAL MODEL FOR TIME DEPENDENT BEHAVIOUR OF LATERALLY LOADED PILES

G. Murtaza
Department of Civil Engineering, A.M.U., Aligarh, India
Gopal Ranjan
Department of Civil Engineering, University of Roorkee, Roorkee, India
Shamsher Prakash
Department of Civil Engineering, University of Missouri, Rolla, Rolla, USA

ABSTRACT

Rheological models have been used in the field of geotechnical engineering to describe the deformation-time behaviour of soils under stress (1, 2). Various models have been used to analyse clay deformation as a rate process (3, 4), to explain land-slide occurrences (5), to represent time-dependent behaviour of a frozen cohesive soil under lateral stress at constant temperature (6) and similar other phenomenon.

The rheological models usually consist of fundamental units of springs in combination with dashpot and slides. The early treatment (7, 8) considered linear spring element called Hookean model, the dashpot element as it simulates a purely viscous phenomenon termed Newtonian model and the friction slides called yield stress model. The coupling of these elements in different forms yielded a series of general composite rheological models. Further, coupling of these composite models provide multi-composite rheological models, which have been used to explain the various phenomenon.

The importance of time-load-deformation of soil-pile has been well recognized. In case of a pile in soft saturated cohesive soil deposit under lateral load, the soil continuum deforms due to pore water drainage from the macropores and the secondary drainage starts from the micropores into macropores. The micro-structure of plastic soil particles creeps and thus compression, secondary consolidation and creep start at a time. Physically, the soil-pile system can be represented by a rheological model.

A comprehensive experimental study has been carried out on single vertical and batter piles in a soft saturated clay deposit under lateral load. Based upon the load-time-deformation characteristics of the system a rheological model consisting of a non-linear spring simulating the strain softening effect of creeping plastic soil mass and a dashpot with a non-linear viscosity to account for the actual change in viscosity of the system has been developed to predict the behaviour of piles. The rheological constants of the model have been evaluated by utilising the data from two pile load tests. The rheological constants are then utilised to predict the time-deformation history of the pile.

The influence of various factors affecting the rheological constants has been highlighted. Using the suggested rheological model the test data on laterally loaded piles reported in the literature has been analysed and comparison with observed and predicted deformations have been made demonstratiting the universality of the approach.

INTRODUCTION

The study of the mechanical properties of soil-water system with regard to stress-deformation behaviour requires certain assumptions of mathematical description. In addition to the deforming stress, the variation in behaviour may be due to time, temperature and similar other factors. The relationship used to describe the stress - strain - time - temperature behaviour is called its rheological equation of state.

Rheology ascribes to practically all types of material properties concerning their response to applied stresses. As a result, the type of behaviour considered may be perfectly elastic, plastic, elasto-plastic, visco-elastic and visco-plastic. This wide range of behaviour may also include stages where one or more of these types will describe stress-strain-time characteristics of the isothermal system.

Rheological models have been used to describe the deformation - time behaviour under stress. These models usually consist of fundamental units of springs in combination with dashpot and slides. The coupling of these elements in different forms yielded a series of general composite and multi-composite models.

The time-dependent behaviour of soils with regard to stress-strain consolidation, and similar other phenomenon have been explained through suitable rheological models. Not only this, the rheological models have also been used to predict the load-time-deformation behaviour of laterally loaded piles (9).

In the present paper, a rheological model has been proposed to predict the time dependent behaviour of single vertical and batter piles under lateral loads in cohesive soil. Also, the experimental technique has been suggested to evaluate the rheological constants for the system.

LITERATURE REVIEW

There is an increasing interest in developing more realistic rheological model to describe the time - dependent behaviour of soils under stresses. Murayama and Shibata (1) studied the rheological character of clays by proposing a model consisting of a top spring to a Kelvin unit to account for an immediate compression of skeleton. Also, a St. Venant element was introduced by modifying the kelvin unit to represent a threshold stress or bond strength. The rheological properties of clays were investigated using the proposed model. In the analysis, the viscosity of clay was assumed to be a structural viscosity derived from statistical mechanics and based on the frequency of the mutual exchange of position between each water molecule and its void in a bond material containing soil particles. A new formula was developed to explain the deformation strength of clay with this model. This formula worked well to explain the results of tests on compression flow, stress relaxation and long term strength of clays. The proposed rheological model was used to explain flow and stress relaxation of clays by improving and revising some unsatisfactory assumptions and treatments used in their earlier work (10). The mechanism of clay behaviour has been explained by considering statistically the micrometric structure of clay skelton and on the deduction of theories concerning the rheological macrocharacters of clay. The analysis thus obtained agrees well with the results of various experiments.

Christesen and Wu (3) suggested a rheological model formed by parallel coupling of Kelvin and Maxwell units to analyse clays deformation as a rate process. It was considered that the strain under shear stress is a result of slip at particle contacts. Further, it was assumed that the slip obeys the rate process theory. The behaviour of this rheological model was found to agree with experimental results. The model parameters were calculated from the experimental data. These parameters were then used to interpret the mechanism of deformation. Barden (11) suggested a non-linear Kelvin model to explain the actual behaviour of consolidation of clay. However, the solved model consists of a Hookean spring with a non-linear dashpot to incorporate a non-linear viscosity in the proposed theoretical analysis.

Wu, et. al. (4) proposed the analysis of consolidation by Rate Process Theory using a rheological model formed by parallel coupling of a Maxwell and Hookean units. It has been suggested that secondary compression is the result of slow viscous displacements at the soil particle contacts. The primary consolidation is governed by the rate of hydraulic flow and the rate of secondary compression is governed principally by the viscous resistance of the soil skeleton.

Barden (12) investigated the time-dependent deformations of normally consolidated clays and peats on the basis of the Kelvin model with non-linear viscosity. According to him there exists two levels of structures, with primary consolidation the results of drainage of a system of macropores, and secondary consolidation the subsequent drainage of a system of micropores into the macropores. This assumed mechanism is represented by a rheological model consisting of a Kelvin unit with non-linear dashpot.

Komamura and Huang (5) proposed a new rheological model

from uniaxial creep test results to explain land slide occurances. The model consists of a series of Bingham and Kelvin units. This model which is called the visco-plasto-elastic model, was used to explain the state changes of soil based on water content and stress level. Three sub-models, visco-elastic model, visco-plastic model and viscous model were deduced from the original model. The creep and flow behaviour of these three models are based upon the boundaries of the critical stress and consistancies of clay.

Aziz and Loba (6) suggested a Burger's rheological model to represent the time -dependent behaviour of a freozen cohessive soil under lateral stress and at constant temperatures. The tests were conducted to correlate the stress-time and strain-time behaviour of the actual frozen cohesive soil layer with the proposed rheological model in order to establish a stress-strain-time relationship for the soil-ice-water system under investigation.

Wu, et. al. (13) studied the creep deformation of clays. Drained triaxial tests were used to measure stress-strain-time behaviour of clays. Undisturbed as samples of glacial deposits near cleveland, a plastic clay from Nevada and remoulded Grundit clay were used for testing. On the test results, a creep low of the form (equation 1) was obtained:

$$\epsilon = c \quad t^n \qquad \ldots\ldots(1)$$

where,

ϵ = strain

t = time

c and n are material constants.

Displacements around an excavation near Cleveland were computed using the measured properties of the Cleveland soils. A close agreement was observed between the computed and measured final displacements. In these studies, the material constants c and n worked out on the basis of laboratory investigations were used to predict the field behaviour.

The importance of load-time-deformation of soil-pile system has been well recognized. Pouls (14) suggested the procedure to predict both immediate and total final displacement of the pile head under applied lateral load. In the elastic analysis for the lateral displacement of pile head the changed values of soil modulus, E for undrained and drained condition may be used to compute immediate and final displacements. However, it is difficult to determine these values from laboratory tests as both the initial stress state and final stress state cannot be readily estimated with reliability. Moreover, prediction of deformations at any specific time is out of question. Hoadley (15) observed that the load deformation behaviour of soil-pile system was non-linear with significant time-dependent deflections. Hoadley analysed the soil-pile behaviour in terms of equivalent Winkler medium and non-linear behaviour was accounted for by a reduction in the stiffness modulus. The available literature reveals that little attempt has been made to study the non-linear time-load-deformation behaviour of a laterally loaded pile.

THEORETICAL ASPECTS

The problem of a laterally loaded pile can be simulated to a beam resting on a foundation. The soil-pile system can thus be represented through an appropriate rheological model. The system related to the problem under investigation is applicable to piles embedded in soft cohesive soil, which exhibits time-dependent deformations. The resulted deformation is due to the response of the system to loading as an interactional outcome with regard to time. Thus, the rheological model be so chosen as to represent the interactional behaviour.

The proposed model takes into account the time-dependent deformations in addition to shear interaction between the adjacent elements. It consists of a set of two kelvin units placed in series and attached by springs to account for the existance of shear interactions. The first kelvin unit with a spring stiffness K1 and a dashpot of viscosity η_1 takes into account the deformations due to consolidation. The second kelvin with different spring stiffness K2 and viscosity of dashpot η_2 takes into account the deformations due to creep.

Figure 1 represents beam on visco-elastic foundation. Fig.2 shows a small element of the beam under the action of applied load, p, the developed soil reaction is p per unit length. Q and M are respectively shear and moments produced. q is the uniformly distributed load. K1 and K2 are the stiffness of models η_1 and η_2 are the viscosities of the dashpots. G represents the shear interaction between two adjacent elements.

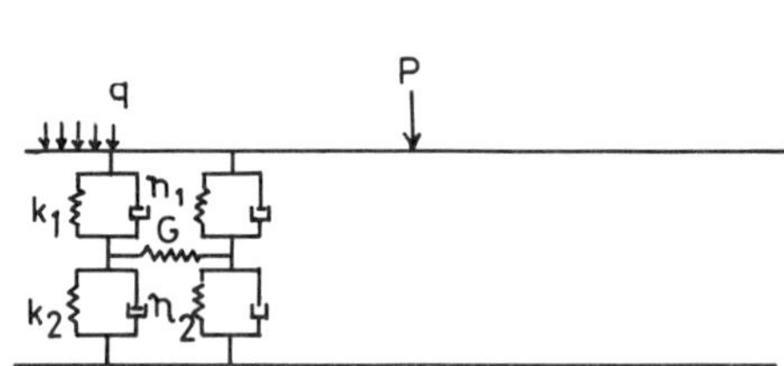

FIG.1. PROPOSED MATHEMATICAL MODEL FOR SOIL-PILE SYSTEM (BEAM ON VISCO-ELASTIC FOUNDATION)

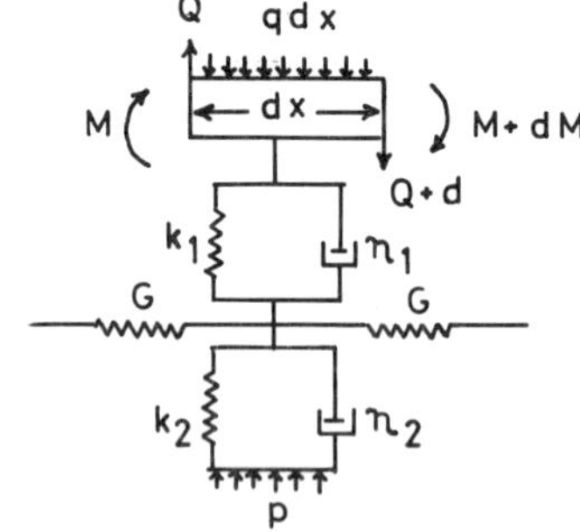

FIG.2. A SMALL ELEMENT OF THE BEAM SHOWN IN FIG.1.

The differential equation based on proposed visco-elastic foundation with shear interaction is given by equation 2.

$$E1 \frac{d^4Y}{dX^4} = - \quad Y(K_1+K2) + \eta_1 \frac{dY1}{dt1} + \eta_2 \frac{dY2}{dt2} - G \nabla^2 Y + q \quad ....(2)$$

The differential equation (2) based on the proposed visco-elastic foundation with shear interaction can be solved for known boundary conditions. Deflection, rotation, shear, moment and soil reaction as a function of time can be determined along the entire length of the pile. However, there is difficulty in determining the soil parameters and separating the deformations due to consolidation and creep. Further, before shear failure under applied load the soil contium deforms due to pore water drainage from the macropores and secondary drainage starts from the micropores into macropores. The micro-structure of plastic soil particles creeps and thus compression, secondary consolidation and creep start at a time. Physically, the entire mechanism of deformation can be better simulated by a non-linear kelvin model consisting of a non-linear spring simulating the strain softening effect of creeping plastic soil mass and a dashpot with a non-linear viscosity to account for the actual change in viscosity of the system. In fact, the viscous resistance increases with time (12). Therefore, non-linear viscosity represents a more realistic picture of the mechanism during primary and secondary compression. Thus, the proposed non-linear kelvin model is adopted to simulate the mechanism of deformation of laterally loaded piles embedded in soft cohesive soils (Fig.3).

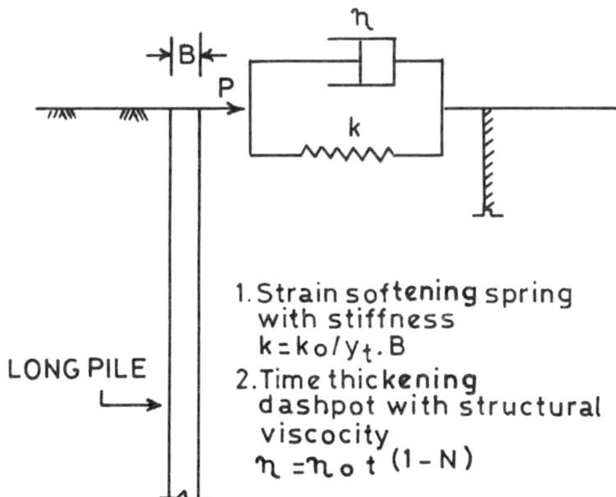

FIG.3. SOIL-PILE SYSTEM REPRESENTED BY RHEOLOGICAL MODEL (TOP BOUNDARY CONDITION)

The derived time-load-deformation relationship(equation3)

$$Y_t = \frac{(P - K_o)}{B\eta_o} \cdot \frac{t^N}{N} \qquad \text{.....(3a)}$$

$$= A\ t^N \qquad \text{.....(3b)}$$

where

$$A = \frac{(P - K_o)}{B\eta_o} \cdot \frac{1}{N} \qquad \text{.....(4)}$$

$$N = (1 - m) \qquad \text{.....(5)}$$

can be solved knowing the rheological constants i.e. K_o, η_o and N.

K_o is a stiffness constant of the spring of the proposed rheological model with load units. To incorporate the non-linear behaviour of soft creeping plastic clay it is assumed that the stiffness of the spring K of kelvin unit decreases with increasing deformation. Thus, K_o the coefficient of the stiffness of the spring is a product of the stiffness and deformation attained at time t of the system under a sustained load and remains constant for a given soil-pile system during the process of deformation. η is a structural viscosity of the proposed dashpot of the units simulating the behaviour of the deforming clay. It increases with the time and the time thickening effect is assumed to vary in the form.

$$\eta = \eta_o t^m \qquad \text{......(6)}$$

where η_o is the initial viscosity of the dashpot with the units of stress-time. According to the analysis η_o remains constant for the given system during the process of deformation. m is an exponent number and it remains constant according to the proposed relationship for all corresponding changes in deformation during the application of load.

Having known the rheological constants, the time-load-deformation behaviour can be obtained.

The above analysis holds good for the case of vertical pile. In case of batter piles under horizontal load, the geometry and end conditions change. However, if the horizontal load acting on pile head is resolved into an axial component and the normal component and the deflections are considered normal to the pile's axis the analysis could be extended to the case of batter piles. The rheological constants will thus be dependent upon the pile angle.

EVALUATION OF RHEOLOGICAL CONSTANTS

The rheological constants have been obtained utilizing the time-load-deformation data on model instrumented piles. Tests were carried out using 19, 22 and 25 mm outer diameter vertical long piles and batter piles in soft cohesive soil. Both the positive and negative batter angles 10°, 20°, and 30° were tested. The horizontal deformation with respect to time were noted to observe the time-deformation behaviour.

The clay used in investigation was a locally available grey coloured clay. The classification of clay as per unified soil classification system is 'CH'. The soil was sundried and pulverized. It was then mixed with predetermined quantity of water and allowed to stand for 24 hours. The clay was than filled in a tank 1mx1mx1.2m high. The piles were jacked using a special jacking arrangement.

The cohesion value of the soil deposits was determined all along the depth of tank using laboratory vane. Soil samples were also collected all through the depth of deposit at 24 cm interval to determine the variation of moisture content. The moisture content in all these tests was varied from 35 percent to 52.37 percent (9).

(a) Vertical Piles

The rheological constants are evaluated by analysing test data of vertical piles subjected to individual and also by incremental sustained lateral loads.

a.1 Computation of Rheological Constants Using Incremental Sustained Lateral Loads:

A single pile test data from test under sustained lateral loads increased in steps, is analysed to determine the rheological constants. Y-t curves for the test data on an arithmatical scale are shown in fig.4 and on long-long scale in fig.5. The values of N obtained from the slope of y-t plot on log-log scale and intercepts A on y-axis are computed from the test data. The values of A, thus obtained are plotted against the corresponding lateral load P (fig. 6). The P-A plot is a straight line. Thus, all the three rheological constants N, K_o and η_o of the time-load-deformation relationship are evaluated. The values of rheological constants thus obtained are tabulated in table 1.

Table 1: Rheological Constants for Incremental Sustained Lateral Loads.

S.No.	Rheological Constants			Soil Properties	
	N	K_o	$\eta_o \times 10^3$ (Kg-min/cm^2)	w %	c (Kg/cm^2)
1.	0.10	0.60	0.085227	47.6	0.2387

The rheological constants are noted to vary with the soil consistency, type of pile and batter angle of the pile and the nature of loading.

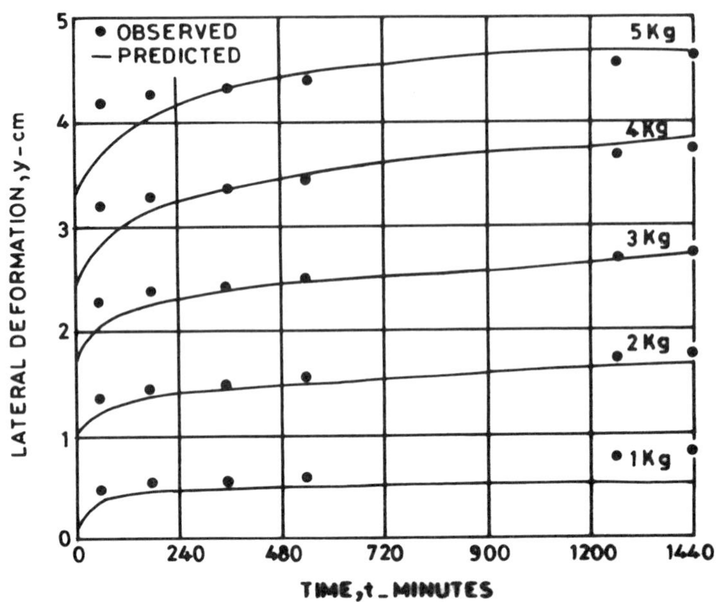

FIG.4. OBSERVED AND PREDICTED y-t PLOTS FOR SUSTAINED LATERAL LOADS

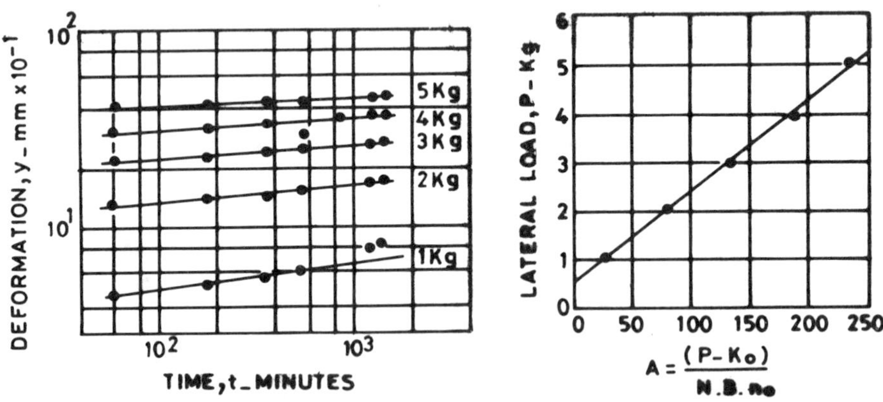

FIG.5. y-t PLOTS ON LOG-LOG SCALE OF SINGLE VERTICAL PILE UNDER INCREMENTAL SUSTAINED LATERAL LOADS.

FIG.6. P-A PLOT FOR INCREMENTAL SUSTAINED LATERAL LOADS

a.2 Computation of Rheological Constants Using Individual Sustained Lateral Loads:

A series of tests under different sustained lateral loads were performed to evaluate the rheological constants of the time-load-deformation relationship developed to describe the deformation pattern of the proposed rheological model. Similar results were obtained. The values of rheological constants thus obtained are shown in table2.

Table 2: Rheological Constants for Individual Sustained Lateral Loads.

S.No.	Rheological Constants			Soil Properties	
	N	K_o (Kg)	$\eta_o \times 10^3$ (Kg-min/cm^2)	W %	c (Kg/cm^2)
1.	.095	0.60	0.05303	50.60	0.1615

The exponential function, N, of the proposed rheological relationship is the rate of deformation on log-log scale which is governed by the interactional behaviour of the system. Thus, for a similar pile N values are expected to very with change in soil characteristics and according to the response of the system. The observations indicate a decrease in N values with the increase in the stiffness of the soil.

The coefficient of stiffness of strain softening spring, K_o is a function of the strength properties of the soil deposit. Test data indicate that with the increase in strength of soil deposit K_o increases.

The coefficient of structural viscosity, η_o increases with the decrease of moisture content of the deposit which in tern increases the strength of the soil, keeping other variables constants.

(b) Batter Piles

The negative and positive batter piles with batter angle of 10°, 20°, and 30° and one vertical pile were tested for incremental sustained loading. The time interval for the application of sustained horizontal load was maintained as 24 hours when another load was applied. The time-dependent-deformation for the period of 24 hours were recorded for each increment of horizontal load. Fig.7 shows the load-deformation plot for positive batter piles. The time-dependent-deformation under 1, 3 and 5 kg loads for +10° batter pile on log-log scale are shown in fig.8. This plot (fig.8) can be utilized to evaluate the two constants defined by the equation 3 and 4 representing an intercept and slope of straight line. In view of three unknown in equation 3(a) at least one more test data is required on the same pile to evaluate all the three constants. Utilizing the record test data, the values of P and A

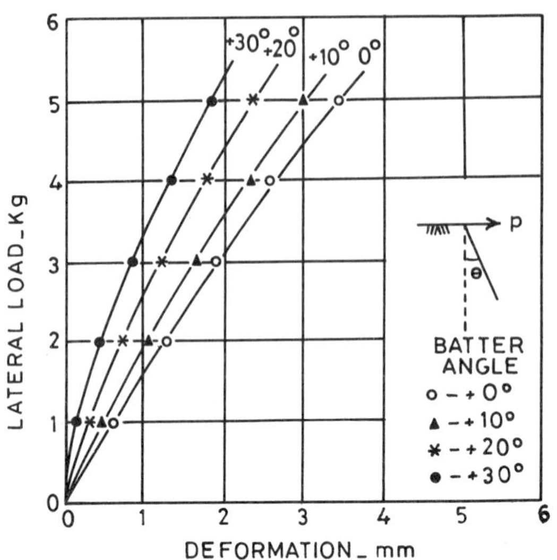

FIG.7. LOAD DEFORMATION CURVES FOR POSITIVE BATTER PILE +10

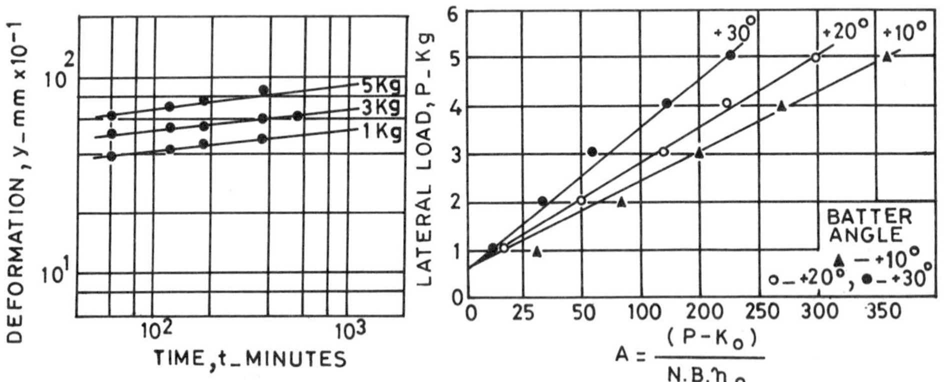

FIG.8. y-t PLOTS ON LOG-LOG SCALE FOR POSITIVE BATTER PILE +10

FIG.9. P-A PLOTS FOR POSITIVE BATTER PILES

reobtained and data plotted (fig.9) and values of rheological constants obtained. Similar plots have been made for piles with other batter angles. The values of the rheological constants obtained for different negative and positive batter piles including the vertical piles as computed from data obtained from model tests are shown in table 3.

Table 3: Rheological Constants for Negative and Positive Batter Piles.

S.No.	Pile Batter Angle,	Rheological Constants N	K_o (Kg)	$\eta_o x10^3$ (Kg-min/cm^2)	Soil Properties Water content w (%)	Cohesive Value, C (Kg/cm^2)	Test
1.	-30	0.1386	0.5196	0.03727	47.6	0.2386	
2.	-20	0.1316	0.5638	0.04607	47.6	0.2387	Incre-
3.	-10	0.1182	0.5909	0.06410	47.6	0.2387	mental
4.	- 0	0.10	0.60	0.085227	47.6	0.2387	load-
5.	+10	0.0948	0.5909	0.1112	48.05	0.1865	ing.
6.	+20	0.0846	0.5638	0.1536	48.05	0.1865	
7.	+30	0.0693	0.5196	0.2475	48.05	0.1865	

The above data indicates that in case of negative batter piles the value of N increases with the increase in the pile batter angle and is maximum for a -30° batter pile whereas it d decreases with the batter angle for a positive batter piles with minimum value for a +30° pile. The trend of the constant η_o is reverse of that N whereas the value of constant K_o is not influenced by the direction of pile batter i.e. negative of positive.

COMPARISON OF PREDICTED AND OBSERVED BEHAVIOUR

Utilizing equations 3 and 4 and the rheological constants from the two load test data, the time-deformation behaviour of a laterally loaded pile is predicted (fig.4). This shows a close fit.

FIELD APPLICATION

A review of literature reveals that the time-load-deformation behaviour on laterally loaded prototype piles in field is very meagre. No data is available on single batter piles. On vertical piles also very little information is available (16, 17). The data available is also inadequate. However, utilizing the available data and making certain assumptions on the pattern of deformation the time-load-deformation behaviour predicted on the basis of proposed analysis (fig.10,11).

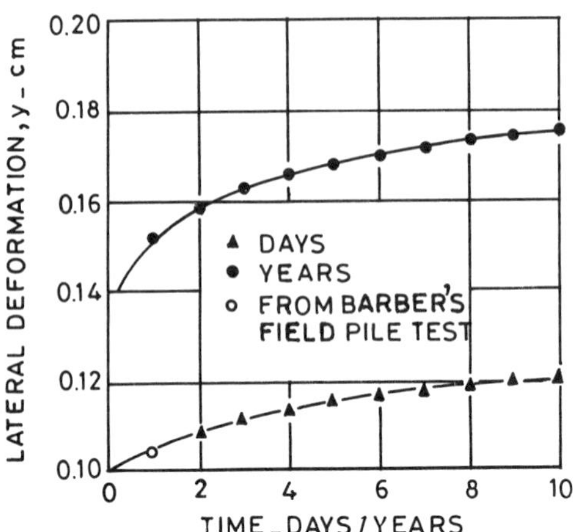

FIG.10. DEFORMATION VERSUS TIME FOR BARBER'S FIELD PILE TEST (1953).

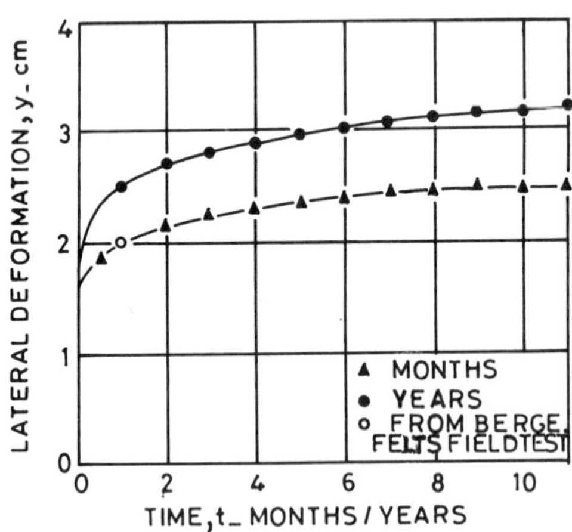

FIG.11. DEFORMATION VERSUS TIME FOR FIELD PILE TEST REPORTED BY BERGFELT (1957)

CONCLUSIONS

On the basis of the study it is concluded that
(a) rheological models can be used effectively to predict the load-time-deformation behaviour of laterally loaded piles.
(b) the proposed visco-elastic analysis is useful to describe the time-load-deformation behaviour of vertical piles and also batter piles with the load acting normal to the pile and the deflections are considered normal to pile axis.
(c) two series of load tests in which deflection recorded with time are needed to evaluate the three rheological constants. Once these contants are estimated, the complete time-load-deformation behaviour can be predicted.
(d) simple laboratory tests need be developed as an alternative to load tests to evaluate the rheological constants.

REFERENCES

1. Murayama, S., and Shibata, T.,(1956), 'On the Rheological Characters of Clay', Transactions of the Japan Society of Civil Engineers, No.40, 1956, pp.1-31.

2. Murayama, S. and Shibata, T.,(1961), 'Rheological Properties of Clays', Proceedings, 5th International Conference on Soil Mechanics and Foundation Engineering, pp.269-273.

3. Christensen, R.W., and Wu, T.H.,(1964), 'Analysis of Clay Deformation as a Rate Process', Journal of the Soil Mechanics and Foundation Division, ASCE, Vol.90, No.SM6, Proc. Paper 4147, Nov., 1964, pp.125-157.

4. Wu, T.H., Resendiz, D. and Neukirchner, R.J.,(1966), 'Analysis of Consolidation by Rate Process Theory', Journal of Soil Mechanics and Foundation Engineering Division, ASCE, Nov. 1966, PP.229.

5. Komamura, Fujiya, and Huang, Rodney, J.,(1974), 'New Rheological Model for Soil Behaviour', Journal of the Geotechnical Engineering Division, ASCE, Vol.100, No.GT 7, Proc. Paper 10675, July, 1974, pp.807-824.

6. Aziz, Khandkar, A.,(1976), 'Rheological Model of Laterally Stressed Frozen Soil', Journal of the Geotechnical Engineering Division, ASCE, Vol.102, No.GT8, Proc. Paper 12136, August, 1976, pp.825-839.

7. Bingham, E.C.,(1922), 'Fluidity and Plasticity', McGraw-Hill Book Co., Inc. New York.

8. Yong, R.N. and Workentin, B.P.,(1966), 'Introduction to Soil Behaviour; The Macmillon Company, New York, Collier Macmillan Limited, London.

9. Murtaza, G., (1978), 'Time Dependent Behaviour of Single Piles Under Lateral Loads in Cohesive Soils', Ph.D.Thesis, Civil Engineering Department, University of Roorkee, Roorkee, India.

10. Murayama, S., and Shibata, T.,(1964), 'Flow and Stress Relaxation of Clays', Rheology and Soil Mechanics Symposium of the International Union of Theoretical and Applied Mechanics, Grenoble, France, Apr., 1964, pp.99-129.

11. Barden, L.,(1965), 'Consolidation of Clay with Non-linear Viscosity', Geotechnique Volume XV- pp.345-362.

12. Barden, L.,(1969), 'Time Dependent Deformation of Normally Consolidated Clays and Peats', Journal of Soil Mechanics and Foundation Division, ASCE, Vol.95, No.SMI Jan.1969, pp.1-29.

13. Wu, T.H., EI Refai, A.N.A.A., and Hsu, J.R.,(1978),'Creep Deformation of Clays', Journal of the Geotechnical Engineering Division, ASCE, Vol.104, No.GT 1, Proc. Paper 13476, January, 1978, pp.61-76.

14. Poulos, Harry, G., (1975), 'Lateral Load-Deflection Prediction for Pile Groups', Journal of the Geotechnical Engineering Division, January, 1955, pp.19-34.

15. Hoadley, P.J.,(1975), 'Behaviour of Steel Piles Under Lateral Load and Moment', Second Australia - New Zealand Conference on Geo-mechanics, Brisban, 1975, The Institution of Engineers, Australia National Conference Publication No. 75/4, pp.190-194.

16. Barber, E.S.,(1953), 'Discussion, Symposium on Lateral Load Tests on Piles', ASTM, Special Technical Publication No.154, pp.96.

17. Bergefelt, A.,(1957), 'The Axial and Lateral Load Bearing Capacity and Failure by Buckling of Piles in soft Clay', Proceedings, Fourth International Conference on Soil Mechanics and Foundation Engineering, Vol.2, pp.8-13.

THE VISCOPLASTIC BEHAVIOUR OF BENTONITE

PIERRE-YVES HICHER
Laboratoire de Mécanique des Sols-Structures
CNRS UA 850, 92290 Chatenay-Malabry France

ABSTRACT

An experimental programme was performed on a remolded Bentonite in order to investigate its time-dependant behaviour. Monotonic as well as cyclic undrained triaxial tests, creep tests and stress- relaxation tests have been analysed on effective stress basis and, as a result, existence of viscoplastic mechanisms and long term behaviour of Bentonite may be proposed and investigated along different effective stress and strain paths. A damage law was introduced for failure conditions.

INTRODUCTION

Numerous studies have already analysed the time-dependant behaviour of clays in many aspects: secondary compression, creep tests, strain rate effect...

This peculiar behaviour has been related to the clay structure and mainly to the existence of an adsorbed water layer around the particles. In a simplified analysis, two types of contact exist between particles:

- a solid-solid contact which involves friction,
- a contact between the adsorbed water layers which creates a viscous effect.

When stresses are applied, the reorientation of the structure by relative displacements of particles mobilizes both types of contacts and eventually redistributes them.

An experimental program composed of monotonic triaxial tests at different strain rates, cyclic triaxial tests at different frequencies, undrained creep tests and stress-relaxation tests was performed on a remolded Bentonite in order to investigate its stress-strain-time behaviour. We present here the results of all these tests and we analyse them in terms of viscoplastic mechanisms.

TESTING PROGRAMME

Tested Clay

All tests were performed on a remolded Bentonite whose Atterberg Limits are: LL = 105% and PL = 51% and whose Clay Fraction is 69%. A mineralogical study gave 100% of Montmorillonite and the activity is .78.

Specimen Preparation

The samples were prepared from a clay slurry mixed at a water content of twice the liquid limit and consolidated in a double drainage consolidometer up to a vertical stress of 100 kPa. The time of consolidation was three weeks.

After removing the samples, specimens with the required dimensions (h = 7cm, d = 3.5cm) were trimmed and set in the triaxial cell. An isotropic stress of 200 kPa was then applied for two days, i.e. until the end of the primary consolidation.

Test Conditions

No anti-friction system was used and porous plates were set directly at the two sides of the samples. Tests were performed in undrained conditions and pore pressure was measured at the bottom. Vertical load and vertical displacement were measured outside the cell except during stress-relaxation tests where a load cell was set inside the triaxial cell in order to avoid the problem of friction between the piston and the cell. The load cell was rigid enough to prevent noticeable vertical strain.

In order to insure a complete saturation of the samples, an initial pore pressure of 300 kPa was imposed.

MONOTONIC UNDRAINED TRIAXIAL TESTS

Influence of Strain Rate on Stress-Strain Relationship

In figure 1 we present the stress-strain curves of three undrained triaxial tests performed at constant strain rate: 6 10^{-7}/s., 6 10^{-6}/s. and 1.5 10^{-4}/s. An increase in strain rate produced an increase in strength at any level of strain. The maximum strength q_f expressed by the maximum of deviatoric stress $q = \sigma_1 - \sigma_3$ increased with the strain rate. The requisite strain to generate maximum strength is independent of the strain rate (around 10% for each test).

In plotting the results in diagram $q/q_f - \varepsilon_1$, we find that the three curves are close to each other, which suggests a viscous effect independent of the level of stress or strain. We have already presented this particular behaviour in a remolded Kaolinite (7).

Effective Stress Paths

The effective stress paths, plotted in a p',q plane, are also strain rate dependant (fig.2a). They present a regular evolution, shifting to the right when the strain rate is larger. The relationship between pore pressure increase and strain seems to be independant of strain rate for strains smaller than 5%. This is no longer the case when the strain rate is too high due to the fact that the pore pressure ceases to be homogeneous inside the sample and, consequently, one has to be careful in analysing tests results on an effective stress basis when strain rate is large. For this study the pore pressure was measured at the base of the sample. By fixing a small pressure transducer in the middle of some samples, we were able to show that above a strain rate of 10^{-4}/s., a difference between the two measurements was noticeable, which did not allow us to make a worthwhile interpretation of the tests.

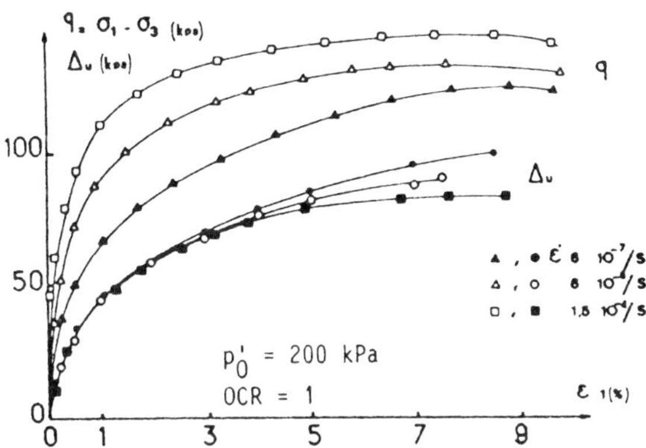

Figure 1. Undrained triaxial tests at different strain rates

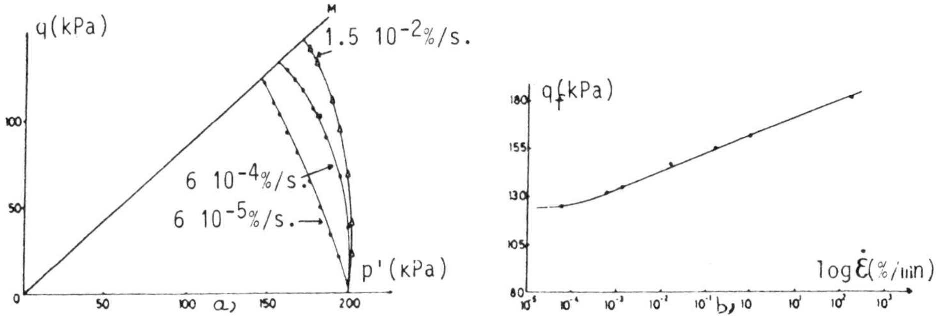

Figure 2. Influence of strain rate: a) on effective stress path, b) on maximum strength

Maximum Strength and Effective Parameters

In Figure 2b we have plotted the values of q_f obtained from tests at different strain rates ($\dot{\varepsilon}$). The relationship between q_f and log$\dot{\varepsilon}$ is linear for 10^{-7}/s. < ε < 10^{-2}/s. with a slope equal to 0.1. For smaller values of ε the slope of the curve decreases gradually, allowing us to assume the existence of an asymptotic value of q_f which we call the "long-term strength" q_s of the Bentonite. This value has been determined roughly around 120 kPa for a normally consolidated sample with a consolidation pressure of 200 kPa. It represents the shear strength of Bentonite for "very slow" tests ($\dot{\varepsilon} \simeq 0$).

If the effective stress paths depend on the strain rate, they all finish on the same critical line q = Mp' . Thus the effective friction angle is not affected by the strain rate. This can be analysed as the result of the complete mobilisation of the frictional contacts between particles. For the Bentonite M = .87 and ϕ = 21°.

Undrained Triaxial Tests on Oversonsolidated Samples

We present in Figure 3 some test results on overconsolidated samples with a constant strain rate of 6.10^{-6}/s.. The influence of the strain rate has not been studied. However, creep tests and cyclic tests were performed on samples at different overconsolidation ratios and the results of monotonic tests will later be used as tests of reference.

As for normally consolidated samples, all of these have developed kinematic discontinuities and deformation at failure appeared to be smaller for overconsolidated samples than for normally consolidated ones.

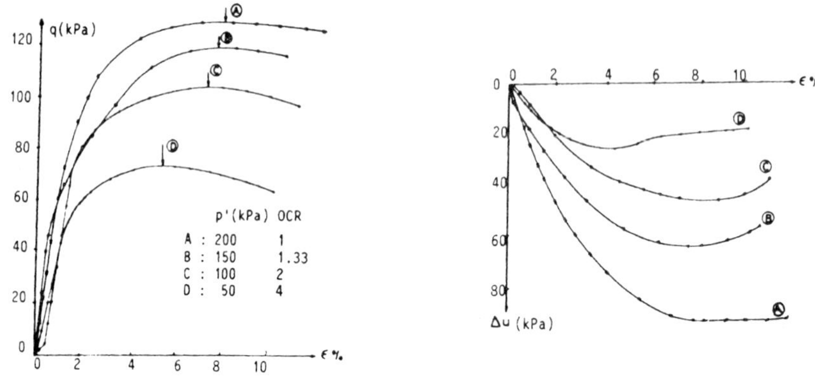

Figure 3. Undrained triaxial tests at different OCRs.

UNDRAINED CREEP TESTS RESULTS

A deviatoric stress q_{cr} was applied in undrained conditions on an isotropically consolidated sample in the triaxial cell and was maintained constant while the vertical deformation and the pore pressure were recorded with time (4,12). While this is not a real creep test because the effective stresses are not constant due to the evolution of pore pressure with time, we may still call them "undrained creep" tests for reasons of convenience and for the fact that the two words associated with each other describe accurately the reality of these tests. We define the stress level as the ratio between q_{cr} and the maximum strength q_f measured at a conventional strain rate of $6.10^{-6}/s$.

Evolution of Deformations with Time

In Figure 4 we present the evolution of vertical deformation with time for samples with different OCRs. All the tests have been stopped after 10000 mn (7 days) if the samples did not fail before. The stabilisation of the deformation was not completely achieved, but the strain rate at the end of the tests was very low: $\dot{\varepsilon} < 10^{-7}/mn$.

For tests performed at stress ratio q_{cr}/q_f smaller than 85%, the curves ε_1-t show a continuous decrease of $\dot{\varepsilon}$ leading to the stabilization of the deformation (primary creep). For higher stress levels, failure occured and, after a phase where $\dot{\varepsilon}$ was still decreasing, the curves exhibited a progressive increase of $\dot{\varepsilon}$ until failure (tertiary creep). No intermediate phase at constant $\dot{\varepsilon}$ (secondary creep) was observed. We noticed that normally consolidated samples were able to support higher stress levels without failure.

We have analysed our results using the Singh-Mitchell theory (10), which can be summarised by the following equation for primary creep:

$$\varepsilon(t,q_{cr}/q_f) = \varepsilon(t_o,q_{cr}/q_f) + A/(1-m).\exp(\alpha q_{cr}/q_f)(t^{1-m}-1) \quad (1)$$

The linearity of the relations in the typical diagrams (Fig.4d) were reasonably well observed. For tests at low stress levels the parameters m, α, A were found independent of the stress level but dependant on the overconsolidation ratio: m varies from .95 for OCR = 1 to .78 for OCR = 4. We must take account that a value of m<1 leads to infinite deformations. In fact, after a certain time, m increases to value above 1. This change in value took place earlier for normally consolidated samples.

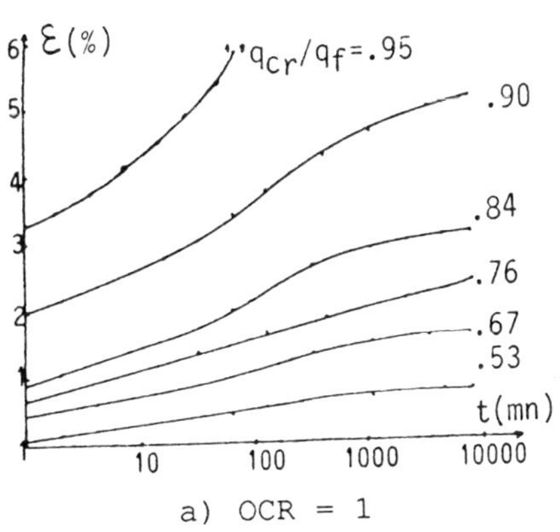

a) OCR = 1

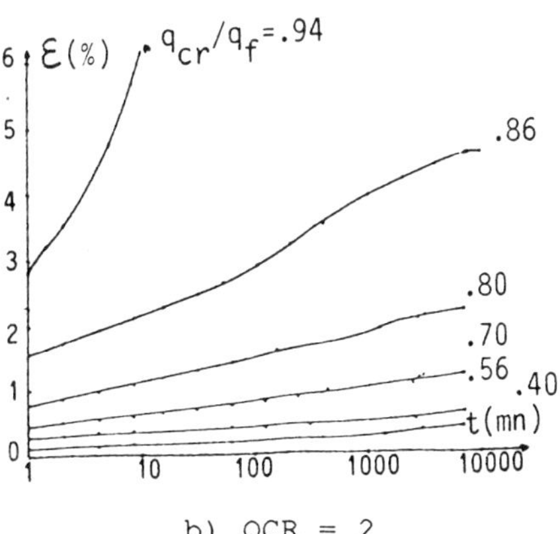

b) OCR = 2

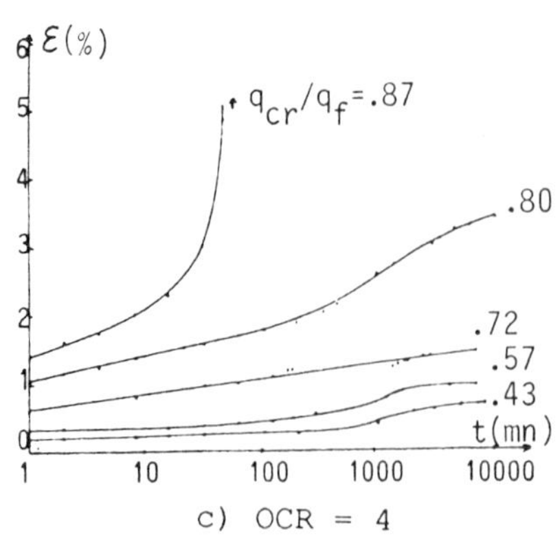

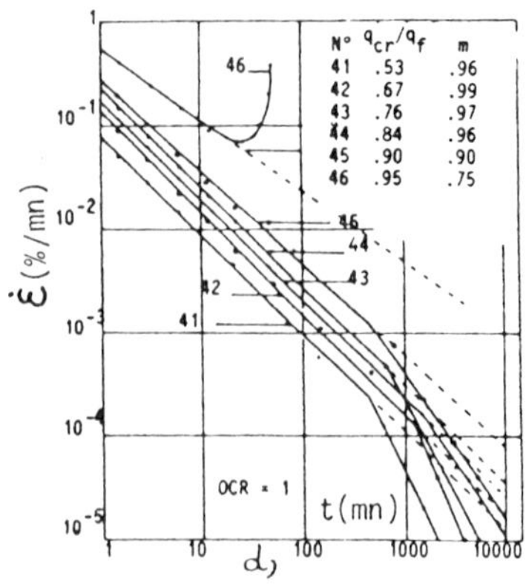

Figure 4. Undrained creep test results

For tests where failure occured, the values of m during primary creep tended to increase while increasing the stress level.

All these remarks prove that the Singh-Mitchell equations can be used only in a limited interval of time and in a limited interval of stress and that the parameters depend on the initial state of the clay (OCR).

Evolution of Effective Stresses with Time

The pore pressure continuously increased with time for all tests. This increase is more pronounced when the stress level is higher and the OCR is lower. The consequence is a reduction of the mean effective stress with time. The effective stress path in p',q plane is an horizontal straight line. The pore pressure increase rate regularly decreased so that the effective stress paths tend to stabilized points (Fig.5).We can see that all these final points define curves whose shapes are identical to the ones corresponding to monotonic loading tests at constant strain rate and which are located on the left.

These curves, called equilibrium state lines (2,9), can be considered as the effective stress paths for monotonic tests at very low strain rate and thus as representative of the long-term behaviour of Bentonite, i.e. elastoplastic behaviour without time effect. We define also the long-term strength as the intersection of the equilibrium state curves with the critical line q = Mp' determined by monotonic tests at constant strain rate, since we noticed above that the critical line was not affected by strain rate.

For normally consolidated samples the long-term strength q_s is equal to 122 kPa, in agreement with the asymptotic value obtained from the relationship between q_f and $\log\dot{\varepsilon}$.

For tests with $q_{cr} > q_s$, failure occured after the effective stress path crossed the critical line. An analysis of these results will be made later on.

An other experimental method was used in order to determine the value of the creep limit of Bentonite. It consisted in increasing the creep stress step by step, the duration of each step always kept the same (here 100 mn.). The axial deformation and the pore pressure were recorded and the test results are presented in Figure 6. We can observe a very distinct threshold, characteristic of an important increase of the mean strain rate by step $a = (\varepsilon_2-\varepsilon_1)/(t_2-t_1)$, for a given value of q_{cr}. This abrupt change in the value of a indicates the passage between creep stress level leading to equilibrium and creep stress level leading to failure. Therefore the creep limit corresponds to the threshold point. For normally consolidated samples a value of q_s = 124 kPa has been determined by the use of this method, in accord with the long term strength determined above. Also for overconsolidated samples the results fit well with the ones obtained from classical creep tests: q_s = 95 kPa for p'_o = 100 kPa (OCR = 2) and q_s = 70 kPa for p'_o = 50 kPa (OCR = 4). The stress level q_s/q_f decreases when increasing OCR. This can indicate a quantitative change in the influence of strain rate, in agreement with a tendency to reach faster the equilibrium state for normally consolidated samples during creep tests. It can also be the result of pore pressure migration inside the samples, which are more pronounced when the clay is overconsolidated and dilates at a high stress level.

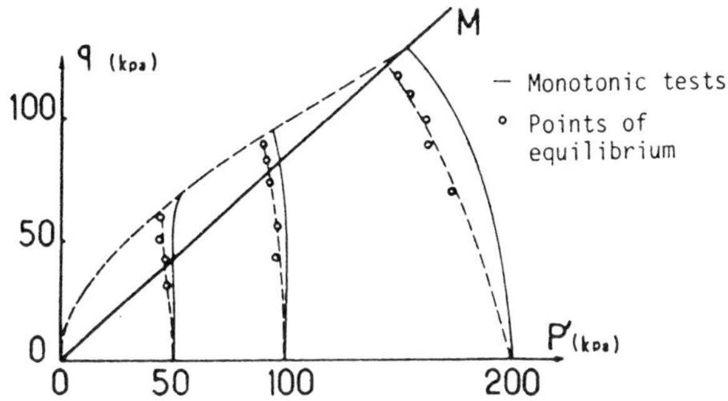

Figure 5. Equilibrium lines for undrained creep tests

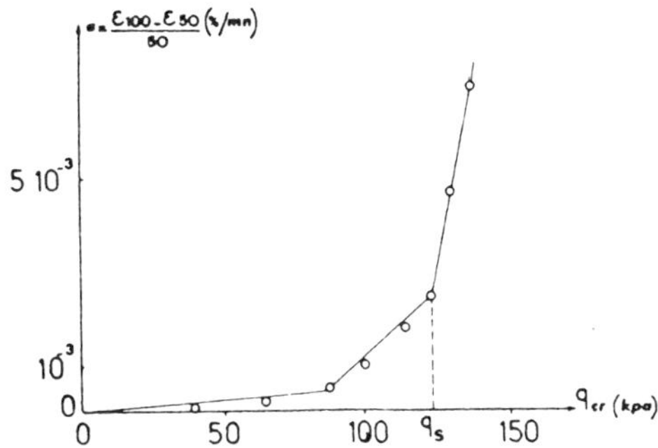

Figure 6. Determination of creep stress limit

STRESS RELAXATION TESTS

Three stress relaxation tests in undrained condition have been performed on normally consolidated samples. They have been first subjected to a monotonic undrained triaxial loading at constant strain rate $\dot{\varepsilon} = 6.10^{-6}$/s.; then the axial deformation has been stopped and the evolution of deviatoric stress q and pore pressure with time have been recorded. We observed an immediate decrease of q which continued at lower rate until the end of each test (1440 mn.). The decrease was initially linear with logt and after 600 to 800 mn. the slope progressively diminished without reaching an equilibrium state (Fig. 7). The tests at ε = 2% and 4% did not show any pore pressure variation, while the test at 6% presented a slight increase of u which slowly reached a constant value at the end of the test (Δu = 10 kPa).

The effective stress paths in the p',q plane are straight lines with a slope +3 for the two tests at ε = 2% and 4%. The final points do not exactly represent equilibrium states but are almost on the equilibrium line defined by creep tests, which represents the undrained long term behaviour of Bentonite (Fig.8).

The fact that stress relaxation tests do not generate pore pressure variation can be related to the results of monotonic tests showing that the evolution of pore pressure with strain is independent of strain rate for axial deformation smaller than 5%. We have plotted the isodeformation lines in p',q plane (Fig.8). The slope is constant and equal to +3 as long as $\varepsilon_1 <$ 5%, then decreases when strain value increases, tending to become parallel to the critical state line. We observe the same pattern for effective stress paths during stress-relaxation tests.

SYNTHESIS OF STRESS-STRAIN-TIME BEHAVIOUR

All the results presented above allowed us to investigate the undrained behaviour of Bentonite along different stress and strain paths. They lead to a consistent framework of viscoplastic behaviour with the following characteristics.

The monotonic tests at constant strain rate produce a set of curves (one for each strain rate) with increasing slope when the strain rate increases. All these curves can be reduced to a single one if we express them in a $q/q_f-\varepsilon_1$ diagram

Monotonic tests, creep tests and stress-relaxation tests produce a set of effective stress paths in p',q plane which permits the determination of the long term behaviour expressed by a single curve representing the equilibrium points of creep and stress-relaxation tests and the monotonic stres path for an undrained triaxial test at very small strain rate. We can then define the long term strength q_s as the intersection of this curve with the critical state line, which was found to be independent of $\dot{\varepsilon}$.

If we report the value of q_s as q_f in the $q/q_f-\varepsilon_1$ relationship, we are able to define the stress-strain relationship at $\varepsilon = 0$, i.e. the elastoplastic behaviour of Bentonite. The influence of viscosity can be represented by the influence of ε at any level in reference to the inviscid part.

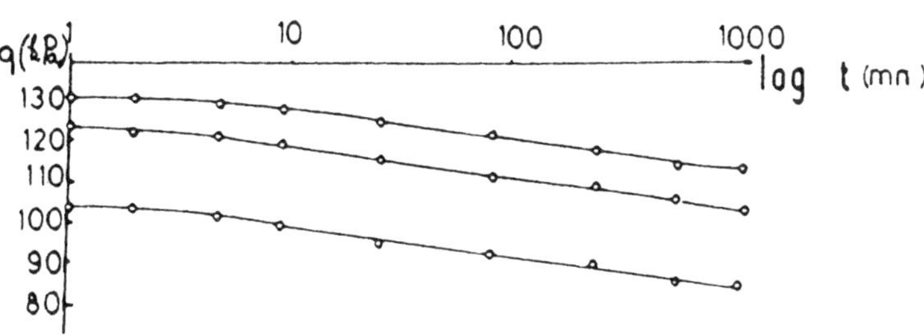

Figure 7. Stress-relaxation test results

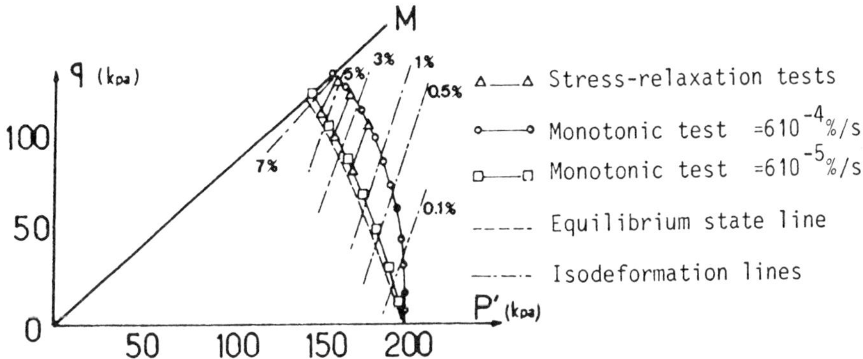

Figure 8. Stress-strain relations for different undrained tests

CYCLIC TRIAXIAL TESTS

One-way cyclic triaxial tests have been performed on normally and overconsolidated samples in undrained condition. All the tests have been continued until the samples reached a state of equilibrium or failure (3,12). Typical results are presented in Figure 9. Pore pressure increased with number of cycles for OCR = 1 and 2 and was almost constant for OCR = 4 and 5. The number of cycles at equilibrium states was typically between 1000 and 2000 for OCR = 1, 2 and 1500 and 2500 for OCR = 4,5. The evolution of permanent deformation ε_p with number of cycles N followed the same pattern as ε with t during creep tests, with a progressive decrease of the slope to equilibrium or a decrease followed by an increase to failure. Therefore we propose an analysis of cyclic test results on the same basis as creep test results.

Evolution of Permanent Deformation with Number of Cycles
A phenomenological approch can be proposed similar to the one of Singh-Mitchell for creep tests. We define first the increase of permanent deformation per cycle ε^*, which represents the slope of the curve ε_p-N. In Figure 9d we can see the evolution of $\log\varepsilon^*$ with logN and the influence of the cyclic stress level q_{cyc}/q_f. All these results are similar to the ones obtained with creep tests if we replace $\dot{\varepsilon}$ by ε^* and t by N. The evolution of permanent deformation can be expressed by the following equations:

$$\varepsilon_p(N, q_{cyc}/q_f) = \varepsilon_{p1}(1, q_{cyc}/q_f) + A/(1-m).\exp\alpha q_{cyc}/q_f.(N^{1-m}-1),$$
if $m \neq 1$

$$\varepsilon_p(N, q_{cyc}/q_f) = \varepsilon_{p1}(1, q_{cyc}/q_f) + A\exp\alpha q_{cyc}/q_f.\mathrm{Log}N, \text{ if } m=1 \quad (2)$$

m, A and α are not intrinsic parameters, since they depend on the cyclic stress path (one-way loading for this study), on the frequency (see below) and on OCR.

The equation (2) lead to the stabilization of permanent deformation only if $m > 1$. We have found a mean value of $m = .75$ at the beginning of the tests, but after a certain number of cycles (between 500 and 1000) m increased above 1 for all tests leading to equilibrium.

Evolution of Effective Stresses
For normally consolidated or lightly overconsolidated samples, pore pressure increased with number of cycles to a stabilized value when the clay reached the state of equilibrium. We can define in p',q plane a line of equilibrium as we did for creep tests. For tests leading to failure the effective stress path crossed the critical state line. The cyclic stress limit can therefore be taken as the intersection between the equilibrium line and the critical state line (Fig.10).

For overconsolidated samples, the equilibrium line coincides with the monotonic stress path because the variation of pore pressure during cyclic loading was negligible. For stress levels so that effective stres paths crossed the critical state line, failure occured after a certain number of cycles. The cyclic stress limit can also be considered as the intersection between the equilibrium line and the critical state line.

Influence of the Frequency of the Cycles
The influence of the frequency can be observed in Figure 11. The permanent deformation is larger for the same number of cycles when the frequency is smaller. The equilibrium state is reached sooner but the final deformation, for the same cyclic stress level, is independent of the frequency. For the example

presented in Figure 11 the equilibrium state was reached after 1000 cycles for f = .1 Hz and 15000 cycles for f = 2 Hz. The pore pressure increase followed the same pattern and the effective stresses at equilibrium are also independent of the frequency.

The viscous effect increases the mechanical properties of Bentonite. As a result, smaller deformations at high frequency for a same number of cycles occur but with a delay in obtaining the equilibrium state which can be considered as independent of the frequency and representing the long-term behaviour of Bentonite under one-way cyclic loading.

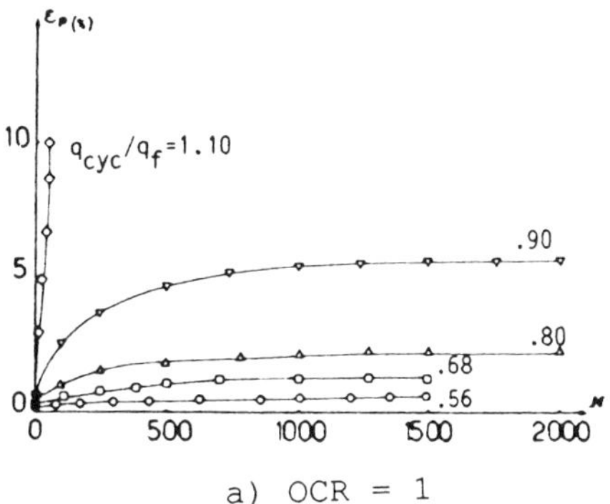

a) OCR = 1

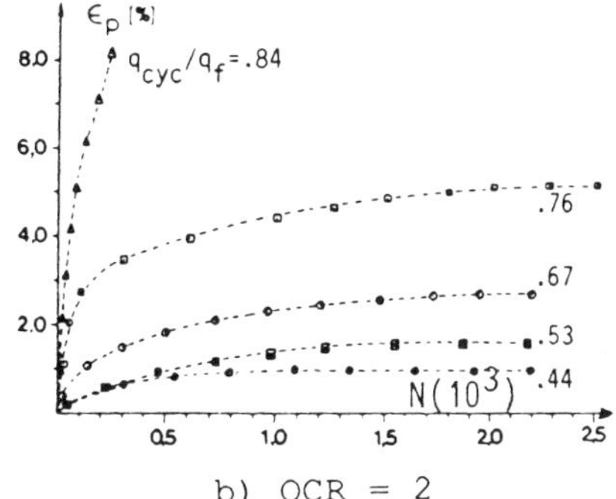

b) OCR = 2

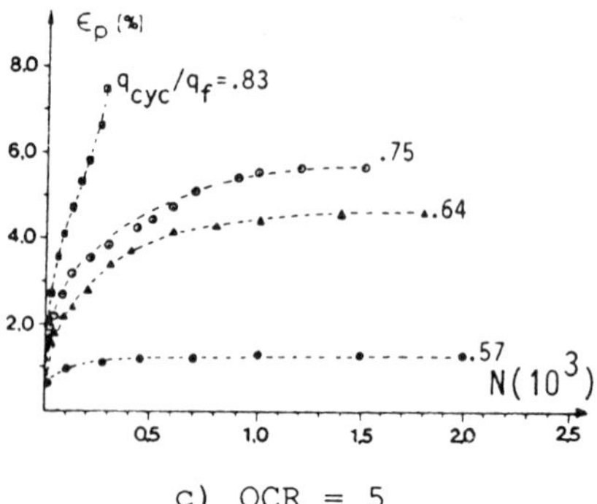

c) OCR = 5

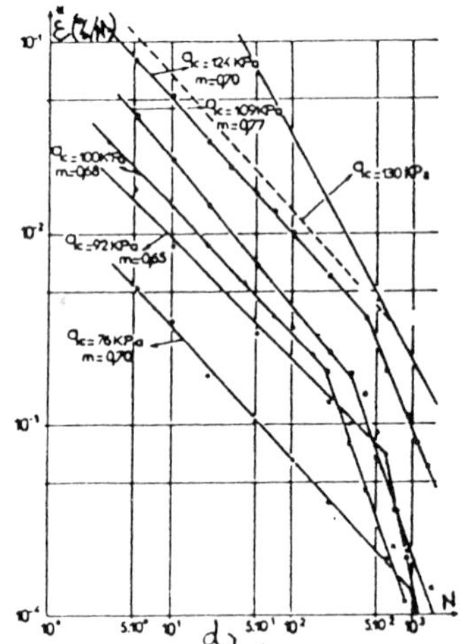

d)

Figure 9. One-way cyclic test results

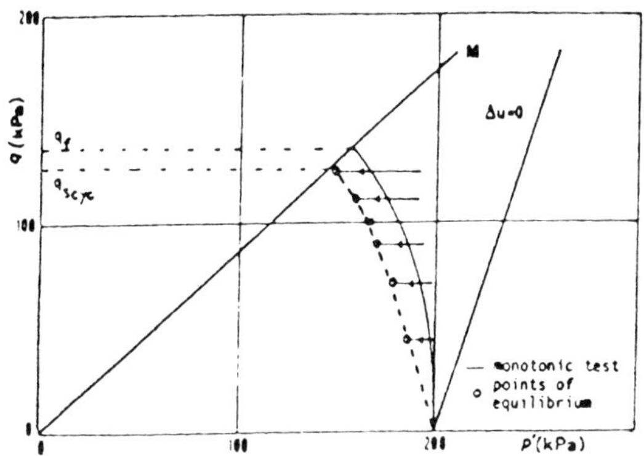

Figure 10. Equilibrium line for cyclic tests

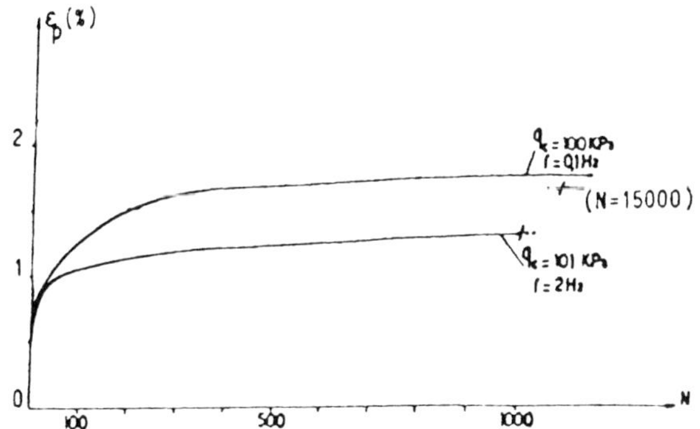

Figure 11. Influence of the frequency in cyclic tests

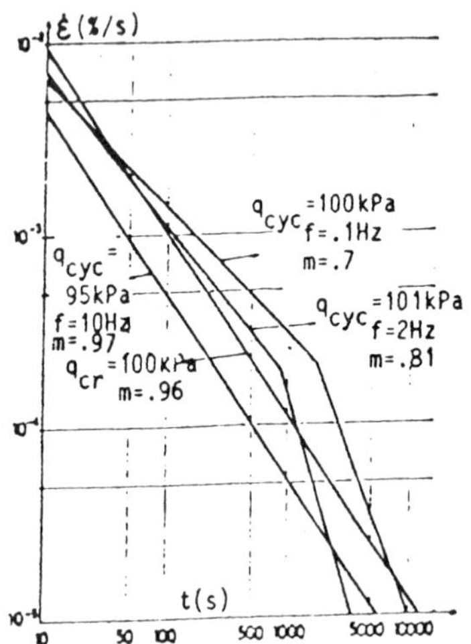

Figure 12. Evolution of permanent deformation with time or number of cycles

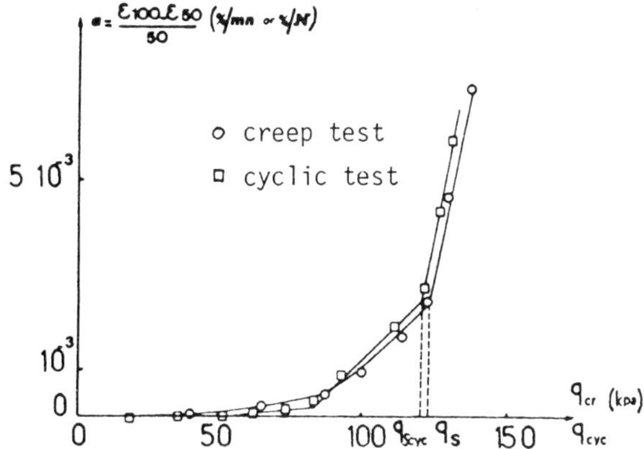

Figure 13. Determination of cyclic stress limit

COMPARISON BETWEEN CREEP AND CYCLIC TEST RESULTS

Evolution of Deformation with Time

In Figure 12 we have drawn the evolution of log$\dot{\varepsilon}$ and logε* with logt and logN (N = t.f) from creep tests and cyclic tests at different frequencies. The slope of the curves (parameter m) varies from one test to an other, m_{cyc} increases with frequency up to a value close to m_{cr} for f = 10 Hz at the same stress level.

The permanent deformations at equilibrium states are very close; only the time for reaching them varies and can increase from 2.5 hours at f = .1 Hz up to 5.5 days for creep test. The cyclic tests can thus be considered creep tests with the use of a "pseudo cyclic viscosity".

Evolution of Effective Stresses with Time

For creep and cyclic tests we have been able to define an equilibrium state line in p',q plane. In the case of Bentonite, the two lines are very close, expressing the fact that, at same stress level, creep and cyclic tests lead to a same final value in effective stresses.

Comparison of Creep Stress Limit and Cyclic Stress Limit

As a consequence of the statement made above, the two limits are also very close if we characterize them as the intersection between the equilibrium state line and the critical state line.We have seen for creep tests an other method to determine this limit, by increasing step by step the creep stress level. We have used the same technique for cyclic tests (Fig.13). Here also creep and cyclic limits have been found very close, which confirms the analysis made above.

We must observe, however, that these quantitative

correspondances between creep and cyclic tests cannot be extended without caution to other clays. The same procedure applied to a Kaolinite did not confirm these results, but showed a value of the cyclic limit lower than the creep limit, as well as larger deformations and pore pressure increase during cyclic tests. On a qualitative level, however, the comparison could still be made and the same conclusions could be drawn (6).

A DAMAGE LAW FOR CREEP AND CYCLIC TESTS

Creep and cyclic tests leading to the failure of the samples exhibit a first phase with a progressive decrease of $\dot{\varepsilon}$ or ε^* and a second phase where these terms increase until failure which is characterised by the existence of kinematic discontinuities inside the samples. We think that this second phase corresponds to a progressive development of strain localizations. This can be interpreted in terms of progressive accumulation of damage with time or number of cycles and, as a consequence, of reduction of mechanical properties. The damage is not located in the whole volume, but concentrated inside zones of strain localization.

We have tried to build a damage law by making the following assumptions:

- damage can be expressed by a scalar D, representing a density of fissurations in the damaged zone. As proposed for metal fatigue, we define an "active" deviatoric stress $q^* = q(1-D)$, by considering that a consequence of the damage is a reduction of the section on which the deviatoric stress is applied: $S^* = S(1-D)$. D can vary from 0 to 1.
- equations (1) and (2) reproduce adequately enough the behaviour of clay during creep and cyclic tests as long as the structure is not damaged. When the relationship between $\log\dot{\varepsilon}$ and $\log t$, or $\log\varepsilon^*$ and $\log N$, ceases to be linear, the damage starts to accumulate and the increasing difference between the prolongation of the straight line (slope m) and the experimental curve is representative of the increasing damage. If we assume now that the difference between the two lines is only due to the evolution of q which has to be replaced by q in the precedent equations, we can calculate an evolution of D with time or number of cycles. The following equations correspond well to the experimental curves (Fig.14):

$$D = D_f(1 - (t/t_f)^{-kcr}) \quad \text{or} \quad D = D_f(1 - (N/N_f)^{-kcyc}) \qquad (3)$$

with t_f = time to failure and N_f = number of cycles to failure. D_f has been introduced to express the fact that, when the maximum damage is obtained, the strength of the clay is not reduced to zero, but to a residual value (residual friction angle).

For Bentonite we obtain : $k_{cr} = k_{cyc} = .3$, $D_f = .5$

- We must also define a criterion which will indicate the beginning of damage development. Considering our results on normally consolidated samples, we have observed that all the tests leading to failure had stress paths crossing the critical state line, while all the stabilized stress points were located under this line. Thus a damage criterion can be : $q/p' > M'$ with M' close to M. This procedure has been used by Aubry and all (1) on the basis of these experimental results. However, for overconsolidated samples, equilibrium states have been found above the critical line during creep tests. Other tests are needed for a better definition of this criterion.

- D is an internal parameter which in general cannot be identified directly as a measured variable (as stress, strain or pore pressure).However the evolution of deformations with time or number of cycles in damaged samples follows the same pattern. Moreover, the value of permanent deformation (ε_i) corresponding to the loss of linearity in the relationship between log$\dot{\varepsilon}$ (respt. logε*) and logt (respt. logN) is constant for all tests and depends only upon OCR: 6.5% for OCR = 1, 3% for OCR = 2 and 2.5% for OCR = 4 or 5. For normally consolidated samples, ε_i was obtained when the effective stress path reached the critical state line, corresponding well to the definition of the beginning of damage. We assume therefore that D is dependent upon the value of permanent deformation. Besides, we have found that the evolution of $\dot{\varepsilon}$ and ε^* with t and N during tertiary phases could be expressed by the following equations:

$$\dot{\varepsilon}(t_f - t) = \text{cste} \quad \text{or} \quad \varepsilon^*(N_f - N) = \text{cste} \tag{4}$$

This relationship was already proposed for creep tests by several researchers (5,11). Using equations (3) and (4), an expression of the damage law can be proposed, as follows:

$$D = D_f(1 - (\dot{\varepsilon}/\dot{\varepsilon}_i)^{-k}) \quad \text{or} \quad D = D_f(1 - (\varepsilon^*/\varepsilon^*_i)^{-k}) \tag{5}$$

with k = .3 and D_r = .5 for Bentonite.

The influence of existing damage in a sample of Bentonite on its mechanical properties can be seen in Figure 15. It was submitted to a cyclic test in the following conditions:
$q_{cyc}/q_f = .64$, $q_{cyc}/p' = .9 > M'$, N = 1500, $\varepsilon_p(N{=}1500) = 2.6\%$.
D, measured by equation (5) is equal to .07 at the end of the cyclic test. Then a monotonic undrained triaxial test was performed on this sample and compared to the result of a same test on an intact sample. The precycled sample presented a decrease in maximum strength of 7.5% and this reduction can be expressed by using the influence of the damage in the following way:

$$q_{fd} = q_f(1 - D) \tag{6}$$

where q_{fd} is the maximum strength of a damaged clay sample (Fig.15). This analysis can explain the reduction of maximum strength after cyclic loading presented elsewhere (6,8).

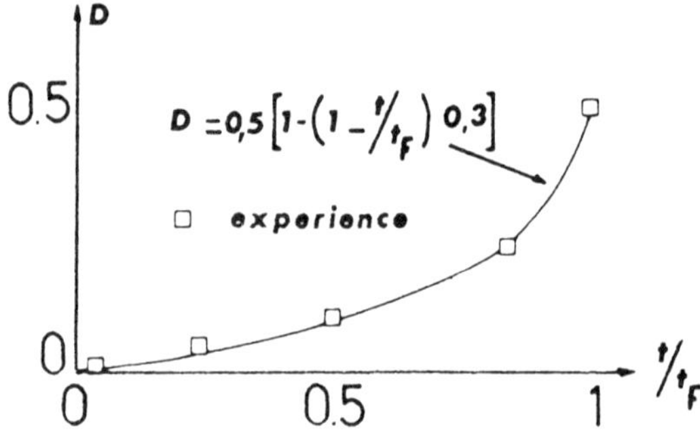

Figure 14. Evolution of damage during creep test

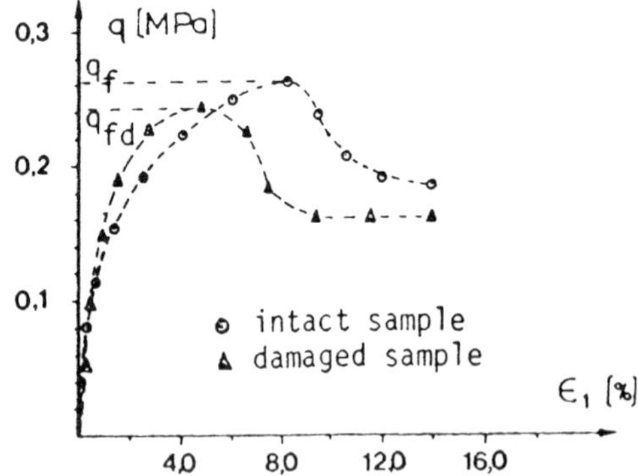

Figure 15. Influence of damage on maximum strength

CONCLUSION

We have widely investigated the time dependancy of Bentonite along different stress and strain paths. The main results lead to the following conclusions:

- The influence of strain rate during monotonic undrained triaxial tests can be expressed by a linear relationship between q_f and $\log\dot{\varepsilon}$ with a slope equal to .1. Its effect is the same at any level of stress and the curves q/q_f-ε_1 have been found to be independent of $\dot{\varepsilon}$. The effective stress paths are also influenced by the strain rate but not by the friction angle.
- Creep tests leading to equilibrium states and stress-relaxation tests allowed us to determine the long-term behaviour of Bentonite in terms of deformations and effective stresses. Combined with the monotonic test result, they allowed us to define the elastoplastic behaviour of Bentonite (at very small strain rate) and to characterise the influence of viscosity along different stress and strain paths.

- Results of one-way cyclic tests presented many similarities with the ones of creep tests: evolution of permanent deformation ε_p and pore pressure with time or number of cycles followed the same pattern. The equilibrium state line and the cyclic stress limit were determined on the same basis. An analytical relationship between ε_p and N was proposed in the same form as the Singh-Mitchell equation for creep tests.
- Failure during creep and cyclic tests has been explained by a progressive development of damaged zones inside the samples. A damage law was proposed using a scalar D which continously increases with time or number of cycles. By assuming that D was only dependant on ε_p, we have proposed a damage law identical for creep and cyclic tests. A monotonic test performed on a damaged sample showed that the damage law could be used to predict the reduction of maximum strength after cyclic loading.

REFERENCES

1. Aubry D., Kodaissi E., Meimon Y., A Viscoplastic Constitutive Equation for Clays including a Damage Law. 5th Int. Conf. on Num. Meth. in Geom., 1985, Nagoya, Japan.
2. Akai K., Adachi T., Ando N., Existence of a Unique Stress-Strain-Time Relation of Clays. Soils and Foundations 15, 1, 1975, pp 1-16.
3. Chamsai P., Contribution à l'étude du comportement mécanique des argiles saturées. D.I. Thesis, 1983, E.C.P.
4. El Gindy A. E., Contribution à l'étude du comportement mécanique des argiles avec surfaces de faiblesse et plus particulièrement les argiles prédécoupées. D.I. Thesis, 1982, E.C.P.
5. Finn W.D.L. and Shead D., Creep and Creep Rupture of an Undisturbed Sensitive Clay. 8th ICSMFE, 1.1, 1973, pp. 135-142, Moscow.
6. Hicher P.Y., Comportement mécanique des argiles saturées sur divers chemins de sollicitations monotones et cycliques. Application à une modélisation élastoplastique et viscoplastique. Thèse d'Etat, 1985, Univ. Paris VI.
7. Hicher P.Y., El Hosri M.S., Homsi M., Cyclic Properties of Soils within a large Range of Strain Amplitude. 3rd Int. Conf. on Soils Dyn. and Earthquake Eng., 1987, Princeton.
8. Lee K.L. and Focht J.A., Strength of Clay Subjected to Cyclic Loading. Marine Geotechnology, Vol. 1, 3, 1976, pp. 165-184.
9. Murayama S. and Shibata T., Flow and Stress Relaxation in Clays. IUTAM Symp. on Rheology and Soil Mechanics, 1964, pp. 99-129, Grenoble.
10. Singh A. and Mitchell J.K., General Stress-Strain-Time Function for Soils. J. of Geot. Eng. Div., ASCE, 94, SM1, 1968, pp. 21-46.
11. Vaid Y.P. and Campanella R.G., Time-dependant Behaviour of Undisturbed Clay. J. of Geot. Eng. Div., ASCE, 103, GT7, 1977, pp. 693-709
12. Voyiatzoglou C., Contribution à l'étude de la fatigue et du fluage des argiles saturées. D.I. Thesis, 1980, E.C.P.

STRESS STRAIN TIME CONSTITUTIVE MODEL

Eduardo Rojas
Instituto de Ingeniería, UNAM
Apdo Postal 70-472, Coyoacán, 04510
México, D. F., MEXICO

ABSTRACT

In order to study the viscous behavior of the Mexico City clay, two series of stress controlled triaxial undrained tests, (using different stress rates) were carried out using a natural normally consolidated clay. According to these results, a viscous function has been considered and it has been added to a non-linear second order constitutive model. The parameters of the model can be found by using the results of two monotonous triaxial drained tests (for the elasto-plastic part) and two creep test (for the viscous one). Knowing these parameters, the model is able to predict the behavior of the soil at any stress rate. A comparison between theoretical and experimental results is made and finally some conclusions are given.

INTRODUCTION

Mexico City was foundated over the ruins of the ancient aztec's capital empire, wich was located in the middle of a big lake. The Spanish conquistadores progressively drained the lake as the city began to grow. Nowadays this lake has almost completely disappered but the foundations and earth construction problems have not. One of the big foundation problems in Mexico City is the sink end tilt of heavy buildings, wich involves the viscous behavior of the Mexico City clay. This study was carried out in order to introduce the viscous behavior of the Mexico City clay on a general non-linear second order constitutive model.

MATERIAL AND METHODS

All specimens tested were obtained from an unaltered exploration program performed at the east of the city. Some of the most important characteristics of this clay are the following: specific weight = 2.30, plastic limit = 75%, liquid limit = 350 %, volumetric weight = 1 150 kg/m^3.

The natural water content varies from 300 to 400 % for the soft layers. In Table 1, some important characteristics of each sample are given.

TABLE 1
Some characteristics of each soil sample

Test	Natural Water Content W_i (%)	Water Content after consolidation W_c (%)	Voids Ratio after consolidation e_c	Saturation Degree G_w	Stress Rate σ
CU.1H	309.9	188.9	4.7	98.9	2 kg/h
CU.1D	301.9	168.0	3.8	99.3	2 kg/d
CU.3D	292.9	168.5	3.9	97.5	2 kg/3d
CU.6D	327.1	209.0	4.8	98.9	2 kg/6d
EU.1H	363.1	204.8	4.8	98.6	-2 kg/h
EU.1D	298.8	161.1	3.8	99.0	-2 kg/d
EU.3D	308.7	173.0	4.1	98.9	-1 kg/3d
EU.6D	308.7	183.3	4.3	98.7	-2 kg/6d

C = compression U = undrained d = day

E = extension h = hour

All samples were trimmed from a soil mass obtained at 15 m depth, where the preconsolidation pressure was estimated on 70 kPa.

All samples were trimmed using a thin wire. The initial dimensions of the samples were: diameter = 3.6 cm, height = 8.5 cm. All test samples were provided with comb-shaped filter paper. An isotropic consolidation pressure of 160 kPa was applied in only one step and drainage was allowed during four days. Furthermore, a back-pressure of 200 kPa was used in all tests. At the end of the fourth day, drainage was closed and then began the loading of the sample with a monotonous stress rate. For the application of the loads, the following rates were chosen: 2 kg/hour, 2 kg/day, 2 kg/3 days and 2 kg/6 days. For each stress rate both compression and extension tests were performed except for test EU.3D where a rate of 1 kg/3 days was applied.

TEST RESULTS

The results of these tests have been ploted in figures 1.a, 1.b and 1.c In figure 1.a the axial strain ε_1 *versus* the deviatoric stress $Q = \sigma_1 - \sigma_3$ are presented. From this figure, it can be observed that the strength at failure seems to be approximately the same, even if it could not be confirmed for the extension tests as the top of the triaxial chamber always separated from the sample before failure could be reached (ϕ>45°). It can be observed that the viscous behavior of all tests -

(except test EU.3D) is in agreement with the stress rate imposed to each test.

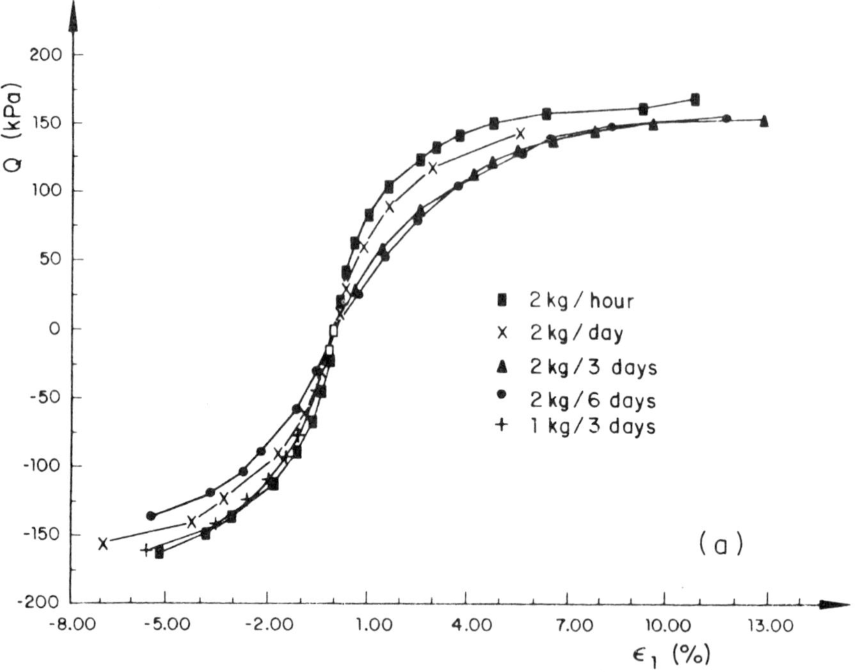

In Figure 1.b the axial deformation ε_1 has been ploted *versus* the pore pressure divided by the consolidation pressure. For the compression tests a logical behavior of the pore pressure against the stress rate can be observed. In contrast, for extension tests, pore pressure behaves very different according to the stress rate. On the other hand, it seems that the stress increment plays a very important role as it can be observed from test EU.3D (-1 kg/3 days).

In general, it is considered that the elasto-plastic behavior of a material occurs instantaneously while the viscous behavior is related with time. On the other hand, it is also accepted that the pore pressure is only produced by the elasto-plastic behavior of the material while the viscous one have no effect on it. This means that even if both elasto-plastic and viscous strains are generated by a deviatoric stress, only the first one will be responsible of the pore pressure increase. Furthermore, this increase will occur instantaneously for a fully saturated soil. For a partially saturated soil this will be approximatelly true, depending on the saturation degree.

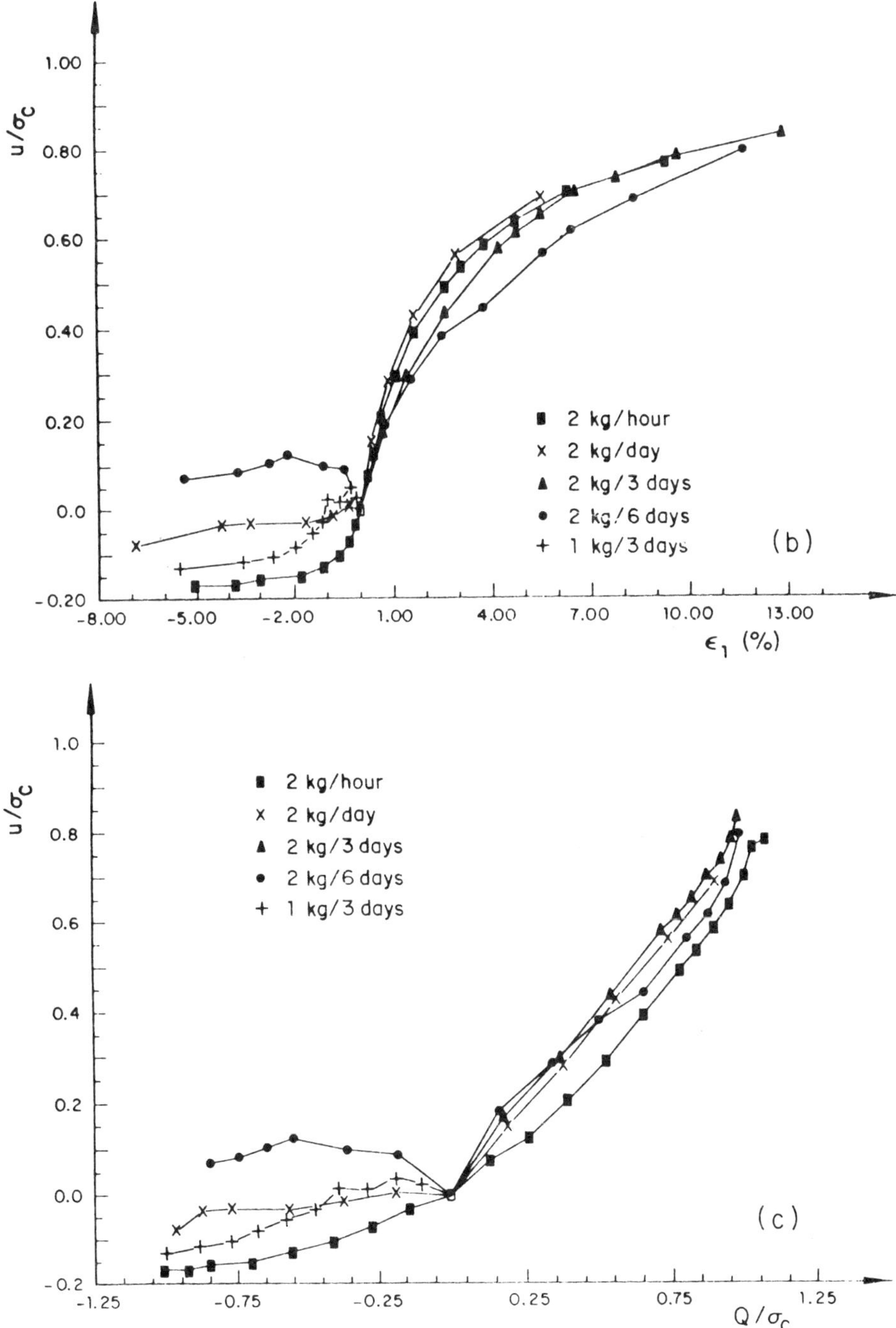

Figure 1. Compression and extension monotonous triaxial tests at different stress rates.

In order to prove these considerations, Figure 1.c was constructred, plotting the deviatoric stress *versus* the pore pressure increase. From this figure, it can be observed that, even if the points obtained from all the compression tests can not be join thogether by one line, all these points follow approximately the same tendency, and it could be said that in every compression test, pore pressure has been generated nearly instantaneously.

In contrast, points obtained on extension tests present a big dispersion and it can not be said that also in this case the pore pressure is generated instantaneously. Therefore, a big difference of behavior exists between compression and extension monotonous tests, and only for the case of compression tests we can distinguish between elasto-plastic and viscous behavior. That is to say, the constitutive model proposed here only will be valid for compression tests.

THE CONSTITUTIVE MODEL

The model presented here has been initially developed by Felix Darve [1] and some generalizations had been introduced since then (Vauillat [2] and Rojas et al [3]). Tha basic idea of the model is to establish a relationship between the stress, strain and time increments by means of a tensorial function $\underset{\sim}{F}$, that is

$$\underset{\sim}{F}\ (d\underset{\sim}{\sigma}\ ,\ d\underset{\sim}{\varepsilon}\ ,\ dt) = 0 \tag{1}$$

The tensorial function F will depend on all the stress-strain history of the material, by means of some state variables. All thermal effects will be neglected.

Then, the strain increment tensor can be decomposed in an elasto-plastic part and a viscous one

$$d\underset{\sim}{\varepsilon} = d\underset{\sim}{\varepsilon}^{ep} + d\underset{\sim}{\varepsilon}^{v} \tag{2}$$

Therefore, the elasto-plastic part will be independent of time and expression (2) can be rewritten as

$$d\underset{\sim}{\varepsilon} = \underset{\sim}{G}\ (d\underset{\sim}{\sigma}) + \underset{\sim}{C}\ dt \tag{3}$$

The tensorial function $\underset{\sim}{G}$ represents an homogeneous function of degree one and its development has been presented in different papers (Darve et al [4], Rojas et al [3]).

For the development of the viscous part, it will be considered that the previous stress-strain history applied to the material has no effect on the determination of $\underset{\sim}{C}$, and only the current state of stress and strains will determine its value. Obviously, this consideration restreints the generalization of the model, but the study of the influence of the stress-strain history on the viscous behavior of a material has only been partially studied.

According to some experimental results, Singh and Mitchell [5], proposed the following expression for the determination of the viscous strain when a deviatoric strain $q = \sigma_1 - \sigma_3/\sigma_f$ is applied (σ_f = deviatoric stress at failure) and when a time t has elapsed:

$$\varepsilon_1 = A\ e^{\alpha q}\ (\frac{t_1}{t})^m \quad (4)$$

where t_1 is the unity of time and A, α and m represent the parameters of the model. Integrating equation (4) it can be found:

$$\varepsilon_1 = \frac{A}{1-m}\ e^{\alpha q}\ (t^{1-m} - 1) + \varepsilon_u \quad (5)$$

where ε_u is the axial strain observed during the unit time. At this step, another important consideration will be introduced. As most of natural soils are not fully saturated, it will be considered here, that the elasto-plastic deformation of the material is produced at the unit time wich can be chosen of 1 min 1 hour, etc (according to the experimental results) and that the viscous behavior begins to appear after that elasto-plastic deformation. That is to say, ε_u will be the elasto-plastic deformation wich was defined as $d\tilde{\varepsilon}^{ep} = \tilde{G}\ (d\tilde{\sigma})$.

The parameters of the elasto-plastic part can be computed from the results of two triaxial monotonous drained test (one in compression and the other in extension). They can also be found by an indirect way using the results of two monotonous undrained tests as it was done here. The parameters of the viscous part can be found with the results of at least two creep tests carried out at different deviatoric stress and the same consolidation history.

Knowing the parameters of the model, we are able to predict the behavior of the soil at any impossed stress rate.

COMPARISON BETWEEN THEORETICAL AND EXPERIMENTAL RESULTS

As stated before t_1 (unit of time) can be chosen to any value. Observing the results of Fig 1.c, it was considered that most of the elasto-plastic behavior of the soil appears during the first hour after the application of the load. Implicity it was also considered that the viscous behavior begins to appear at the end of this first hour. Therefore in order to obtain the elasto-plastic parameters of the soil, the experimental results of tests CU.1H and EU.1H were used.

These results have been ploted in Figs 2.a, 2.b, 2.c and 2.d. The elasto-plastic parameters of the model have been chosen in order to adjust as best as possible the theoretical results with the experimental ones. The viscous parameters have been obtained from 3 creep test each one affected by a different deviatoric strain. Figures 3.a and 3.b show these results in axes t *vs.* ε and $\sigma_1-\sigma_3/\sigma_f$ *vs.* ε, respectively. From these figures parameters m, α and A were obtained.

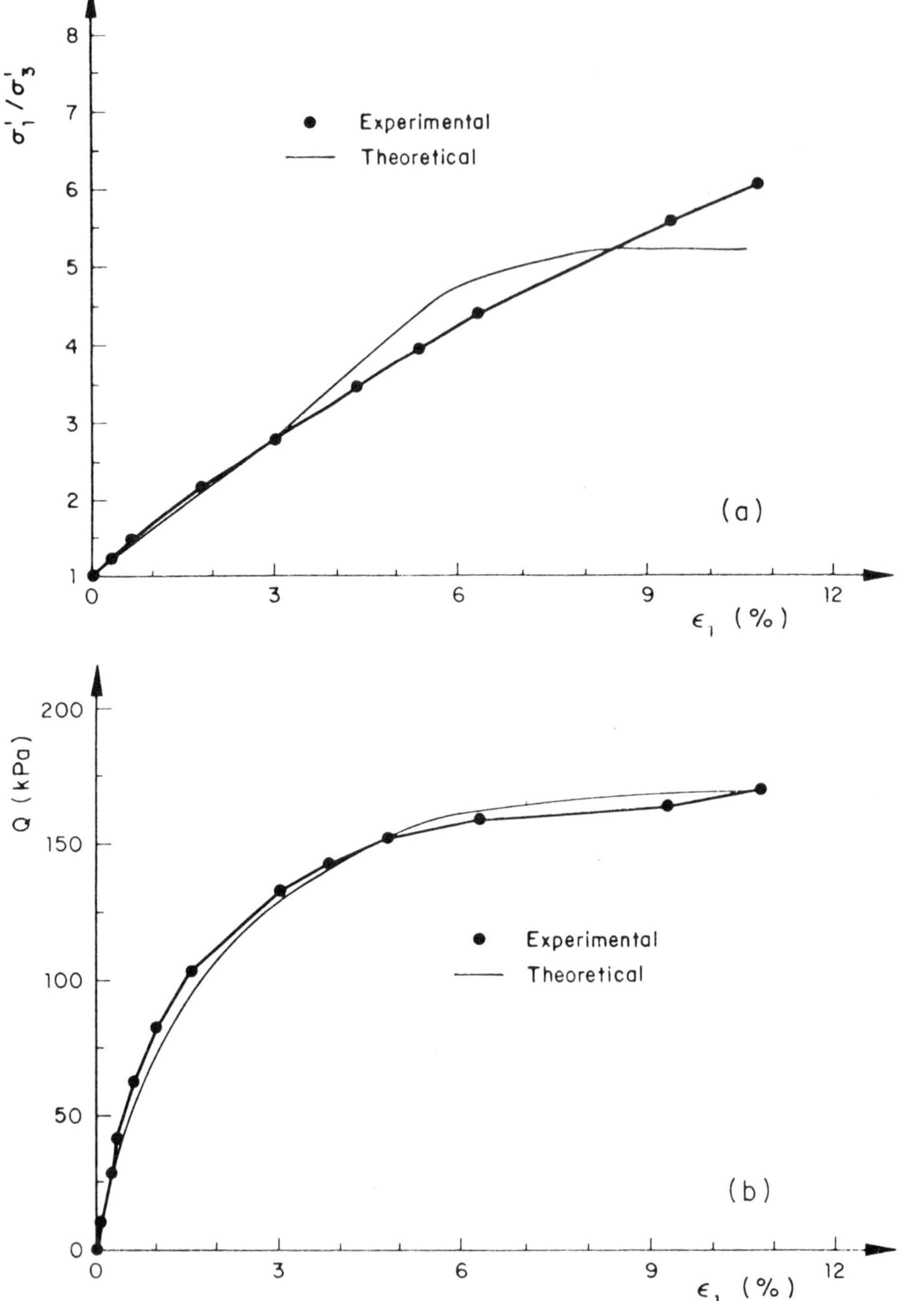

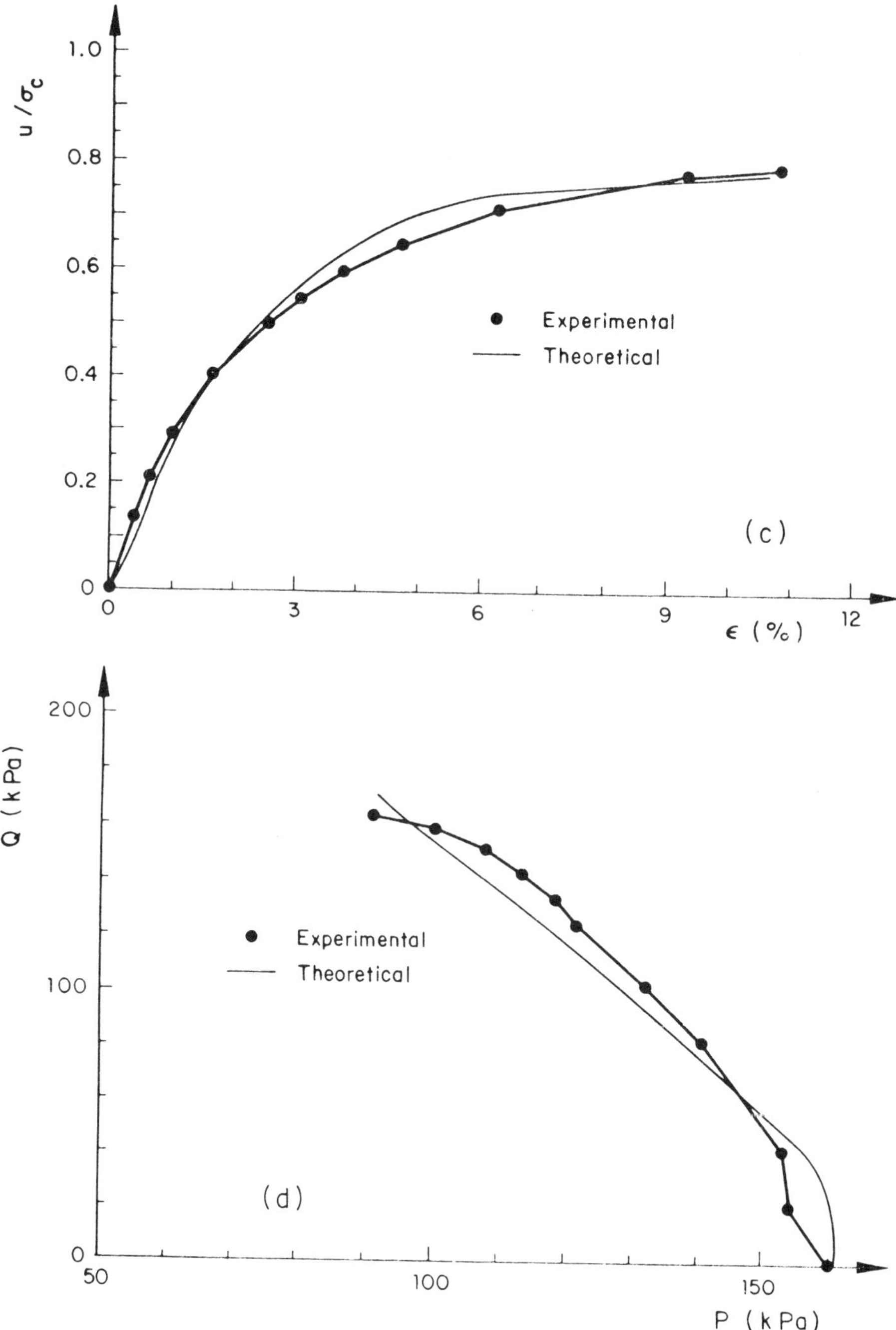

Figure 2. Calibration of the elasto-plastic parameters of the constitutive model using CU.1H and EU.1H test results.

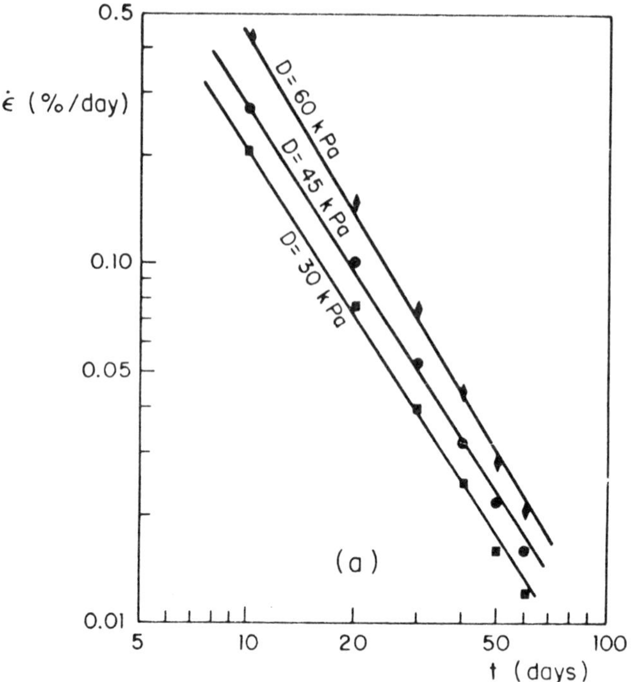

At this stage we are able to predict the behavior of this soil at any stress rate superior or equal to the stress rate used to compute the elasto-plastic parameters. In figures 4.a, 4.b and 4.c we are comparing the theoretical and experimental results of test CU.3D and in Figures 5.a, 5.b and 5.c such of test CU.6D, tested at 2 kg/3 days and 2 kg/6 days, respectively.

As it can observed from these comparisons, there is a general good agreement between theoretical and experimental results. It can be added that if $\sigma_1-\sigma_3/\sigma_3$ *vs.* u/σ_c values had been ploted a unique curve should be obtained for every stress rate. This unique curve should be very near of the curve obtained from test CU.1H used on the elasto-plastic parameters computation as it was considered that the viscous behavior does not induce any change in pore pressure.

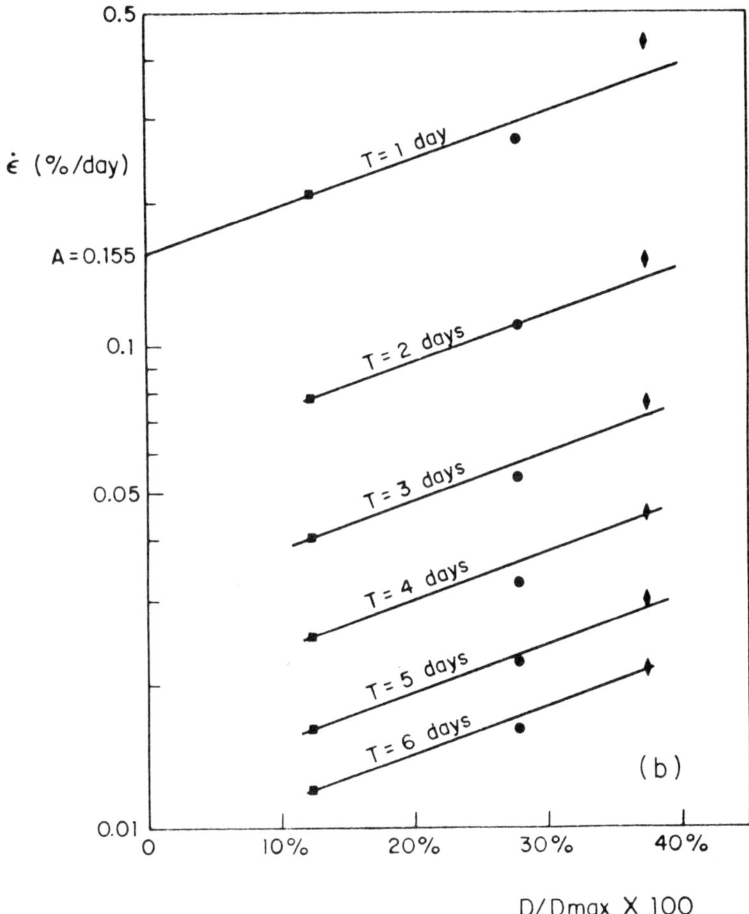

Figure 3. Computing the viscous parameters from three creep tests.

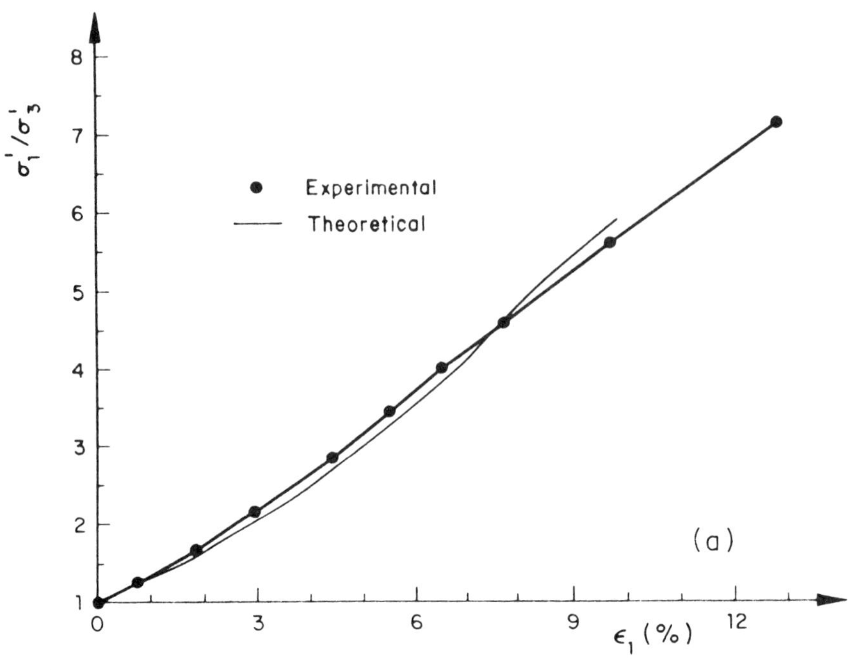
σ_1'/σ_3'
8
7
6
5
4
3
2
1
Experimental
Theoretical
(a)
0
3
6
9
12
ϵ_1 (%)

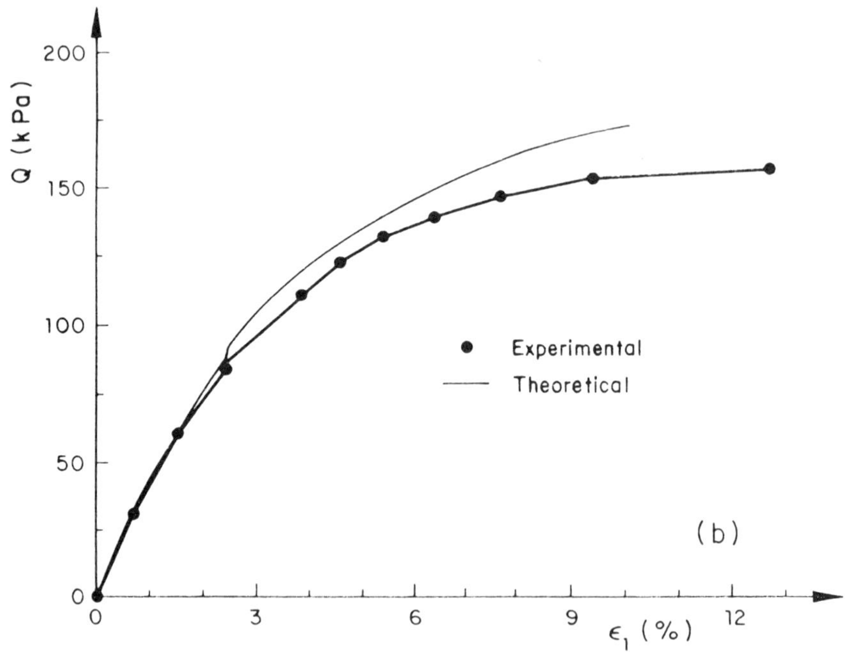
Q (kPa)
200
150
100
50
0
Experimental
Theoretical
(b)
0
3
6
9
12
ϵ_1 (%)

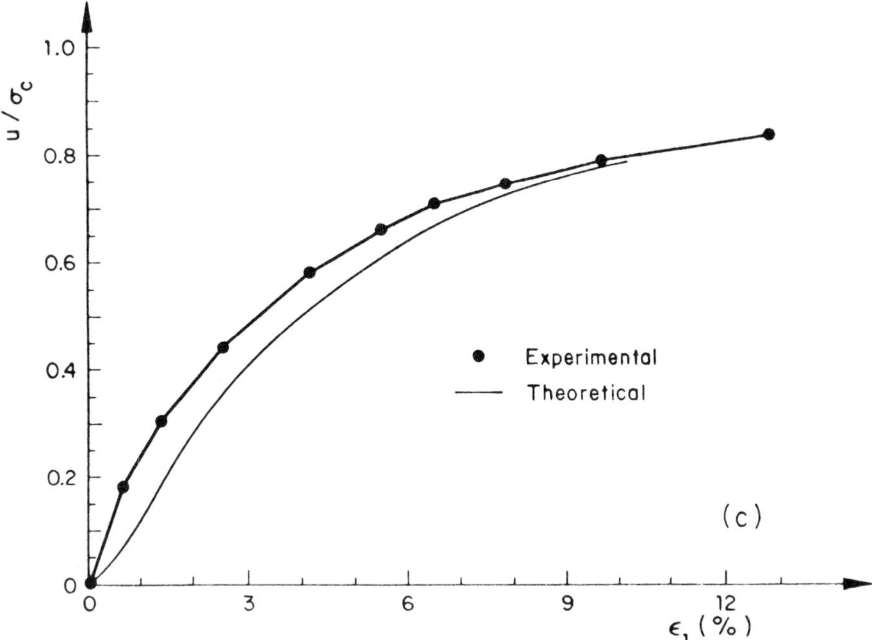

Figure 4. Comparison between theoretical and experimental tests results for test CU3.3

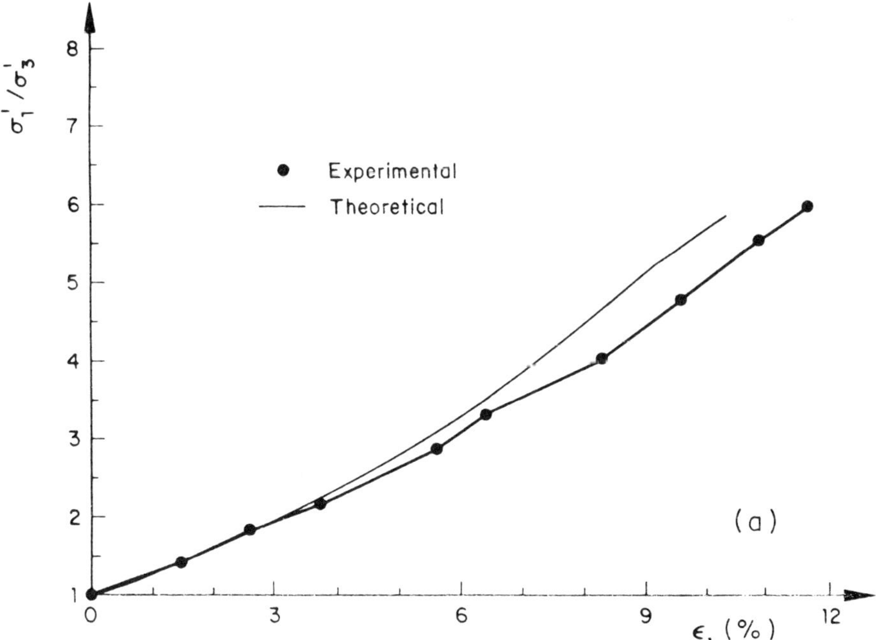

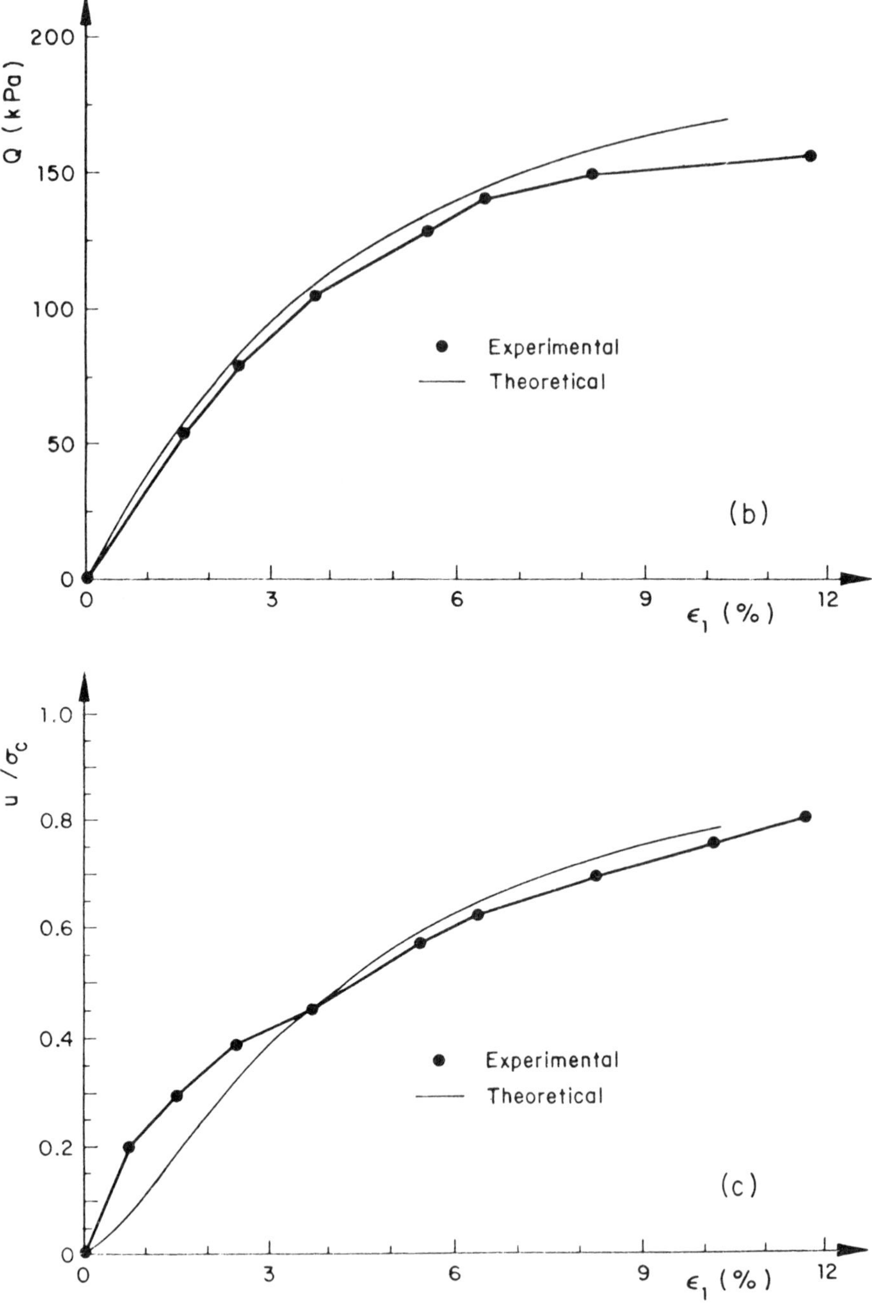

Figure 5. Comparison between theoretical and experimental tests results for test CU6.4.

CONCLUSIONS

1. In the case of soils wich are not fully saturated, its elasto-plastic behavior does not take place instantaneously, but it is defered with time.

2. Apparently, in extension tests the homogenization of the pore pressure takes much more time than in compression tests. This phenomenon makes it difficult to establish a limit between elasto-plastic an viscous behavior for these tests.

3. For the natural Mexico City clay and for the load increments values used here, it was estimated that most of the elasto-plastic behavior takes place during the first hour after loading.

4. The generality of the constitutive model presented here is restreinted as the stress-strain history is considered not to influence the viscous behavior of the soil.

5. In monotonous compression tests, good agreement between theoretical and experimental results was obtained.

ACKNOWLEDGEMENT

All tests presented here were carried out at the Instituto de Ingeniería, UNAM, by Mr. Guillermo Hiriart. His care and patience are gratefully acknowledged.

REFERENCES

1. Darve, F., Une formulation incrémentale des lois rhéologiques, applications aux sols, Thése d'Etat. Grenoble, 1978

2. Vauillat, P., Propritēs visqueuses d'une argile, expériences et formulation incrementale, Thése de Docteur Ingenieur, Paris 1975

3. Rojas, E., Romo, M. P., Hiriart, G., Stress path influence on Mexico City clay behavior, 2nd International Conference on Constitutive laws for Engng. Mat., Tucson, 1987, pp 1289-1296. Ed. Elsevier

4. Darve, F., Rojas, E., Flavigny, E., On a description of the cyclic behavior of clays, 5th International Conference on Numerical Methods in Geomechanics, Nagoya

5. Singh, A., Mitchell, J. K., General Stress-Strain-Time Functions for Soils, J. Soil Mech. Found. Div., ASCE, vol 94, SM1, 1968, pp 21-46

6. Jaime, A., Romo, M. P., Ovando, E., Características del suelo en el sitio Central de Abastos Oficinas, Informe 413, Instituto de Ingeniería, UNAM, 1987

TIME DEPENDENT SHEAR DEFORMATION OF CLAY

Y.P. VAID
Department of Civil Engineering
University of British Columbia
2324 Main Mall, Vancouver, B.C., Canada V6T 1W5

ABSTRACT

A unified treatment of the undrained shear deformation of clay is considered in the time dependent domain, utilizing the hypothesis of an equation of state. Results from a comprehensive series of tests on a clay under a variety of time loading histories are presented in support of the proposed hypothesis.

INTRODUCTION

Saturated clays, like most engineering materials, undergo shear deformations that are dependent on time. Although manifestations of such behaviour have been recognized and sometimes accounted for in practice (e.g. in adjusting vane strengths), little systematic treatment of clay response under generalized time loading histories has been pursued. The behaviour under constant rate of strain and creep deformation under constant stress, for instance, are treated as totally unrelated. There should be an intimate link between the behaviour in the two tests if time was added as an additional variable in influencing the stress-deformation response. This would also permit a rational consideration of shear deformations under generalized time loading histories.

This paper presents a comprehensive study of undrained shear deformation response of a saturated clay in the time dependent domain. The behaviour of the clay in the undisturbed normally consolidated state is determined in the triaxial test under a variety of time loading histories. This consisted of loading identical specimens under constant rate of strain, constant rate of stress, creep under constant and decreasing stresses, including discontinuities in creep stress or constant rate of strain part way into the loading process. Creep stress levels were chosen so as to encompass creep rupture in the time deformation response. Influence of the level of effective confining pressure on the time dependent response is also investigated. In addition, possible differences in the nature of the time effects between the clay in the undisturbed and the remolded destructured states are explored on a limited scale.

EXPERIMENTATION

Material Tested

A natural clay (Haney clay) was used in the study. Haney clay is a postglacial marine clay with illite as the predominant clay mineral. Some physical properties of the clay are given in Table 1.

TABLE 1

Physical Properties of Haney Clay

Liquid limit	44%
Plasticity index	18%
Clay fraction	50%
Natural water content	40 ± 0.5%
Porewater salinity	∿2.0 g/litre
Sensitivity	6 to 10
Maximum past pressure	∿3.5 kgf/cm^2

The clay was block sampled from an open pit. In order to minimize natural material variability, all test specimens were trimmed from blocks taken from the same horizon.

Remolded destructured clay specimens were trimmed from a large sample that was consolidated one dimensionally from slurry in a large oedometer. The slurry was made by mixing natural clay with water at twice the liquid limit. A thorough mixing was ensured by the use of a solids pump. The slurry was consolidated under an effective stress of 1 kgf/cm^2.

Tests Performed

Undrained triaxial tests were carried out on the undisturbed clay specimens normally consolidated hydrostatically to a stress σ'_c of 5.25 kgf/cm². A limited number of tests were performed on specimens with σ'_c = 6.25 kgf/cm². Apart from the commonly performed constant rate of strain and constant stress creep tests, tests were carried out in which neither strain rate nor stress was held constant. Thus stress, strain and strain rate were continuously (also a single discontinuity in stress or rate in some cases) varying during the deformation process.

Only a limited number of undrained tests were performed on the remolded clay. Hydrostatic consolidation for these specimens was done under σ'_c = 4.25 and 5.25 kgf/cm². These tests also included constant rate of strain, constant stress creep and some tests under other generalized time loading histories.

Test Procedures

Triaxial specimens were 3.5 cm dia. x 7.5 cm long. Special triaxial cells with low friction seal were used. This enabled confident external measurement of axial load. All test variables were monitored electronically. High speed digital data acquisition system was employed that was particularly essential to capture behaviour in the region of rapidly changing deformation rates under some loading patterns. This is mandatory particularly in creep tests where small variations in stresses or material have a large effect on the response. The testing program was carried out in a constant temperature environment (maximum variation ± 0.25°C) in order to eliminate influence of temperature variations on the time dependent response.

EQUATION OF STATE

For metals deforming under isothermal conditions, a unique relationship is assumed to exist among the instantaneous values of stress σ, strain ϵ and strain rate $\dot{\epsilon}$,

$$f(\sigma, \epsilon, \dot{\epsilon}) = 0 \tag{1}$$

regardless of the manner in which these parameters varied in arriving at the current state (1). That the stress is a function of current strain and strain rate only, as implied in Eq. 1, has been frequently used in the study of strain-time behaviour of metals. This concept, which is referred to as the strain hardening creep law (or the equation of state), if often used to determine creep behaviour under varying stresses from information obtained under constant stress creep. Also, the existence of a unique $\sigma,\epsilon,\dot{\epsilon}$ law has been used to predict creep behaviour of metals and plastics from test data obtained from loading under constant rate of strain (1,2).

If the concept of equation of state is considered applicable to the undrained deformation of clay, it would imply

$$q = f(\epsilon, \dot{\epsilon}) \tag{2}$$

in which q = normalized deviator stress $(\sigma_1-\sigma_3)/\sigma'_c$ and ϵ and $\dot{\epsilon}$ are axial strain and strain rate respectively. For the conditions of the triaxial test, q is a meausure of the maximum shear stress and ϵ and $\dot{\epsilon}$ are directly proportional to shear strain and shear strain rate respectively.

Although the concept of equation of state has been widely used for metals, experimental evidence supporting its validity is scarce, particularly under loading histories involving all $\sigma,\epsilon,\dot{\epsilon}$ varying with time.

BEHAVIOUR OF UNDISTURBED HANEY CLAY

Characteristic Behaviour

Figure 1 shows characteristic features of the measured undrained deformation response under a variety of time loading histories. The time variation of each of the three variables q, ϵ and $\dot{\epsilon}$ is illustrated. In all loading modes, ϵ was an increasing function of time, but the time rate of its accumulation varied with the test type and the characteristics of the soil.

Constant rate of strain shear (Fig. 1a) represents conventional triaxial tests. Strain rate is constant, ϵ increases linearly and q nonlinearly with time. Because of the strain softening nature of the clay tested, q represented both increase and a later decrease with time during the deformation process. Faster the strain rate, the higher was the position of the resulting stress-strain curve.

Shear under constant rate of loading (Fig. 1b) resulted in all ϵ, $\dot{\epsilon}$ and q varying with time. The stress was essentially a linear function of time initially, but decreased somewhat with time in later stages due to increase in sample area with straining. Both ϵ and $\dot{\epsilon}$ increased almost exponentially. The higher the rate of loading, the stiffer was the observed stress-strain response.

Constant stress creep (Fig. 1c) represented deformation under constant q and continuously decreasing $\dot{\epsilon}$. Creep under constant load on the other hand involved both q and $\dot{\epsilon}$ decreasing. This type of behaviour was observed at q levels less than 0.518 in constant stress creep.

In constant stress creep rupture (Fig. 1d) ϵ accumulated initially at a decreasing rate until $\dot{\epsilon}_{min}$ under constant q. Thereafter $\dot{\epsilon}$ increased continuously until rupture. This behaviour was observed at q levels in excess of 0.518. Creep rupture under constant load represented $\dot{\epsilon}$ history similar to that under constant stress creep in addition to continuously decreasing q.

Step creep (Fig. 1e) and creep rupture (Fig. 1f) represent deformation histories similar to Figs. 1(c) and 1(d) simulating sudden discontinuities in q and hence in ϵ and $\dot{\epsilon}$ part way into the constant stress or constant load creep.

Thus the data base obtained represents arrival of the clay to any current $\sigma,\epsilon,\dot{\epsilon}$ state by a range of time histories of each variable. Apart from strain accumulation in traditional constant q or constant $\dot{\epsilon}$ tests, several other arbitrary histories in q and $\dot{\epsilon}$ have been included. Moreover, the response of the clay is considered over the full strain range, including the strain softening region identified in the constant rate of strain shear.

Stress-Strain-Strain Rate Response

A convenient way to test the validity of the hypothesis expressed by Eq. 2 will be to look at the stress-strain response at a fixed $\dot{\epsilon}$ where at current q and ϵ should be uniquely related. Each such unique relationship will depend on the selected $\dot{\epsilon}$. This is conveniently determined by the conventional constant rate of strain undrained tests.

Stress-strain response observed in four constant rate of strain tests is illustrated in Fig. 2 by solid lines. Current q and ϵ values at

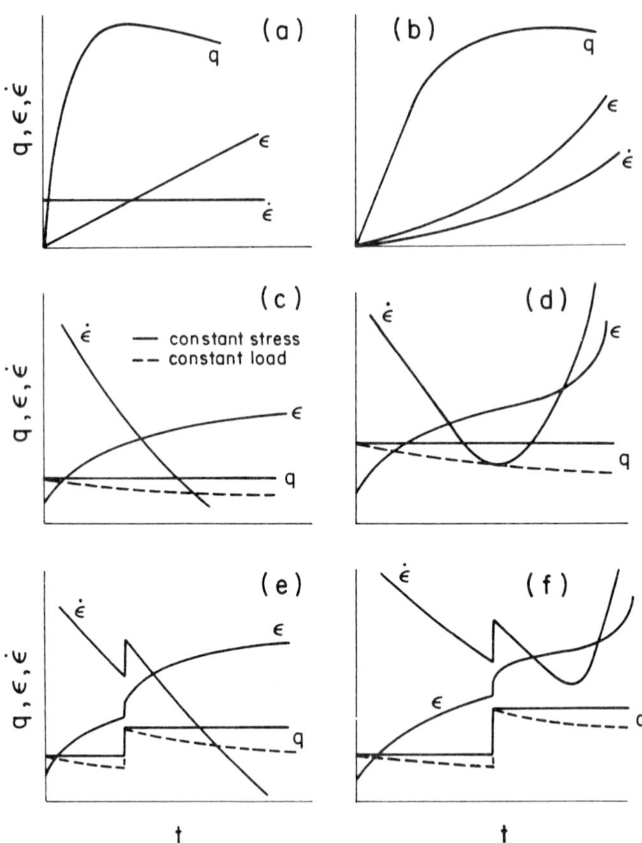

Fig. 1. Undrained behaviour of undisturbed Haney clay under various time loading histories.

the current $\dot{\epsilon}$ equal to those selected in Fig. 2 for deformation under other loading histories are also plotted by data points on the respective curves. An excellent agreement with constant $\dot{\epsilon}$ curves clearly furnishes evidence in support of a unique stress-strain-strain rate relationship for the clay tested. Further examination of test data at several other constant $\dot{\epsilon}$ yielded confirmations similar to those shown in Fig. 2. The validity of the unique $q, \epsilon, \dot{\epsilon}$ relationship not only in the strain hardening but also in the strain softening region is noteworthy.

The data shown in Fig. 2 constitutes results from tests at both consolidation stresses. The effect of consolidation stress level is thus accounted for by the use of normalized shear stress q. Such normalized behaviour for normally consolidated clays is widely recognized in conventional undrained stress-strain and strength studies (3).

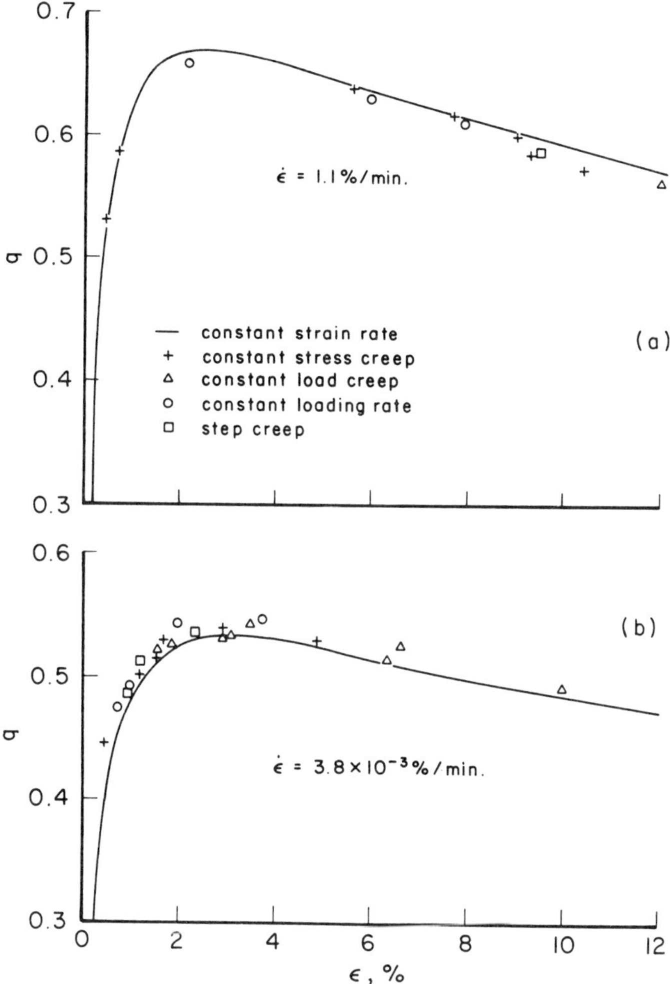

Fig. 2. Unique stress-strain response of undisturbed Haney clay at several constant strain rates.

Direct Confirmations in Specific Test Types

Stress-strain curves from two constant rate of strain tests are shown in Fig. 3 by solid curves. Results of a third test initially commenced at the smaller of the two rates but suddenly increased to the higher value after an accumulated strain of about 0.8% is also shown by data points. That this specimen after increase in $\dot{\epsilon}$ mimics the behaviour of the specimen tested at the higher rate is a confirmation of the existence of the unique $q, \epsilon, \dot{\epsilon}$ relationship.

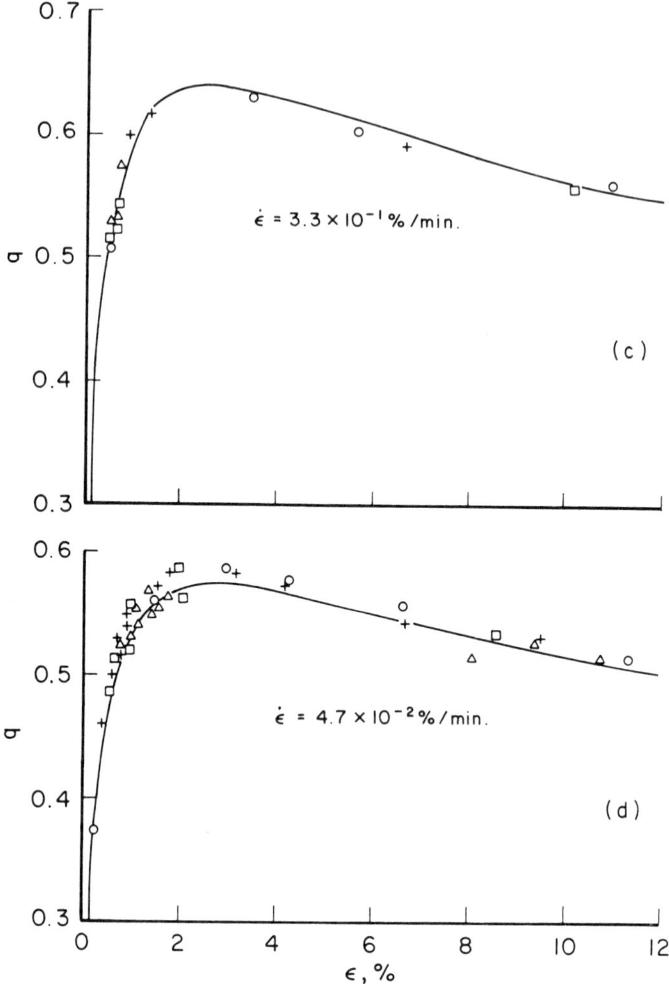

Fig. 2. Cont'd... Unique stress-strain response of undisturbed Haney clay at several constant strain rates.

Results of a constant stress (q_1) creep and a constant stress (q_2) creep rupture test are illustrated in Fig. 4 as strain-time curves. The data points represent results from a step creep test. In this test the specimen was allowd to creep under q_1 for the first 13 minutes whereafter the creep stress was suddenly increased to q_2. The strain-time response predicted after the stress increment assuming validity of the unique $q,\epsilon,\dot{\epsilon}$ relationship is labelled as the predicted curve in Fig. 4. This predicted curve would simply be the part beyond 'a' of the strain time curve under creep stress q_2 translated horizontally to 'b' by an amount

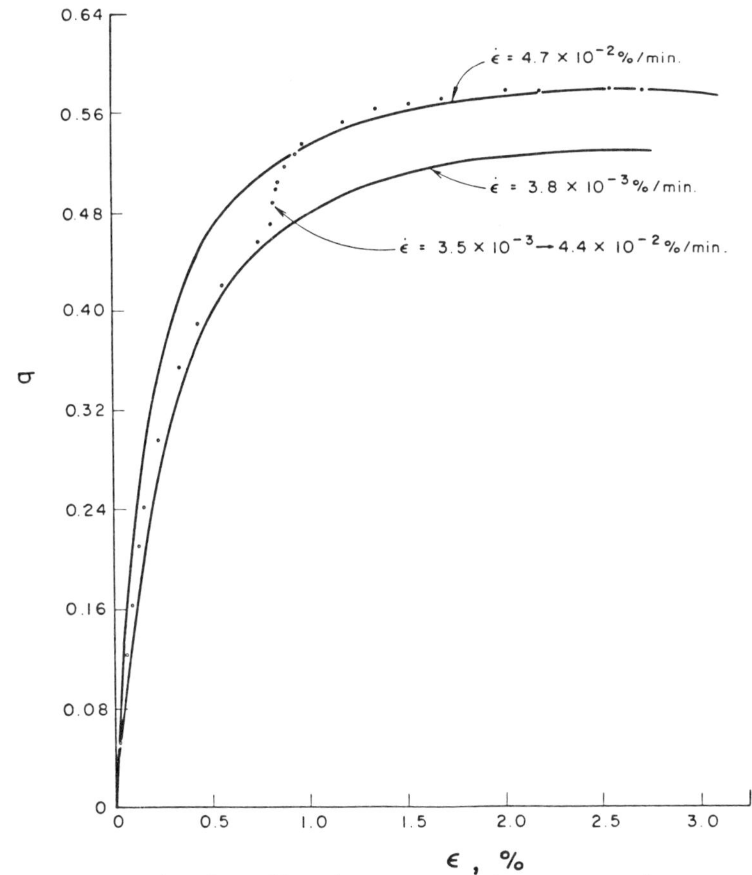

Fig. 3. Observed and predicted stress-strain response due to step change in constant rate of strain.

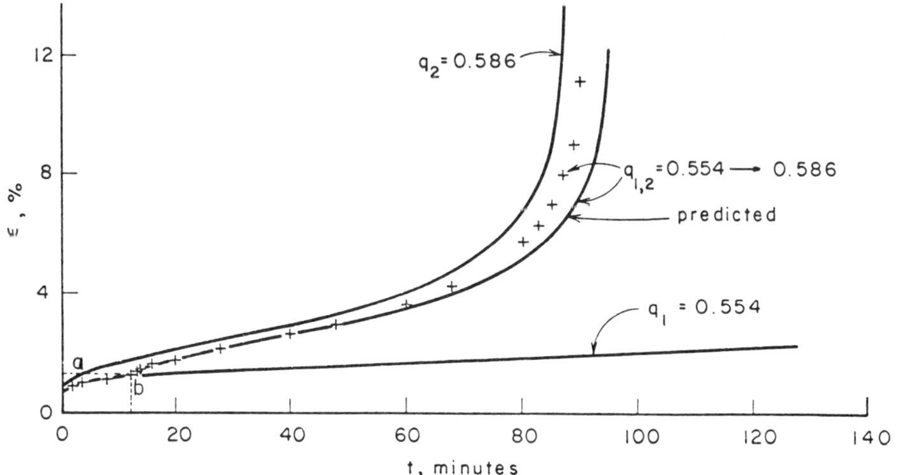

Fig. 4. Observed and predicted stress-strain response due to step change in stress in constant stress creep.

'ab'. Excellent agreement between observed and predicted strain-time response may be noted.

Creep Response Derived from Constant Strain Rate Data and Vice-Versa

This is illustrated in Fig. 5 assuming unique $q, \epsilon, \dot{\epsilon}$ relationships for the clay. Results of constant stress creep tests when plotted in the form of

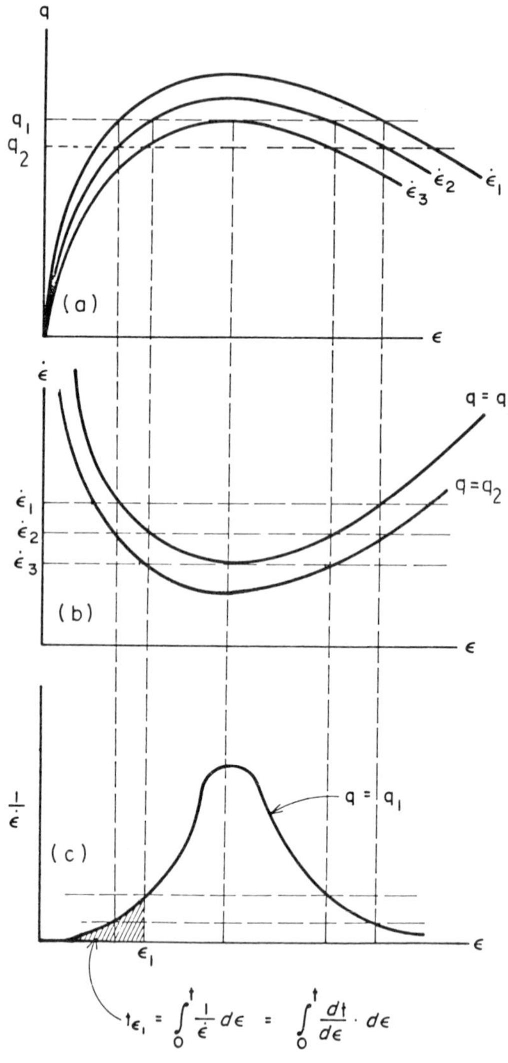

Fig. 5. Prediction of stress-strain behaviour under constant rate of strain from constant stress creep data and vice-versa.

Fig. 5b enable predictions of clay behaviour under constant rate of strain (Fig. 5a). Such successful predictions have already been demonstrated in Fig. 2 at several constant strain rates. If a constant rate of strain test was carried out at a strain rate equal to the minimum creep rate of a constant stress creep test under q_1, then the peak stress in the constant rate of strain test would be q_1 and will occur at a strain equal to that at minimum creep rate in the creep test (see Fig. 5a and 5b). Experimental evidence in support of this may be seen in Fig. 6 where data showing peak q (q_m) vs $\dot{\epsilon}$ in constant rate of strain tests

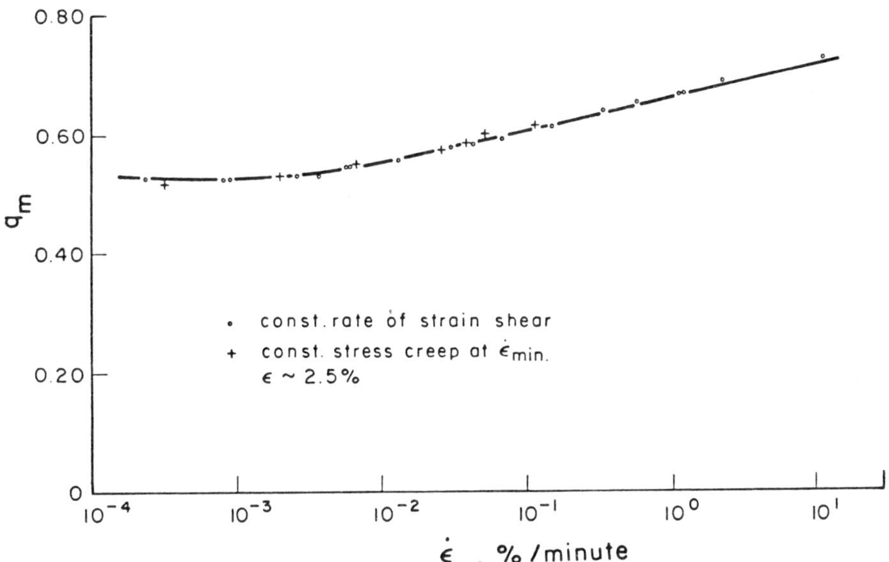

Fig. 6. Rate dependence of undrained strength of undisturbed Haney clay in constant rate of strain shear and constant stress creep.

and q vs. $\dot{\epsilon}_{min}$ in creep test lie along a unique curve. Axial strain at peak q in constant $\dot{\epsilon}$ shear and at $\dot{\epsilon}_{min}$ in constant stress creep was essentially constant in the neighbourhood of about 2.5% regardless of constant $\dot{\epsilon}$ or q in these tests. The relationship in Fig. 6 thus holds at constant ϵ, and would be expected if uniqueness of $q, \epsilon, \dot{\epsilon}$ was valid. Strain rate dependence of undrained strength ($q_m/2$) reflected by Fig. 6 is a well recognized characteristic of clays.

Contant strain rate shear data in Fig. 5a when plotted in the form of Fig. 5b enables prediction of strain time behaviour in constant stress creep tests. In this figure the time $t_{\epsilon 1}$ required for accumulation of strain ϵ_1 under creep stress q_1, is given by the shaded area under the curve, $1/\dot{\epsilon}$ vs ϵ until time $t_{\epsilon 1}$. Strain-time prediction for two creep tests are shown in Fig. 7. Good agreement between predicted and measured response may be noted.

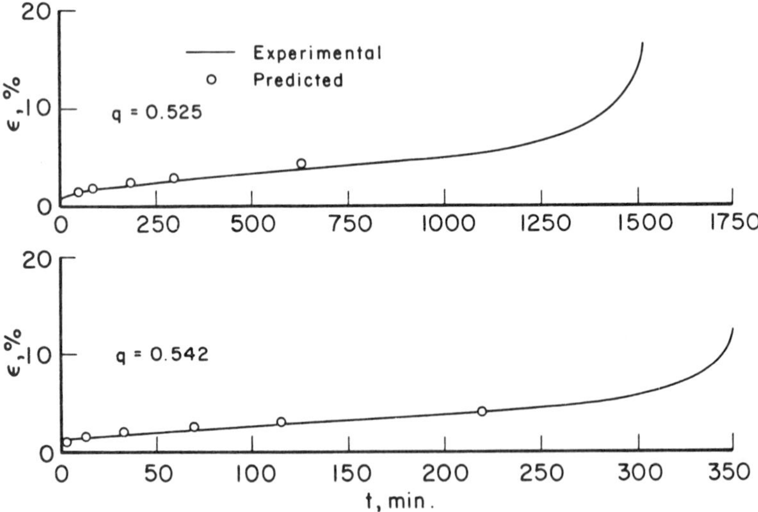

Fig. 7. Observed and predicted strain-time response in constant stress creep.

BEHAVIOUR OF REMOLDED CLAY

Clay in the remolded state was not tested extensively. Only a limited number of tests were carried out in each of the categories illustrated in Fig. 1. Nevertheless, the time dependent shear deformation response had all the general characteristics observed for the clay in the undisturbed state.

The remolded clay after hydrostatic consolidation to identical effective stress had a water content about 4% lower than that for the undisturbed clay. This apparently reflects the destructuring of the random cardhouse structure of the undisturbed clay on remolding. Much reduced strain softening following peak stress in constant rate of strain shear was a further evidence of destructuring on remolding.

The relationship between rupture life and minimum creep rate in constant stress creep was virtually unaltered on remolding (Fig. 8).

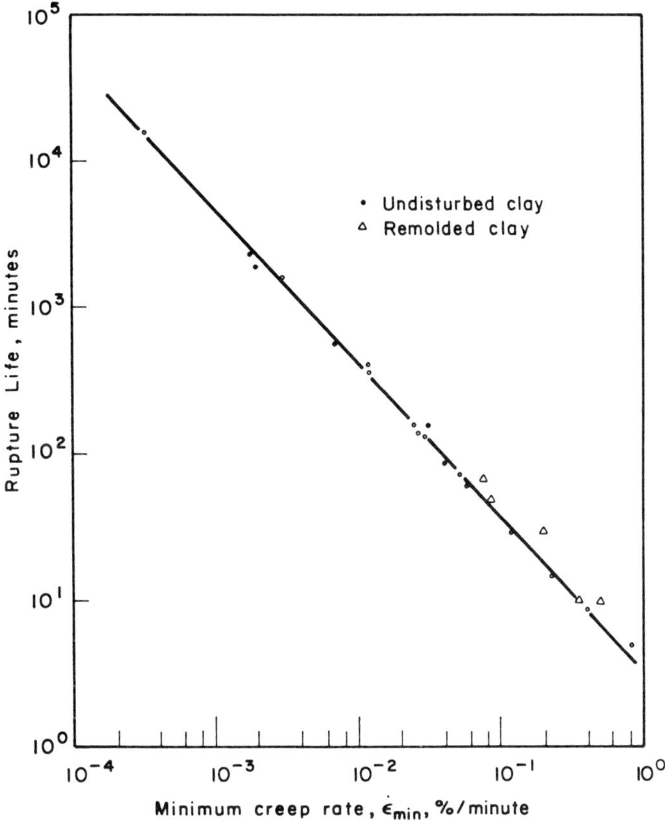

Fig. 8. Relationship between rupture life and minimum creep rate for undisturbed and remolded Haney clay.

Unlike undisturbed clay, a very narrow range of creep stresses (q = 0.546 - 0.528) transformed clay response from rupture in only 50 min to no rupture. Such a characteristic seems to be related to a very small post peak strain softening nature of the remolded clay. This explains the lack of data in Fig. 8 in the region of greater rupture life. Linear relationships between log rupture life and log minimum creep rate have also been reported for metals and for other soils (4,5). However, unlike the data presented for Haney clay, the reported relationships suffer from a very large data scatter.

The existence of a unique stress-strain-strain rate relationship for the remolded clay is illustrated in Fig. 9. Stress-strain response at

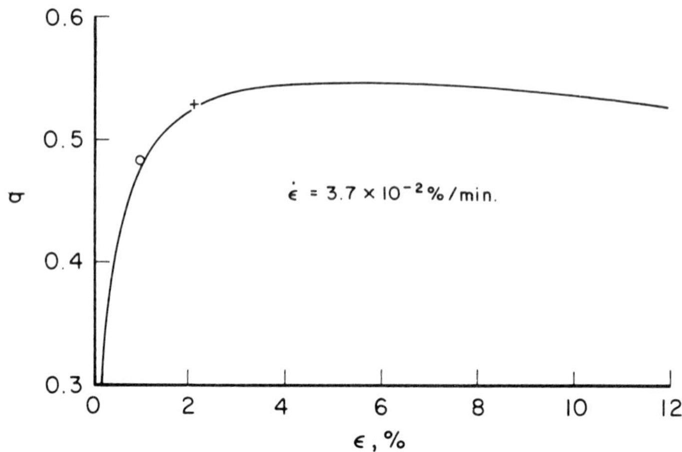

Fig. 9. Unique stress-strain response of remolded Haney clay at a constant strain rate.

constant $\dot{\epsilon} = 3.5 \times 10^{-2}$%/min is shown together with stress-strain data at identical $\dot{\epsilon}$ in tests with other time deformation histories. Although data is limited, validity of a unique $q, \epsilon, \dot{\epsilon}$ relationship is clearly indicated. This relationship may be compared with that for the undisturbed clay at approximately the same $\dot{\epsilon}$ in Fig. 2d. Remolded stress-strain response is located below that for the undisturbed soil and is not much susceptible to strain softening.

Relationship similar to that in Fig. 6 for the undisturbed clay was also found valid for the remolded clay. This is shown in Fig. 10. Creep data in the region of low $\dot{\epsilon}_{min}$ could not be obtained for the remolded clay for reasons explained earlier. The data in Fig. 10 represents a strain level of about 4.5% at which peak stress in constant $\dot{\epsilon}$ tests and $\dot{\epsilon}_{min}$ in constant stress creep tests occurred.

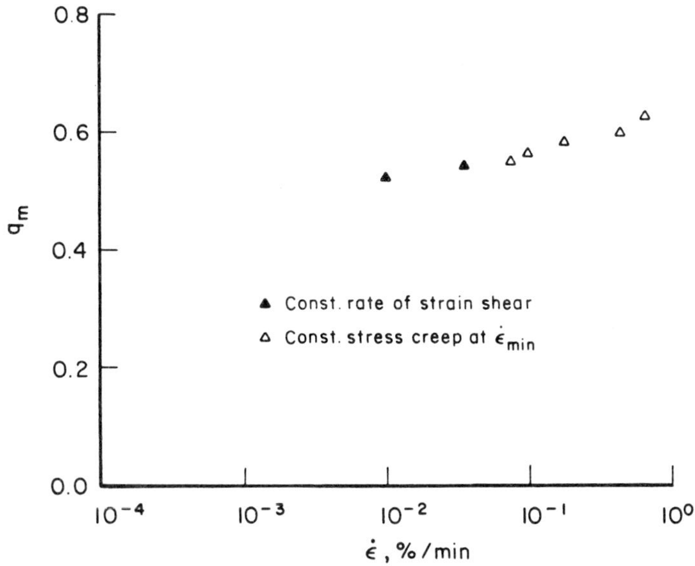

Fig. 10. Rate dependence of undrained strength of remolded Haney clay in constant rate of strain shear and constant stress creep.

CONCLUSIONS

Shear deformation of a saturated clay can be described in the time dependent domain by an equation of state. A comprehensive series of undrained tests on a normally consolidated undisturbed clay under generalized time loading history show that the current shear stress is a function of current shear strain and shear strain rate only and is independent of the past deformation history.

Most of the time dependent response aspects of the clay in the remolded state were found in general similar to that of the same clay in the undisturbed state.

ACKNOWLEDGMENTS

This research was supported by a grant from the Natural Science and Engineering Research Council of Canada. The assistance of Kelly Lamb in preparation of the manuscript and of Richard Brun in drafting figures is gratefully acknowledged.

REFERENCES

[1] Lubahn, J.D. and Felgar, R.P., Plasticity and Creep of Metals, John Wiley and Sons Inc., New York, 1961.

[2] Pao, Y.H. and Marin, J., Prediction of Creep Curves from Stress Strain Data, Proc. Am. Soc. for Testing Materials, 52, 1952, pp. 51-57.

[3] Ladd, C.C., Foott, R., Ishihara, K., Schlosser, S. and Poulos, H., Stress Deformation and Strength Characteristics, Proc. 7th Int. Conf. Soil Mech. Found. Eng., Tokyo, 2, 1977, pp. 421-494.

[4] Monkman, I.C. and Grant, N.J., An Empirical Relationship Between Rupture Life and Minimum Creep Rate in Creep Rupture Tests, Proc. Am. Soc. for Testing Materials, 56, 1956, pp. 593-620.

[5] Saito, M. and Uezawa, H., Failure of Soil Due to Creep, Proc. 5th Int. Conf. Soil Mech. Found. Engng., Paris, 1, 1961, pp. 315-318.

RHEOLOGICAL PECULIARITY OF CLAYEY SOILS DEFORMATION UNDER SWELLING

A.A.MUSTAFAYEV, Professor of Civil Engineering, ACE Institute, Baku, USSR

SYNOPSIS The results of the experimental studies of the mechanism of the rheological process in swelling clayey soils have been presented in this paper. On the bases of these results it has been determined, that the deformation of clayey swelling is a rheological process: the mechanism of the said process can be interpreted with sufficient from the point of view of practical application, accuracy in terms of the linear hereditary creep of Boltzmann-Volterr.

The results of the long laboratory experiments have proved, that the swelling of clayey soils is a rheological process, i.e. it is the temporal expansion of deformations at constant values of water content and pressure. That's why the temporal variation of the stressed-strained state of these soils can be interpreted in terms of the appropriate theory of creep. It has been shown, that Boltzmann-Volterr theory of linear hereditary creep with the kernel of Abel type is sufficiently precise from the point of view of practical application to describe the mechanism of clayey soils swelling within the wide range of compacting pressure variations.

Inspite of the fact, that the foundation engineering on swelling clayey soils has achieved certain success, it's scientific base - swelling soils mechanics, is considerably falling behind. The design model of swelling soils has not been developed and the mechanism of time-dependent variations of the stressed-strained state of these soils in terms of the methods of deformation continuum mechanics has not been determined yet.

Meanwhile, the problems of the mechanics of swelling clayey soils are of a particular importance for developing of well founded technique for the forecasting of the swelling deformations, going on in the bases of the engineering structures.

The swelling process, taking place at the continuous moistening of the soil mass, can be represented as that, consisting of two samultaneous non-stationary processes(Mustafayev A.A., Chigniyev G.D., Nazirova G.D., 1974; Mustafayev A.A., Chigniyev G.D., 1977; Mustafayev A.A., 1980). The first one is the result of the water absorption by the pores of the soil and the beginning of negative tensile effective stresses in it's skeleton. In the said process the beginning of swelling deformation and the moment of it's stabilization comes coincide respectively with the beginning of percolation and the cessation of water inflow into the thickness of soil. As to the value of the volume deformation of soil, caused by the mechanical moving of the soil's particles apart, due to the thickening of the water film, it directly depends upon the volume of water, participating in the process. A discussion of the problem will be found in the literature of the subject.

In the second process water is absorbed by the mineral aggregates themselves, with their density being higher, than the mean density of soil. The temporal development of deformation in this case is going on slower, than the filtrational process, hence the volume of swelling soil should be considerably larger than the volume of water, coming into the soil mass when moistened. In this process the swelling doesn't always start with the moistening of the soil thickness, and it's stabilization comes as a rule, when a sufficient time is up since the cessation of water inflow to the soil . The intravolumetric processes going on in the aggregates of soil particles seem to fall behind the fast-moving front of moistening. Such a complecated physico-chemical and mechanical process results in the onset and the development of the rheological processes in the said soils - i.e. the temporal expansion of swelling at the constant values of water content and load - the phenomenon of creep. To determine the mechanism of the rheology of swelling soils, the appropriate experimental study has been done on the basis of which the author of the present paper has obtained the families of swelling curves at constant values of compacting pressures, the stress variations curves at the constant values of deformation, as well as the graphs of the compacting pressures against the swelling deformations for the definite values of deformation time (the isochrone creep curves). All the said graphs have been plotted at different but constant during the experimental period, values of water content, i.e. from the natural to the saturated state of the soil. The deformability of the soils under study, has been examined with the consolidometers on the samples 40 cm^2 in area and 35 mm in height, cut out of the swollen block samples taken from the typical construction sites of Azerbaijan. Three varieties of swelling samples have been examined (A,B,C).

The soil samples have been preconsolidated under the influence of pre-set external loads in the consolidometers untill the complete stabilazation of deformation has been reached. Then, by means of special device a rated amount of water has been supplied being constant for the whole experimental period. The variations of soil deformation have been observed for 100 days.

The samples under study can be reffered to the firm clays of the marine origin. The montmorillonite is the most frequent occurance in the mineralogical composition of the said soils (50-60%) with the content of kalloysite being 2-5%. The content of kaolinite is 15-17%. The plasticity index varies within the limits of 20-40; with density being 26,6-27,2 kH/m^3 and porosity - 38-42%.

The analyses of the curves, plotted, has been showed, that the temporal variations of stressed-strained state of swelling clayey soils should be interpreted by Boltzmann-Volterr's theory of linear hereditary creep (Mustafayev A.A. and El-Hansy Ruoby M.M., 1984).

According to this theory, the stressed state at a given moment is determined not only by the deformation, existing at the moment, but by all the proceeding history of soil deformation (Vyalov S.S., 1978).

The variation of the relative swelling of clay in terms of the theory at issue, can be described by means of the integral equation:

$$\mathcal{E}_{sw}(t) = \frac{1}{E_o}\left[\sigma(t) + \int_0^t K(t-\tau)\sigma(\tau)d\tau \right] \quad (1)$$

including the expression of the creep kernel $K(t-\tau)$, characterising accurate up to constant factor the rate of soil deformation at a constant value of stress, equal to unit.

$$\frac{1}{E_o}K(t) = \frac{1}{\sigma}\frac{d\mathcal{E}_{sw}(t)}{dt} \quad (2)$$

If we write $R(t-\tau)$ for the resolvent of the kernel of the integral equation (1), then the variation of time-dependent swelling deformation will be determined in terms of the following expression:

$$\sigma(t) = E_o\left[\mathcal{E}_{sw}(t) - \int_0^t R(t-\tau)\mathcal{E}_{sw}(\tau)d\tau \right] \quad (3)$$

Assuming in (3) $\mathcal{E}_{sw}(t) = \mathcal{E}_{sw}(\tau) = const$ and having differentiated both parts with respect to t, we'll obtain:

$$E_o R(t) = -\frac{1}{\mathcal{E}_{sw}}\frac{d\sigma(t)}{dt} \quad (4)$$

Therefore, the resolvent of the creep of kernel, which characterizes the rate of temporal variations of pressure, necessary for keeping of the constant unit deformation going, as well as the kernel of creep, may be obtained experimentally.

In order to check the possibility of interpreting the mechanism of the rheology of swelling soils by means of the theory of linear hereditary creep, the results of the experiments, carried out, have been processed by the said theory (Mustafayev A.A. and El-Hansy Ruoby M.M., 1984

It has been determined, that the peculiar behaviour of clayey soils in the course of swelling, may quite satisfactory be characterised by the exponential kernel, of

Abel type.

$$\kappa(t-\tau) = \delta(t-\tau)^{-\alpha} \quad (5)$$

where α, δ - the rheological parameters of the soil, with $0 < \alpha < 1$. Assuming that in (1) $\sigma(t) = \sigma(\tau) = const$ and $\kappa(t-\tau) = \delta(t-\tau)^{-\alpha}$ the following can be obtained

$$\varepsilon_{sw}(t) = \frac{\sigma_o}{E_o}\left(1 + \frac{\delta}{1-\alpha} t^{1-\alpha}\right) \quad (6)$$

According to (6) at $t=0$, we have $\varepsilon_{sw}(0) = \sigma_o / E_o$; the rate of deformation can be expressed as

$$\frac{d\varepsilon_{sw}}{dt} = \frac{\sigma_o}{E_o} \delta t^{-\alpha} \quad (7)$$

Hence, it follows: at $t=0$, $d\varepsilon_{sw} : dt = \infty$, at $t \to \infty$ one has $d\varepsilon_{sw} : dt = \to 0$, which is in a completely agreement with the mechanism, obtained experimentally. In order to determine the rheological parameters of the swelling clayey soils the following procedure should be recommended. One has to logarithmate both parts of the expression (7) to obtain:

$$\ln \frac{d\varepsilon_{sw}}{dt} = \ln \frac{\sigma_o}{E_o} \delta - \alpha \ln t$$

As the experiments have shown, the curve, described by the formula, mentioned above, (7), becomes the straight line on the logarithmic network (fig.1) That is why, if one plots the experimental points on the logarithmic network of coordinates, then the slope of the resultant straight line will determine the value of the parameter α, while the y -intercept, cut off by the said straight line, enables the evaluation of δ-parameter. For the soils under study the values of α and δ vary within the limits of δ = = 0,027-0,054 day^{-1}; α =0,81-0,95.

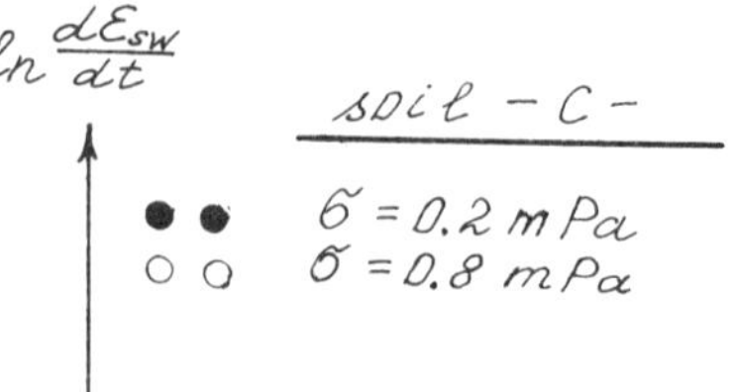

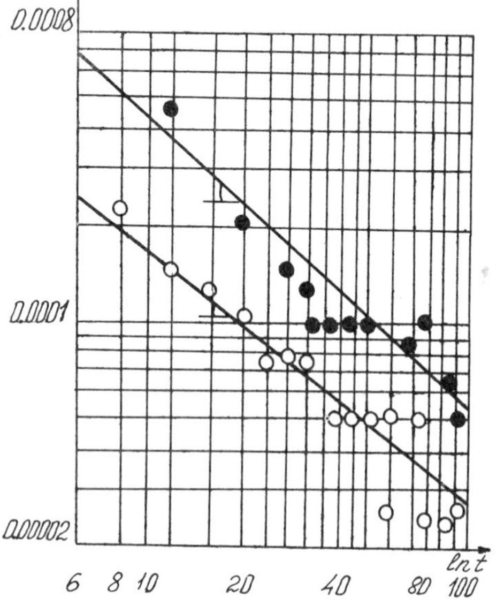

Fig.1. The Straightening of the Experimental Curves $\varepsilon_{sw} = f(t)$ on the Logarithmic Grid.

It is natural, that the value of these parameters will depend upon the water content - i.e. the density of soil. According to the experiments the increase of water content in the soil is accompanied by the decrease of α and δ values. Table 1 contains the values of the rheological parameters of the examined soils.

Table - 1

The Relationship Between the Values of the Rheological Parameters of Clayey Soils and Their Water Content.

Soil A			Soil B			Soil C		
$\omega\%$	α	δ day^{-1}	$\omega\%$	α	δ day^{-1}	$\omega\%$	α	δ day^{-1}
14	0,8160	0,3258	17	0,7035	0,14904	12	0,9100	0,3904
16	0,7922	0,2196	19	0,5771	0,0831	14	0,8912	0,2877
18	0,7464	0,1045	21	0,5456	0,0725	16	0,82703	0,13383
20	0,75398	0,07401	23	0,6362	0,0469	18	0,77536	0,07954

Using the experimental values of rheological parameters one has evaluated the relative deformation of swelling at different periods of time by formula (6), and on the basis of data, obtained, the families of the curves of swelling have been plotted for various values of soil water content.

Fig.2 shows the experimental points and the theoretical curves of swelling, calculated from the formula (6) for different values of compac - ting pressures at the water content ω = 20%.

Similar comparisons have been made for all the values of soil water content, used in the experiments. On the basis of swelling curves the relationships between relative swelling and compacting pressure for the period t = 96 days are plotted in fig.2 (left side).

As is seen from fig.2, the formula of the linear theory of hereditary creep interprets satisfactory enough, the process of swelling in clays. The maximum error at the initial period of swelling has been found to be no more than 6-8%.

Fig.3 presents the variation curves of temporal relative swelling at different water contents of soil, plotted on the basis of formula (6), for value of compacting pressure σ = 0,1 MPa. The experimental points are marked on these curves. As is seen from this figure, formula (6) describes quite satisfactory the process of swelling in clayey soils at different values of water content.

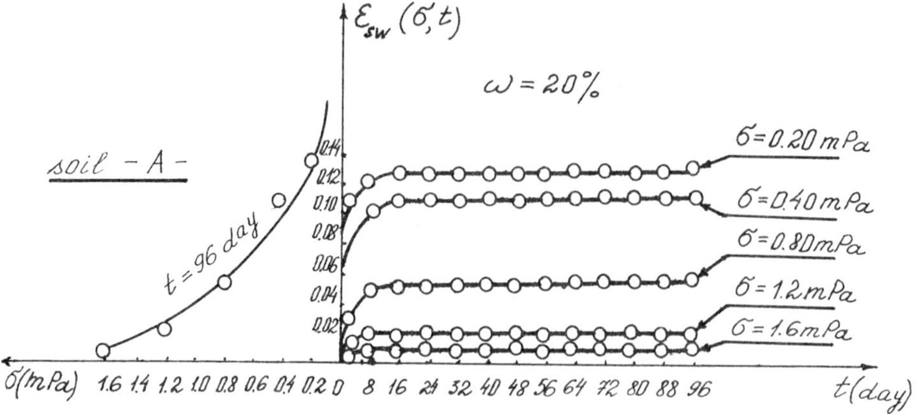

Fig.2. The Experimental and Theoretical Curves of Swelling at Different Values of Pressure

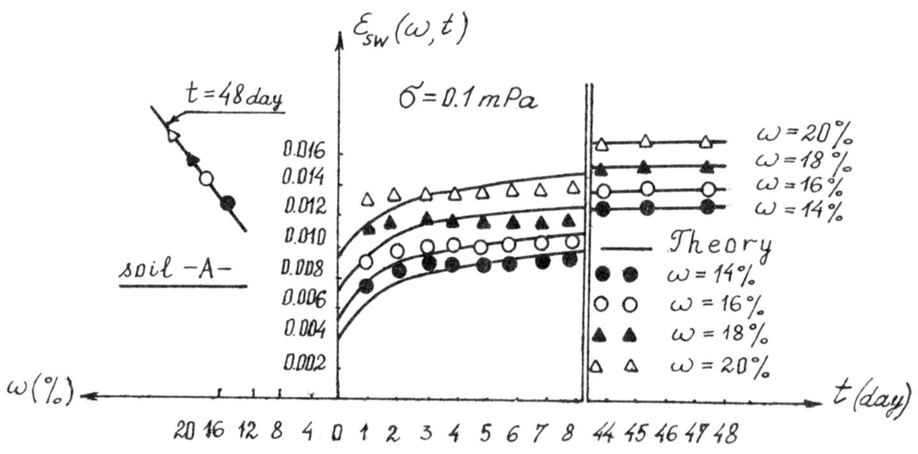

Fig.3. The Theoretical Curves of the Temporal Variation of Relative Swelling at Different Values of Water Content, Plotted on the Basis of Formula 6.

On the basis of the experimental creep curves the curves of compacting pressure variations have been plotted at definite constant values of the relative swelling of soil (fig.4). The curves of pressure variations have made it possible to construct, according to (4), the curves of the resolvent of the kernel of creep at various values of water content. The similar curves have been plotted, proceeding from the accepted deformation law. The comparison of the curves at issue has proved, that the law, accepted for the variations of the compacting pressures (3), gives satisfactory results. As a result it has been established, that the mechanism of variation of the resolvent of the accepted kernel of creep, agree within the experimental data for all the examined values of water content of the swelling soil under study. The experimental data give the opportunity to determine the fact, that the accepted type of the kernel of creep is in confirmity with it's resolvent. Since the rheology of swelling soils can be quite satisfactory interpreted in terms of the linear theory of hereditary creep, there is no need in determining the resolvent experimentally.

CONCLUSION

It has been determined on the basis of the experiments, that the deformation of clayey swelling is a rheological process; the mechanism of the said process can be interpreted with sufficient, from the point of view of practical application, accuracy in terms of the li- hereditary creep of Boltzmann-Vollterr.

The kernel Abel type of the integral equation of the theory at issue approximates the deformation of clayey soils under swelling within the wide range of the compacting pressure variations.

The families of the curves of the kernel of creep and their resolvent make it possible to determine the mechanism of variations of the stressed-strained state of clayey soils, when swelling.

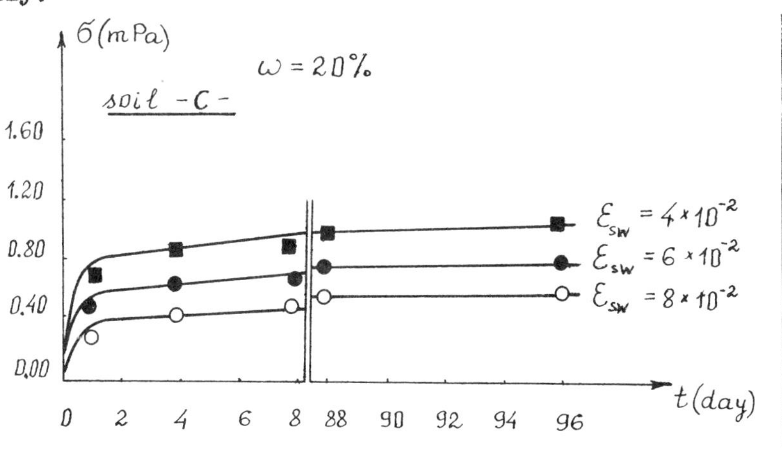

Fig.4. The Curves of the Compacting Pressure Variations at Constant Relative Swelling of Soil Mass.

REFERENCES

Mustafayev A.A., Chigniyev G., Nazirova G.D. (1974) About the rheological nature of swelling deformations in clayey soils and the settlement in loess soil. Bases, foundations and soil mechanics., (3);

Mustafayev A.A.,Chigniyev G. (1977), The relationship of rheological deformation of swelling in clayey soils and the methods of forecasting it for the foundation of structures. Proc. 1st Nat. Sym. on Exp.Soils, Kanpour.

Mustafayev A.A., (1980), Rheology of swelling soils and deformation forecast in the foundation of structures. Int.Con.Swel., Denver.

Mustafayev A. A., El-Hansy Ruoby M.M. (1984), The theory of heredity of the clayey soils deformation of swelling.Proc.6th Conf. on Soil Mech. and Found. Engg, Budapest.

Vyalov S.S. (1978), The rheological principles of soil mechanics. Visshaya Shcola Moscow.

AN ELASTOPLASTIC–VISCOPLASTIC BOUNDING SURFACE MODEL FOR ISOTROPIC COHESIVE SOILS

VICTOR N. KALIAKIN
Solid Mechanics Division
Sandia National Laboratory
Livermore, California 94550, USA

ABSTRACT

A generalized three-dimensional constitutive model for isotropic cohesive soils, based on the concept of the bounding surface in stress space, is developed within the framework of coupled elastoplasticity-viscoplasticity and critical state soil mechanics. The prominent feature of the bounding surface concept is the fact that inelastic deformations can occur for stress points located within the bounding surface. The consideration of viscoplastic characteristics sets the current model apart from previous bounding surface formulations for soils and introduces rate and time effects. The coupling between plasticity and viscoplasticity for stress states within the bounding surface differentiates the present work from the classical formulation of pure viscoplasticity (no coupling), or from formulations involving plasticity and viscoplasticity with a yield surface (coupling only for states on the yield surface). Incremental constitutive relations applicable to isotropic cohesive soils are developed. A minimum number of parameters are introduced and the predictive capabilities of the model are evaluated.

INTRODUCTION

The purpose of this paper is to present a generalized three–dimensional constitutive model based on the concept of the bounding surface in stress space, and developed within the framework of coupled elastoplasticity-viscoplasticity and critical state soil mechanics. The notion of such a soil model was introduced by Dafalias [1]. It differs from classical yield surface elastoplasticity–viscoplasticity formulations in that the stress is assumed to be continuously at an inelastic state, with the possibility of plastic-viscoplastic coupling, either within or on the bounding surface. Furthermore, unlike some other time dependent formulations [2–5], this model is not restricted to normally consolidated cohesive soils. The model thus represents a novel approach to simulating the time related behavior of soils.

The prominent feature of the bounding surface concept is the prediction of inelastic deformations for stress points within or on a bounding surface in stress space at a pace depending on the proximity of the actual stress point to a properly defined "image" point on the surface itself. The image point is specified by an appropriate mapping rule which becomes the identity mapping if the stress state lies on the surface. The normal to the surface at the image point defines the direction of loading–unloading. At the image point a "bounding" plastic modulus is defined by means of the consistency condition for the bounding surface. The actual plastic modulus is a function of this bounding modulus and of the distance in stress space between the actual stress point and its "image" on the bounding surface. Thus, unlike classical yield surface viscoplasticity, inelastic states are not restricted only to those lying on a surface. A more detailed description of the bounding surface concept is given in [6]; application of the concept to a rate independent formulation for isotropic cohesive soils is discussed in [7]. A microscopic basis for the current elastoplastic–viscoplastic formulation is presented in [1,8].

FORMULATION FOR ISOTROPIC COHESIVE SOILS

In the subsequent development tensors are presented in indicial form following the summation convention over repeated indices. Compressive stresses and strains are positive, and only small deformations are considered. The material is defined in terms of the effective stress tensor σ_{ij} and a single internal variable which accounts for the nonconservative nature of soil by keeping track of the past loading history.

The dependence of the bounding surface on σ_{ij} is expressed in terms of the following three stress invariants:

$$I = \sigma_{kk}\,, \quad J = \sqrt{\frac{1}{2}\, s_{ij}\, s_{ij}}\,, \quad \alpha = \frac{1}{3}\sin^{-1}\left[\frac{1}{2}\sqrt{3}\left(\frac{s_{ij}\, s_{jk}\, s_{ki}}{J^3}\right)\right] \tag{1}$$

where s_{ij} and α $(-\pi/6 \le \alpha \le \pi/6)$ represent the deviatoric part of σ_{ij} and the "Lode" angle [9], respectively. A meridional section of the surface (i.e., for a given value of α) is shown in Fig. 1. The actual stress point (I, J) is related to its "image" value $(\bar{I}, \bar{J})$ on the bounding surface itself through a "radial mapping" rule [1,10] which is analytically expressed by

$$\bar{I} = b\left(I - C I_o\right) + C I_o\,, \qquad \bar{s}_{ij} = b\, s_{ij} \quad \Rightarrow \quad \bar{J} = b J\,, \quad \bar{\alpha} = \alpha \tag{2}$$

where C represents a model parameter $(0 \le C < 1)$ and I_o represents the intersection of the bounding surface with the positive I-axis. Using CI_o as the projection center (Fig. 1), the

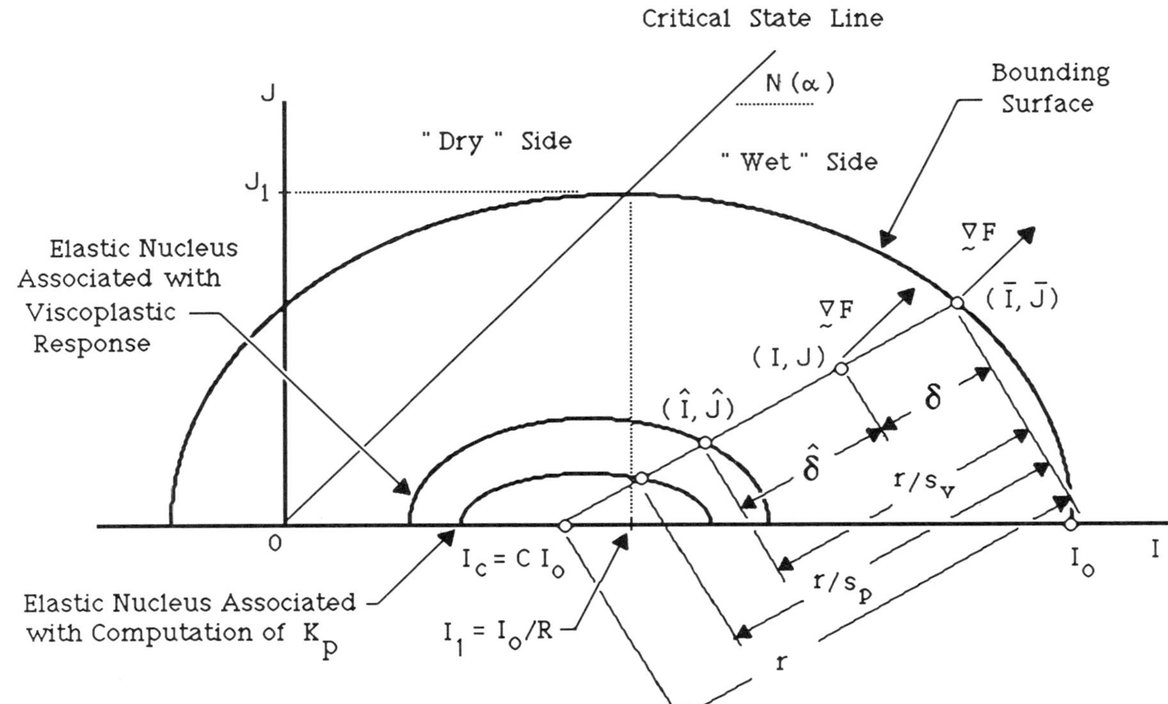

Figure 1. Schematic Illustration of the Radial Mapping Rule and of the Bounding Surface in Stress Invariants Space

image stress is obtained by the radial projection of the actual stress onto the bounding surface (hence the name "radial mapping").

The bounding surface is assumed to undergo isotropic hardening. The hardening is controlled by a single scalar internal variable which measures the inelastic change in volumetric strain. This variable is defined as the inelastic rate of the total void ratio e, given by

$$\dot{e}^i = -(1 + e_{in})\, \dot{\varepsilon}^i_{kk} = -(1 + e_{in}) \left(\dot{\varepsilon}^v_{kk} + \dot{\varepsilon}^p_{kk}\right) \tag{3}$$

where e_{in} represents the initial void ratio corresponding to the reference configuration with respect to which engineering strains are measured. For natural strains, e must be substituted for e_{in} in Eq. (3) as well as in all subsequent expressions. Based on the above discussion, the bounding surface is analytically defined by

$$F\left(\bar{I}, \bar{J}, \bar{\alpha}, e^i\right) = 0 \tag{4}$$

From Eqs. (1) and (4), it follows that

$$\frac{\partial F}{\partial \bar{\sigma}_{ij}} = F_{,\bar{I}}\, \delta_{ij} + \frac{1}{2J} F_{,\bar{J}}\, s_{ij} + \frac{\sqrt{3}\, F_{,\alpha}}{2bJ \cos 3\alpha} \left[\frac{1}{J^2} \left(s_{ik} s_{kj} - \frac{1}{2} \frac{(s_{ij} s_{jk} s_{ki})\, s_{ij}}{J^2} \right) - \frac{2}{3} \delta_{ij} \right] \tag{5}$$

where a comma indicates partial differentiation with respect to the index which follows.

The strain rate is additively decomposed into an elastic and inelastic part, the latter consisting of a delayed (viscoplastic) and an instantaneous (plastic) part. Denoting the infinitesimal strain tensor by ε_{ij}, it follows that:

$$\dot{\varepsilon}_{ij} = \dot{\varepsilon}^e_{ij} + \dot{\varepsilon}^i_{ij} = \dot{\varepsilon}^e_{ij} + \dot{\varepsilon}^v_{ij} + \dot{\varepsilon}^p_{ij} \tag{6}$$

where the superscripts e, i, v, and p denote the elastic, inelastic, viscoplastic and plastic components, respectively, of ε_{ij}. A superposed dot indicates a material time derivative or rate.

The response associated with the elastic strain rate is given by

$$\dot{\varepsilon}^e_{ij} = \left[\frac{2G - 3K}{18\, KG} \delta_{ij} \delta_{kl} + \frac{1}{4G} (\delta_{ik} \delta_{jl} + \delta_{il} \delta_{jk}) \right] \dot{\sigma}_{kl} \tag{7a}$$

$$\dot{\sigma}_{ij} = \left[(K - \frac{2}{3} G)\, \delta_{ij} \delta_{kl} + G\, (\delta_{ik} \delta_{jl} + \delta_{il} \delta_{jk}) \right] \dot{\varepsilon}^e_{kl} \tag{7b}$$

where K and G represent the elastic bulk and shear moduli respectively.

The rate equation for $\dot{\varepsilon}_{ij}^{v}$ is based upon a generalization of the viscoplastic theory of Perzyna [11]. According to this theory, the viscoplastic strain rate is a function of the "distance" in stress space of the current stress from the stress on the boundary of a quasi-static elastic domain. In the present development, an "elastic nucleus" – a region of purely elastic response around the projection center CI_o (Fig. 1) – constitutes this elastic domain. The "distance" of the actual stress point from the elastic nucleus is represented by the "normalized overstress" $\Delta\widehat{\sigma}$:

$$\Delta\widehat{\sigma} = \frac{\widehat{\delta}}{r - \frac{r}{s_v}} = \frac{s_v}{b\,(s_v - 1)} - 1 \tag{8}$$

where s_v (> 1) denotes a model parameter which defines the size of the elastic nucleus, and $\widehat{\delta}$ and r represent Euclidean distances (Fig. 1). The exact role of $\Delta\widehat{\sigma}$ in the rate equations is reflected in a proper continuous scalar function ϕ of the overstress in such a way that $\phi > 0$ when $\Delta\widehat{\sigma} > 0$ and $\phi \le 0$ when $\Delta\widehat{\sigma} \le 0$. On the basis of the above discussion and assuming an associated flow rule, it follows that

$$\dot{\varepsilon}_{ij}^{v} = \langle \phi \rangle \frac{\partial F}{\partial \bar{\sigma}_{ij}} \tag{9}$$

where $\partial F/\partial \sigma_{ij}$ is explicitly given by Eq. (5), and the symbols $\langle\ \rangle$ denote the Macaulay brackets. A functional form for ϕ is given in a subsequent section.

The plastic response is given by

$$\dot{\varepsilon}_{ij}^{p} = \langle L \rangle \frac{\partial F}{\partial \bar{\sigma}_{ij}} \tag{10}$$

where L represents a scalar loading index; loading, neutral loading, and unloading occur when $L > 0$, $L = 0$, and $L < 0$, respectively. Within the framework of the radial mapping model, L is defined by [12]:

$$\begin{aligned} L &= \frac{1}{K_p}\left\{ F_{,\bar{I}}\,\dot{I} + F_{,\bar{J}}\,\dot{J} + \frac{1}{b} F_{,\alpha}\,\dot{\alpha} - \langle\phi\rangle\,\overline{K}_p \left[\frac{1}{b} - C\left(1 - \frac{1}{b}\right)\frac{F_{,\bar{I}}}{F_{,I_o}}\right]\right\} \\ &= \frac{1}{\overline{K}_p}\left\{ F_{,\bar{I}}\,\dot{\bar{I}} + F_{,\bar{J}}\,\dot{\bar{J}} + F_{,\alpha}\,\dot{\alpha} \right\} - \langle\phi\rangle \end{aligned} \tag{11}$$

Since it accounts for the coupling of plastic-viscoplastic hardening for states on and within the bounding surface, Eq. (11) represents a key step in the development of the present model [1]. The quantities K_p and $\overline{K}_p$ represent the scalar plastic moduli associated with the actual and "image" (i.e., for b = 1) stress states respectively, and allow prediction of loading not only in conjunction with stable (hardening) response, but also for unstable (softening) response as well [6]. Assuming L > 0, and using Eqs. (3), (4) and (9) – (11) along with the consistency condition $\dot{F} = 0$, it follows that

$$\overline{K}_p = 3\left(1 + e_{in}\right) F_{,e^i} F_{,\bar{I}} \tag{12}$$

The feature which distinguishes this bounding surface formulation from classical elastoviscoplasticity formulations is that K_p is obtained not from a consistency condition, but from the following relation which depends upon $\overline{K}_p$ and upon the distances δ and r (Fig. 1):

$$K_p = \overline{K}_p + H \frac{\delta}{\langle r - s_p \delta \rangle} = \overline{K}_p + H \left\langle \frac{b}{b-1} - s_p \right\rangle^{-1} \tag{13}$$

The model parameter s_p represents a second elastic nucleus parameter (Fig. 1), and H represents a hardening function which defines the shape of stress-strain curves for points within the bounding surface. Further details regarding H are given in a subsequent section.

After suitable manipulation, the constitutive relations in inverse form are given by

$$\dot{\sigma}_{ij} = D_{ijkl} \dot{\varepsilon}_{kl} - V_{ij} \tag{14}$$

Explicit expressions for the fourth rank incremental stiffness tensor D_{ijkl} and for the second rank tensor of viscoplastic contribution V_{ij} are given in [13].

A SPECIFIC FORM OF THE BOUNDING SURFACE

The bounding surface is explicitly defined by

$$F = \left(\bar{I} - I_o\right)\left(\bar{I} + \frac{R-2}{R} I_o\right) + \left(R-1\right)^2 \left(\frac{\bar{J}}{N}\right)^2 = 0 \tag{15}$$

where R represents a constant model parameter which completely defines the shape of this elliptical surface (Fig. 1). The slope of the critical state line (CSL) in stress invariants space is defined by N, whose variation is given by [14]:

$$N(\alpha) = \frac{2k}{1 + k - (1-k)\sin 3\alpha} N_c \tag{16}$$

where N_e=N(−π/6) and N_c=N(π/6) represent the values of N associated with triaxial compression and extension, respectively, and $k=N_e/N_c$. The CSL intersects the bounding surface at the point $(I_1, J_1) = (I_o/R, J_1)$ where, as required, $F_{,\bar{I}} = 0$.

The dependence of F = 0 on e^i is introduced through I_o. An expression for dI_o/de^i is thus sought. Denoting by λ and κ the slopes of the consolidation and swell/recompression lines in e-ln I space, respectively, [15], it follows that

$$\frac{dI}{de^e} = -\frac{\langle I - I_L \rangle + I_L}{\kappa}, \qquad \frac{dI_o}{de} = -\frac{\langle I_o - I_L \rangle + I_L}{\lambda}, \qquad \frac{dI_o}{de^i} = -\frac{\langle I_o - I_L \rangle + I_L}{\lambda - \kappa} \tag{17}$$

where the first equation also applies for $I = I_o$, and I_L represents the value of I and/or I_o below which the relation between I (or I_o) and e changes smoothly from logarithmic to linear. I_L, which is typically set equal to the atmospheric pressure, is not related to the bounding surface concept but was introduced into the formulation to prevent excessive softening from occurring for small values of I (or I_o). Noting that $\dot{e}^e = -(1 + e_{in})\,\dot{\varepsilon}_{kk}{}^e$, and using the first of Eqs. (17) in conjunction with the relationship $\dot{I} = \dot{\sigma}_{kk} = 3K\,\dot{\varepsilon}_{kk}{}^e$ (Eq. 7b), yields the following expression for the elastic bulk modulus K:

$$K = \frac{(1 + e_{in})\left(\langle I - I_L \rangle + I_L\right)}{3\,\kappa} \tag{18}$$

It is evident that were it not for the presence of I_L, K would equal zero for I = 0.

THE HARDENING FUNCTION

The hardening function H (Eq. 13), which defines the shape of the response curves during inelastic hardening (or softening) for points within the bounding surface, is given by:

$$H = \frac{(1 + e_{in})}{\lambda - \kappa}\frac{p_a}{2}\left[h(\alpha)\,z^{0.02} + h_o\left(1 - z^{0.02}\right)\right]\left\{a + \mathrm{sgn}(n_p)\,[n_p]^{1/w}\right\} \tag{19}$$

where e_{in}, λ and κ are as previously defined, and p_a represents the atmospheric pressure which is used to non-dimensionalize H. The variable z is defined by $z=J/J_1=JR/NI_o$ (Fig. 1) and is a "weighting factor" with respect to h(α) and h_o. The quantity h_o, which represents a hardening parameter associated with states in the vicinity of the I-axis (i.e., for z ≈ 0), was included in the formulation to assure continuity when the stress point crosses this axis. The variation of h with α is given by an equation similar to Eq. (16) with h(α), h_c and h_e

substituted for $N(\alpha)$, N_c and N_e, respectively. Typically $h_o = (h_c + h_e)/2$ and does not enter into the parameter calibration process. The quantity n_p represents the component in the p-direction of the equivalent unit outward normal in triaxial stress space, where $p = (\sigma_1 + 2\,\sigma_3)/3 = I/3$ and $q = \sigma_1 - \sigma_3 = \pm\sqrt{3}\,J$. The word "equivalent" is used because even if the stress state is not triaxial, an equivalent state can be defined in terms of the above relations involving p, q, I and J. Letting $\eta = q/p$, n_p ranges in value from +1 (for $\eta = 0$ and $p > 0$) to -1 (for $\eta = 0$ and $p < 0$). When the "image" stress contacts the CSL, $n_p = 0$. The quantities "a" and "w" represent model parameters which, in conjunction with n_p, control the variation of H as a function of η [8,16].

RESPONSE UNDER UNDRAINED CONDITIONS

Under ideal undrained conditions the assumption of a saturated soil mass along with incompressible fluid and solid phases yields $\dot{\varepsilon}_{kk} = 0$. Substituting Eqs. (5), (7a), (9) and (10) into Eq. (6), and imposing the condition $\dot{\varepsilon}_{kk} = 0$ yields an expression for the change in I:

$$\dot{I} = -9\,K\left(\langle\,\phi\,\rangle + \langle\,L\,\rangle\right)\,F_{,\bar{I}} \tag{20}$$

Eq. (20) illustrates the fact that under undrained conditions the change in I is no longer independent. Substituting Eq. (20) into Eq. (11) and assuming $L > 0$ yields

$$\begin{aligned} L &= \frac{F_{,\bar{J}}\,\dot{J} + \frac{1}{b}F_{,\alpha}\,\dot{\alpha} - \langle\,\phi\,\rangle\left\{9\,K\left(F_{,\bar{I}}\right)^2 + \overline{K}_p\left[\frac{1}{b} - C\left(1 - \frac{1}{b}\right)\frac{F_{,\bar{I}}}{F_{,I_o}}\right]\right\}}{K_p + 9\,K\left(F_{,\bar{I}}\right)^2} \\ &= \frac{F_{,\bar{J}}\,\dot{\bar{J}} + F_{,\alpha}\,\dot{\alpha}}{\overline{K}_p + 9\,K\left(F_{,\bar{I}}\right)^2} - \langle\,\phi\,\rangle \end{aligned} \tag{21}$$

The constraint on $\dot{I}$ given by Eq. (20) thus results in L being controlled by $\dot{J}$ and $\dot{\alpha}$ only.

In a typical undrained triaxial creep test, $J \geq 0$ but $\dot{s}_{ij} = 0$, implying $\dot{J} = 0$. With $C \geq 0$, $b \geq 1$, $F_{,I_o} < 0$, and observing that for such states $\dot{\alpha} = 0$ and $F_{,\bar{I}} > 0$, it follows from Eq. (21) that $L < 0$. As a result Eq. (5), in conjunction with Eqs. (6), (7a), (9), (10) and (20), leads to

$$\dot{I} = -9\,\langle\,\phi\,\rangle\,K\,F_{,\bar{I}}\ , \qquad \dot{e}_{ij} = \langle\,\phi\,\rangle\,\frac{1}{2J}\,s_{ij}\,F_{,\bar{J}} \tag{22}$$

where e_{ij} represents the deviatoric part of the strain tensor. An explicit expression for ϕ is given in the following section. Eqs. (22) describe the well-known phenomena of the increase of e_{ij} and decrease in I (with a corresponding pore pressure increase) under undrained creep. This decrease in I is shown schematically in Fig. 2 by a sequence of arrows emanating from the point of initiation of creep; the dashed lines depict the corresponding expansion of the bounding surface and of the elastic nucleus.

IDENTIFICATION AND DETERMINATION OF PARAMETERS

Associated with the most general form of the model are sixteen parameters, the values of which fall within fairly narrow ranges and are determined using a well-defined calibration procedure [12,16]. With a single set of parameter values the model predicts the behavior of soils at any overconsolidation ratio (OCR), subjected to either monotonic or cyclic compression and/or extension loading under either drained or undrained conditions.

Elastoplastic Model Parameters

The values of the twelve parameters in this category are determined by matching the results of standard laboratory experiments of duration short enough to ensure negligible viscoplastic effects. The traditional material constants include the elastic shear modulus G (or, alternatively, Poisson's ratio ν) and the critical state parameters λ, κ and M (the values of M associated with triaxial compression and extension are denoted by M_c and M_e, respectively; M is related to N through $M = 3\sqrt{3}\,N$). The elastic bulk modulus K is defined in terms of κ and I by means of Eq. (18), and G is either determined explicitly or is computed from κ and a constant ν (in the latter case, G is an increasing function of I and consequently invalidates the existence of an elastic potential). The surface configuration parameters consist of the shape parameter R (Eq. 15), the elastic zone parameter s_p (Eq. 13), and the projection center parameter C (Eq. 2). In the current formulation different elastic nuclei are assumed for purposes of computing $\Delta\hat{\sigma}$ (Eq. 8) and K_p (Eq. 13). Since both nuclei have the projection center as their center of homology (Fig. 1), it follows that the selection of C influences the magnitude of both quantities. The hardening parameters h_c, h_e, a and w enter the expression for K_p (Eq. 13) through the function H (Eq. 19). They control the degree of plastic hardening (or softening) that occurs at stress states within the bounding surface but have no effect on undrained triaxial creep response. With the possible exception of C, the elastoplastic parameters are inactive during the determination of the viscoplastic parameters.

Viscoplastic Model Parameters

The viscoplastic contribution enters the constitutive relations through the continuous scalar overstress function ϕ (Eq. 9), defined by:

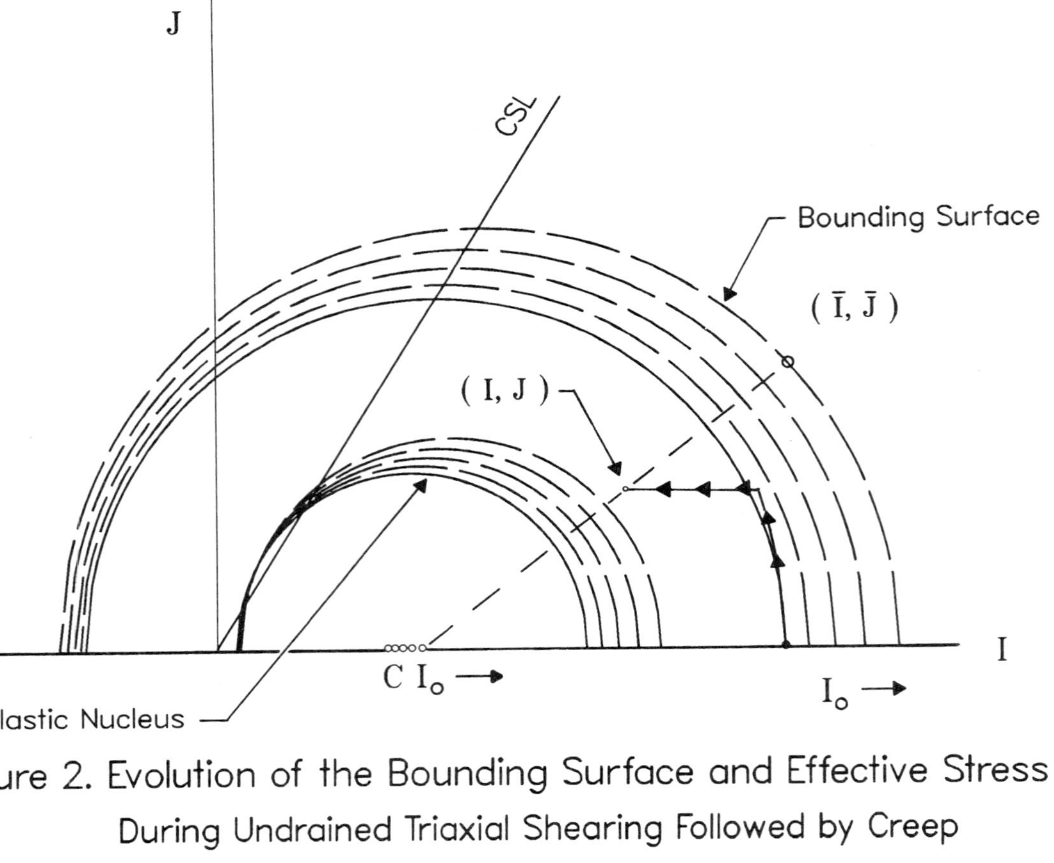

Figure 2. Evolution of the Bounding Surface and Effective Stress During Undrained Triaxial Shearing Followed by Creep

$$\phi = \frac{1}{\widehat{V}} \left\langle \Delta\widehat{\sigma} \right\rangle^{n} \tag{23}$$

where

$$\widehat{V} = V \frac{\exp\left(-J/NI\right)}{1 + \left\langle \left[\frac{2}{3} e_{ij}^{i} e_{ij}^{i}\right]^{0.5} - \varepsilon_m \right\rangle} \tag{24}$$

and I, J and N are as previously defined, e_{ij}^{i} represents the inelastic deviatoric strain tensor, and $[2\, e_{ij}^{i}\, e_{ij}^{i}/3]^{0.5}$ represents the accumulated inelastic deviatoric strain. The viscoplastic model parameters, which are determined by matching the results of at least one long term laboratory experiment, include the viscoplastic zone parameter s_v ($1 < s_v < \infty$) which defines $\Delta\widehat{\sigma}$ (Eq. 8), and the parameters n, V and ε_m. Note that it is the reciprocal of $\widehat{V}$ which appears in the expression for ϕ, and thus in the equation for $\dot{\varepsilon}_{ij}^{v}$ (Eq. 9).

The parameter ε_m represents the axial strain corresponding to the minimum axial strain rate and gives $\widehat{V}$ the capability to account for the tertiary creep phase (which terminates with rupture of the material). More precisely, if creep rupture is to be predicted analytically, a suitable value for ε_m must be chosen to cause a rapid decrease in $\widehat{V}$ and thus a rapid increase in predicted strain at a particular time. If, on the other hand, no evidence of creep rupture is observed experimentally, ε_m should be set equal to an artificially large value such that the Macaulay brackets in the denominator of Eq. (24) always yield zero and $\widehat{V}$ does not experience a drastic reduction in magnitude. It is important to point out that the value chosen for ε_m is determined independent of the other viscoplastic parameters.

Suitable values for s_v (and possibly for C) are determined by matching predicted values of the maximum change in I (and thus in the pore pressure) with those observed experimentally. This determination is performed independent of the values of the remaining viscoplastic parameters [12]. Increases in s_v enlarge the elastic nucleus (Fig. 1), reduce the value of $\Delta\widehat{\sigma}$ and thus slow the viscoplastic evolution of the bounding surface (and the pore pressure build–up and the axial strain development under undrained creep conditions). An increase in C results in the movement of the projection center to larger positive values of I (Fig. 1). This has nearly the same effect on the predictions as does an increase in s_v. However, both parameters are typically necessary in order to accurately predict time dependent response of the material.

Finally, values for the parameters V and n are determined by matching the predicted pore pressure– and axial strain time histories (obtained by integrating Eqs. 22 [12]) with those observed experimentally. For relatively small values of V the response is nearly inviscid throughout the loading history; i.e., the viscous response occurs very rapidly. If, on the other hand, V is large, the viscoplastic strain is greatly reduced, resulting in little change in the overall response with time. Increases in n have a similar effect on the response as do increases in V, though variations in the latter have a greater influence on the initial slope of the response curves.

VERIFICATION OF THE MODEL

To verify the adequacy of the model, the constitutive equations, along with such enhancements as local iteration, sub-stepping and radial return [17], were incorporated into a modular system of FORTRAN 77 subroutines [18]. The modular design facilitates simple and inexpensive incorporation of the subroutines into new and existing programs for the analysis of earth structures [19,20].

Simulation of Undrained Triaxial Response

Extensive undrained triaxial tests were performed by Shen et al. [21] on undisturbed specimens of a fine–grained, organic silty clay known as San Francisco Bay Mud. The testing program consisted of: (i) A total of nine undrained triaxial strength tests, performed on normally consolidated specimens. The isotropic consolidation pressure (σ_c = 2.0, 3.0, and 4.0 kg/sq cm) and the period of consolidation (T_c = 1, 3, and 7 days) were varied in these tests. Typical experimental results are depicted by discrete symbols in Fig. 3; and, (ii) A group of nine creep tests, performed using the same values of σ_c and T_c as used in the strength tests. However, in the creep tests a strength test was not performed following consolidation. Instead, the drainage was closed and the ensuing increase in pore pressure was measured continuously for eight days. During this period the isotropic consolidation pressure was retained on the specimen and no axial strain was detected. Typical experimental results are depicted by discrete symbols in Figs. 4 and 5. In all the creep tests, following an initial period of increase, the rate of pore pressure build–up decreased with time. For any given T_c the amount of pore pressure build–up increased with σ_c. Also, for any given σ_c, the pore pressure build–up decreased with an increasing T_c ; i.e., with the "age" of the specimen. This is explained by the fact that "older" specimens exhibit greater secondary consolidation and thus greater rearrangement of particles. The resulting reduction in rearrangement potential gives older specimens a lower potential for subsequent pore pressure build–up. Fig. 5 shows that if, for a given period of consolidation the pore pressure is normalized by σ_c, the resulting experimental points fall in fairly narrow bands.

For purposes of calibrating the model parameters, e_{in} and the traditional material constants (λ = 0.37, κ = 0.10, M_c = 1.49, and G = 60 kg/sq cm) were taken directly from [21]. The shape parameter R (= 2.90) was determined by matching the experimental undrained stress paths for the strength test associated with T_c = 1 day (the loading rate employed in the numerical simulations was identical to that used in [21]). The resulting simulations are shown in Fig. 3 in the form of continuous curves. Since the experimental results showed no

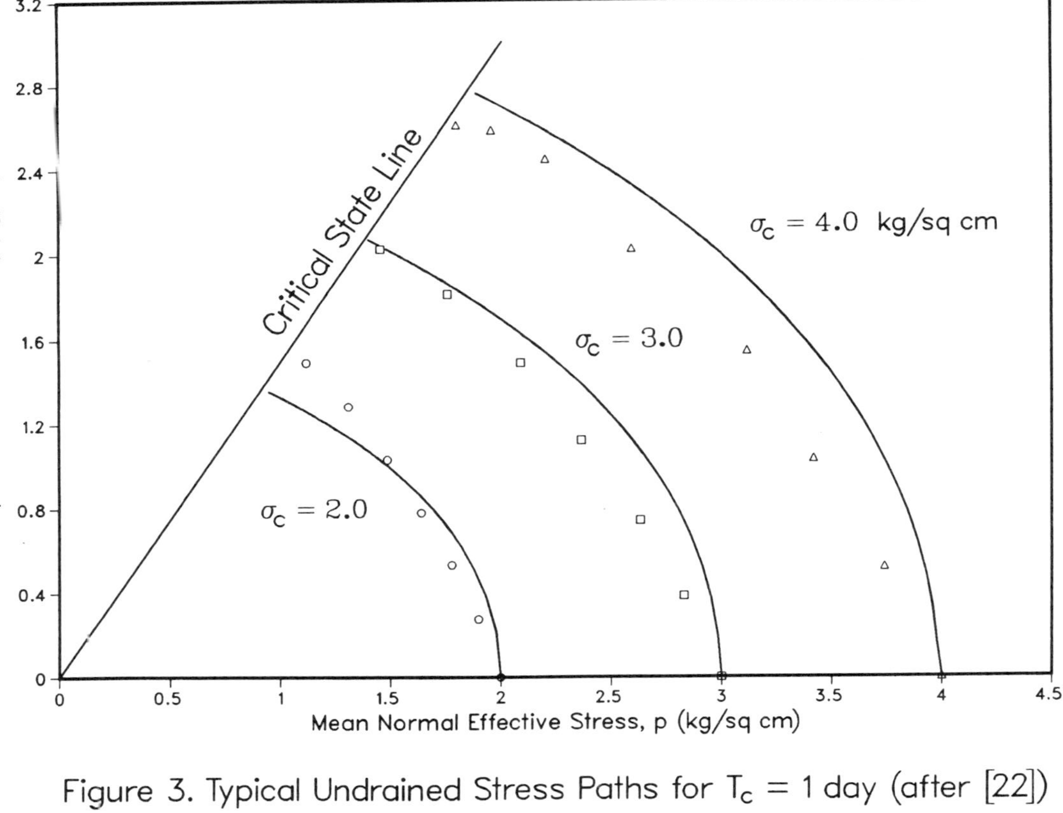

Figure 3. Typical Undrained Stress Paths for $T_c = 1$ day (after [22])

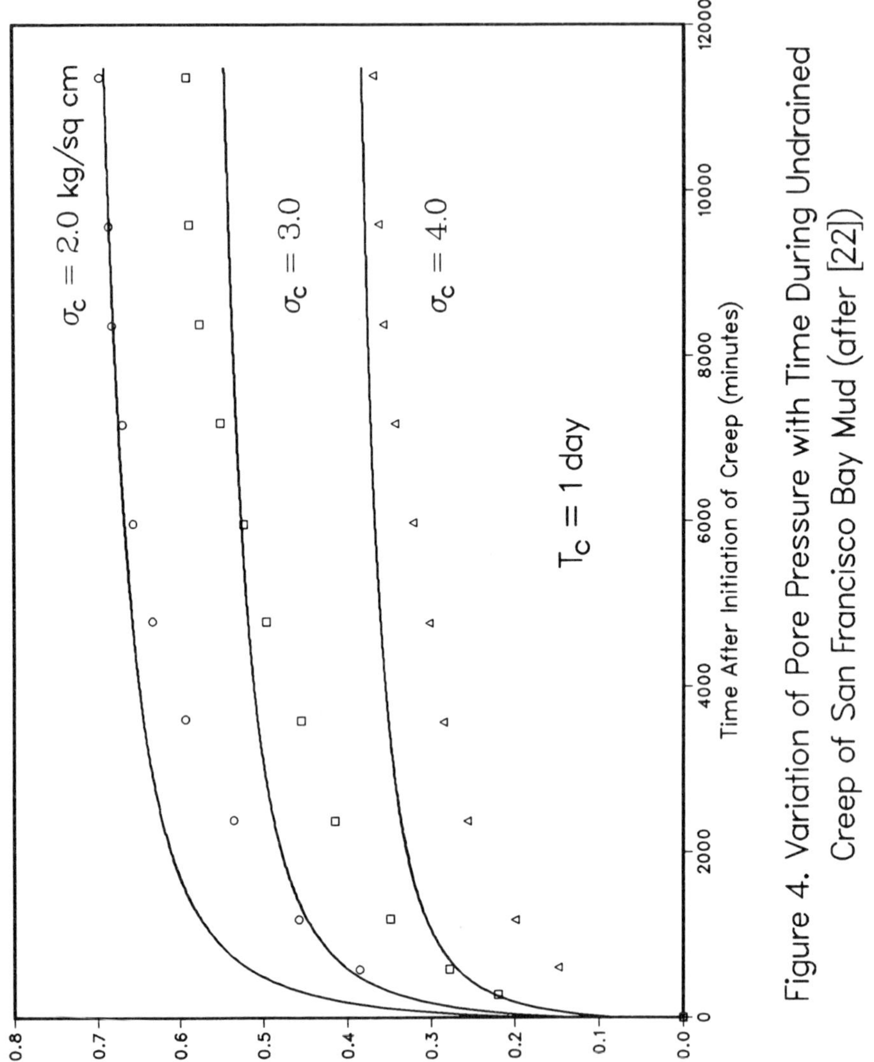

Figure 4. Variation of Pore Pressure with Time During Undrained Creep of San Francisco Bay Mud (after [22])

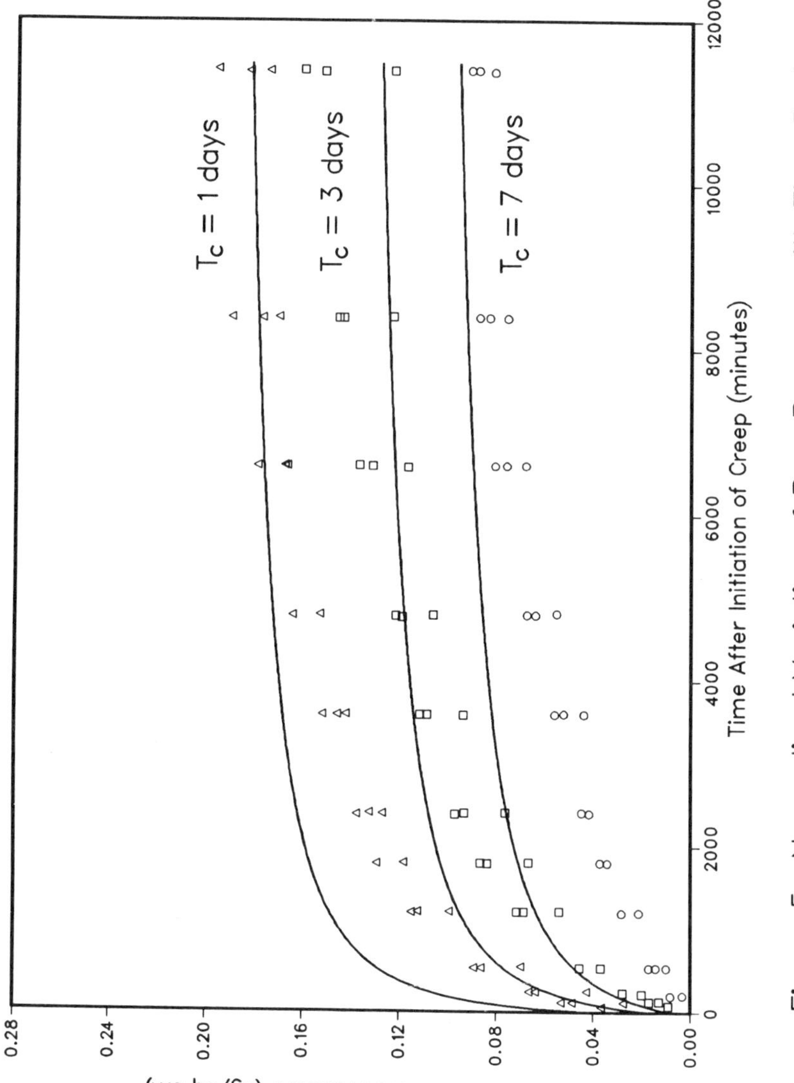

Figure 5. Normalized Variation of Pore Pressure with Time During Undrained Creep of San Francisco Bay Mud (after [22])

significant increase in strain leading to creep rupture, the parameter ε_m was set to an arbitrarily large value of 35%. Values for the parameters C (= 0.20) and s_v (= 2.40) were determined by matching the changes in p measured during undrained creep. The final two viscoplastic parameters (V=9x10^4 kg–min/sq cm and n = 3.2) were determined by matching numerical predictions (generated by numerically integrating the first of Eqs. 22) with experimental pore pressure time histories. The simulations of undrained triaxial behavior obtained using these parameter values are shown in Figs. 3–5 in the form of continuous curves. With the exception of the initial stages of pore pressure increase, the overall agreement between model simulations and experimental results is quite acceptable, and shows the model to be capable of simulating the effects of sample age (under drained conditions) and undrained creep response.

ACKNOWLEDGEMENT

The research reported herein was conducted, in part, under National Science Foundation Grant CEE–82169995.

REFERENCES

1. Dafalias, Y. F., Bounding Surface Elastoplasticity - Viscoplasticity for Particulate Cohesive Media, Deformation and Failure of Granular Materials, eds., P. A. Vermeer and H. J. Luger, A. A. Balkema, pub., Rotterdam, 1982, pp. 97-107, from the I.U.T.A.M. Symposium on Deformation and Failure of Granular Materials, Delft, the Netherlands.

2. Adachi, T. and Oka, F., Constitutive Equations for Normally Consolidated Clay Based on Elasto-Viscoplasticity, Soils and Foundations, J. Japanese Soc. Soil Mech. and Found. Engrg., 1982, **22**, No. 4, 57-70.

3. Nova, R., A Viscoplastic Constitutive Model for Normally Consolidated Clay, Deformation and Failure of Granular Materials, eds., P. A. Vermeer, and H. J. Luger, A. A. Balkema, pub., Rotterdam, 1982, pp. 287-295, from the IUTAM Symposium, Delft.

4. Oka, F., Elasto/Viscoplastic Constitutive Equations with Memory and Internal Variables, Computers and Geotechnics, 1985, **1**, 59-69.

5. Sekiguchi, H., Theory of Undrained Creep Rupture of Normally Consolidated Clay Based on Elasto-Viscoplasticity, Soils and Foundations, Jap. Soc. Soil Mech. and Found. Engrg., 1984, **24**, No. 1, 129-147.

6. Dafalias, Y. F., Bounding Surface Plasticity. I Mathematical Foundation and the Concept of Hypoplasticity, J. Eng. Mech., ASCE, 1986, **112**, No. 9, 966-987.

7. Dafalias, Y. F. and Herrmann, L. R., "Bounding Surface Plasticity II: Application to Isotropic Cohesive Soils," J. Eng. Mech., ASCE, 1986, **112**, No. 12, 1263-1291.

8. Kaliakin, V. N., Bounding Surface Elastoplasticity-Viscoplasticity for Clays, dissertation presented to the University of California, Davis, in partial fulfillment of the requirements for the degree of Doctor of Philosophy, December 1985.

9. Zienkiewicz, O. C. and Pande, G. N., Some Useful Forms of Isotropic Yield Surfaces for Soil and Rock Mechanics, Chapter 5 in Finite Elements in Geomechanics, ed., G. Gudehus, J. Wiley and Sons, 1977, pp. 179-190.

10. Hashiguchi, K. Constitutive Equations of Elastoplastic Materials with Elastic-Plastic Transition, J. App. Mech., ASME, 1980, **47**, 266-272.

11. Perzyna, P., Fundamental Problems in Viscoplasticity, Adv. in Ap. Mech., 1966, **9**, 243-377.

12. Kaliakin, V. N. and Dafalias, Y. F., Elastoplastic–Viscoplastic Bounding Surface Model for Cohesive Soils – I. Theory, J. Eng. Mech., ASCE, forthcoming publication.

13. Kaliakin, V. N. and Dafalias, Y. F., Elastoplastic–Viscoplastic Bounding Surface Model for Cohesive Soils – II. Applications, J. Eng. Mech., ASCE, forthcoming publication.

14. Gudehus, G., "Elastoplastische Stoffleichungen fur trockenen Sand," Ingenieur – Archiv, 1973, **42**.

15. Schofield, A. N. and Wroth, C. P., Critical State Soil Mechanics, McGraw–Hill, London, 1968.

16. Kaliakin, V. N. and Dafalias, Y. F., A Simplified Bounding Surface Model for Isotropic Cohesive Soils, Int. J. Num. Anal. Meth. in Geomech., forthcoming publication.

17. Herrmann, L. R., Kaliakin, V. N., Shen, C. K., Mish, K. D. and Zhu, Z-Y, Numerical Implementation of a Plasticity Model for Cohesive Soils, J. Eng. Mech., ASCE, 1987, **113**, No. 4, 500-519.

18. Kaliakin, V. N. and Herrmann, L. R., Guidelines for Implementing the Elastoplastic – Viscoplastic Bounding Surface Model for Isotropic Cohesive Soils, Dept. of Civil Engin. Report, University of California, Davis, 1987.

19. Kaliakin, V. N., and Herrmann, L. R., Numerical Implementation of the Elastoplastic–Viscoplastic Bounding Surface Model for Isotropic Cohesive Soils – The EVALVP Computer Program, Dept. of Civil Engin. Report, University of California, Davis, 1987.

20. Herrmann, L. R., and Kaliakin, V. N., User's Manual for SAC-2, A Two-Dimensional Nonlinear, Time Dependent, Soil Analysis Code Using the Bounding Surface Elastoplasticity–Viscoplasticity Model, Volumes I and II, Dept. of Civil Engin. Report, University of California, Davis, 1987.

21. Shen, C. K., Arulanandan, K., and Smith, W. S., Secondary Consolidation and Strength of a Clay, J. Soil Mec. Found. Div., ASCE., 1973, **99**, No. SM1, 95-110.

EFFECTS OF PARTIAL DRAINAGE ON THE LATERAL DEFORMATION OF CLAY FOUNDATIONS

HIDEO SEKIGUCHI, TORU SHIBATA AND MAMORU MIMURA
Disaster Prevention Research Institute,
Kyoto University, Uji, Kyoto, Japan

ABSTRACT

Coupled stress-flow analyses in terms of the method of finite elements are performed. A plane-strain elasto-viscoplastic constitutive model for clays is implemented into the analysis procedure. The calculated results are presented in chart form so that the effects of embanking speed or partial drainage on lateral soil movements are readily assessed. The performances of a wide variety of natural soils loaded by embankments are reviewed in detail. It is found that the nature of the soil deposits is well reflected in the pattern and magnitude of their lateral deformations.

INTRODUCTION

The problem of lateral deformation of soft foundations under embankments and coastal fills has had increasing attention. A unique feature of the problem lies in that it relates not only to the problem of contained plastic flow or ground failure, but also to the problem of multi-dimensional consolidation. This means that classical soil-mechanics approaches, in terms of the method of limit equilibrium or the oedometric method of consolidation are almost invalid for the problem of predicting lateral soil movements.

Another interesting feature of the problem stems from the geological background of alluvial deposits. That is to say, the layered nature of such soil deposits exerts a profound influence on the pattern and even magnitude of the lateral deformation that develops when the deposit is loaded by an embankment or a coastal fill.

The purpose of the present paper is to present a rational framework for assessing lateral deformations of embankment foundations. For this purpose, results from elasto-visco-plastic consolidation analyses in terms of the method of finite elements will be presented in chart form in the first part of the paper. Emphasis will be placed on quantifying the effects of embanking speed or partial drainage upon the lateral soil movements. The second part of the paper will focus the stratification of natural soil deposits and will substantiate the introductory remark made in the above paragraph.

Compressive stresses and compressive strains are taken as positive throughout the paper.

FRAMEWORK FOR ASSESSING LATERAL SOIL MOVEMENTS

Basic Parameters

Consider a long embankment constructed on the bed of soft clay (Fig. 1(a)). The base width of the fill and its height from the ground surface are denoted by B and h. The thickness of the soft foundation is denoted by H. Due to the weight of the fill, the foundation block immediately below the fill will deform in a manner such as shown in Fig. 1(a). Here, ρ_{CL} represents the surface settlement at the center of the embankment, V_ρ represents the volume lost in settlement and V_δ stands for the volume gained in lateral displacement. The lateral displacement, δ, will hereafter be taken as positive when it is directed away from the embankment. The net reduction in the volume of the foundation block may be expressed as $V_{net}=V_\rho - V_\delta$. This may also be expressed in the following dimensionless form:

$$V_{net}/V_o = (V_\rho/V_o) - (V_\delta/V_o) \qquad (1)$$

Here, V_o is the volume of the foundation block per running meter. Note that those volumetric parameters defined above will be used below to quantify the overall degree of partial drainage of soft foundations.

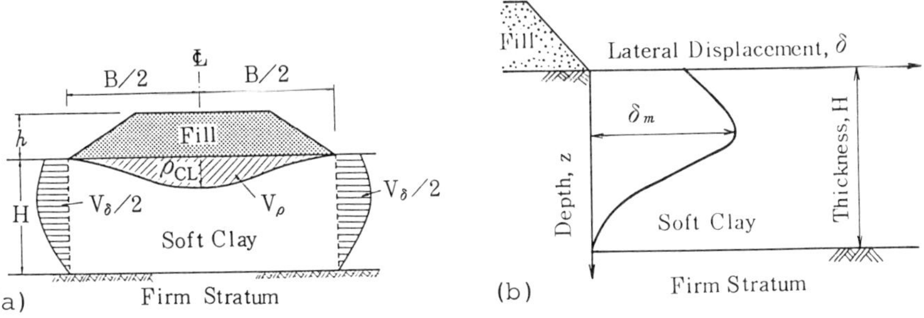

Figure 1. Cross-section of an embankment-foundation system together with principal symbols indicated.

It is also convenient for later discussions to define the maximum value in a given, vertical profile of lateral displacement at or very near the toe of the embankment (see Fig. 1(b)). In this paper such a (local) maximum of the lateral displacements is denoted by δ_m.

Distribution of Lateral Displacements

The distribution of lateral displacements within an embankment foundation at a given time is best illustrated in the form of contours of equal lateral displacement. Such an example is given in Fig. 2. The results are based on a coupled stress-flow analysis using the method of finite elements, in which a plane-strain version (1) of the elasto-viscoplastic constitutive model for clay (2, 3) is implemented. Only the right-hand side of the embankment-foundation system is shown in Fig. 2, in view of the symmetry of the system considered. Note that the largest lateral displacement occurs at point A, below the approximately midside of the slope. Consider next a vertical line through point B, running in close proximity to the toe of the embankment. In this particular profile, the lateral displacements take a local maximum, δ_m, at a point just exemplified by point B. It is noteworthy that such a particular maximum, δ_m, approximates numerically to the largest lateral displacement such as exhibited at point A.

In Fig. 2 it should also be noted that a local maximum of another kind is realized at point C. That is to say, the following relation holds at point C:

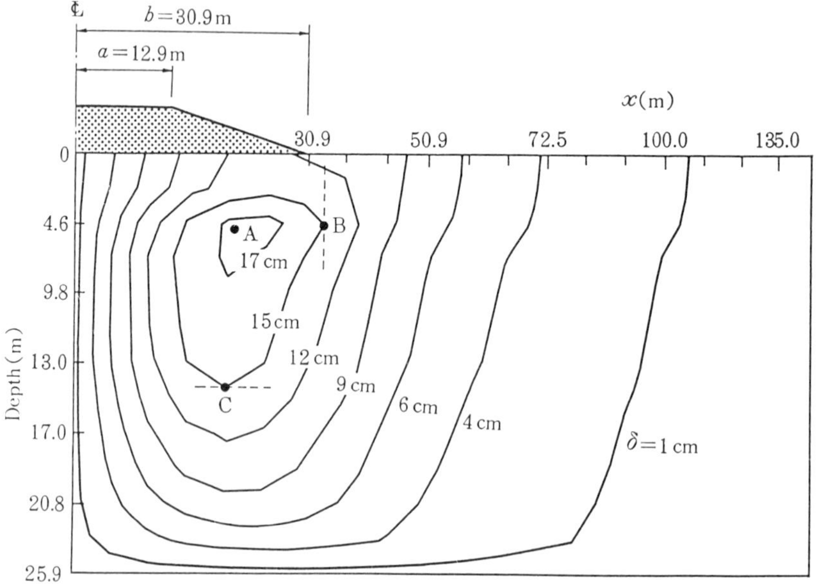

Figure 2. Calculated contours of equal lateral displacement.

$$\varepsilon_h = -\partial\delta/\partial x = 0 \qquad (2)$$

Here, ε_h is the horizontal strain and x denotes the horizontal co-ordinate. Thus the lines joining such points as A and C represent the loci of zero lateral strain, inside which the lateral strains are expansive and outside which the lateral strains are compressive. A series of related finite-element analyses suggest that a workable expression for the loci of zero lateral strain is as follows:

$$x = \pm[(a^2+b^2)/2]^{1/2} \qquad (3)$$

where a is the half of the crest width of the embankment and b is the half width at the embankment base.

It should be mentioned here that the expression (3) is obtained by refering to the corresponding expression for the semi-infinite, undrained, elastic body subjected to embankment loading. Namely, the loci in the case of an undrained elastic ground take the following analytical form:

$$x^2 - z^2 = (a^2 + b^2)/2 \qquad (4)$$

where a and b are the shape parameters for the embankment loading (see Fig. 3). There are some factors invalidating Eq. (4) for more realistic ground conditions. These include the presence of a rigid base or firm strata below the clay bed as well as the occurrence of partial drainage even during construction stage. Note that the just mentioned is the background of suggesting Eq. (3) for realistic soil conditions.

Partial Drainage as Affected by Embanking Speed

The purpose of this section is to relate the partial drainage of a clay foundation to the embanking speed as well as the consolidation capability of the clay foundation.

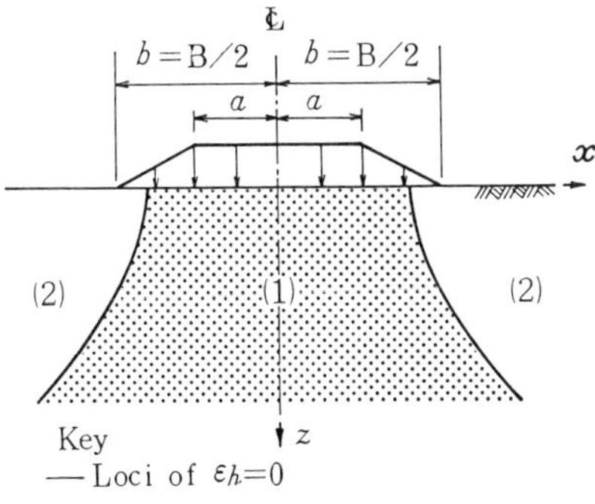

Figure 3. Loci of zero lateral strain in a semi-infinite undrained elastic body.

Consider that an embankment is constructed on a homogeneous bed of clay at a constant rate of loading, $\dot{q}$, to a prescribed intensity of loading, q_{ec}, and thereafter it is left to stand at that constant load intensity. In general, the degree of partial drainage within the clay foundation depends on the rate of loading relative to its consolidation or drainage capability. It is appropriate herein to introduce a time factor, T_{ec}, as being such a rate parameter. That is to say,

$$T_{ec} = c_v \, t_{ec}/H_d^2 \qquad (5)$$

where t_{ec} is the elapsed time to the end of construction of the embankment from its commencement of embanking, c_v is the coefficient of (one-dimensional) consolidation of the clay foundation and H_d is the maximum length of drainage of the clay foundation.

The next thing to do is to define the overall degree of drainage of the clay foundation in terms of a relevant measure. For this purpose, we introduce the following parameter:

$$U_v(t) = V_{net}(t)/(V_{net})_f \qquad (6)$$

Here, $U_v(t)$ stands for the degree of consolidation at any instant of time, t, in terms of the net volume-changes of the foundation block discussed in Fig. 1(a), and $(V_{net})_f$ denotes the final, net volume-changes that are reached if the intensity of loading is maintained at $q=q_{ec}$ after the end of construction .

The physical meaning of the new parameter U_v can clearly be seen from Fig. 4. Here, the normalized volume-changes gained in lateral deformation are drawn against the normalized volume-changes lost in settlement after the stoppage of four different rates of embanking. The B/H ratio involved is equal to 2, and the load level adopted is equal to $q_{ec}/\sigma_{vc}'=1.8$, where σ_{vc}' is the vertical consolidation pressure. The broken lines on this figure schematically show the behaviour during

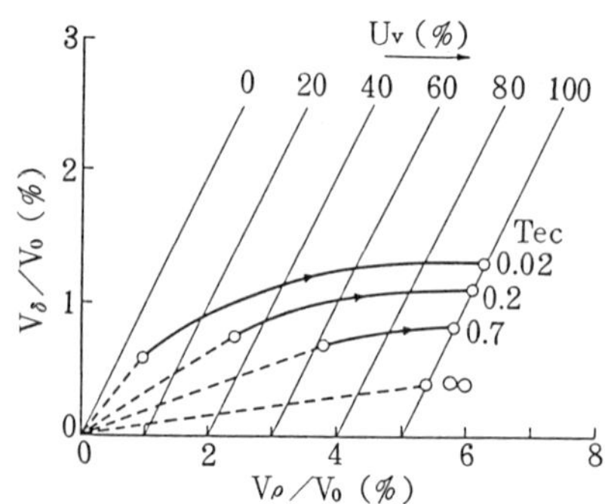

Figure 4. Calculated performance of displacement volumes.

the construction stage. Note that the performance with $T_{ec} = \infty$ stands for the perfectly drained performance, and this is computationally realized here by rendering the coefficient of permeability, k, of the foundation clay infinitely large in value. It is seen that in this particular example, all the final points fall on the line of V_{net}/V_o = 5%, irrespective of the T_{ec} value. This is a direct consequence of the present constitutive model (1) and is compatible with what has been observed for many clays (4). It is thus logical to define the degree of consolidation in terms of the net volume-changes in the form of Eq. (6). Indeed, the lines of equal U_v in Fig. 4 are drawn on the basis of the above reasoning.

Let $(U_v)_{ec}$ be the degree of (elasto-viscoplastic) consolidation at the end of construction, in the sense stated above. The calculated relationship between $(U_v)_{ec}$ and the corresponding time factor, T_{ec}, for the B/H ratio of 2 is shown in Fig. 5. Note that calculations at other B/H ratios of 3, 4 and 6 yield curves essentially the same as in the case of B/H=2, although they are omitted on Fig. 5 for brevity. Instead, the theoretical relationship between the end-of-construction degree of consolidation and the time factor obtained by Lumb (5) within the framework of one-dimensional elastic consolidation is presented in Fig. 5. It is of interest to note that both curves are remarkably similar despite their totally different sets of assumptions.

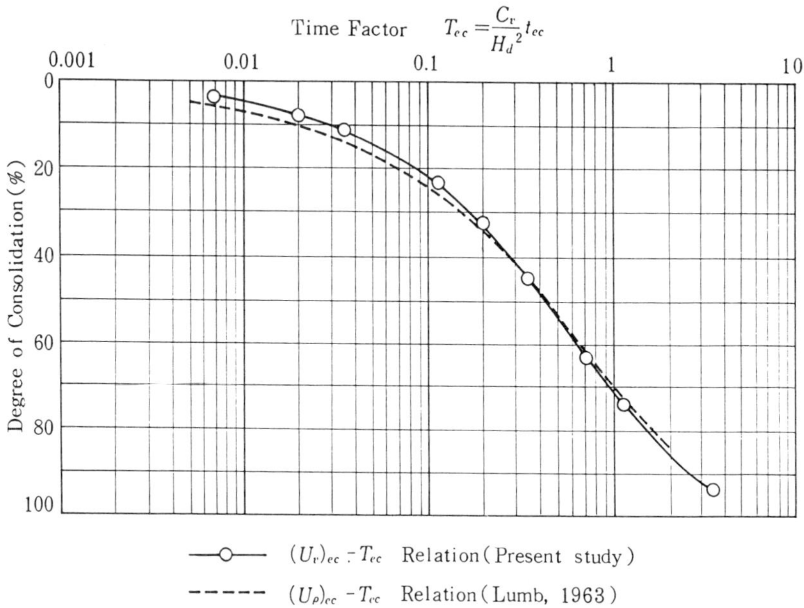

Figure 5. Calculated relationship between the degree of consolidation and the time factor.

Effects of Partial Drainage on Lateral Soil Movements

The calculated effects of partial drainage (or embanking speed) on the lateral soil movements can be summarized in the form of Fig. 6. Here, the ratios of the volume gained in lateral deformation to the volume lost in settlement at the end of construction, are drawn against the corresponding degrees of consolidation in terms of the net volume-changes of the foundation blocks with B/H ratios of 2, 3, 4 and 6. It is seen that for a given B/H ratio, the lateral deformation develops more rapidly as the degree of consolidation in terms of the net volume-changes, $(U_v)_{ec}$, is less than 30%.

From Fig. 6 it is also noted that for a given value of $(U_v)_{ec}$, the lateral deformation tends to be suppressed with increasing B/H ratio, except for the undrained case where the value of V_δ/V_ρ is always unity by definition.

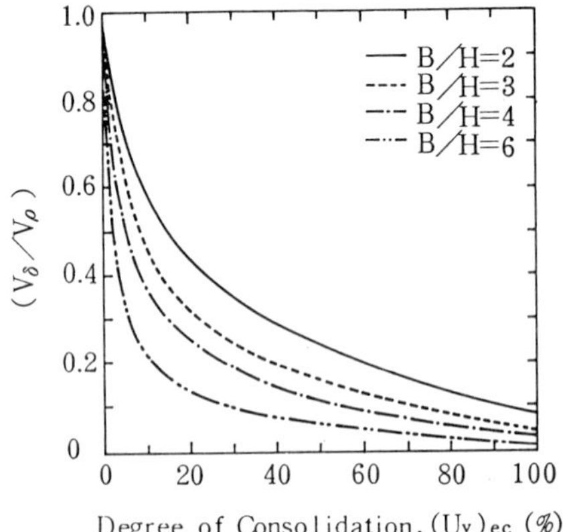

Figure 6. The ratio of displacement volumes plotted against the degree of consolidation.

PERFORMANCES OF LATERAL DEFORMATION IN NATURAL SOIL DEPOSITS

Introductory Remarks

The performances of lateral deformation in natural soil deposits are discussed in this chapter. The underlying idea is that the variety of soil-forming processes is well reflected in the stratification of each deposit as well as in the nature of the constituent soils.

Let us first make a brief review of the case histories compiled by Tavenas et al. (6). From the information given in their Table 1, we take up the lateral deformability factors, $(\delta_m/H)_{ec}$, for a total of 21 embankments and depict them in the form of Fig. 7. Here, δ_m is the maximum lateral displacement in a vertical profile through the toe of a given embankment, H is the thickness of the soft foundations and the subscript, ec, means the end of construction, as defined before. We classify the status of each embankment as follows: "Constructed to failure" or "Very close to failure" or "Stable", on the basis of the description by Tavenas et al. (6) and the related references. Also, we arrange all the embankments in five groups, in view of the construction sites on a global scale. It is then clear that the case histories covered are concerned with rather restricted regions in the world. Care should be taken in this regard, however, that the apparent trend would be owing principally to the availability of the published case histories. In other words, the trend encourages us to collect more information from sources effective in the other regions as well.

Another aspect to be noted in Fig. 7 is the scope in deformability. At the one extreme, the koda test embankment (site 7) exhibits the lateral deformability factor as high as

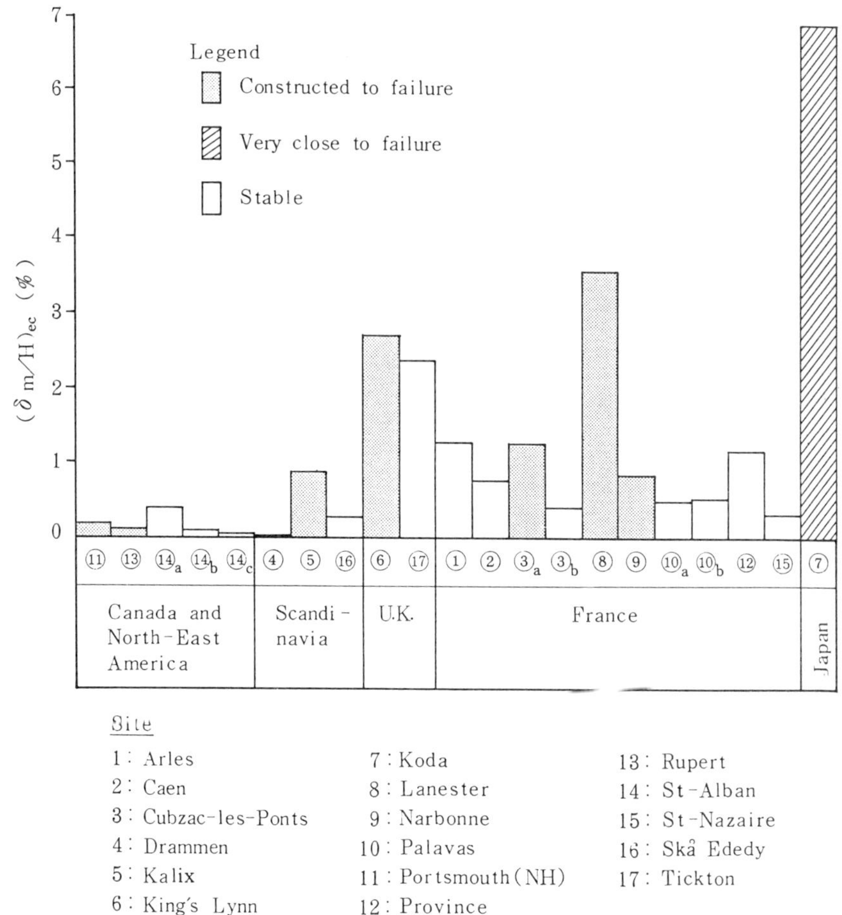

Figure 7. Lateral deformability factors at 17 test sites.

7%. In contrast, the Portsmouth test embankment (site 11) has the lateral deformability factor as low as 0.17%, although it was brought to eventual failure. Such a remarkable difference in the lateral deformability seems to come primarily from the difference in the nature of the soil deposits. In the following sections this interesting aspect will be discussed fully.

The Deposits of Soft Soils Selected

A total of nine deposits of soft soils are selected for the present discussion. Their sources of information are summarized in Table 1, together with the principal data on the embankments constructed on the deposits (7-15). The columnar sections below the ground level are shown in Fig. 8, relative to the mean sea level (M.S.L.). Columnar section 1 represents a borehole log that was taken from a small-scale deposit of peat located between hills. Columnar sections 2 and 3 both feature the large-scale lowlands, in which there exist the thick beds of soft clays overlain by the highly compressible peats. Columnar sections 4, 5 and 6 indicate the deposits of soft, slightly organic clays, with clay crusts. Columnar section 7 is drawn for the deposit of the highly sensitive clay that was presumably subjected to leaching. Columnar

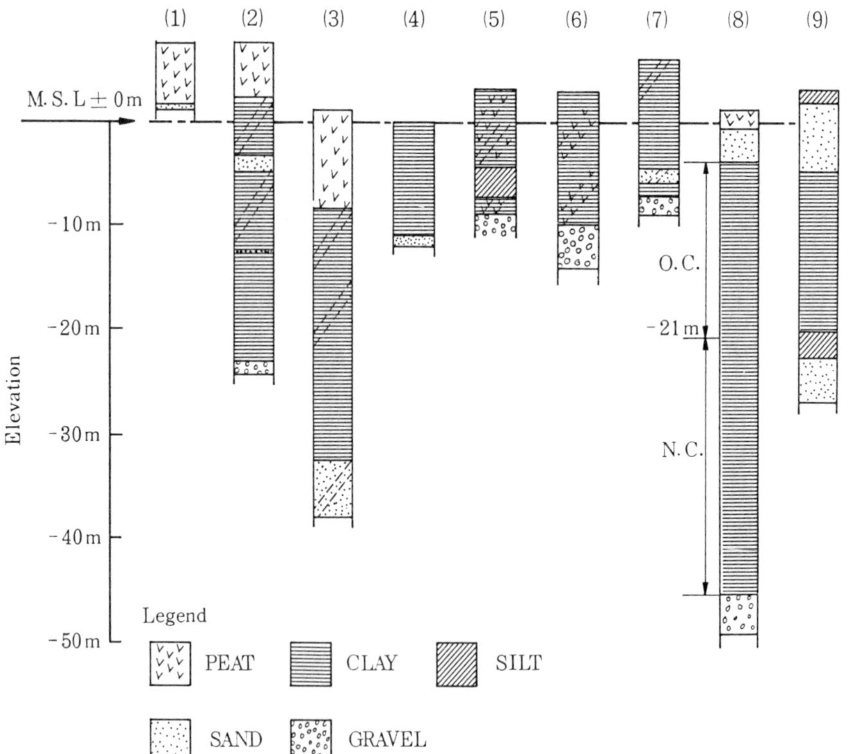

Figure 8. Stratification of the soil deposits selected.

Table 1
Summary of the nine deposits of soft soils selected

Column. Sec. No.	Site	Nation	B (m)	H (m)	Source of Data
1	Koda	Japan	24	6.0	Muromachi & Watanabe(7)
2	Ebetsu	Japan	63	28.9	J.H.P.C.(8)
3	Atcafalaya Levee	U.S.A.	72	36.0	Kaufman & Weaver(9)
4	Rio de Janeiro	Brazil	40	11.3	Ramalho-Ortigao et al.(10)
5	River Thames	U.K.	47	12.0	Marsland & Powell(11)
6	Cubzac-les-Ponts	France	43	9.0	Magnan et al.(12)
7	Portsmouth	U.S.A.	71	13.4	Ladd(13)
8	Boston	U.S.A.	81	45.6	Lambe(14)
9	Kanda	Japan	62	23.3	J.H.P.C.(15)

section 8 features the very thick bed of Boston blue clay (14, 16). Note that the upper half of the blue clay is overconsolidated to unusually high extents, compared with an ordinary deposit of alluvial clay (Fig. 9). Indeed, the presence of the sandy glacial till below the blue clay is revealing concerning the process of formation of this particular deposit.

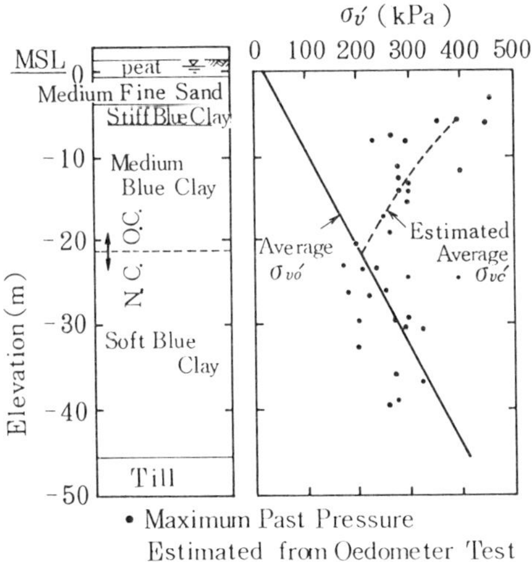

Figure 9. Distribution of soil properties at the Boston test site (adapted from D'Appolonia et al. (16)).

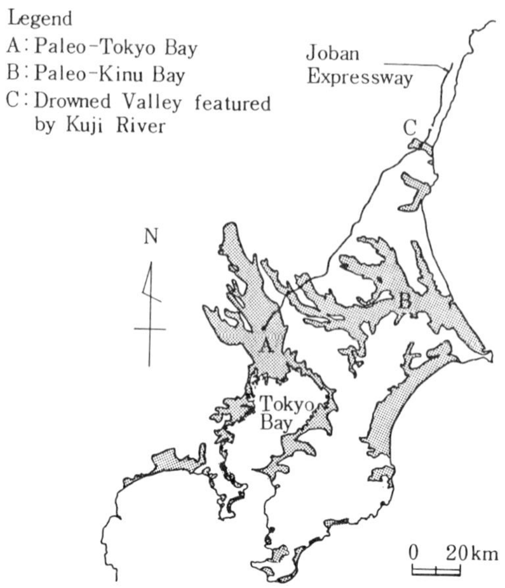

Figure 10. Drowned valleys at 6000 years B.P. in the Kanto district, Japan (adapted from Endo et al. (17)).

Columnar section 9 in Fig. 8 depicts a borehole log that was taken from a past drowned valley (marked C on Fig. 10), in the Kanto district, Japan (15, 17). Note that in this deposit the thick bed of marine clay is overlain by the naturally sedimented sand.

It will thus be evident that the soil deposits selected here cover a comprehensive range of alluvial deposits of clays and peats.

The Stress-Deformability Performances and Discussion

Pressure-deformability curves: The performances of the eight deposits loaded by the embankments are shown in Fig. 11. Here, the observed maximum lateral displacement in a vertical profile through the toe of each embankment is plotted against the applied load intensity for the construction phase. For the Ebetsu test embankmen the performance during the holding period and the second filling stage is also indicated. The performance of the Atchafalaya levee is not shown in Fig. 11, because it was concerned solely with the test raising of the existing bank and the preceding lateral soil movements due to the existing bank were not reported in the literature (9). By closely examining the pressure-deformability curves in Fig. 11 in the light of the soil profiles shown in Fig. 8, we can come to a conclusion that those pressure-deformability curves well reflect the nature of the soil deposits concerned.

Practical implications: The pressure-deformability curves shown in Fig. 11 include those from the four test embankments that were actually brought to failure: Rio de Janeiro (10); River Thames (11); Cubzac-les-Ponts (A) (12); and Portsmouth (13). In the case of the Rio de Janeiro test embankment as well as the River Thames test bank, the stiffness factor, $\Delta q/\Delta\delta_m$, tends to decrease remarkably with increasing intensity of loading, q, until the eventual failure of the embankment is reached. This immediately suggests that for these particular kinds of soft deposits, the monitoring of

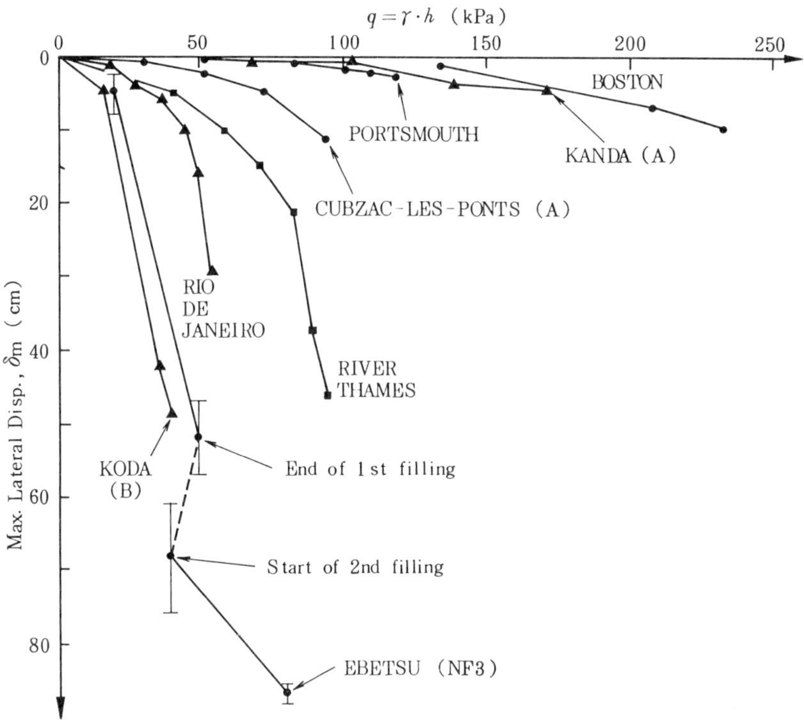

Figure 11. Pressure-deformability curves for eight deposits.

lateral soil movements is an effective means for identifying the impending failure of the embankment-foundation system.

The above statement can be reinforced from Fig. 12, which indicates the reported degradation in overall stiffness of the soft foundations below the River Thames test bank (11, 18). Note here that the test bank was brought to failure by regularly placing 0.33 meter-thick lifts at one-day intervals (11). The resulting increment in lateral displacement, $\Delta\delta$, over that one-day interval is indicated in Fig. 12(a) as a function of the height of the bank, h, from the original ground level (11). The associated relationship between the stiffness factor, $\Delta h/\Delta\delta$, and the fill height, h, is shown in Fig. 12(b), after Shibata and Sekiguchi (18). It is seen that at higher levels of loading the stiffness factor, $\Delta h/\Delta\delta$, tends to decrease linearly with increasing height of the bank, h, thus enabling one to assess the failure height, h_f, in advance of the eventual failure (18).

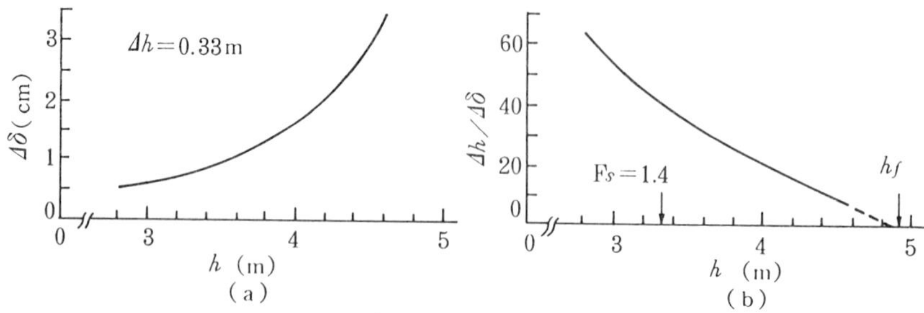

Figure 12. Performance of the River Thames test bank.

Such an observational procedure of failure prediction does not seem to be applicable, however, to deposits of brittle nature. A case-history implying this is with the Portsmouth test embankment that was built on the highly sensitive clay. Indeed, Ladd (13) reports that the test embankment underwent eventual rupture, without any noticeable signs of failure. The pressure-deformability curve given in Fig. 11 also is compatible with the statement made by Ladd and is only barely indicative of the degradation in stiffness before failure.

The performance of the Cubzac-les-Ponts (A) test embankment is also worth discussing. The deposit is featured by a 8 meter-thick, slightly overconsolidated, soft organic clay that has a natural water content as high as 200% at its weakest portion (12). The pressure-deformability curve depicted in Fig. 11, however, suggests that the overall stiffness of the deposit is moderate. In this regard, it is important to recognize that the soft organic clay actually is covered with a 1.8 meter-thick, overconsolidated clay crust, and that the embankment was brought to failure rather rapidly in 8 days (19). If the loading were performed more slowly, then the passage of the foundation soils from the overconsolidated to the normally consolidated state would have been more dominant, thus causing more remarkable reduction in the overall stiffness.

It may now be instructive to set a reference bearing capacity, in such a way that a soil deposit having a lower bearing capacity exhibits the highly ductile behaviour, whereas a soil deposit having a larger bearing capacity undergoes the rather brittle behaviour. The results summarized in Fig. 11 suggest that such a reference bearing capacity can be taken at around 100 kPa.

In essence, the above discussion emphasizes the importance of allowing for the deformability or the nature of the soil deposit as part of the strategy for monitoring the embankment stability.

Performances of Partial Drainage and Discussion

The measured relationships between the volume gained in lateral deformation and the volume lost in settlement are shown in Fig. 13 for the peat deposit (Koda) and for the deposits of soft clays overlain by peats (Ebetsu and Atchafalaya levee). In Fig. 13(a), the performances during the construction stage (or the first filling stage) are depicted, whereas in Fig. 13(b) the performances after the end of construction (or the end of the first filling stage) are also indicated. Symbols E and S on Fig. 13(b) stand, respectively, for the end of the first filling phase and the start of the second filling phase. What is most notable from Fig. 13 is that the behaviour of the soft foundations is far from undrained, or isochoric in a more rigorous sense, even during the loading stages.

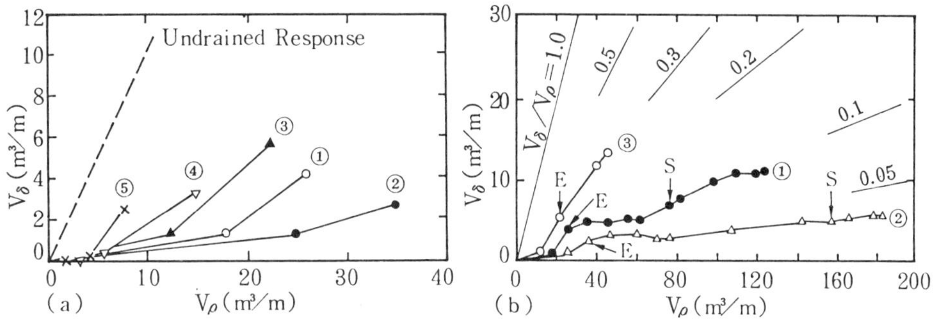

Legend ① Ebetsu (NF3)
② Ebetsu (RF), with sand drains
③ Atchafalaya Levee (TS2)
④ Koda (B)
⑤ Koda (A), with sand drains

Figure 13. Performances of the displacement volumes of the deposits characterized by the presence of peats.

The ratios of the volume gained in lateral deformation to the volume lost in settlement at the end of construction, or at the end of the first filling stage, are plotted in Fig. 14 against the B/H ratios of the five embankments indicated. For purposes of comparison, the theoretical results discussed in Fig. 6 are also indicated on Fig. 14.

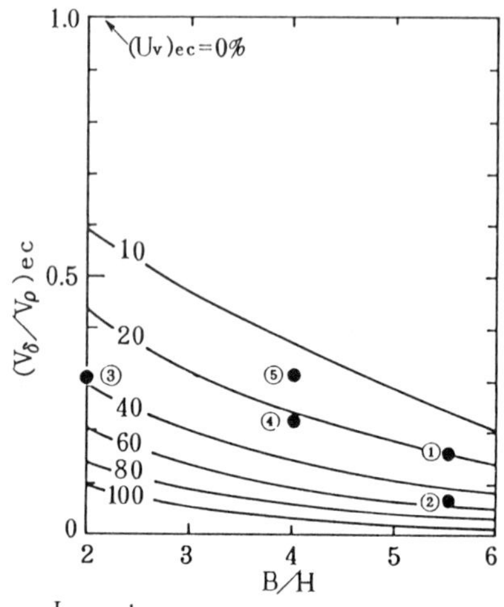

Figure 14. The ratio of displacement volumes plotted against the B/H ratio, with the lines of equal degree of consolidation in terms of net volume-changes.

Let us first discuss the performances of the Ebetsu test embankment. The selection of the thickness of soft foundations, H, for this test site deserves attention, because there exist the intercalated sands in the clay bed (see columnar section 2 in Fig. 8). In short, we have adopted the thickness (H^*=11.3 m) from the ground surface to the the upper sand layer at M.S.L.-3.6 m, in view of the inclinometer readings available, instead of the total thickness of the soft foundations, H=29.5 m on average. It should also be mentioned regarding the test section (RF) that the sand drains were installed down to the level of the upper sand layer, and that the reinforcement of the fill itself was made using steel strips. A comparison between the field performance data plotted on Fig. 14 clearly shows that in this particular site, the sand-drain treatment of the soft foundations coupled with the fill reinforcement was highly effective in suppressing the lateral flow. In this regard, it may be appropriate to mention that in the test section marked RF, the fill was successfully constructed, in two stages, to the height of 8.0 m, whereas in the untreated section (NF3) the fill was raised to the height of 3.5 m with much difficulty (8).

In the case of the Koda test site, however, no beneficial effects of installing sand drains can be seen from the field performance data plotted on Fig. 14. This may be ascribed to the fact that the embankment width relative to the thickness of the peat layer was rather narrow at the Koda test site, as compared with the Ebetsu test site.

The field performance data of the test section 2 of the Atchafalaya levee plotted on Fig. 14, suggests that significant net volume-changes were accompanied by the ground deformation. This suggestion would be interesting, in view of the reported fact (9) that the test section was designed at a factor of safety equal to 1.1 and was actually marginal in stability at the final stage of the filling work. A clue for re-examining the above suggestion in the future would be to assess the degree of saturation of the foundation soils (in particular, of the peaty soils), and to make clear how much the porewater was really squeezed out of the foundation soils.

CONCLUSIONS

A framework for assessing the lateral soil movements has been developed, based on the coupled stress-flow analyses using the method of finite elements and based on a detailed study of the field performance data.

The framework facilitates a general understanding of the problem of lateral soil movements, before conducting individual numerical analyses for specific configurations of embankments on specific kinds of soft soils, at specific sites. This perspective becomes particularly important, in view of the following main findings of the present research: The nature or stratification of the deposits of soft soils is well reflected in their pressure-deformability performances (Fig. 11); and in many cases a significant drainage is accompanied by the lateral soil movements, even during the loading stages (Figs. 13 and 14).

REFERENCES

1. Sekiguchi, H., Nishida, Y. and Kanai, F., A plane-strain viscoplastic constitutive model for clay. Proc. 37th Nat. Conf., JSCE, 1982, 181-182 (in Japanese).

2. Sekiguchi, H., Rheological characteristics of clays, Proc. 9th Int. Conf. Soil Mech. Found. Eng., Tokyo, 1977, 1, 289-292.

3. Sekiguchi, H., Nishida, Y. and Kanai, F., Analysis of partially drained triaxial testing of clay. Soils and Foundations, 1981, 21, 3, 53-66.

4. Schofield, A. N. and Wroth, C. P., Critical State Soil Mechanics, McGraw-Hill, London, 1968.

5. Lumb, P., Rate of settlement of a clay layer due to a gradually applied load. Civil Eng. Publ. Wks Rev, 1963, March, 315-317.

6. Tavenas, F., Mieussens, C. and Bourges, F., Lateral displacemants in clay foundations under embankments, Canadian Geotech. Jour., 1979, 16, 532-550.

7. Muromachi, T. and Watanabe, S., Deformation of soft peat foundation under embankment. Railway Technical Research Report, 1963, 364, 1-49 (in Japanese).

8. The Japan Highway Public Corporation, Report on the performances of Ebetsu Trial Embankment, 1979 (in Japanese).

9. Kaufman, R. I., and Weaver, F. J., Stability of Atchafalaya levees. J. Soil Mech. Found. Div., ASCE, 1967, 93, SM4, 157-176.

10. Ramalho-Ortigao, J. A., Werneck, M. L. G. and Lacerda, W. A., Embankment failure on clay near Rio de Janeiro. J. Geotech. Eng., ASCE, 1983, 109, 11, 1460-1479.

11. Marsland, A. and Powell, J. J. M., The behaviour of a trial bank constructed to failure on soft alluvium of the River Thames. Proc. Int. Symp. on Soft Clay, Bangkok, 1977, 1, 505-525.

12. Magnan, J. P., Mieussens, C. et Queyroi, D. D., Etude d'un remblai sur sols compressibles-Le remblai B du site experimental de Cubzac-les-Ponts. Rapports de Recherche LPC N, 1983, 127, Laboratoire Central des Ponts et Chaussees, Paris.

13. Ladd, C. C., Test embankment on sensitive clay. Proc. Specialty Conf. on Performance of Earth and Earth-Supported Structures, ASCE, 1972, 1, 101-128.

14. Lambe, T. W., Predictions in soil engineering. Geotechnique, 1973, 23, 2, 149-202.

15. The Japan Highway Public Corporation, Report on the performances of Kanda Trial Embankment, 1981 (in Japanese).

16. D'Appolonia, D. J., Lambe, T. W. and Poulos, H. G., Evaluation of pore pressures beneath an embankment. J. Soil Mech. Found. Div., ASCE, 1971, 97, SM6, 881-897.

17. Endo, K., Sekimoto, K., Takano, T., Suzuki, M. and Hirai, Y., Alluvium of the planes of Kanto. URBAN KUBATA, 1983, 21, 26-43 (in Japanese).

18. Shibata, T. and Sekiguchi, H., A method of predicting failure of embankment foundation based on elasto-viscoplastic analyses. Proc. of JSCE, 1980, 301, 93-104 (in Japanese).

19. Leroueil, S., Magnan, J. P. et Tavenas, F., Remblais sur Argiles Molles. Technique et Documentation, 1985, Lavoisier, Paris.

TIME DEPENDENT DEFORMATION OF SAND AS MEASURED BY ACOUSTIC EMISSION

Yasuo TANAKA* and Kiichi TANIMOTO**
*Research Associate, ** Professor Emeritus
Department of Civil Engineering,
Kobe University, Nada, Kobe, JAPAN

ABSTRACT

This paper describes the time dependent behaviour of saturated sand during the isotropic consolidation and the anisotropic consolidation in triaxial chamber. The behaviour was studied by the routine deformation measurements and also by measuring the acoustic emission (AE) released from the soil. The study by the acoustic emission measurement indicated that there were considerable movements of soil grains after reaching the steady maximum consolidation stress and the rate of movements decreasing with time. The anisotropic consolidation tests showed more movements of soil grains as compared with the isotropic tests and this was clearly indicated by the acoustic emission measurement.

INTRODUCTION

The time dependent deformation of clayey soil is well recognised. For example, the researchers are well aware of the effects of the secondary consolidation time period on the subsequent stress-strain behaviour of clay. However there seems to be much less attention being paid on the time dependent deformation of sandy soil. Thus triaxial tests to examine the deformation properties of sandy soil, for instances, are often carried out without specifying the details of the time required for the consolidation.

Recently Tatsuoka et al. (1) have reported that there is a significant increase in liquefaction resistance when sandy soil was left under sustained pressure for prolonged period of time. Mulilis et al. (2) have also reported the importance of time for leaving the sandy specimen under confining stress. These papers have shown that even for sandy soil there is some effect of time dependent compression on the subsequent deformation and strength behaviours of soil but the mechanism which control the behaviour is not clearly understood.

In this paper, the deformation of sand was studied by carrying out a series of triaxial consolidation test with a special attention to the emission of acoustic energy (AE). This technique of AE measurement has been shown to be a powerful tool to investigate the micro-structural behaviour of sandy soil, (3),(4). Since the AE should represent the sliding of grains, the stress state which start to emit the acoustic energy should define the boundary between the elastic and plastic behaviour of soil. Based on this concept, the yield locus of pre-stressed sandy soil was successfully determined using the AE measurements by Tanimoto and Tanaka (3), (4).

TEST APPARATUS AND TEST METHODS

The details of the triaxial test apparatus which is capable of measuring the AE during shear have been described elsewhere (4), and for the sake of completeness a brief description of the apparatus will be given here. Fig. 1 shows a schematic view of the apparatus. The triaxial specimen with a diameter of 50 mm is seated on the lower pedestal in which centre an AE sensor is placed. The apparatus is capable of shearing the specimen either in compression or extension mode. Other test arrangements are the same with the standard triaxial apparatus except that the axial loading was made by using an air cylinder to minimise the mechanical noises during shear. All measurements such as axial and volumetric deformations were taken automatically using a personal computer.

As to the AE measurements, the method employed here is to count the number of the pulses exceeding a threshold level and this level was set to

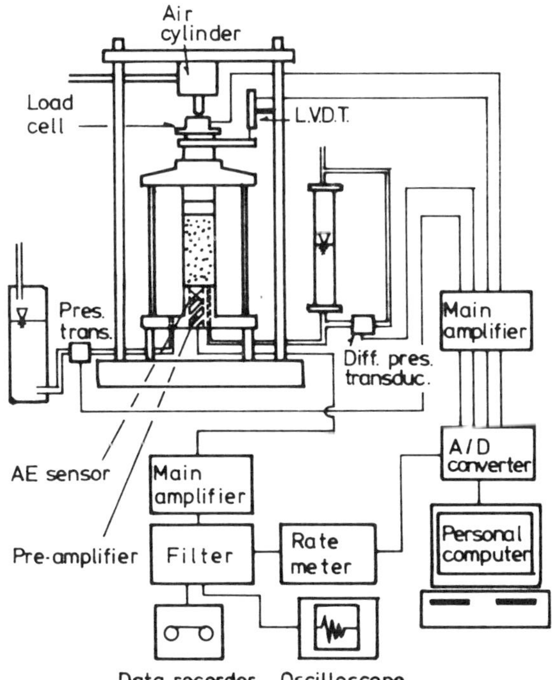

Fig. 1 Triaxial test apparatus

be slightly higher than the background noise. The number of AE counts registered over a specified period of time is termed here as the AE count rate and the total number of AE counts accumulated from the start of test as the cumulative AE counts.

The soil for the test was a well graded sand which was taken from a deposit of decomposed granite. The average particle size was 0.41 mm with the coefficient of uniformity of 29. The triaxial specimen was formed by placing the air-dried soil loosely into a mold and the resulting dry density of the specimen was approximately 1.6 Mg/m^3. The specimen was saturated by introducing de-aired water from the bottom under the vacuum. In order to ensure the saturation, the specimens were given a back pressure of 160 kPa.

The Isotropic consolidation was carried out by increasing both the axial and lateral stresses in small equal steps to the maximum pressure of

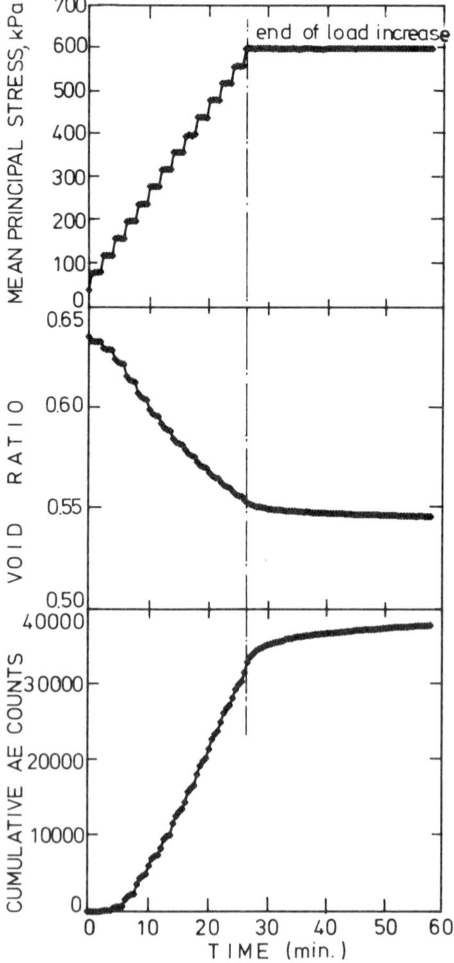

Fig. 2 A typical result of isotropic consolidation tests

600 kPa. At each step, the load was maintained for 2 minutes and then the next loading was applied. For the anisotropic consolidation, the triaxial specimens were consolidated by keeping the ratio between the vertical and horizontal stresses to 1 to 0.46. This ratio was chosen, after a set of preparatory experiments, in order to consolidate the specimens with Ko condition. Similar to the isotropic test, the loading was made in small steps and at the each step the load was held constant for 2 minutes. The maximum consolidation pressure was 640 kPa in terms of the mean principal stress. When the loading step reached maximum, the vertical and horizontal stresses were kept constant.

TEST RESULTS

ISOTROPIC CONSOLIDATION

A typical example of isotropic consolidation tests is shown in Fig.2. The upper most figure shows the loading sequence, and the changes of void ratio and cumulative AE counts with time are shown in the middle and lower figures respectively. As can be seen from the figure, the volume change of soil occurred without much delay at each loading. At the end of last consolidation steps, the rate of volume changes decreases and it seems to be almost negligible. It is also evident that the AE counts starts to decrease at the end of consolidation, but the rate of its changes shows that there still be non-negligible AE counts being registered.

The compression curve obtained during the isotropic loading is shown in Fig. 3. In the figure, the changes of cumulative AE counts with the mean principal stress, p, are also shown. The compression of the specimen increases after the p value exceeds about 100 kPa which seems to correspond to the maximum pre-stressing level reached during the saturation procedure by vacuuming. At this stress level, the AE counts starts to increase and the trend of its increase seems to match the shape of e-log p curve as shown.

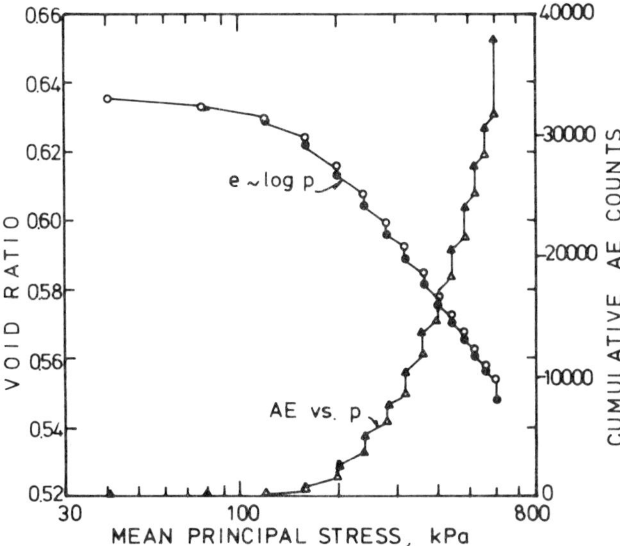

Fig. 3 Changes of void ratio and cumulative AE counts with confining stress

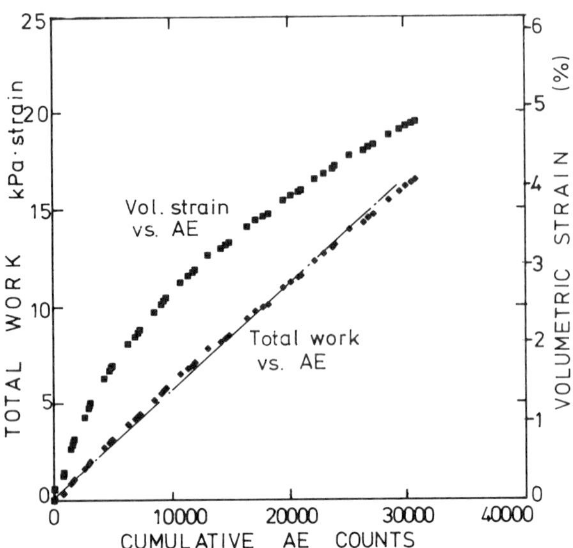

Fig. 4 Relationships among volumetric strain, total work and AE

As mentioned earlier, the AE would represent the movement of soil grains which is irrecoverable work. The sudden increase of compression characteristic indicates that the specimen is in normally consolidated state and the starting of AE counts at that stress level do indicate that the irrecoverable, plastic deformations of soil structure have started. It may be however appropriate here to show that the AE count is not a simple reflection of the soil movement.

In Fig.4, the relationship between the cumulative AE counts and the volumetric strain is depicted and it is clear that the relationship is not linear. Also shown in the figure is the relationship between the cumulative AE counts and the total work, W, done to the specimen by external force and the relationship between them is linear. The total work was calculated by using the following equation which is based on the equations suggested in Critical State Soil Mechanics, (5).

$$W = \int (p \; d\varepsilon_v + q \; d\varepsilon_s) \qquad (1)$$

where p and q are the mean principal stress and the principal stress differences respectively, and $d\varepsilon_v$ is the increment of volumetric strain for each loading and the $d\varepsilon_s$ is the increment of shear strain.

Since q was zero for the isotropic loading, the total work done was calculated based on the volumetric strain and the value of p. Also it may be stated that the AE should represent the dissipated form of energy so that the only plastic strain can be used to compute the dissipated energy. However it was assumed here that the amount of elastic strain is negligible as compared with the plastic strain of soil. The linear relationship between the cumulative AE counts and the total work therefore shows that the AE count is to represent the dissipated energy and not the soil movement itself.

The volumetric changes and the AE as measured under the constant maximum consolidation pressure are depicted as a function of time in Fig. 5 and the origin of the time axis represents the beginning of holding the pressure constant. The values of the volumetric strain and the AE count are the increments after the start of constant pressure. Both the volumetric changes and the AE decrease with time and the trend is nearly the same. Since the value of p is constant during this period, the cumulative AE counts should be simply interpreted as the cumulative volumetric strains.

The variation of AE count rate , i.e., AE counts over 30 seconds, with time for the same period is shown in Fig. 6. It may be noted that the AE count rate represents the gradient of the cumulative AE counts versus time curve and the rapid decreasing of it indicates that the rate of soil movements is decreasing with time. For the isotropic consolidation tests, the AE count rate became negligible usually after 30 minutes from the start of constant pressure.

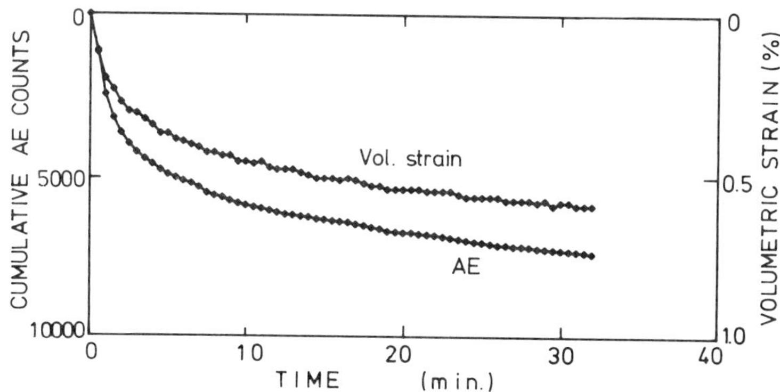

Fig. 5 Changes of volumetric strain and AE with time under constant isotropic stress

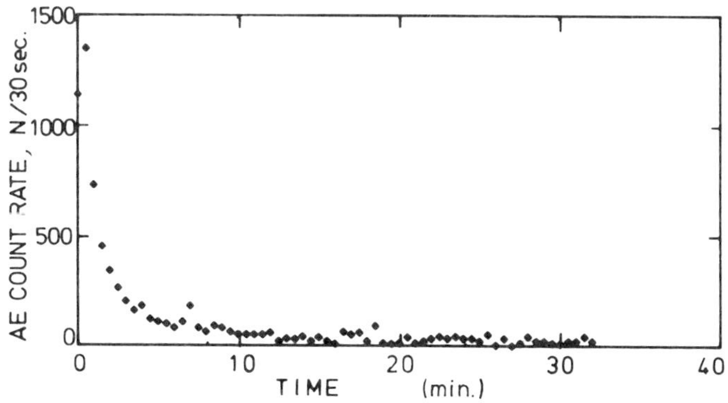

Fig. 6 Changes of AE count rate with time under constant isotropic stress

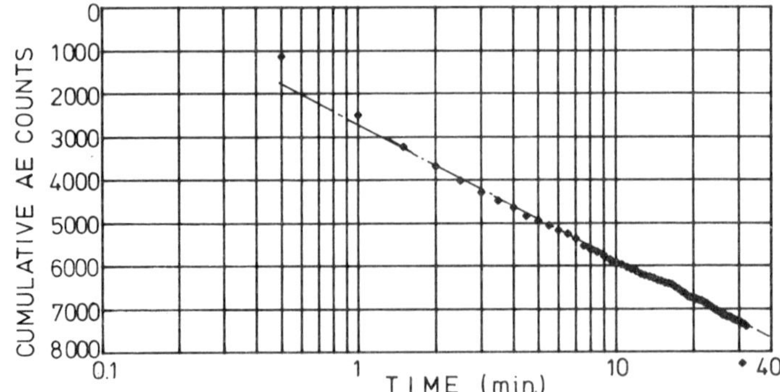

Fig. 7 Relationship between cumulative AE counts and logarithmic time under constant isotropic stress

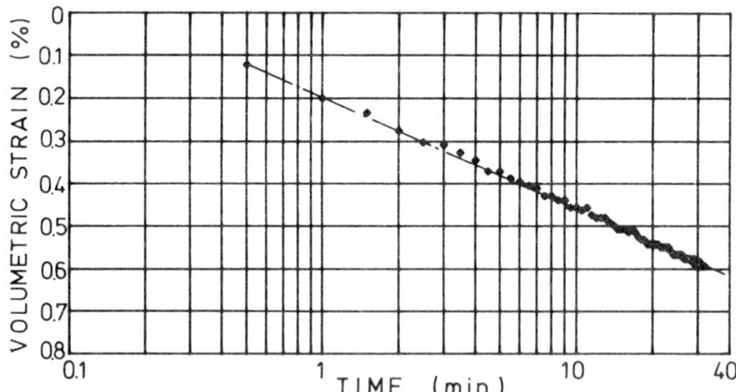

Fig. 8 Relationship between volumetric strain and logarithmic time under constant isotropic stress

The logarithmic time variations of the volumetric strains and the cumulative AE counts are shown in Fig. 7 and 8 respectively. It is clear that the variation of both of them with logarithmic time is almost linear. Thus this indicates that the nature of deformation taking this period is very similar to the secondary compression of clayey soils. The negligible AE count rate as registered after 30 minutes does indicate the rate of soil movement is decreasing but, because of its logarithmic change, it will register some dissipating acoustic energy when the observation is to be made over much prolonged period.

ANISOTROPIC CONSOLIDATION

Fig. 9 shows a typical example of the anisotropic consolidation. The loading sequence, the variations of the void ratio and the cumulative AE counts with time are shown from the top to bottom of the figure respectively. The void ratio changes rapidly at each loading and the cumulative AE count increases accordingly. After reaching the maximum stress level, there is only a small changes of the volumetric strain with time while the changes of the cumulative AE counts with time is more pronounced.

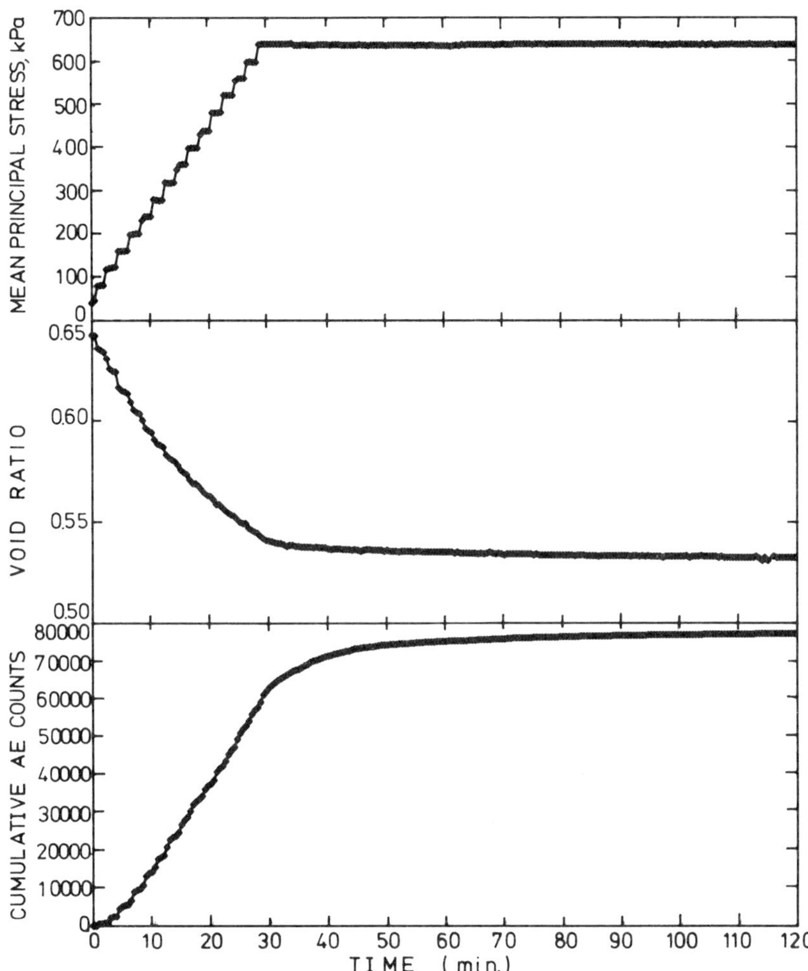

Fig. 9 A typical result of anisotropic consolidation tests

The compression curve obtained from the anisotropic consolidation is shown in Fig. 10 together with the changes of the cumulative AE counts with load. Similar to Fig. 3 of the isotropic test, the AE starts to increase after the mean principal stress exceeds about 100 kPa which corresponds to the maximum stress level reached during the sample preparation. Also shown in the figure is a typical compression curve as obtained from the isotropic test. It may noted that the compression curve from the anisotropic test shows slightly lower void ratios as compared with the isotropic test for the same mean principal stresses.

A comparison of the compression characteristics between the isotropic and anisotropic consolidation is made in Table 1. The table shows that the amount of compression during the load increments was larger in the anisotropic consolidation giving an average value of the void ratio change

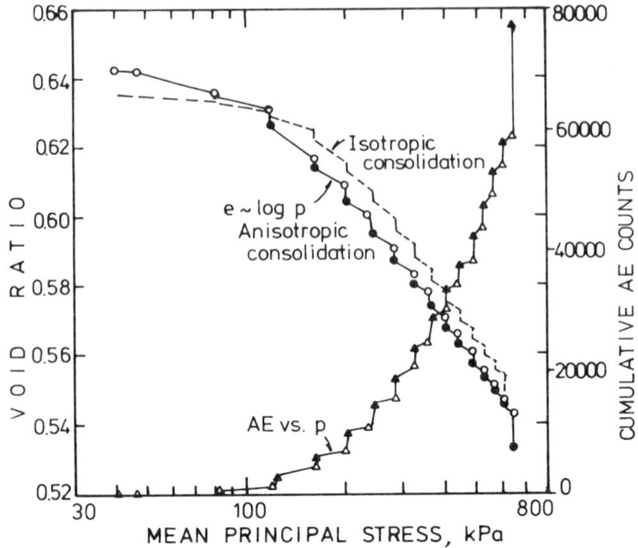

Fig.10 Changes of void ratio and cumulative AE counts with confining stress

TABLE 1
Summary of void ratio changes during the triaxial consolidation tests

Test No.	e_0	e_1	e_f	$e_0 - e_1$	$e_1 - e_f$	Remark
I-1	0.646	0.566	0.556	0.080	0.010	Isotropic
I-2	0.633	0.571	0.562	0.062	0.009	Consolidation
I-3	0.631	0.552	0.542	0.079	0.010	Tests
I-4	0.635	0.556	0.546	0.079	0.010	
I-5	0.637	0.558	0.549	0.079	0.009	e_0 :initial stage
I-6	0.643	0.564	0.554	0.079	0.010	e_1 :end of load
I-7	0.639	0.561	0.551	0.078	0.010	increments
I-8	0.633	0.548	0.539	0.085	0.009	e_f :end of test
Average	0.637	-----	-----	0.078	0.0096	
A-1	0.637	0.532	0.522	0.105	0.010	Anisotropic
A-2	0.642	0.533	0.523	0.109	0.010	Consolidation
A-3	0.639	0.534	0.524	0.105	0.010	Tests
A-4	0.633	0.531	0.520	0.102	0.011	
A-5	0.631	0.535	0.525	0.096	0.010	
A-6	0.647	0.543	0.534	0.104	0.009	
A-7	0.643	0.543	0.533	0.100	0.010	
A-8	0.635	0.531	0.521	0.104	0.010	
Average	0.638	-----	-----	0.103	0.010	

of 0.103 as compared with the average of 0.078 for the isotropic case. It is also noted the change of void ratio under the steady maximum pressure is smaller for the isotropic case. However this difference seems to be very small.

The relationship between the cumulative AE counts and the volumetric strain and also the one with the total work as computed using Eq.(1) are presented in Fig. 11. As can be seen from the figure, the AE counts linearly varies with the total work done by the external force. For the anisotropic consolidation, both the shear strain and volumetric strain were measured and thus the AE counts were larger than the isotropic case.

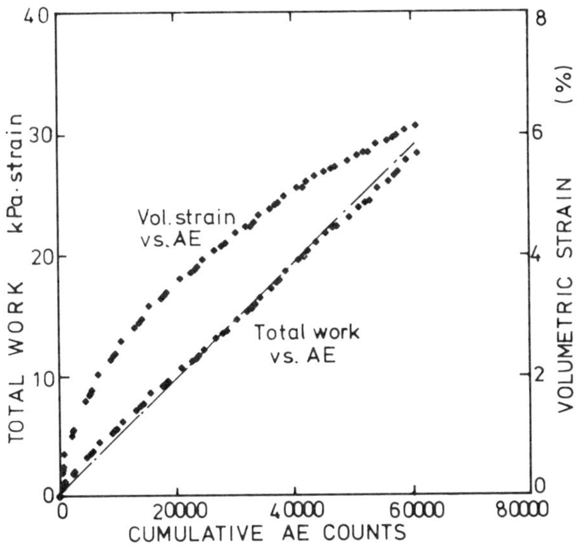

Fig.11 Relationships among volumetric strain, total work and AE

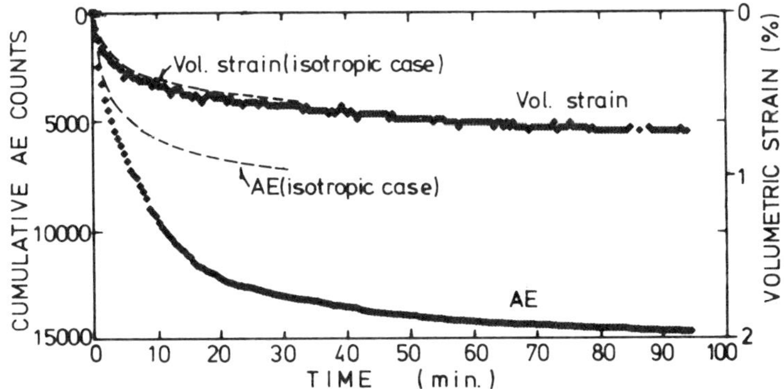

Fig.12 Changes of volumetric strain and AE with time under constant anisotropic stresses

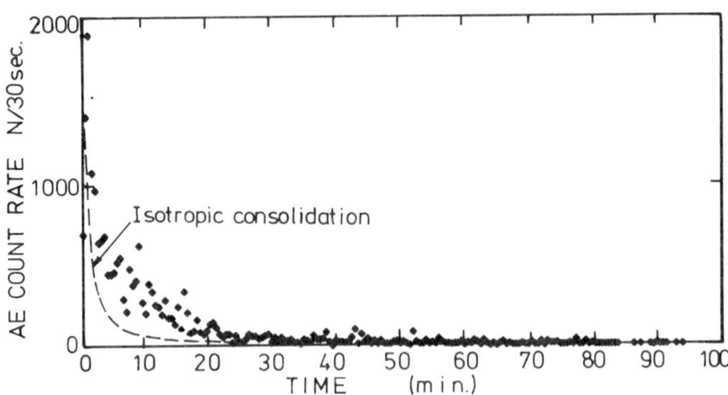

Fig.13 Changes of AE count rate with time under constant anisotropic stresses

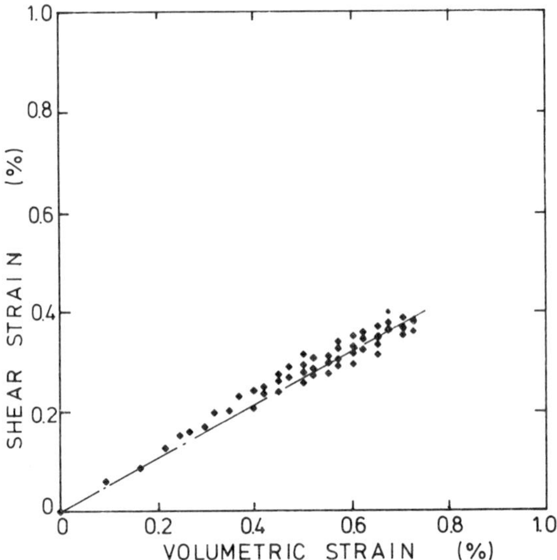

Fig.14 Relationship between volumetric strain and shear strain under constant anisotropic stresses

The volumetric strain and the cumulative AE count increased gradually with time while the maximum loading being held and the variations of these with time are shown in Fig. 12. Similar to Fig. 5 of the isotropic test, there is time dependent behaviour of soil and these changes seem to take longer time to reach the steady level as compared with the isotropic tests. The difference between the anisotropic tests and the isotropic tests is more clearly seen by examining how the AE count rate varies with time. In Fig. 13, the AE count rates from the both tests are compared and it is apparent that the AE count rate of the anisotropic test case takes longer time to come down to an insignificant level. Fig. 14 shows the relationship between the volumetric and shear strains during this period. As can be seen, the shear strain increased almost linearly with the volumetric strain during the anisotropic loading. Therefore, due to the anisotropic loading, more movements of soil grains in a form of shear strain must have been mobilised in addition to the volumetric compression, and it would result in larger AE counts.

CONCLUSIONS

In this paper, the behaviour of sandy soil during the isotropic and anisotropic consolidation in triaxial chamber was examined and the measurement of acoustic emission was used to study the microscopic changes of soil structure. The test results indicate that there were considerable movements of soil grains after reaching the steady maximum consolidation stress and the rate of movements decreasing with time. The characteristics of this compression was very similar to those of the secondary compression of clayey soils and the emission of acoustic energy strongly indicates that soil grains are moving to a more stable position during this period.

The anisotropic consolidation tests showed more movements of soil grains as compared with the isotropic tests and this was clearly shown by the larger AE counts measured during the anisotropic consolidation. An examination of the strain components under the constant maximum stress showed that both the shear and volumetric type of deformations continued with time and it took longer for the movements of soil grains to cease.

REFERENCES

1. Tatsuoka, F., Kato, H., Kimura, M. and Pradhan, T.B.S., Liquefaction strength of sands subjected to sustained pressure. Soils and Foundations, 1988, Vol.28, No.1, pp. 119-31

2. Mulilis, J.P., Mori, K., Seed, H.B. and Chan, C.K., Resistance to Liquefaction due to sustained pressure, Proc. of ASCE, J. of Geotech. Div., 1977, Vol.103, GT7, pp. 793-97

3. Tanimoto, K. and Tanaka, Y., A method of determining yield locus of sandy soil, Proc. 11th Int. Conf. on SMFE, 1985, Vol.2, pp. 1069-72

4. Tanimoto, K. and Tanaka, Y., Yielding of soil as determined by acoustic emission, Soils and Foundations, 1986, Vol.26, No.3, pp 69-80

5. Schofield, A. and Wroth, P., Critical State Soil Mechanics, McGraw-Hill, London, 1968, pp. 103-105

CREEP AND AGEING EFFECTS ON STRESSES AND DEFORMATIONS OF SATURATED CLAYED SOILS

TRIFON GERMANOV
Dr.Ph.Eng., Assoc. Professor
Secretary of the National Committee for SMFE, University of Architecture and Civil Engineering. 1421 Sofia, Bulgaria

ABSTRACT

The investigations on one-dimensional time-dependent stress-strain state of nearly saturated clayed soils are presented. Long lasting tests are carried out with samples of different types of soils under compression. Results from the tests in an open (drained) system and a closed (undrained) system under constant instantaneously applied loading are presented. A good agreement between the experimental and theoretical results, obtained with the use of the theory of linear creep and ageing is observed. The following conclusions for clayed soil behavior are drawn: the height of the soil sample (layer thickness) effects on the stress-strain state of clayed soils in an open system, change over time of the pore pressure in a closed system, change over time of the coefficient of earth pressure at rest.

INTRODUCTION

Clayed soils are found in almost all regions in Bulgaria. Environment control, soil preservation, development of transport and energetics induced the construction of important machinery and equipment in regions with complex geological conditions, the saturated clayed soils being among them. This is the reason why the study and prognosis of the stress-strain state of the clayed massifs used for foundations, medium or material for erecting buildings and structures are of great importance for improving the methods of designing the foundations.
Unlike the other continuous monophase deformable systems, the stress-strain state of the clayed soils (as complex disperse multi-phased systems) varies with the elapse of long periods of time. On the other hand, due to differences in load intensity are distinguished two relative states in clayed soils, namely

sublimited (when the existing stresses do not exceed the shear strength), and limited, presented here are the investigations related to the sublimited stress state, i.e., the compression phase. The behaviour of nearly saturated soils is examined, their deformations being accompanied by two simultaneously rheological processes: filtration and creep of the soil skeleton.

THEORETICAL CONDITIONS AND RESULTS

Multi-phased clayed soil which changes its stress-strain state over time, subjected to vertical instantaneous loading is investigated. It is supposed that, due to incomplete saturation, the fluid is linearly deformable, while the deformations of the soil skeleton are presented according to the theory of the linear creep. The equation which describes the skeleton condition, according to [2,3] acquires the following form:

$$e_0 - e(t) = \frac{\theta(t)}{1+2K_0} m_v(t,t) - \frac{1}{1+K_0}\int_{\tau_1}^{t} \theta(\tau) m_v(t,\tau)\, d\tau \; ; \qquad (1)$$

where: e_0 and $e(t)$ are the initial and the variable over time voids ratios; $\theta(t)$ is the sum of normal effective stresses at one point of the soil massif; K_0 is the coefficient of the lateral pressure at rest; $m_v(t,\tau)$ is the generalized coefficient of volume deformation.

$$m_v(t,\tau) = m_0(\tau) + \varphi(\tau)\left\{1 - \exp[-\eta(t-\tau)]\right\} \; ; \qquad (2)$$

where $m_0(\tau)$ is the coefficient of the instantaneous consolidation; $\varphi(\tau)$ is the function of ageing (tyxotropic strengthening) of the soil skeleton.

$$\varphi(\tau) = m_1 + \frac{m_h}{\tau} \quad ; \qquad (3)$$

where m_1 is the coefficient of creep (secondary) volume deformation; η - the parameter of creeping speed; m_h - the coefficient of"ageing" volume deformation of the soil skeleton; τ_1- the parameter of the soil skeleton age (the prehistory of the stressed condition).

Examining the pore water and the air dissolved into the water as a component which is deformed as a result of the air bubbles compression [13], the follwing equation is suggested:

$$\frac{1}{\rho_w}\,\frac{d\rho_w}{du_w} = \frac{1 - Sr}{Pa} = m_w \; ; \qquad (4)$$

where: ρ_w is the water density; u_w - the pore pressure (stress of the pore liquid, or natural stress); m_w - the coefficient of linear volume deformation of the pore liquid; Sr - the degree of saturation; Pa - the atmospheric pressure.

Assuming that the fluid filtration in vertical direction along axis z is in accordance with Darcy-Gersevanov's law [13] in one-dimensional stress state the equation of consolidation is, as follows :

$$\frac{\partial^2 u_w}{\partial t_v^2} + f(t_v)\frac{\partial u_w}{\partial t_v} = \beta_o \frac{\partial^3 u_w}{\partial t_v \partial \xi^2} + \varkappa \beta_o \frac{\partial^2 u_w}{\partial \xi^2} ; \tag{5}$$

where:

$$f(t_v) = \varkappa\left(1 + \beta_1 + \frac{\beta_h}{t_v}\right);$$

$$t_v = \frac{c_v}{H^2}; \quad \xi = \frac{z}{H} ; \quad \nu = \frac{H^2}{c_v} ; \quad \varkappa = \eta \frac{H^2}{c_v} ;$$

$$c_v = \frac{(1+e_o)K}{m_o \gamma_w}; \quad \beta_o = \frac{1}{1+Aw}; \quad \beta_1 = \frac{A_1}{1+Aw};$$

$$\beta_h = \frac{A_h}{1+Aw}; \quad Aw = \frac{e_o m_w}{m_o}; \quad A_1 = \frac{m_1}{m_o}; \quad A_h = \frac{m_h}{m_o};$$

H is the thickness of the examined layer; γ_w - the unit weight of the water.

Equation (5) is solved in [10] according to the Fouier's method with the help of confluent hypergeometrical functions.

The vertical deformations (settlements) in an one-dimensional stress state (compression condition) can be defined by applying the practical method cited in [13], under the condition that for each moment the effective stresses will be defined according to the Terzaghi s principle, namely:

$$\sigma'(t,z) = \sigma - u_w(t,z); \tag{6}$$

The solition of equation (5) is given in [7].

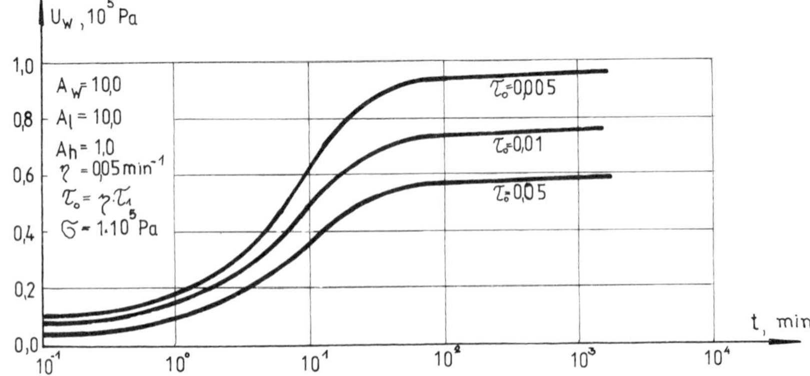

Figure 1. Theoretical curves $u_w(t)$ in a closed system

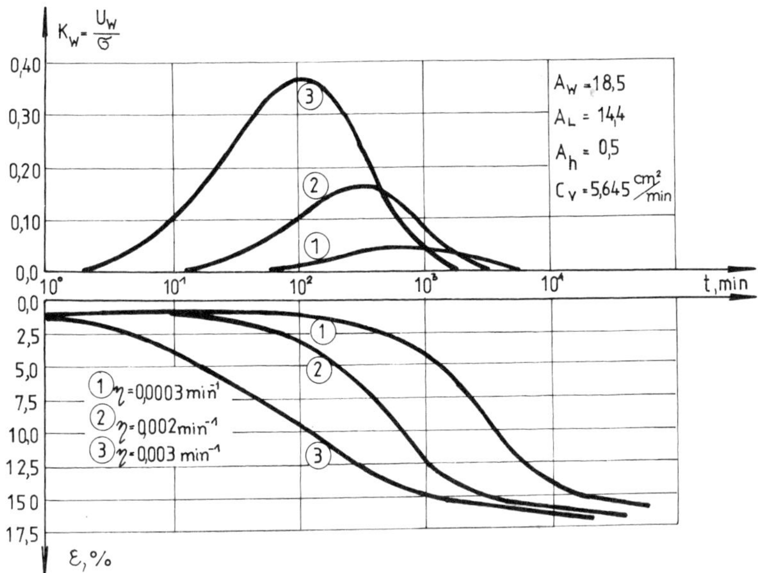

Figure 2. Theoretical curves of the pore pressure coefficient $K_w(t)$ and for relative deformation $\varepsilon(t)$ for different values of the parameter η.

The results, obtained by the theoretical solution of the pore pressure coefficient K_w and the relative deformation ε are presented on Figure 2.

In a closed system (undrained condition) the pore pressure function is determined from the following homogenous differential equation:

$$u_w''(t_n) + (1 + \beta_1 + \frac{\eta \beta_h}{t_n})\ u_w'(t_n) = 0; \qquad (7)$$

where $t_n = \eta t$.

The solution of equation (7) is given in [6]. The graphics of the function $u_w(t)$ in the closed system for different values of the "age" parameter are given on Figure 1.

With observing the principle of the effective pressures, the equation for the horizontal stresses σ_x is:

$$\sigma_x(t) = u_w(t) + K_o'[\sigma_z - u_w(t)]; \qquad (8)$$

in which $K_o' = \frac{\sigma'_x}{\sigma'_z}$ is the coefficient of lateral pressure at rest.

In (8), we accept, that the coefficient of lateral pressure of the fluid is of unit value. Then, the coefficient of the lateral pressure for nearly saturated clayed soils will change in accordance with the following:

$$K_o(t) = K_o + (1 - K_o')K_w(t) \qquad (9)$$

EXPERIMENTAL RESULTS

The one-dimensional stress state is examined by using a oedometer with vertical deformable walls [4]. Cylindrical soil samples with different heights (50 to 200 mm) can be tested by helpof the oedometer, simultaneously measuring the vertical deformations, the pore pressure and the lateral pressure. The main parts of the oedometer are shown on Figure 3. Using this apparatus continuous compression tests may be carried out on different types of soils: clay, loam (sandy clay), loess[9], silt [8], tailings [1] and others.

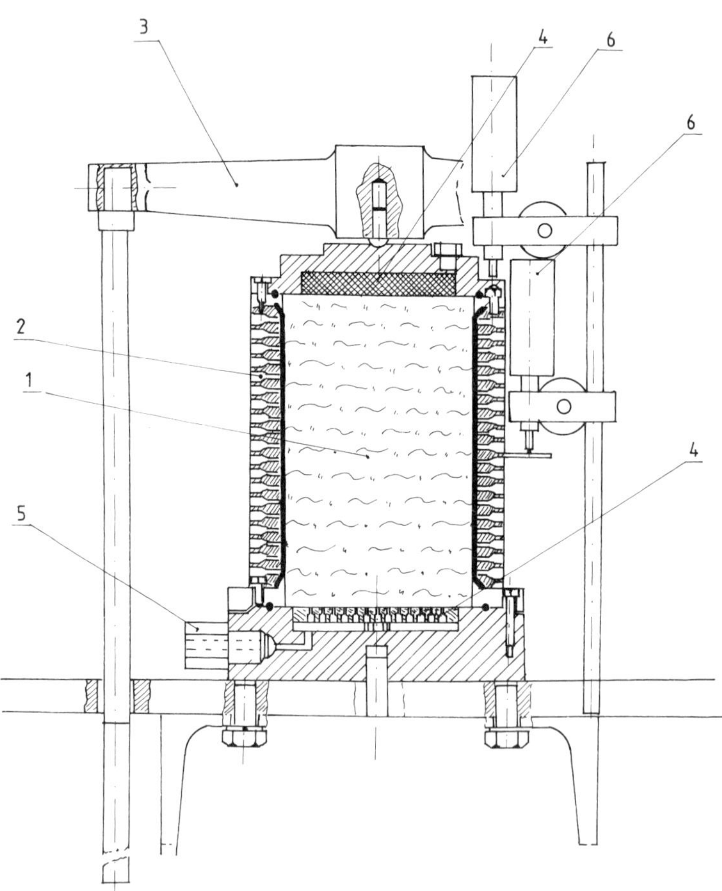

Figure 3. Oedometer without friction along the circular area of the sample: 1. Soil sample 2. Deformable walls (elastic gum cover and light metal rings-meters of the lateral pressure) 3. Loading frame 4. Drainage tiles 5. Pore pressure meter 6. Vertical deformations meters.

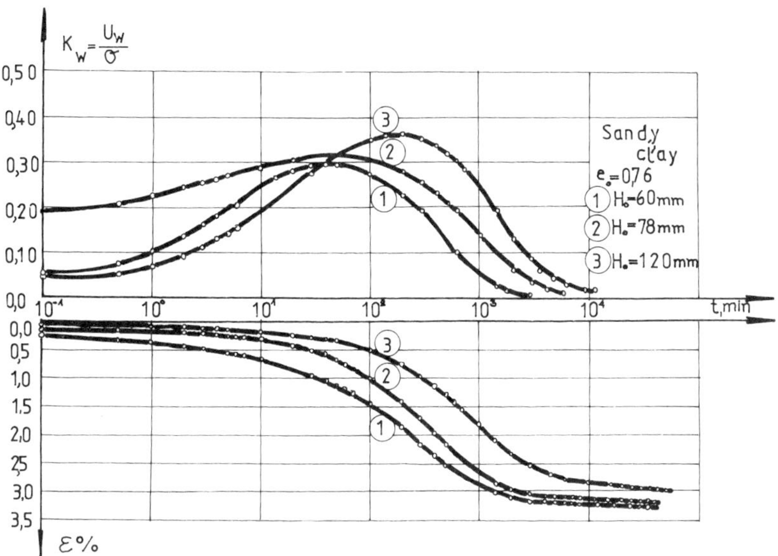

Figure 4. Experimental curves $K_w(t)$ and $\varepsilon(t)$ for a sandy clay with different heights of the samples.

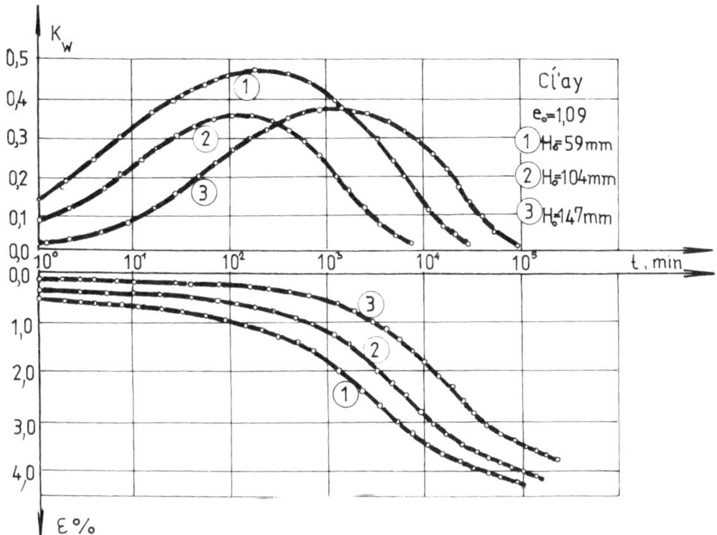

Figure 5. Experimental curves $K_w(t)$ and $\varepsilon(t)$ for a clay with different heights of the soil samples.

Figures 4. and 5. show the experimental curves of sandy clay and clay soils with different heights of the soil samples. Similiarity can be observed in the theoretical and experimental dependences. After a successful selection of the physical parameters according to the method elaborated [5, 13] a good similiarity between the theoretical and experimental results has been observed.

The analysis of the theoretical dependences and experimental results have confirmed the existence of an important influence of the layer thickness upon the stress-strain state of saturated clayed soils with creep and ageing characteristics.

The ageing character [11, 13] is considered as being one of the structural changes in the ageing material (tyxotropic strengthening of clayed soil), which depend solely on some internal processes taking place independently from the active pressures. This fact can explain the decrease in the relative deformation for different heights of the soil samples (layer thicknesses). The increase in layer height leads to an increase in the intensity of the pore pressure and the time for its dispersal is consequently also increased. This reduces the speed of the effective pressure increase. The reduction in the effective pressure induces a decrease in the speed of deformations. Simultaneously, the soil skeleton is strenghtened (ageing occurs) and the relative deformation decreases. The greater the layer height, the greater the possibility for increasing the contacts between the soil particles, which have been loosened at time of loading. This fact, theoretically explained [7] and [12], and confirmed experimentally [7] is of principal importance for predicting the stress-strain state of saturated soil massifs under natural conditions.

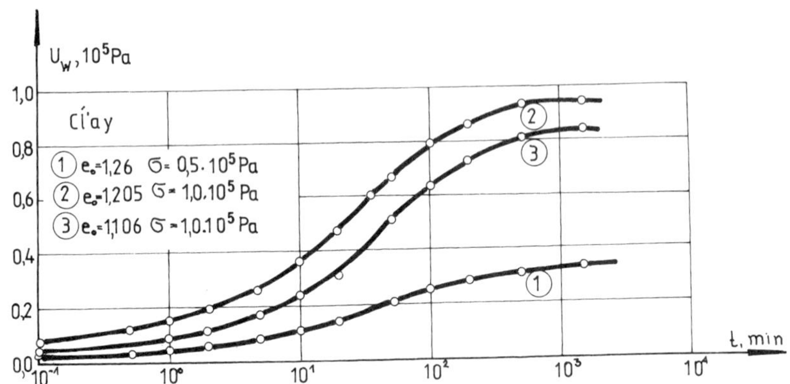

Figure 6. Experimental curves $u_w(t)$ in a closed system

The experimental results under the conditions of a closed system, presented on Figure 6., show that the stress state depends on the elapse of time also. This problem is important when calculating the stability of soil massifs subjected to short-time static loading. In such cases, the initial values of the pore pressure may be relatively lower, as compared to that in a stabilized state. This means that the soil skeleton may bear the greater part of the loading. Therefore, the shear strength of clayed soil and its bearing capacity will increase.

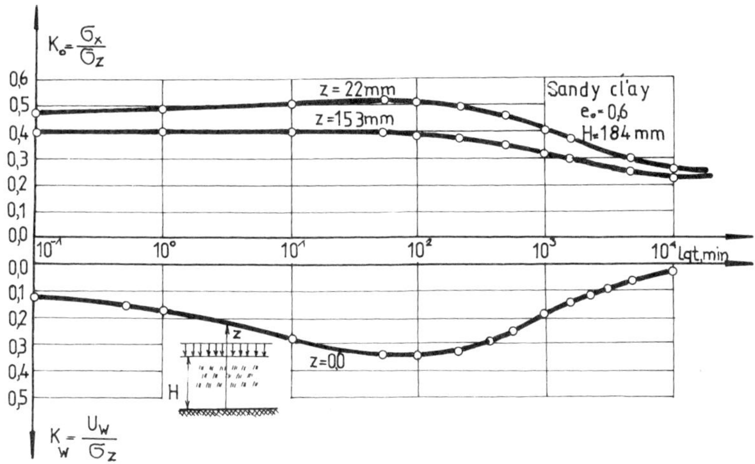

Figure 7. Experimental curves $K_o(t)$ and $K_w(t)$ for a sandy clay in an open system.

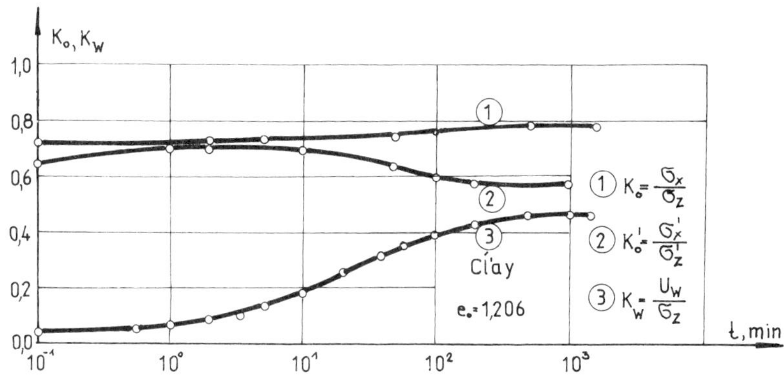

Figure 8. Experimental curves $K_o(t)$ and $K_w(t)$ for sandy clay in an open system

Figures 7. and 8. show the experimental results for the coefficient of pore pressure K_w and the coefficient of lateral pressure at rest K_o in an open system and in a closed system. It can be seen that in the open system (with the presence of drainage) the coefficient of lateral stress changes over time and the graphics of $K_o(t)$ function is similar to that of $K_w(t)$, depending on the height of the layer. In a closed system, the influence of time upon K_o is less expressed.

The experimental results, shown on Figure 9. are also important in the sense that they display that the inter-dependence between full pressures $\sigma_x = f(\sigma_z)$ is non linear, while function $\sigma'_x = f(\sigma'_z)$ is linear in the effective pressure. This fact shows that with lack of pore pressure during the process of compression one can use the theory of linear-deformable media in order to evaluate the stress-strain state of the clayed soils.

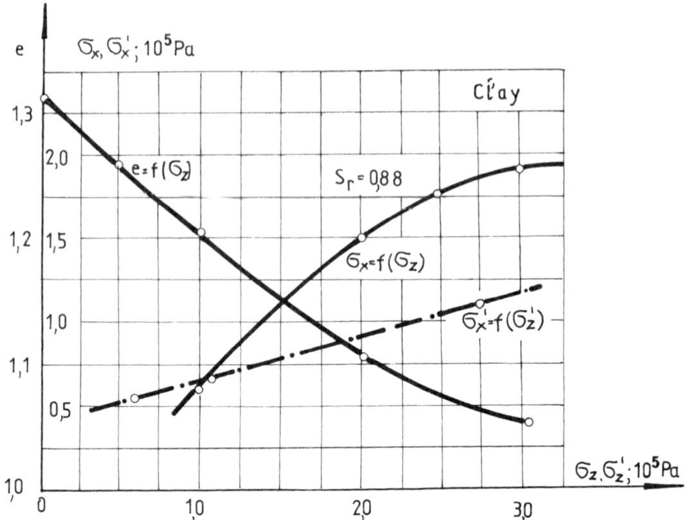

Figure 9. Experimental curves $e = f(\sigma)$; $\sigma_x=f(\sigma_z)$ and $\sigma'_x=f(\sigma'_z)$ in a closed system

CONCLUSION

These experimental investigations conducted show the extreme character of function $u_w(t)$ and the change of relative deformation $\varepsilon(t)$ proportional to the time logarhythm at $u_w(t) \to 0$. This can be theoretically explained when taking into account the nearly saturation and the viscosities of the soil skeleton according to the thoery of linear creep. Thus are presented possibilities for explaining the unstable stress state in a closed system and the change over time in the coefficient of a lateral pressure at rest.

REFERENCES

[1] Abadjiev, C.B., T.S. Germanov, G.T.Markov. Determination of tailings consolidation for a high spigotted upstream tailings dam. Proc.9th ECSFE, v.4.1, Dublin, 1987, pp 335-357

[2] Arutjunjan, N.H. Some problems on the theory of creeping M., 1952 (in Russian)

[3] Florin V.A. Soil Mechanics, vol.II, M.,1961 (in Russian)

[4] Germanov T. Aedometer without lateral friction. Patishta, Sofia, 1978, pp 18-20 (in Bulgarian)

[5] Germanov T. La determination des parametres du fluage dans les soils argileux. Annuaire de l' institut d' arcgitecture et de genie civil, vol.27, Fasc.4, Sofia, 1978,pp 23-34 (in Bulgarian)

[6] Germanov T. On the problem of bearing capacities of the soil base under short-timed static loading. Stroitelstvo No.7, Sofia, 1978, pp 20-22 (in Bulgarian)

[7] Germanov T. Influence of the rheological properties of the soil skeleton on the deformations of multiphase clay soil. Technical Ideas, Bulgarian Academy of Sciences No.3, Sofia 1979, pp 69-74 (in Bulgarian)

[8] Germanov T. Z.Ter-Martirosyan. The influence of the thickness of compacted layer on the stress and strain state of the multi-phase clay soils. Proc. 6th Danube European CSMFE, vol.2, Varna, 1980, pp 89-100

[9] Germanov T. B. Kirov. Influence of waste waters on soil consolidation. Proc. 12th ICSMFE, 9/C/7, San Francisco, 1985, pp 2407-2408

[10] Germanov T. One-dimensional consolidation at the alternuate limit of the layer. Annuaire de l' Inst. d' arch. et de genie civil, vol.32, Fasc.4, Sofia, 1986, pp 29-36 (in Bulgarian)

[11] Rabotnov, Yu.N. Creep structure elements. Science Publishing House, Moskow, 1966 (in Bulgarian)

[12] Tsytovich, N.A., Z.G. Ter-Martirosyan, K.R. Kulkarni. Consolidation of time-hardening soil. Proc. 4th Danube European SCMFE, Bled, 1974,pp 247-253

[13] Tsytovich, N.A., Z.G. Ter-Martirosyan. Applied Geomechanics, M., 1981 (in Russian)

THE TIME DEPENDENT BEHAVIOUR OF NORMALLY CONSOLIDATED CLAY IN THICK HOLLOW CYLINDER TESTS

W F ANDERSON, I C PYRAH
Department of Civil and Structural Engineering
The University
Mappin Street, Sheffield S1 3JD, UK

L S PANG
Scott Wilson Kirkpatrick and Partners
Bayheath House, Rosehill West,
Chesterfield, Derbyshire S40 1JF, UK

F HAJI-ALI
Department of Civil and Structural Engineering
University of Malaya
Kuala Lumpur 22-11, Malaysia

ABSTRACT

Pressuremeter tests in normally consolidated clays have been simulated in the laboratory by expanding a thick hollow cylinder of soil, prepared with known stress history, using an increasing internal pressure and keeping the external pressure constant. Different stress control and strain control expansion techniques have been used, and in addition to stress and strain measurements at the cavity boundary, pore water pressures at the cavity boundary and within the soil mass have been monitored. The experimental data shows similar trends to finite element predictions based on critical state soil mechanics with the inclusion of both consolidation (Biot) and creep (Singh and Mitchell). The results presented form a useful database for assessing the performance of rheological models.

INTRODUCTION

The load-deformation behaviour of a fine grained soil is inherently time dependent. Under most loading conditions the increase in stress is non-uniform resulting in different pore water pressures at different points within the soil mass. This variation causes pore fluid movements resulting in time dependent deformations. To these deformations, due to changes in effective stress, must be added further deformations due to the time dependent properties of the soil skeleton e.g. creep.

The results of pressuremeter tests in fine grained soils are invariably analysed assuming that undrained conditions exist in the soil around the pressuremeter, and that, in the relatively short time (10-30 minutes) it takes to carry out the test, creep is insignificant and can be ignored. However, comparative field studies using the pressuremeter in clay deposits have shown that time dependent phenomena do influence the test results although the extent of this influence is not yet fully understood.

As part of a study of time dependent effects in pressuremeter tests a detailed laboratory scale simulation has been carried out. Thick hollow cylinders of clay have been expanded using increasing internal pressure applied in different ways and at different rates. The results of some of these tests are presented here so that they may be used for the validation of different rheological models.

TEST EQUIPMENT AND PROCEDURES

The tests were carried out in a large diameter triaxial cell which has been modified to accommodate hollow cylindrical specimens with nominal inside and outside diameters of 25mm and 150mm, and a height of 150mm as shown in Figure 1.

Beds of clay were prepared by one-dimensional consolidation of slurries mixed at twice the liquid limit. At the end of consolidation these were sampled to give 150mm diameter specimens; a 25mm concentric hole was subsequently drilled through each specimen. The specimen was mounted in the modified triaxial cell and reconsolidated isotropically using internal and external water pressures equal to the vertical stress applied during the initial one dimensional consolidation (i.e. 200 kN/m^2).

At the end of reconsolidation the drainage valves were closed and the top platen rigidly fixed in position so as to maintain a globally undrained radial plane strain condition during expansion. The expansion test was carried out with the outer boundary of the specimen subjected to a stress equal to the consolidation pressure.

Stress-control expansion tests were carried out by applying a constant increment of pressure for a fixed time interval. Magnitudes of pressure increment used in different tests were 10 kN/m^2, 20 kN/m^2 and 30 kN/m^2,

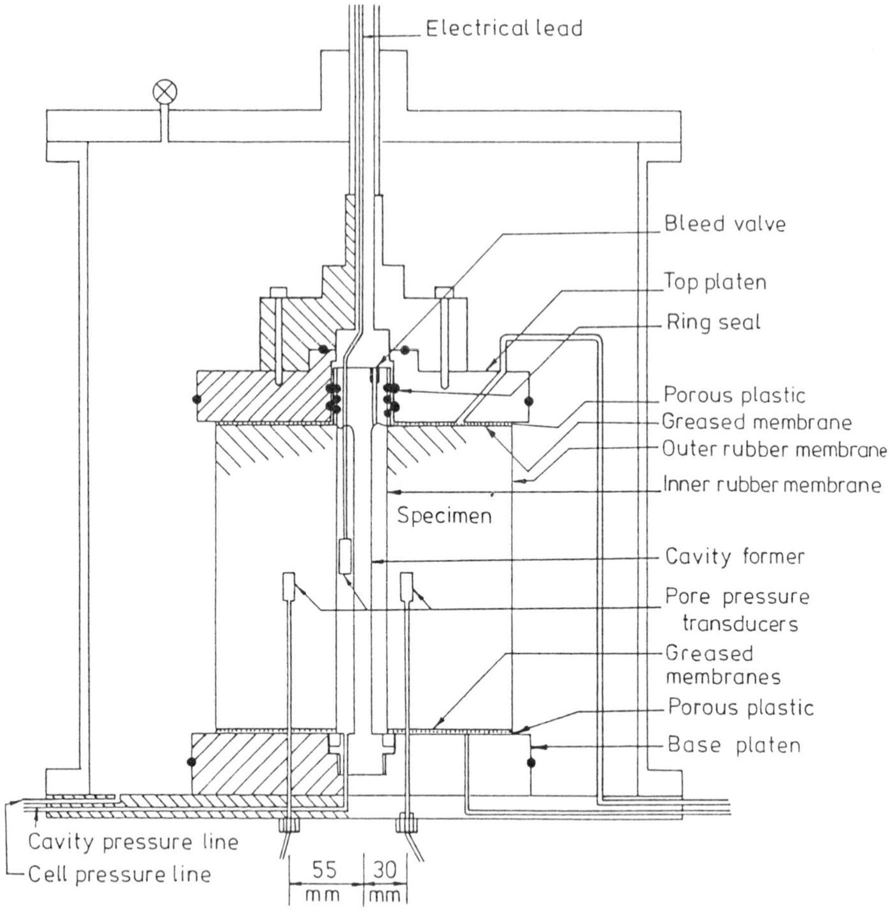

Figure 1. Equipment for hollow cylinder cavity expansion tests

with each increment being applied for 1 minute. Another series of tests was carried out in which a fixed pressure increment of 10 kN/m² was applied, but different holding items were used in each test. The holding times used were 30 seconds, 1 minute, 2 minutes and 'until creep ceased'. The 'creep ceased' criterion was defined as the time when less than 0.005% radial cavity strain was monitored in any 1 minute time interval.

Strain controlled tests were carried out using a commercial pressuremeter control system to provide radial cavity strain rates of 0.2%/minute, 0.4%/minute, 1%/minute, 2%/minute and 4%/minute.

During the expansion tests pore water pressures were measured at the cavity boundary and within the soil at the positions shown in Figure 1.

The two transducers for monitoring pore water pressures in the soil mass were installed in the clay slurry prior to consolidation. Initial response times in the stress-controlled tests were less than 10 seconds and improvement of the monitoring system led to response times of 4 to 5 seconds in the strain controlled tests.

MATERIAL PROPERTIES

Although three different clays have been used in this study and trends summarised elsewhere [1], [2], the results presented in this paper will be confined to pottery clay. Conventional classification tests, effective stress triaxial compression tests and oedometer tests have been carried out to give the basic soil properties and critical state parameters; These are presented in Table 1.

TABLE 1
Properties of pottery clay

Index Properties	
Liquid limit, %	40
Plastic limit, %	23
Plasticity index, %	17
% finer than 2 μm	45
Activity	0.38
Critical State Parameters	
κ	0.025
λ	0.101
e_{cs}	1.265
M	1.10
G , kN/m^2	6300
k , m/s	3.38×10^{-10}
Creep Parameters	
A , %/min	5.25×10^{-3}
α	5.4
m	1.00

In addition, series of undrained triaxial creep tests have been carried out at constant, but different, deviatoric stress levels and the results interpreted using the Singh and Mitchell [3] creep model. This is defined in terms of three parameters, A, α and m and the empirical equation giving the axial creep strain rate (R) in terms of the deviator stress level ($\bar{D}$) and time (t) is

$$R = A\,[\exp(\bar{\alpha}.\bar{D})]\left[\frac{t_1}{t}\right]^m$$

where $\bar{D} = \dfrac{(\sigma_1 - \sigma_3)}{(\sigma_1 - \sigma_3)_{failure}}$

$\bar{\alpha} = \alpha\,(\sigma_1 - \sigma_3)_{failure}$

t_1 = reference time, usually equal to unity

t = time (period over which deviator stress has been acting)

Values of the creep parameters are also reported in Table 1.

RESULTS

In the stress control expansion tests the increase in volume of the cylindrical cavity above its original value (73.6 cm^3) was monitored at the end of each pressure increment prior to raising the pressure to its next value. Figure 2 shows the expansion curves obtained with the pressure increment held constant at 10 kN/m^2 but the holding time varied. The

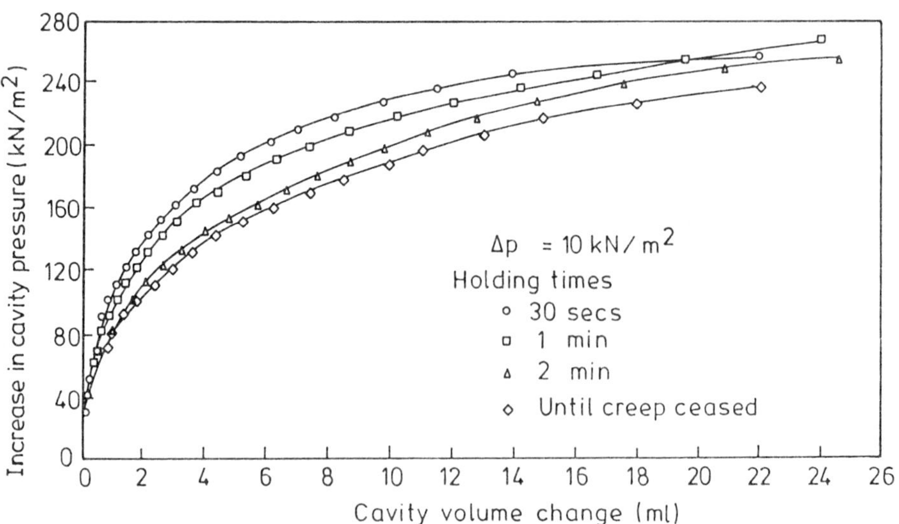

Figure 2. Expansion curves for stress control tests with different holding times

cavity pressure is plotted as the increase in pressure above the consolidation pressure (200 kN/m²). Figure 3 shows the expansion curves obtained using a constant holding time of 1 minute, but varying the magnitude of the pressure increment.

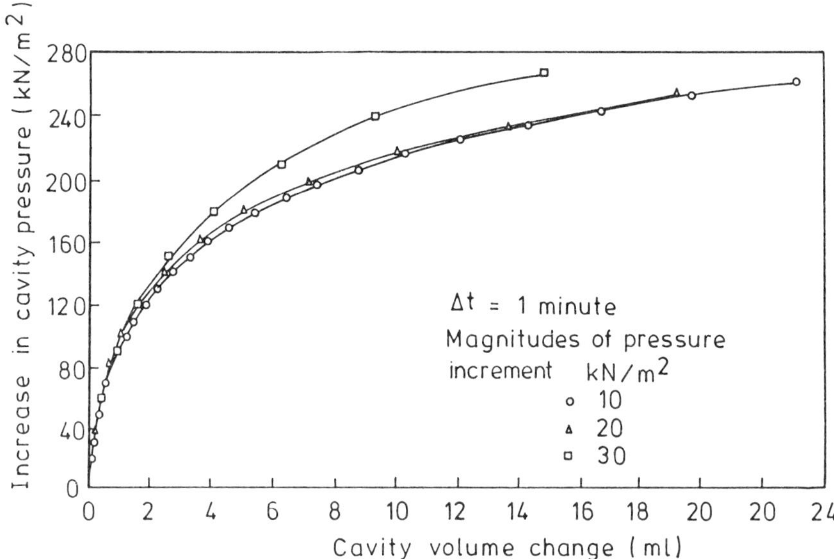

Figure 3. Expansion curves for stress control tests with different pressure increments

From Figures 2 and 3 it can be seen that time dependent phenomena are affecting the expansion curves. Pressuremeter expansion curves are usually interpreted to obtain shear stress-strain curves. Derived values of shear modulus and undrained shear strength from these cavity expansion tests have been found to vary depending on the magnitude of pressure increment and holding time [1].

Pore water pressures monitored at the cavity boundary at the end of each pressure increment during the stress control tests are plotted in Figures 4 and 5. From these it can be seen that the faster the expansion, i.e. the shorter the holding time or the greater the pressure increment, the greater the excess pore water pressure monitored at the end of each pressure increment. This difference can be attributed to local consolidation around the expanding cavity for even in the fastest test (Δt = 30 secs) dissipation of excess pore water pressure occurs at the cavity boundary (Figure 6).

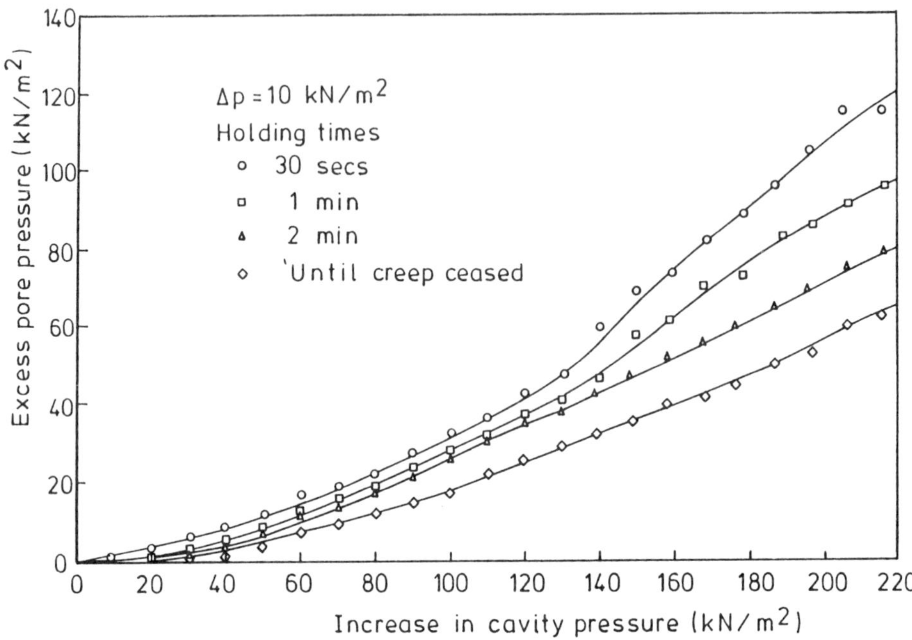

Figure 4. Excess pore water pressure measured at the cavity boundary for stress control tests with different holding times

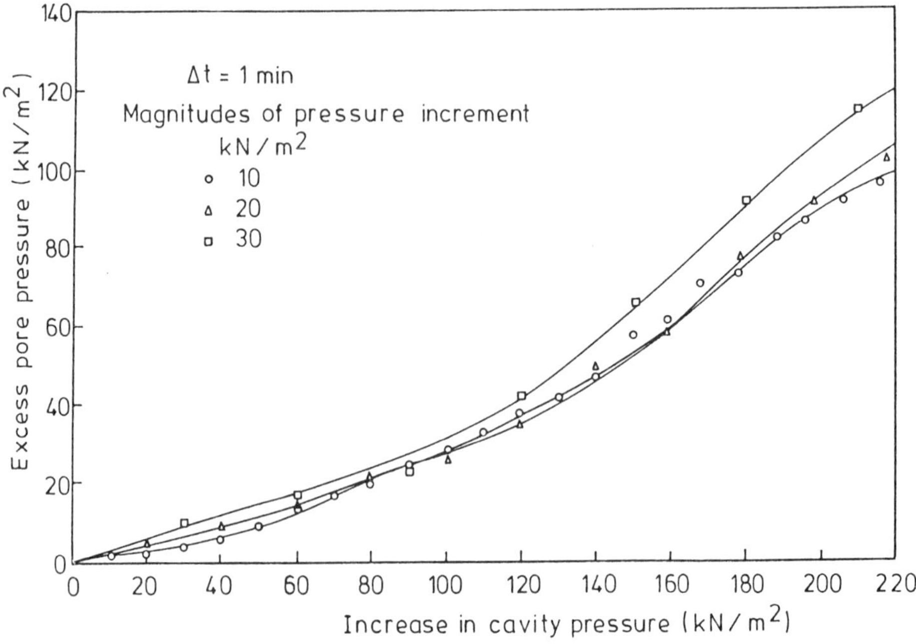

Figure 5. Excess pore water pressure measured at the cavity boundary for stress control tests with different pressure increments

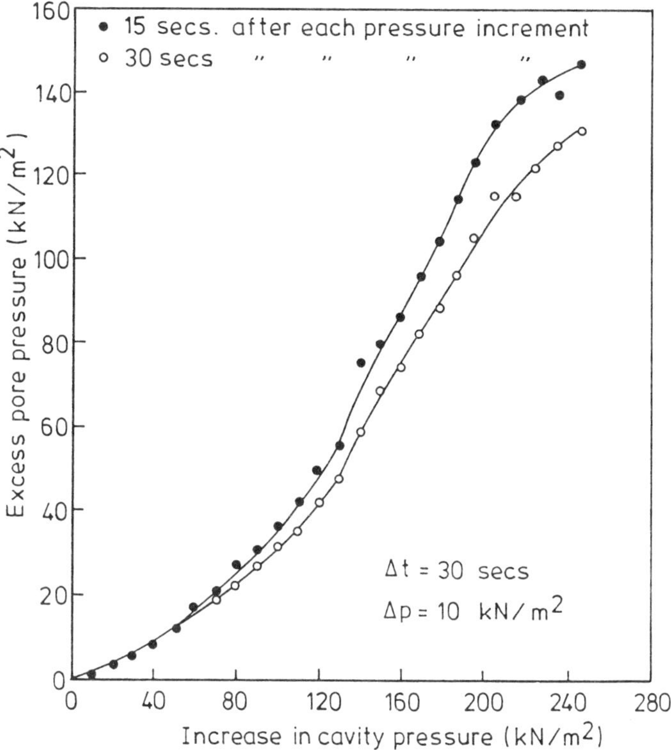

Figure 6. Dissipation of excess pore water pressure at the cavity boundary

The build up of excess pore water pressure throughout the specimen was a function of the radial distance from the expanding cavity and the expansion technique used, as shown in Figures 7 and 8.

In the strain control tests the cavity expansion was monitored by measuring the radial movement of the cavity boundary at three points at the mid-height using strain gauged feelers; the expansion curves are plotted in Figure 9 as increase in pressure against radial cavity strain. As with the stress control tests, the excess pore water pressure measured at the cavity wall depended on the rate of strain, with the highest excess pore water pressures being generated in the fastest test as shown in Figure 10. The variation of pore water pressure across the specimen also depended on strain rate, the values for the fastest and slowest tests being shown in Figure 11.

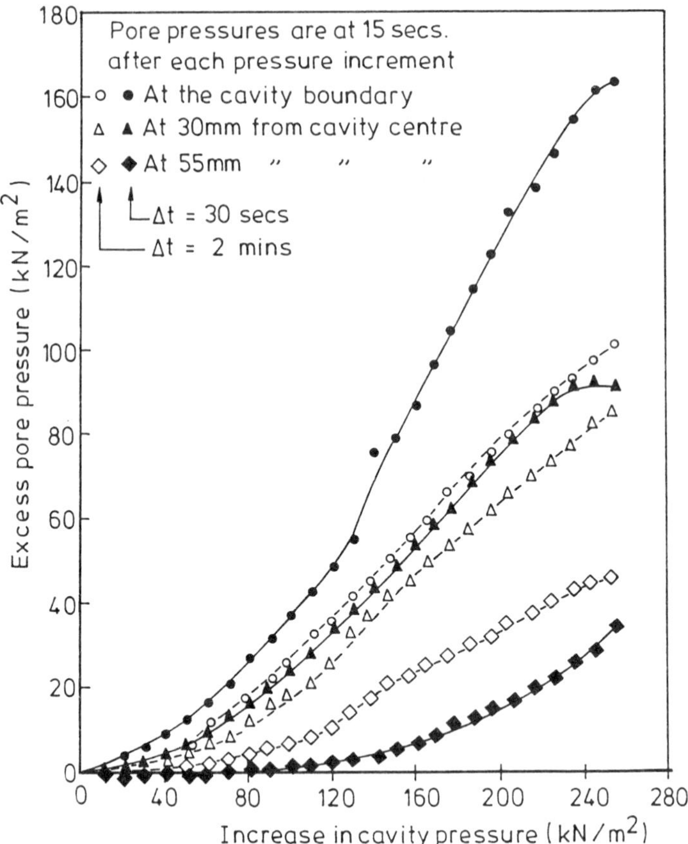

Figure 7. Build up excess pore water pressure at different positions with the specimen in stress control tests carried out with different holding times (Δp = 10 kN/m²)

NUMERICAL MODELLING

The numerical analyses were carried out using a modified version of the finite element program CAMFE, developed by Carter [4]; the program was extended to include creep as well as consolidation. Details of its use for simulating stress control and strain control cavity expansion has been reported elsewhere [5,6].

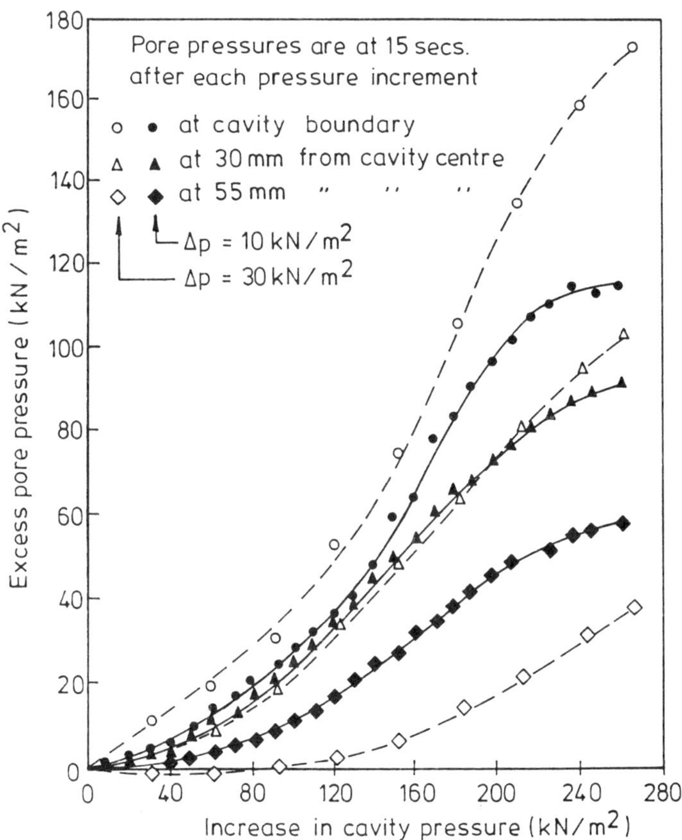

Figure 8. Build up of excess pore water pressure at different positions within the specimen in stress control tests carried out with different pressure increments (Δt = 1 minute)

Figure 12 shows a comparison of experimental results for one stress control test with numerical predictions made using different assumptions about time dependent phenomena. The closest prediction to the experimental data at higher strain levels is when it is assumed that both consolidation and undrained deviatoric creep are occurring during expansion. For all stress control tests the trends of the numerical predictions based on consolidation plus creep deairing were identical to those found in the experiments, but the absolute values were different [1]. The effects of consolidation are to increase the displacement of the cavity boundary and give an increase in soil strength. Creep effects, however, dominate the later stages of the test and appear to have the opposite effect on the deduced undrained strength.

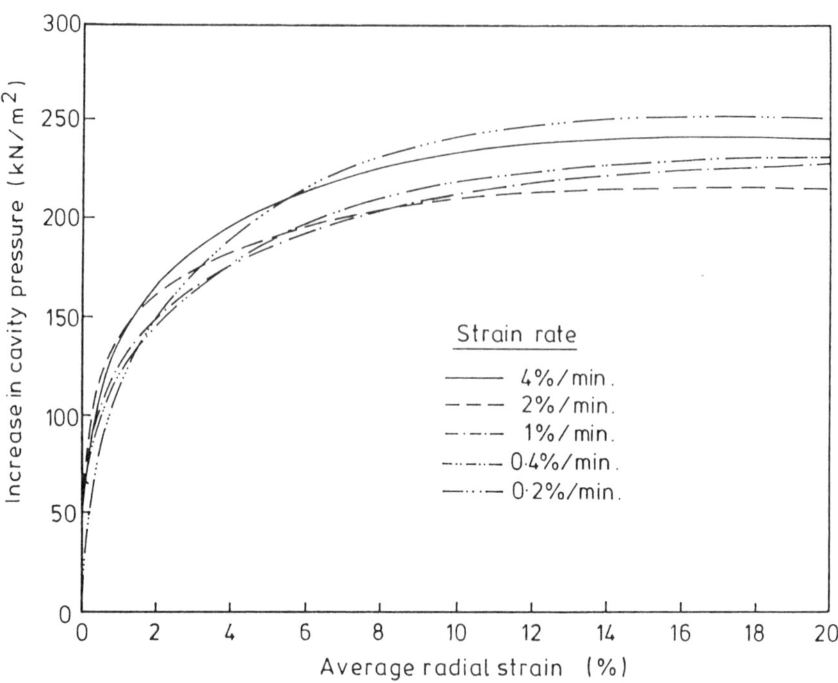

Figure 9. Expansion curves for strain control tests

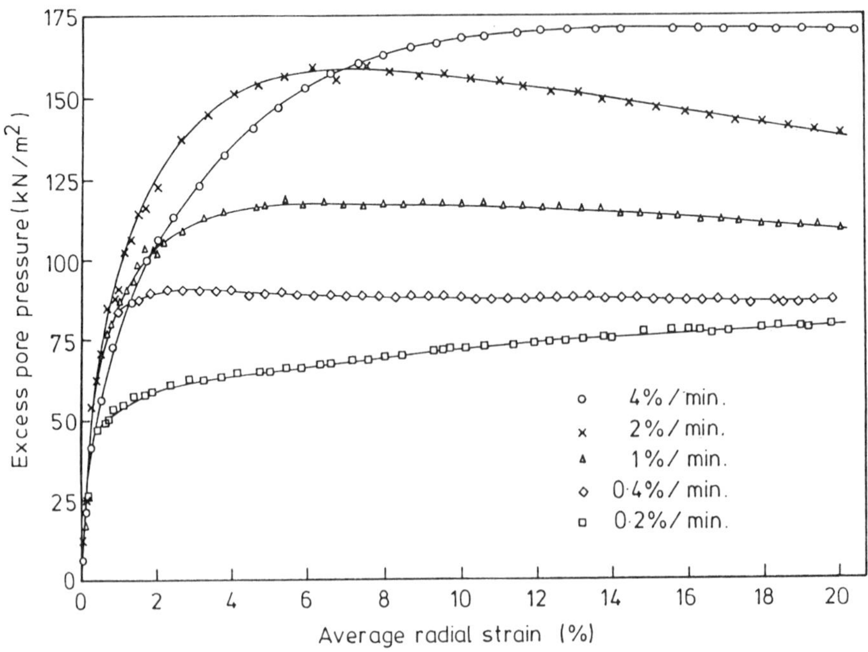

Figure 10. Excess pore water pressure measured at the cavity boundary in strain control tests

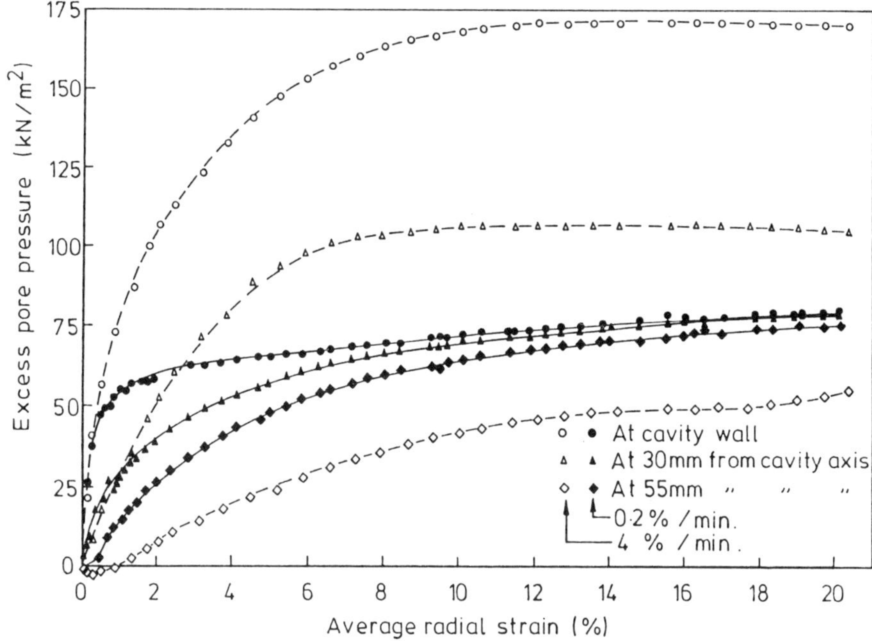

Figure 11. Build up of excess pore water pressure at different positions within the specimen in strain control tests

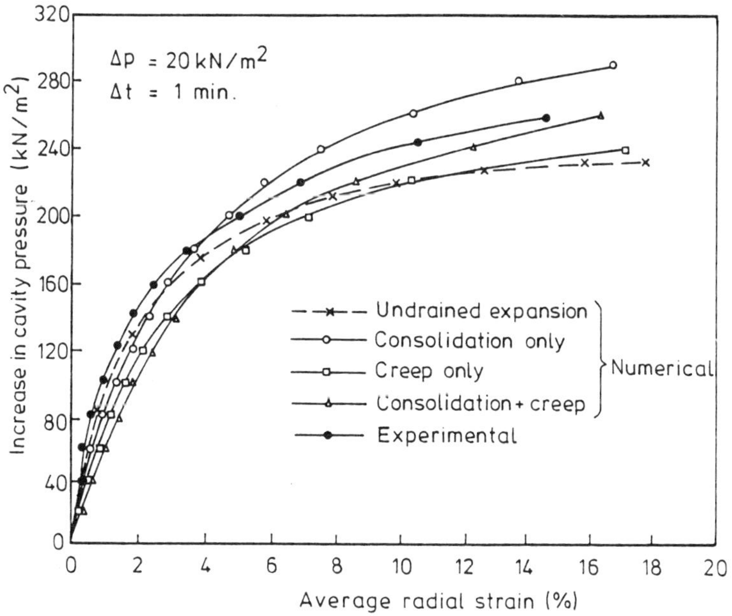

Figure 12. Comparison of experimental expansion curve and numerical predictions for a stress control test

When experimental and numerical results are compared for the strain control expansion tests the agreement is not so good as for the stress control tests. However it is clear that in the strain control tests consolidation is a more dominant phenomenon than creep [6]. Comparison between the experimental and numerically generated pore water pressures for the strain control tests indicates similar trends, but the gradients across the specimen are much greater in the predictions than in the experiments (Figure 13).

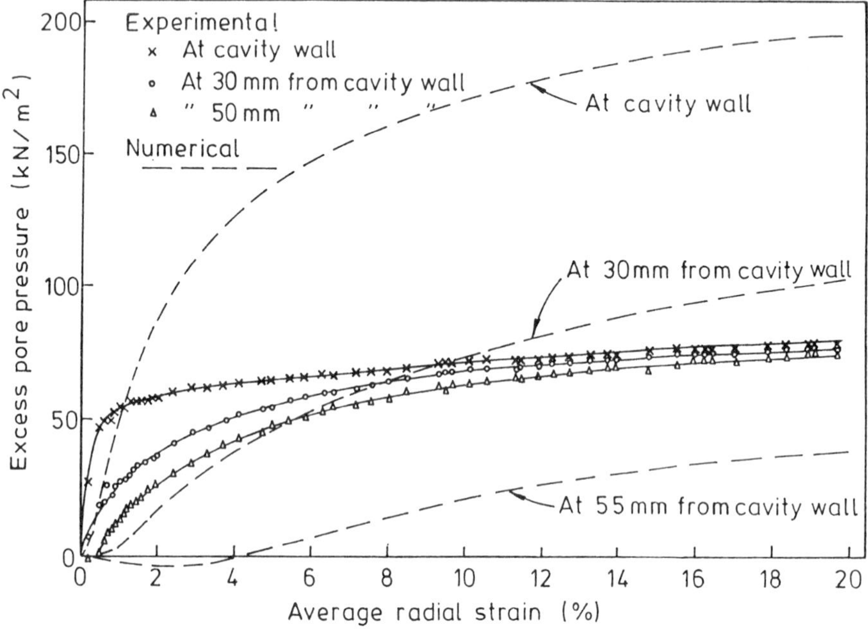

Figure 13. Comparison of experimental pore water pressures and numerical predictions for a strain control test (0.2%/min)

Discussion

Both experimental and numerical results have shown that plane strain expansion of a 25mm diameter cylindrical cavity in a clay, even if carried out reasonably quickly, cannot be considered undrained. The local consolidation which occurs affects the results, as does deviatoric creep, and these phenomena combine to affect the expansion curve which is obtained when different expansion techniques are used. Figure 14 shows the different expansion curves obtained when identical specimens of pottery clay were taken to failure in similar times but using different expansion techniques. The implications of this for standardisation of pressuremeter tests are discussed elsewhere [1].

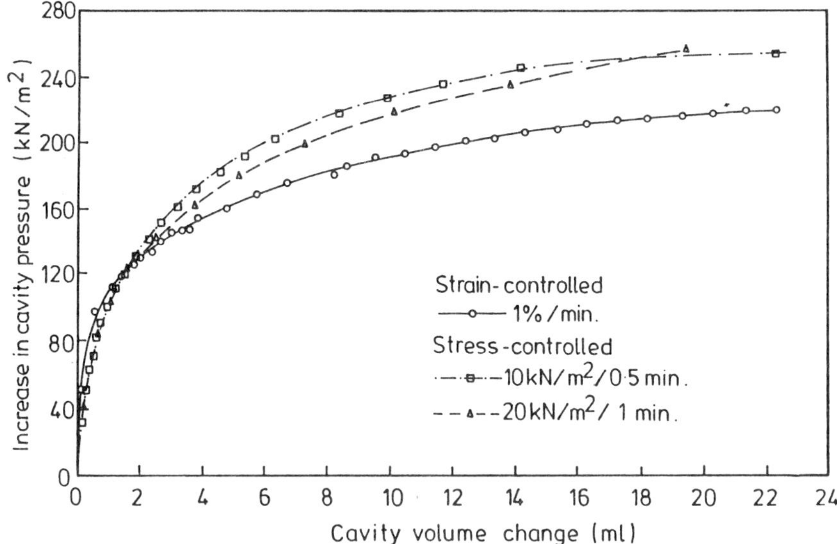

Figure 14. Comparison of experimental results obtained from similar specimens tested using different expansion techniques

The soil model used in this study to predict time dependent behaviour is relatively simple in that consolidation and creep are assumed to be two independent processes. More sophisticated rheological models,taking into account the interdependence of these time dependent processes, may prove more realistic; the data presented here may be used to calibrate these models.

REFERENCES

1. Anderson, W.F., Pyrah, I.C. and Haji Ali, F., Rate effects in pressuremeter tests in clays. Proc. ASCE, 1987, **113**, **GT11**, 1344-1358.
2. Anderson, W.F., Pyrah, I.C. and Pang, L.S., Strain rate effects in the pressuremeter test. Proc. Int. Symposium on Goetechnical Engineering of Soft Soils, Mexico City, August 1987.
3. Singh, A. and Mitchell, J.K., General stress-strain-time function for soils. Proc. ASCE, 1968, **94**, **SM1**, 21-46.
4. Carter, J.P., CAMFE A computer program for the analysis of a cylindrical cavity expansion in soil. Report CUED/SOILS/TR52, University of Cambridge, 1978.

5. Pyrah, I.C., Anderson, W.F. and Haji-Ali, F., The interpretation of pressuremeter tests - Time effects for fine grained soils. Proc. 5th Int. Conf. on Numerical Methods in Geomechanics, Nagoya, 1985, 1629-1636.

6. Pyrah, I.C., Anderson, W.F. and Pang, L.S., Effects of test procedure on constant rate of strain pressuremeter tests in clay. Proc. 6th Int. Conf. on Numerical Methods in Geomechanics, Innsbruck, 1988, 647-652.

RHEOLOGICAL REGULARITIES IN FROZEN SOIL MECHANICS AND THEIR APPLICATION IN ENGINEERING CALCULATIONS

S.S.VYALOV
Moscow Civil Engineering Institute
Yaroslavskoye road, 26, 129337 Moscow, USSR

M.E.SLEPAK
Research Institute of Bases and Underground Structures, Gosstroy USSR
Pushkinskaya Str., 26, 103828 Moscow, USSR

ABSTRACT

The rheological constitutive equations of frozen soil derived using hardening creep theory are reported. In contrast to traditional equations the proposed equations describe simultaneously the creep deformation development and the long-term strength decreasing. These equations relate to the known regularities of frozen soil deformation including the availability of all three creep stages with progressive flow stage resulting in failure, the effects of positive and negative dilatation, etc. In under ultimate region the proposed equations are simplified and result in the usual power form. Computer realization of proposed equations is done on the basis of finite element method. It is shown that the utilization of simplified modification of these equations makes the problem easier through decreasing of its dimensions.

INTRODUCTION

Frozen soils have very marked rheological properties, i.e. they are able to develop creep deformations and to decrease due to this fact their strength (1,2,3). Many problems of engineering geocryology are connected with the prediction of frozen soil stress-strain behaviour. A calculation of bases and foundations, an analysis of slope stability on permafrost, a calculation of mine ice-soil retaining structures, etc. are the examples of such problems, which are usually solved using some rheological models. Many rheological models are known to-day (4-8). However most of them are too complicated and large experimental work is needed to determine the model parameters. It is of great interest to construct such rheological model, which describes the general regularities of frozen soil behaviour and at the same time contains minimum amount of experimentally determined parameters. It is shown below, that this problem can be solved using some of the technical theories of creep, namely the hardening creep theory.

GENERAL ASSUMPTIONS

Most of technical theories of creep assume the strain tensor ε_{ij} to be the sum of instantaneous-elastic strain ε_{ij}^{e} and completely irreversible creep strain ε_{ij}^{c}:

$$\varepsilon_{ij} = \varepsilon_{ij}^{e} + \varepsilon_{ij}^{c}. \tag{1}$$

The ε_{ij}^{e} tensor is connected with the stress tensor σ_{ij} by Hook's law

$$\sigma_{ij} = A_{ijk\ell}\,\varepsilon_{k\ell}^{e}, \tag{2}$$

where $A_{ijk\ell}$ - is the tensor of elastic constants.

The creep strain rate $\dot{\varepsilon}_{ij}^{c}$ is determined by the equations of creep hardening theory which in the most general way are given as follows (9):

$$\dot{\varepsilon}_{ij}^{c} = f_{ij}(\theta, \sigma_{k\ell}, q_1, \ldots, q_n), \tag{3}$$

where θ - is frozen soil temperature;

$q_1, \ldots, q_n$ - set of hardening parameters.

For isotropic soils the relation (3) yields the dependence on stress invariants. According to (5) in equations (3) we consider the dependence on the first stress tensor invariant and the second deviator invariant. For simplicity we assume n to be 1 and q_1 to be (9):

$$q_1 = \bar{\gamma}_i = \int_0^t \hat{\gamma}_i\,dt, \tag{4}$$

where $\hat{\gamma}_i$ - is intensity of shear creep strain rate.

Taking into account the above assumptions the equations (3) can be presented as follows:

$$\dot{\varepsilon}_{ij}^{c} = \dot{\varepsilon}^{c}\delta_{ij} + \dot{\bar{\gamma}}_i/(2\tau_i)(\sigma_{ij} - \sigma\delta_{ij}), \tag{5}$$

where $\dot{\varepsilon}^c = \frac{1}{3}\dot{\varepsilon}^c_v$;

$\dot{\varepsilon}^c_v$ - volume creep strain rate;

σ - mean hydrostatic pressure;

τ_i - tangential stress intensity;

δ_{ij} - Kroneker's symbols.

Two unknown functions $\dot{\bar{\gamma}}_i$ and $\dot{\varepsilon}^c$ determing shear and volume creep strain rates consequently are given in the equations (5).

SHEAR CREEP EQUATIONS

$\dot{\bar{\gamma}}_i$ is assumed to be the following function:

$$\dot{\bar{\gamma}}_i = \frac{\alpha A^{1/\alpha}}{\bar{\gamma}_i^{1/\alpha - 1}}\left(1 + \left(\frac{\bar{\gamma}_i}{A}\right)^{1/\alpha}\frac{1}{t_f}\right)^2. \tag{6}$$

This function is discussed below and here we note that parameters α, A, t_f in general depend on stresses and temperature. It will be shown that α and A are the deformation parameters, t_f being the parameter of long-term strength. So the equation (6) in contrast to the traditional creep equations covers both the development of creep strains and the frozen soil strength variation with time.

Let us analyse the proposed relation. First of all under conditions of constant temperature and stresses the parameters α, A, t_f are also constant so the equation (6) can be integrated:

$$\bar{\gamma}_i = A\left(\frac{t}{1 - t/t_f}\right)^{\alpha}, \tag{7}$$

where t is the time, hour.

This equation describes the frozen soil creep behaviour under constant stresses and temperature (Fig. 1). If $t \ll t_f$ the equation is simplified giving the usual power form (2-4) (curves 6-8, Fig. 1):

$$\bar{\gamma}_i = A t^{\alpha}. \tag{8}$$

In contrast, if $t \to t_f$ then $\bar{\gamma}_i \to \infty$ (curves 1-3, Fig. 1), then t_f can be identified as time to failure under given stresses. It is easy to find that the second derivative $\ddot{\bar{\gamma}}_i < 0$ while $t < t^* = (1-\alpha)t_f/2$ i.e. the deformation proceeds with a decreasing rate and this corresponds to so called non-steady creep stage (section OA, Fig. 1). When $t = t^*$ then $\ddot{\bar{\gamma}}_i = 0$ i.e. the creep curve is nearly a straight line close to the moment $t = t^*$; this corresponds to steady creep stage with practically constant rate (section AB, Fig. 1). Finally $\ddot{\bar{\gamma}}_i > 0$ if $t^* < t < t_f$ i.e. strain rate continuously increases and the progressive flow stage with failure at $t = t_f$ is simulated (section BC, Fig. 1).

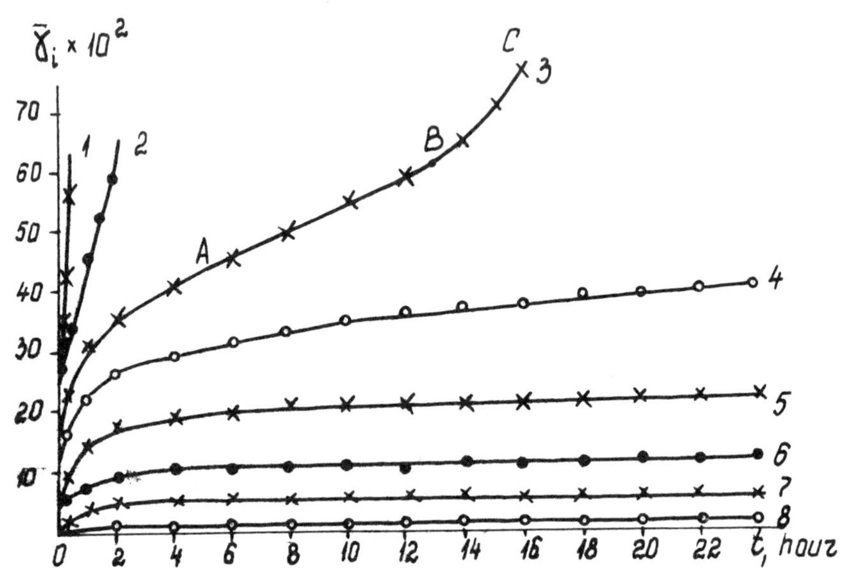

Figure 1. Shear creep curves of frozen kellovey silt at a temperature of -10°C (symmetrical triaxial compression, σ = 30 kg/cm²), τ_i being (kg/cm²): 1-43,3; 2-39,0; 3-34,7; 4-30,3; 5-26,0; 6-21,6; 7-17,3; 8-8,66.

Equation (7) allows to predict the frozen soil creep strains in all three creep stages including the progressive flow stage resulting in failure. Earlier this equation has been used for α = 0,5 (10). Note, that equation (7) is the simplest among all possible equations describing the mentioned effects. Equation (6) generalizes the equation (7) for the changing stresses and temperature.

Tests under various loading conditions can be used for the determination of the parameters of equations (6), (7). The simplest way to determine the above parameters is using data of creep experiments conducted under constant stresses. Numerous experiments (2-5) demonstrate creep curves of frozen soils derived from various tests (uniaxial and triaxial compression, uniaxial extention, simple shear, etc.) having analogous character. For example, we use the frozen Kellovey silt triaxial test results (11) for the determination of parameters of the equations (6), (7). These results were derived using the apparatus of symmetrical triaxial compression at a temperature of -10°C under various hydrostatic pressures σ (15, 30 and 60 kg/cm^2) and various tangential stresses intensities τ_i. The results of these experiments under σ = 30 kg/cm^2 are shown on the Fig. 1. Analogous creep curves occurred under other σ. According to equation (7) the initial creep curves are replotted into "$\lg \gamma_i - \lg(t/(1-t/t_f))$" plots on the Fig. 2. Time to failure t_f which is necessary for the replotting is determined directly from curves of Fig. 1 (for failed samples, curves 1-3) or by extrapolation with use of Vyalov's logarithmic long-term strength equation (1):

$$\tau_i = \beta \ln(t_f/B). \tag{9}$$

As one can see from Fig. 2 experimental curves are straightened in these plots so the validity of equation (7) is justified. Analogous straightening occurred at other σ. Tangents of the derived straight lines slope angles determine the α values, points of intersection with ordinate axis determining the A values. According to derived data α increases with τ_i increasing and decreases with σ increasing. For the first approximation α is assumed to be α_{av} = const, where α_{av} - the average value of α. The dependence of A on τ_i at various σ is shown on the Fig.3.a. As one can see the A value is practically independent from σ. The A dependence on τ_i can be considered as power function

$$A = (\tau_i/a)^{1/m} \tag{10}$$

The relation (10) is justified by straightening of the initial "$A - \tau_i$" curve in the logarithmic plots (see Fig. 3.b).

Test results with the same soil, as in (11) (Kellovey silt, θ = -10°C), are given in (4) for other test conditions (uniaxial compression and extention, simple shear). Analysis of these results similar to given above justifies the validity of the equation (7) for the tests in question. Values of the parameters a, m, α of the equations (7), (10) proved to be close to the values determined from triaxial tests so one can admit the existence of the unique values of these parameters. Mean values of the parameters a, m, α for all test conditions are as follows:

$$a = 60{,}6\ \frac{\text{kg}}{\text{cm}^2}\ \text{hour}^{m\alpha}; \quad m = 0{,}39; \quad \alpha = 0{,}14. \tag{11}$$

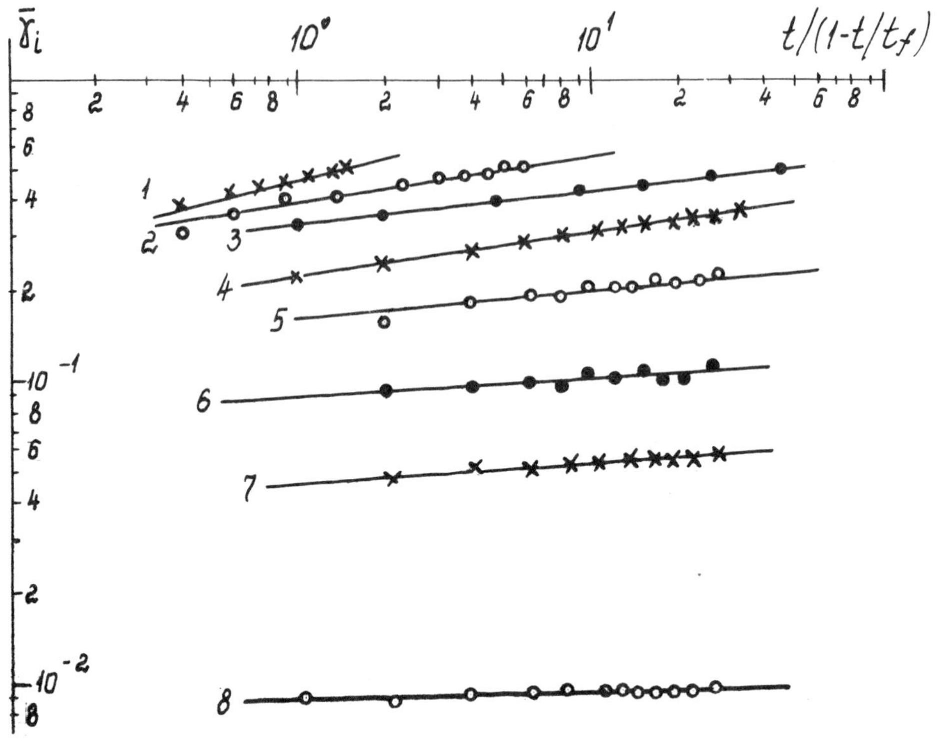

Figure 2. Shear creep curves of frozen Kellovey silt in logarithmic plots. The designations are the same as on the Fig. 1

So the determination of deformation parameters of equations (7), (10) is completed.

It was shown above that the long-term strength equation is absolutely necessary while using of equations (6),(7). Transform the logarithmic equation (9) used above to describe long-term strength curves under all test conditions. The long-term strength curves derived in (4,11) are shown on Fig.4. In accordance with general assumptions we shall describe these curves using the invariants σ and τ_i. Besides the parameter B of equation (9) is assumed to be constant being independent from test condition, and parameter β is assumed to be a function from the ratio σ/τ_i then the equation (9) results in the form

$$\ln(t_f/B) = \frac{\beta(\sigma/\tau_i)}{\tau_i}, \tag{12}$$

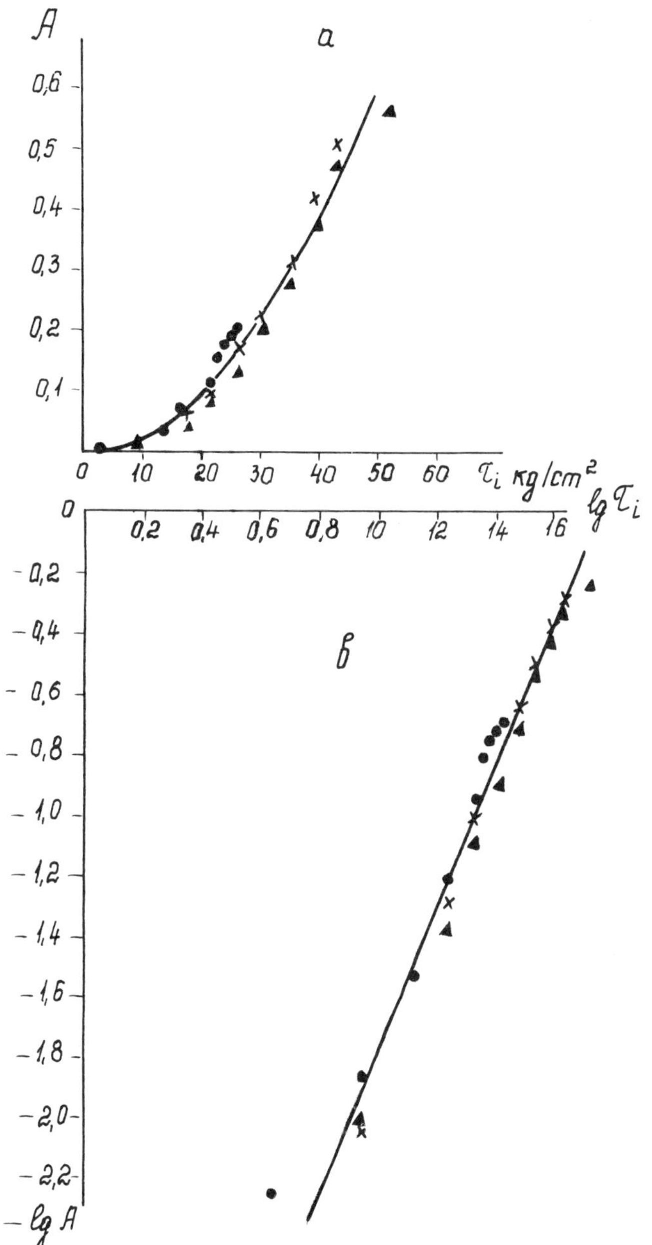

Figure 3. The dependence of parameter A on τ_i in usual (a) and in logarithmic (b) plots, σ being (kg/cm²): • – 15; × – 30; ▲ – 60.

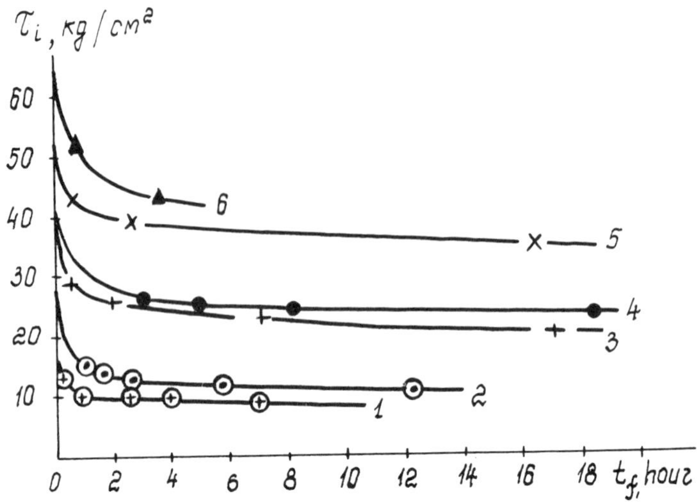

Figure 4. The long-term strength curves of frozen Kellovey silt at a temperature of -10°C. 1 - uniaxial extention; 2 - simple shear; 3 - uniaxial compression; 4,5,6 - triaxial compression, σ being 15 kg/cm², 30 kg/cm², 60 kg/cm² consequently.

where parameter B determined in (4) from uniaxial compression test results is as follows

$$B = 4{,}157 \cdot 10^{-4} \text{hours.} \tag{13}$$

Write (12) in the form

$$\tau_i \ln(t_f / B) = \beta(\sigma / \tau_i) \tag{14}$$

and mark the experimental points on the diagram in the "$\tau_i \ln(t_f/B) - \sigma/\tau_i$" plots, where B is determined according to (13) (see Fig. 5.a). As one can see the experimental points for all test conditions are plotted near the unique curve. So the validity of the equation (12) is justified. Analytical description of this curve having S-like tracing can be done for example by use of the following function

$$\beta(\sigma/\tau_i) = \frac{b}{\pi} \operatorname{arcctg}\left[\frac{1}{\delta}\left(c - \frac{\sigma}{\tau_i}\right)\right]. \tag{15}$$

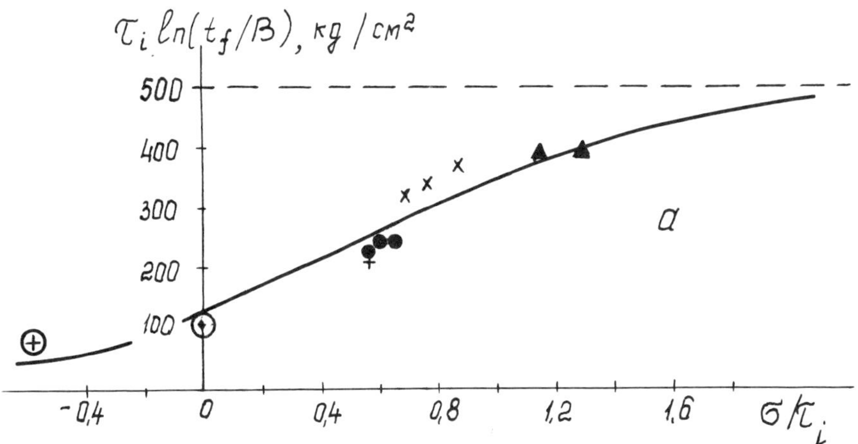

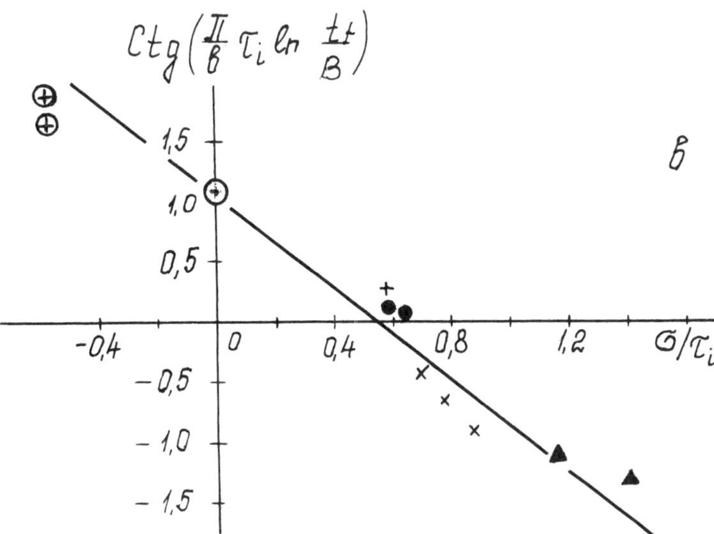

Figure 5. The long-term strength curves of frozen Kellovey silt at a temperature of -10°C in generalized plots The designations are the same as on the Fig. 4

Then equation (12) results in the form

$$\ln(t_f/B) = \frac{b}{\pi \tau_i} \operatorname{arcctg}\left[\frac{1}{\delta}\left(C - \frac{\sigma}{\tau_i}\right)\right]. \qquad (16)$$

Analyse the validity of this equation. First of all it is evident that the function $F(\tau_i, \sigma)$ in the right hand part of (16) satisfies general requirements

$$\frac{\partial F}{\partial \tau_i} < 0; \quad \frac{\partial F}{\partial \sigma} > 0. \qquad (17)$$

Further consider some particular cases. If $\tau_i \to \infty$ then $F \to 0$ i.e. $t_f \to B$. B is usually very small so we have practically $t_f \to 0$ which agrees with the known experimental facts. If $\sigma \to +\infty$ then $F \to b/\tau_i$ i.e. b is the ultimate value of β under $\sigma \to +\infty$. One can assume b to be 500 kg/cm^2 as shown on Fig. 5.a.

Analyse now the derived equation when $\tau_i \to 0$ i.e. under hydrostatic loading. It is easy to see that under hydrostatic compression ($\sigma > 0$) $t_f \to +\infty$ i.e. there is no failure, while under hydrostatic extention ($\sigma < 0$) the equation (16) results in the form:

$$\ln(t_f/B) = -\frac{\delta b}{\pi} \cdot \frac{1}{\sigma} \qquad (18)$$

i.e. in this case we also have the logarithmic law of long-term strength applied to σ. Under simple shear and uniaxial compression and extention equation (12) results in the form (9) with constant β .

The above analysis of the derived long-term strength equation shows that this equation agrees with the known facts on long-term failure of frozen soils. The determination of parameters of the equation (16) is carried out (with b = 500 kg/cm^2) by straightening of the curve of Fig. 5.a in plots shown on Fig. 5.b. Finally we have: $B = 4{,}157 \cdot 10^{-4}$ hour; b = 500 kg/cm^2; $\delta = 0{,}538$; $C = 0{,}570$.

So the shear creep function of frozen soils can be written in the form (6) taking into account (10), (16).

VOLUME CREEP. CONSTITUTIVE RHEOLOGICAL EQUATIONS

Usually (5,11) it is considered that the hydrostatic component of frozen soil volume strain is negligible and the volume creep strain rate $\dot{\varepsilon}^c$ is connected with $\dot{\gamma}_i$ by the relation

$$\dot{\varepsilon}^c = \lambda \dot{\bar{\gamma}}_i , \tag{19}$$

where λ - is dilatation coefficient.

According to (5,11) the λ value essentially depends on frozen soil deformation stage. In the non-steady creep stage which is accompanied by healing of structure microdefects and hence by contraction of soil we have $\lambda > 0$. In the progressive flow stage which is accompanied by intensive development of microdefects and by dilatation of soil we have $\lambda < 0$. In the simplest case let us assume that

$$\lambda = \begin{cases} \lambda_1 > 0, \text{ under } & \bar{\gamma}_i < \bar{\gamma}_i^* \\ -\lambda_2 < 0, \text{ under } & \bar{\gamma}_i \geqslant \bar{\gamma}_i^* , \end{cases} \tag{20}$$

where $\bar{\gamma}_i^*$ is the $\bar{\gamma}_i$ value at the moment of the deformation process transition into the progressive flow stage. One can derive from (7), (10), that

$$\bar{\gamma}_i^* = \left(\frac{1-\alpha}{1+\alpha} t_f \right)^{\alpha} \left(\frac{\tau_i}{a} \right)^{1/m} . \tag{21}$$

Then general equations (5) result in the form

$$\dot{\varepsilon}_{ij}^c = \left(\lambda \delta_{ij} + \frac{\sigma_{ij} - \sigma \delta_{ij}}{2\tau_i} \right) \dot{\bar{\gamma}}_i , \tag{22}$$

where λ is determined from (20), (21), and $\dot{\bar{\gamma}}_i$ is determined from (6), taking into account (10),(16)

Note that parameters of the derived equations depend in general on temperature. According to (4) we consider the parameters a and b to be the unique parameters depending on temperature and connected by the relation

$$a(\theta) = a_0 \, b(\theta), \tag{23}$$

where a_0 = const. The dependence of b on θ can be considered linear (4):

$$b = b_0 + b_1 |\theta| . \tag{24}$$

The general system of constitutive equations (20)-(22), (6),(10),(16) must be considered together with the equations (23),(24). These constitutive equations derived from hardening creep theory are valid under actual temperature and loading conditions and describe all known peculiarities of frozen soil deformation and failure including the dependence of frozen soil strength on loading time, the availability of all three deformation stages, the non-linear character of deformations, the effects of positive and negative dilatation, etc. though these equations are derived with some simplifications.

SIMPLIFIED MODIFICATION OF CONSTITUTIVE EQUATIONS

If deformation proceeds in under ultimate stage $\bar{\gamma}_i << \bar{\gamma}_i^*$ then the proposed equations are simplified

$$\dot{\varepsilon}_{ij}^{c} = \dot{\bar{\gamma}}_i/(2\tau_i)\left(\sigma_{ij} - \delta_{ij}\sigma\left(1 - 2\lambda_1\tau_i/\sigma\right)\right), \tag{25}$$

$$\dot{\bar{\gamma}}_i = \alpha\left(\frac{\tau_i}{a}\right)^{1/m\alpha}\frac{1}{\bar{\gamma}_i^{1/\alpha-1}} \tag{26}$$

If in addition stresses in frozen soil are changed in proportion to unique parameter, i.e. the Iljushin simple loading condition is satisfied then

$$2\lambda_1\frac{\tau_i}{\sigma} = K = const \tag{27}$$

Introducing a new parameter (5)

$$\nu = \frac{1-K}{K+2} \tag{28}$$

which serves as Poisson coefficient, we have

$$\dot{\varepsilon}_{ij}^{c} = \dot{\bar{\gamma}}_i/(2\tau_i)\left(\sigma_{ij} - \frac{3\nu}{1+\nu}\delta_{ij}\sigma\right), \tag{29}$$

$$\dot{\bar{\gamma}}_i = \alpha\left(\frac{\tau_i}{a}\right)^{1/m\alpha}\frac{1}{\bar{\gamma}_i^{1/\alpha-1}} \tag{30}$$

So the general equations result in the usual power equations (12) if the additional assumptions are made. These equations can also be considered coupled with (23),(24) under variable temperature conditions.

COMPUTER REALIZATION OF PROPOSED EQUATIONS

Computer realization of proposed equations is done using the finite element method coupled with the usual time step procedure. Some results of pile behaviour in permafrost are shown below as an illustration. Circular elastic pile 6 m long and 40 cm diameter was assumed to be installed in frozen silt, θ being -0,5°C. It was shown that upper part of pile initially was subject to about 90% of the applied load. The lower part of a pile and its bottom began to work gradually in time. The settlement of a pile under loading of 300 KN was 2,2 cm a year later.

Computer realization of simplified equations (29),(30) is strongly simplified if the instantaneous strains are negligible though these equations are valid under simple loading condition only. This loading type occurs for example in absolutely rigid and flexible plate problems (5) and in absolutely rigid pile problem (12). The solution of such problems results (if temperature remains constant with reference to space variables and changes in time only) in the form of production of time functions and space variables functions (12), time functions and the dependence on load, temperature, and parameters a_0, α being analytically determined. Only space variables functions are unknown. The model problem of non-linear elasticity with power law of hardening is considered for determination of these functions. Thus for this class of problems the dimensions of initial problem are decreased and the problem itself results in the problem independent on time.

CONCLUSIONS

1. The rheological constitutive equations of frozen soil derived using hardening creep theory are reported.

2. In contrast to traditional equations the proposed equations contain both deformation and strengthening parameters and describe simultaneously the creep deformation development and the long-term strength decreasing. These equations are valid either at constant stresses and temperature and under their actual variation with time.

3. The general constitutive equations are derived with some assumptions but they relate to the known regularities of frozen soil deformation including the availability of all three creep stages with progressive flow stage resulting in failure, the effects of positive and negative dilatation,etc.

4. In under ultimate region the proposed equations are simplified and result in the usual power form.

5. Computer realization of proposed equations is done on the basis of finite element method. It is shown that the utilization of simplified modification of these equations makes the problem easier through decreasing of its dimensions.

REFERENCES

1. Vyalov, S.S., Rheologicheskie Svoistva i Nesyshaya Sposobnost Merzlikh Gruntov, AN USSR, Moscow, 1959 (in Russian)

2. Andersland, O.B., Anderson, D.M. (ed.), Geotechnical Engineering for Cold Regions, McGraw-Hill, New York, 1978.

3. Johnston, G.H. (ed.), Permafrost Engineering Design and Construction, John Wiley & Sons, 1981.

4. Vyalov, S.S., Gnoshinsky, V.G., Gorodetsky, S.E., Grigorieva, V.G., Zaretsky, Yu.K., Pekarskaya, N.K., Shusherina, Ye.P., The Strength and Creep of Frozen Soils and Calculations for Ice-Soil Retaining Structures, U.S.Army, CRREL, Transl. 76, 1965.

5. Vyalov, S.S., Rheological Fundamentals of Soil Mechanics, Elsevier, 1986.

6. Zaretsky, Yu.K., Stchobolev, A.G., Chumichev, B.D., Vyaskoplastichnost Lda i Merzlikh Gruntov, Nauka, Novosibirsk, 1986 (in Russian).

7. Perzyna, P., Physical theory of viscoplasticity. 1. Mathematical structure. Bull. Acad. Pol. Sci. Ser. Sci. techn., 1973, 21, No 3, 183-188.

8. Naghdi, P.M., Murch, S.A., On the mechanical behaviour of viscoelastic/plastic solids., J. Appl. Mech., 1963, 30, No 3, 321-328.

9. Rabotnov, Yu.N., Polzuchest Elementov Konstruktsy, Nauka, Moscow, 1966 (in Russian).

10. Crishtal, M.A., Gavrilov, G.M., Problemy Prochnosty, Nauka, Moscow, 1978, No 12, 29-32 (in Russian).

11. Zaretsky, Yu.K., Gorodetsky, S.E., Dilatansiya merzlogo grunta i postroenie deformatsionnoy teorii polzuchesti., Gidrotechnicheskoe Stroitelstvo, 1975, No 2, 15-18 (in Russian).

12. Slepak, M.E., Osadki i napryazhenno-deformirovannoe sostoyaniye plastichno-merzlogo grunta v osnovanii tsentralno nagruzhennoi svai., Reologiya Gruntov i Inzhenernoye Merzlotovedenie, Nauka, Moscow, 1982 (in Russian).

DETERMINATION OF RHEOLOGICAL PROPERTY PARAMETERS OF FROZEN BASES

U.S.Mirenburg,L.N.Khrustalyov

The USSR NCSMFE,Gosstroy USSR,Pushkinskaya Str.26

Moscow 103828 USSR.

ABSTRACT

Manifestation of rheological property parameters of frozen bases provides impossibility of straight experimental determination,precise enough,of maximum term meanings of strength or bearing capacity and deformation.Hence,bearing capacity and foundation settlements prognosis in frozen soils is based on mathematical model, which reflects rheological soil properties.Model parameters are determined by relatively short tests.Such a model is presented in this paper,based on phenomenological successive creeping theory and generalized deformation dependence on stresses and power influence duration.Results of experimental model of its parameters on the bases of short tests data are also adduced.In addition, ways of model utilization for prognosis of bearing capacity and piles settlement under constant and variable loads are offered.

INTRODUCTION

In this paper results on investigation of pile bases are considered in the main.But,as our works,tests and literature data analysis have showed,conceptions and forms of dependence one can apply both for stamps and samples of frozen soil.It is not accidentally,since development of deformations and carrying capacity of foundation bases is the result of display of rheological properties of frozen base.The works of Vialov [1,2] and other investigators show that the process of development in time of creep deformations and alterations of strength do not stop for decades.So real and possible duration of frozen soils and foundation tests is much less than elapsing terms of rheological processes and exploitation time of bases. Discrepancy is expressed by difference in succession of bases stress-strain state in tests and in nature. Thus, tests are the models relative to time and loading succession. Hence, as a result, we take parameters of the mathematical expression of dependence of deformations and strength on stress, which are invariant relative to succession and duration of loading.

OPTIMIZATION OF TESTS DURATION

Step-increasing loading tests, where every step is endured till conditional damping of deformations, or tests with equal time duration of every step are widely used at present. Duration of the first method exceeds 30-60 days and preliminary prognosis is not real. Duration of the second method is much less. It can be optimized by accuracy of the result. This is an important factor of test methods. For pile testing an optimum duration is determined by function of total error when Δ is minimized:

$$\Delta = \Delta_n + \Delta_T = \min, \qquad (1)$$

where Δ_n -an error, stipulated by volume limit of experimental data n owing to limitation of duration t_n.

Δ_T -an error, owing to seasonal temperature change of base T, which depends on test duration.

An analysis, carried out by us, showed that an optimum test duration, depending on soil type and temperature in summer and autumn period may change from 8 to 15 days. Thus, taking into account test comfort conditions, duration of all steps is equal to 24 hours.

SELECTION OF CREEP THEORY

Succession of loading is the second factor,which affects on accuracy of determination of rheological parameters.This method represents a family of curves of pile settling development under permanent loads,taking into account data on step-increasing loading.Influence of this factor is represented by figure1,where curves of the settling development under permanent load N_2 (fig.1b)are drawn based on two steps of loading N_1 and N_2 in accordance with different creep theories [3] and methods[4,5].

Building method of these curves is also shown on the figure.According to the method of data processing, quantity of settlements under permanent load N_2 changes more than 4 times.Difference expands,when the ammount of steps increases.It caused choozing of creep theory just for processing of pile tests data.In this connection,tests has been carried out [6],with piles d=18mm submerged into shute d=287mm with 300 mm depth,where shute depth is equal to 600mm,filled up by frozen paste of topsoil loam with humidity equal to 0,25 and density equal to 195 g/cm^3,at temperature 0,8 ± 0,1°C by parallel,constant and step-increasing loads 0,45 ; 0,9; 1,35; 1,8kN.Time duration of constant loadings was equal to 4 days.Six sets has been carried out for realibility of statistical processing.

Under constant loading tests data,in accordance with every theory and method of data processing,calculations were made for ordinates of settling development curves during step-loading S_t^* .Further they were compared with settling development curves S_r^* during step-increasing loading. Thus,depending on loading value,both settlemet value S_r^* and settlement difference $S_r^* - S_t$ were changed considerably,and analysis was carried out with relative deflection

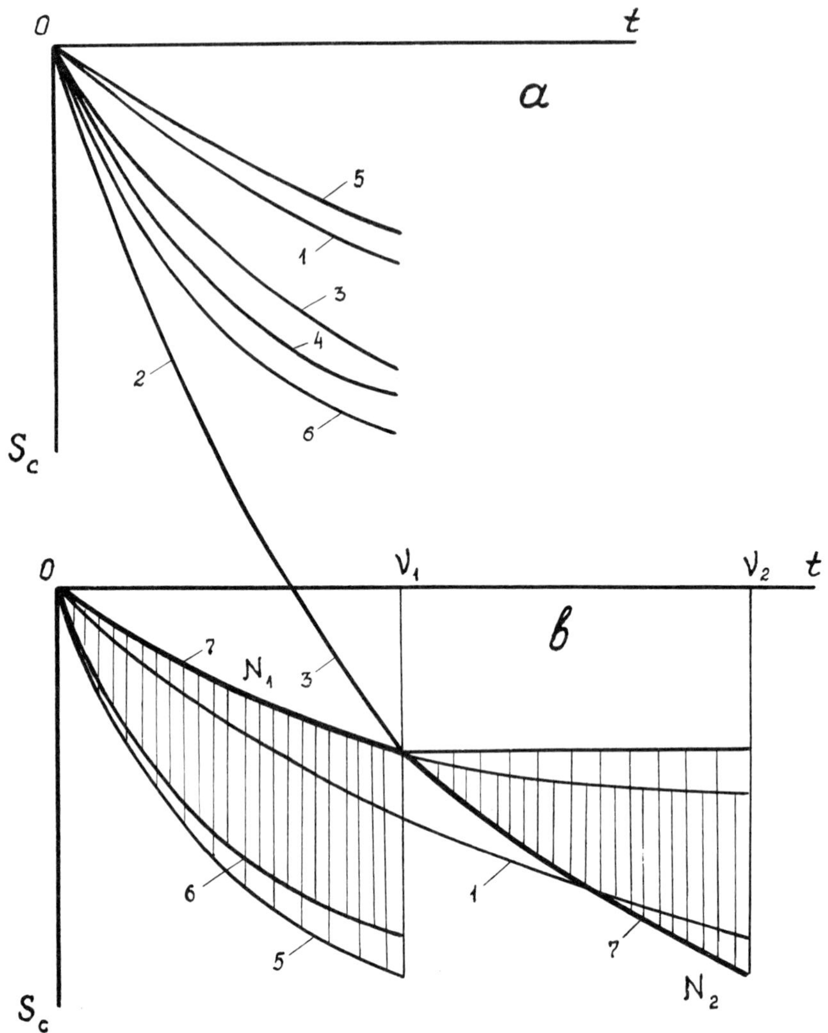

Figure1.Graphic building schemes of settling development curves under constant load N_2, according to step-increasing loading (7) on the basis of different creep theories and data processing methods of pile testing.
Aging theory (1); flowing theory (2); consolidation theory (3) successive creeping theopy (4);data processing method(5) and summation method(6).

$$\delta_i = \frac{S^*_{ri} - S^*_{ti}}{S^*_{ri}}, \qquad (2)$$

since this value is less dependent on loading.

Standard deflection σ served as criteria of tightness estimation

$$\sigma = \sqrt{\frac{\sum_{i=1}^{n} \delta_i^2}{n}}, \qquad (3)$$

and correlation index ρ

$$\rho = \sqrt{1 - \frac{\sum_{i=1}^{n} (S^*_{ri} - S^*_{ti})^2}{\sum_{i=1}^{n} (S^*_{ri} - \bar{S}^*_r)^2}}, \qquad (4)$$

where n – number of experimental points;
$\bar{S}^*$ – medium pile settlement.

Results of calculations are shown in table.

TABLE

Comparison of data processing methods

Data processing methods	σ	ρ
1.Aging theory	1,281	–
2.Flow theory	0,221	–
3.Consolidation theory	0,174	0,813
4.Theory of successivecreeping	0,158	0,886
5.Existing data processing method [4]	0,180	0,786
6.Summation method [5]	0,163	0,858

Comparison,poited below,affords to chooze method of data processing of step loading in favour of successive creeping theory and summation method,which have greater tigthness with experimental data.

Let us consider mathematical form of tests data processing. Development of settlement S under constant loading N_j,which is equal to successive creeping theory can be expressed by:

$$S_j\,(t-\nu_{j-1})=S_{oj}+S_{j-1}(t-\nu_{j-2})+S_j^*(t)-S_{j-1}^*(t) \qquad (5)$$

where $S_j\,(t-\nu_{j-1})$ and $S_{j-1}(t-\nu_{j-2})$ - pile settlement under constant loads N_j and N_{j-1} in time interval $(t-\nu_{j-1})$ and $(t-\nu_{j-2})$;

S_{oj} -instant settlement under load N_j ;

$S_j^*(t)$ -settling development schedule at step j ;

$S_{j-1}^*(t)$ -extrapolated settling development schedule at step (j-1);

ν_{j-1} - the moment of loading N_j.

Extrapolation of settling development schedule at the step follows after approximation of schedule at a step of smooth curve,expressed,for instance,by degree function:

$$S_{j-1}^*(t-\nu_{j-1})=S_{j-1}^*(\nu_{j-1})+a_{j-1}(t-\nu_{j-1})^{\alpha_{j-1}}, \qquad (6)$$

where a_{j-1} and α_{j-1} - parameters.

Approximation and calculation of extrapolated settlement should be done by computers.If it makes manually,labour-intensive calculations can be confronted.In this case you may omit the last two items in formula (5).According to this assumption difference between data processing by method of summation and successive creeping theory method is obtained.Utilization of summation method for data processing with steps time duration equal to 48-72 hours showed,that this method leads to 30 % prognosed settlement icrease with calculated meaning 42 % ,confidential probability α_n=0,85. It also leads to reducing of calculated meanings of utmostly prolonged bearing capacity by 10 % with medium meaning of 4%. These errors,as they appear systematically, can be decreased by appropriate introduction of coefficients,obtained on the basis of statistical tests data processing.

Thus,during pile settlement processing,tested by steps, where time duration was equal to 48-72 hours with confidential probability α_n =0,85 ,introduction of coefficient 0,83 do not lead to reducing of settlement.It decreases error by 16 % ,where ρ =0,977 is an index of correlation of calculated settlements with experimental one. In that way successive creeping theory is used for data processing when step-loading tests are carried out,or when computers are not avaliable,by method of summation,just to reduce laboriosness with introducing statistically substantiated empirical coefficients,which decrease systematical mistakes of this method.

CONCLUSION OF THE MAIN DEPENDENCE

The third main factor,to determine settlement prognosis and bearing capacity of the piles is selection of dependence of these indices on loading and its time duration.Dependence must be easy enough for approximation of tests data, correlation with data and must have a good theoretical conceptions about deformation process of frozen bases. Our data analysis of deformation samples development of frozen soil,stamps and piles [7,8] shows,that the main dependence to be found is B.P.Popov,s dependence [9] ,taking into account instant settlement S_o .

$$S = S_o + \frac{A_{ut} N}{1 - \frac{N}{F_{ut}}} , \qquad (7)$$

and dependence of deformative characteristics A_{ut} and F_{ut} strength characteristics on time in degree and logarithmic form:

$$A_{ut} = A_{uo}\left(\frac{t}{t_o}\right)^{\lambda} , \tag{8}$$

$$F_{ut} = \frac{F_{uo}}{\ln\left(\frac{t}{t_o}\right)} , \tag{9}$$

where A_{uo} , λ , F_{uo} and t_o - parameters, determined during the tests.

Dependence of instant settlement S_o on loading N is approximated by linear function with coefficient of proportionality A_o .

$$S_o = A_o N , \tag{10}$$

Substituting (8)-(10) in (7) we determine:

$$S = A_o N + \frac{A_{uo} N}{1 - \frac{N}{F_{uo}} \ln\left(\frac{t}{t_o}\right)} \left(\frac{t}{t_o}\right)^{\lambda} , \tag{11}$$

We take this dependence for approximation of data and settling prognosis and formula (9) for calculation of bearing capacity. Compliance of dependence (11)to theoretical conceptions and experimental data is confirmed by the following properties:

1. It characterises infinite increasing of settlements

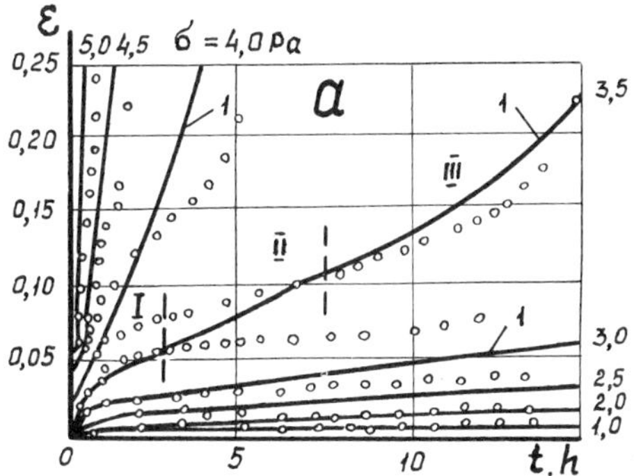

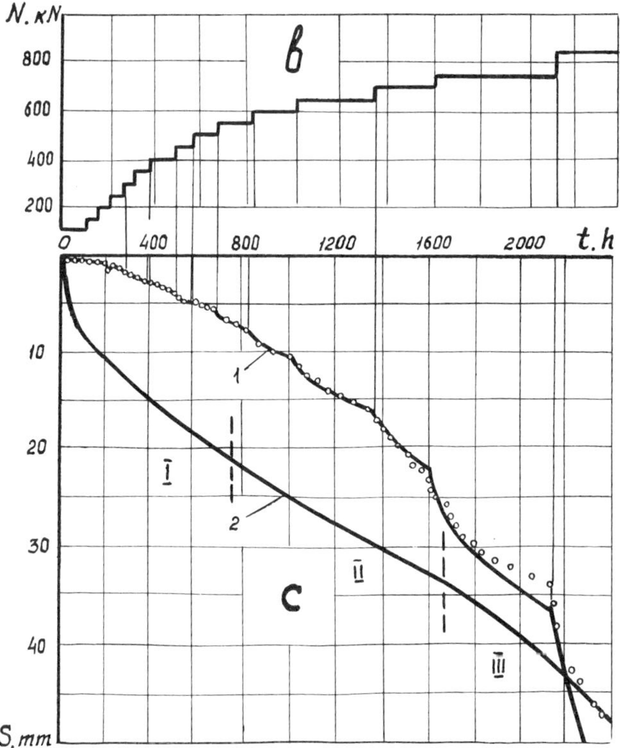

Figure2.Comparison of experimental (○) and calculated creeping curves of frozen sandy loam under step loading (b). Prognosis of pile settling development under constant loading N =650kN (2).Creeping stages:damping(I),established(II),and progressive(III).

with infinite icreasing of time.It corresponds to the results pointed out in works [1.2].

2. When value of loading N approximates to strength F_{ut} ($N \rightarrow F_{ut}$) the formula represents development of flat settlement ($S \rightarrow \infty$).It corresponds to theoretical conceptions reflected in the work [10].

3. If loading ($N \rightarrow 0$)is reduced,the formula fully characterizes linear dependence of settlement on loading $S=(A_o^+ + A_u)$ N.This factor is utilized in calculation of bases [11].

4. When time t is limited by a certain limit, as well as by period of exploitation t ,damping,established and progressive creeping can be expressed by formula(11).It satisfactory correlates with frozen soils tests data by constant loads and piles under step-increasing loadings (fig.2) [7].

5. Long-term pile settlement prognosis during 11 years,based on tests data,satisfactory correlates with the results of levelling of a building,constructed on such piles(Fig.3)[12].

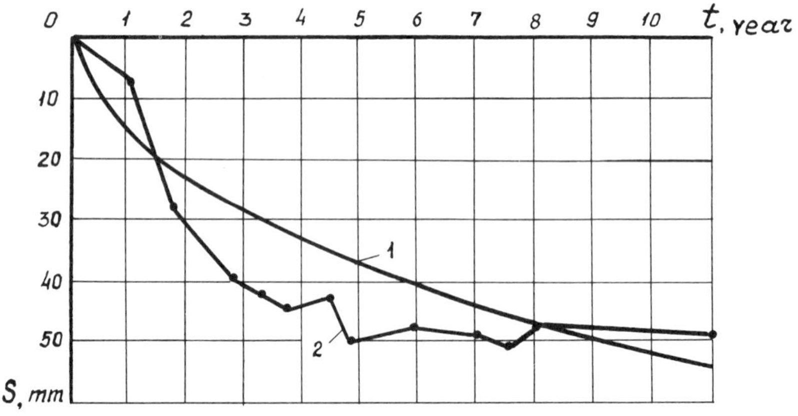

Figure3. Comparison of pile settling (1), predicted by tests data,with the results of levelling of a building, constructed on such piles(2).

6. Satisfactory coincidence [5] is obtained during the comparison of loads by formula(14),causing progressive pile settlements with time t and loadings,causing the same settlements with the same period of time.

Thus, dependence (11) reflects theoretical conceptions about rheological processes and satisfactory correlates with experimental data.

DETERMINATION OF THE MAIN DEPENDENCE PARAMETERS

The following important requirement to dependence is capability of simple determination of its parameters by tests data. Dependence (11) approximates these data. For this purpose tests data are represented in rectified coordinates and by coefficients a and b of straight line $y = a + bx$ of the best approximation to experimental data, necessary data can be determined. Meanings of coefficients a and b are calculated by method of smallest square or graphically. In this connection parameters of formulae (7), (10), (11) can be otained (fig.4). Tests data processing in accordance with [5] is executed as follows:

1. First, instant settlement S_{oj} is apportioned, determined by summation settling increments at the moment of loading. Meanings of this settlement are approximated by expression (10). As a result we find coefficient A_o (fig.4a).
2. Ordinates of experimental points of creep settling development S_c under constant loads N_j, which are equal to step loads, can be determined by successive creeping theory or by summation method (fig.4e).
3. Graphs ordinates of creep settling dependence S under load N for its different time duration t are calculated by settling development curves (fig.4f). These curves, according to (7) we rectify at $x = N$ coordinates, $y = N/S_c$. Further, as a result, one can find $A_{utj} = 1/a_j$ and $F_{utj} = -(a_j/b_j)$.
4. Graph of meanings F_{utj} rectifies according to (9) in coordinates $x = \ln t$, $y = 1/F_{ut}$. By these data we find a and b parameters (fig.4c) and then we determine parameters of formula (11) $F_{uo} = 1/b$ and $t_o = \exp(-ab)$.

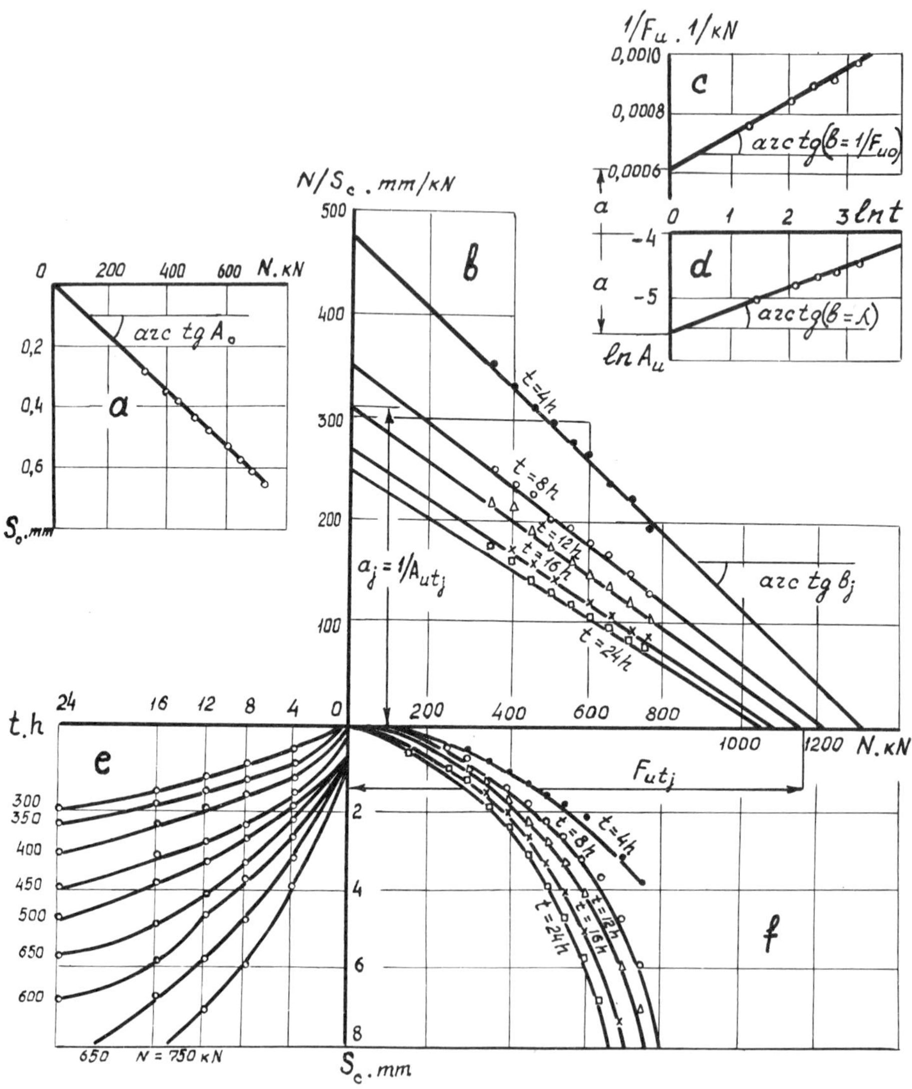

Figure4. Graphic processing of pile tests data: determination of the parameter A_o (a); determination of the paramaters A_{ut} and F_{ut} (b); determination of the parameters F and t_o (c); determination of the parameters λ and A_{uo}(d); settling development curves under loads(e), isochrons(f).

5. In accordance with (8) a graph of meanings A_{utj} rectifies in coordinates lnt $-\ln A_{ut}$ (fig.4d),hence $\lambda = b$ and $A_{uo} = t_o^b \exp a$.

In that way,parameters of formula (11) are easily determined.

PILES CALCULATION

Let us consider the main points of settlement prognosis and bearing capacity of piles.Under permanent loadings N with t_e settlement prognosis is carried out by formula (11) and bearing capacity by formula (9),taking into account soil security coefficient γ_g [13].

$$F_u = \frac{F_{uo}}{\gamma_g \ln(\frac{t_e}{t_o})} . \tag{12}$$

For variable loadings formulae (9) and (11) one should substitute into equations of damage linear summation [1] and successive creeping theory [1,3].Hence,we find calculation conditions in the form of integral [14].It would be better to represent the loading in the form of step graph (fig.2b).Calculations accuracy depends on degree of detailed elaboration of the graph.It must be noted,that intervals of loadings gradation should be reduced under maximum loadings just to cut calculation volume.Thus,for step loading graph calculation condition by bearing capacity can be expressed as:

$$\frac{1}{t_o}\sum_{j-1}^{m}[(V_j - V_{j-1})/\exp\frac{F_{uo}}{\gamma_g \gamma_n \gamma_f N_j}] \leqslant 1 , \tag{13}$$

where γ_n – reliability coefficient [13];

γ_f – reliability coefficient under loading [15];

N_j – standard loading ;

$V_j - V_{j-1}$ – operation time loading j .

Settling development prognosis is given by :

$$S = A_{uo} \sum_{j-1}^{m} \frac{(N_j - N_{j-1}) \tau_j^{\lambda}}{(1- \frac{N_j}{F_{uo}} \ln \tau_j) \; (1- \frac{N_{j-1}}{F_{uo}} \ln \tau_j)} , \qquad (14)$$

where
$$\tau_j = \frac{t_e - V_{j-1}}{t_o} \qquad (15)$$

According to our investigations experimental determination of rheological property parameters of frozen bases affords to increase bearing capacity more than by 1,5 times [16]. Besides,due to registration of variable loadings foundations volume can be reduced by 2 times [17].

CONCLUSION

Methods of determination of rheological property parameters, adduced above, meets modern conceptions on manifestation of these properties.It also satisfactory correlates with experimental data and affords to give proper prognosis of bearing capacity and foundations settlement in frozen soils under constant and variable with time vertical loadings,as well as to get positive effect due to accurate definition of calculated characteristics.

REFERENCES

1. Vialov, S.S., Rheological principles of soil mechanics. Vysshaya shkola Publishers,Moscow,1978,pp.160-72,219-29, 333-39.
2. Vialov,S.S., Experimental stamps settlements on plastic frozen soils.Bases,foundations and soil mechanics.1978,5, pp.26-29.
3. Malinin,N.N.,Applied plastic theory.Mashinostroenije, Moscow,1968,pp.341-59.
4. Guidance on field piles testing in permafrost soils. Stroiizdat,Moscow,1977,pp.17-25.
5. Mirenburg,U.S.,Method of time duration shortening of pile testing in frozen soils.Proc.of Research Inst.for foundations and underground structures,1978,pp.98-106.
6. Mirenburg,U.S.,Khrystalyov,L.N.,Creeping selection theory for investigation and prediction of pile settling and bearing capacity.Reports of IV Symposium on Soil Rheology Samarkand,1982,pp.129-30.
7. Vialov,S.S.,Mirenburg,U.S.,Fokin,V.A.On the possibility of using the results of tests on frozen soils for creep in designing foundations with respect to two limiting states by allowing for the rheological properties of the soils.Hydrotechnical construction in the areas of permafrost and severe climate.Energiya Publishers, Leningrad,1979,pp.27-31.
8. Vialov,S.S.,Mirenburg,U.S.,Settling and carrying capacity of bases,composed of weak soils by allowing for their non-linearity and creep.VI Danube-European Conference on Soil Mechanics and Foundation Construction,Varna,Bulgaria 1980,pp.387-96.
9. Popov,B.P.,Utilization of dimensions analysis for experiments with test loadings.Engineering and geological investigations for hydropower construction,Moscow,1950, Volume2,pp.
10. Gersevanov,N.M.,Pile resistance determination,Petrograd, 1917,Cement,pp.
11. Tsitovich,N.A.,Soil mechanics.Vysshaya shkola Publishers, Moscow,1979,pp.202-18.
12. Mirenburg,U.S.,Fedoseev,U.G.,Prediction of pile foundations settlement in plastic frozen soils.Soil rheology and permafrost engineering,Nauka Publishers, Moscow,1982,pp.159-61.
13. BS&R 11-18-76,Bases and foundations on permafrost soils Stroiizdat,Moscow,1987,pp.15-16.
14. Mirenburg,U.S.,Calculation of variable loading and temperature during foundation calculations on permafrost soils.Bases,foundations and soil mechanics,1984,3, pp.16-18.
15. BS&R 2.01.07-85, Stresses and influence, Stroiizdat, Moscow,1987,p.1.
16. Mirenburg,U.S.,Khrystalyov,L.N.,Determination of optimal quantity of pile tests.Bases,foundations and soil mechanics,1978,5,pp.12-14.
17. Vialov,S.S.,Aleksandrov,U.A.,Gorodetsky,S.E.,Mirenburg, U.S.,Khrystalyov,L.N.,Thermopiles in building at the North.Stroiizdat,Leningrad,1984,p.76-91.

INFLUENCE OF SOIL CREEP ON STRESS STATE OF THE UNDERGROUND STRUCTURES BEING BUILT WITH STRENGTHENING OF THE SURROUNDING MASSIF

N.N.Fotiyeva, A.S.Sammal
Tula Polytechnical Institute
Tula, USSR

and
N.S.Chetyrkin
Research Institute of Bases and Underground Structures
Moscow, USSR

ABSTRACT

A method of consideration of rheological properties of soils when determining the stress state of the underground structures being built with strengthening of the surrounding massif is proposed. It is based on the theory of linear hereditary creep. A difference of stress state of the tunnel lining after preliminary strengthening of rock and in case of grouting through the lining is shown. Examples of computation illustrating development of stresses and displacements in the lining as function of time and rheological characteristics of the massif are given. It is shown that consideration of rheological properties of rock enables to design more economical structures and proves the greater effectiveness of the preliminary strengthening in comparison with the grouting through the lining.

INTRODUCTION

Nowadays when building the underground structures in complicated geological conditions characterized by presence of weak and water-saturated rock special measures, together with lining, are undertaken to strengthen surrounding massif by grouting through the face of a tunnel (preliminary strengthening) or through completed lining. Strengthening by grouting enables to reduce sufficiently anisotropy of rock properties around opening, to raise its modulus of deformation. Thus, a layer of soil is being created around the opening whose deformation properties are different from those of the rest of the massif. The layer is immediate continuation of the massif and its influence on stress state of lining is considerable.

Stress analysis of the underground structures being built with strengthening of the surrounding massif can be carried out on the basis of study of interaction of structure, strengthened layer and soil massif as parts of integrated deformable system. This enables in a number of cases to lighten considerably the structures by reducing its thickness and percentage of reinforcement.

METHOD

For that purpose a method of stress analysis has been developed in Tula Polytechnical Institute (Tula, USSR) based on the solution of plane contact problem of theory of elasticity for two-layered ring of an arbitrary shape (with one axis of symmetry) supporting an opening in weighable medium /1/. An idealization is given on Fig.1.

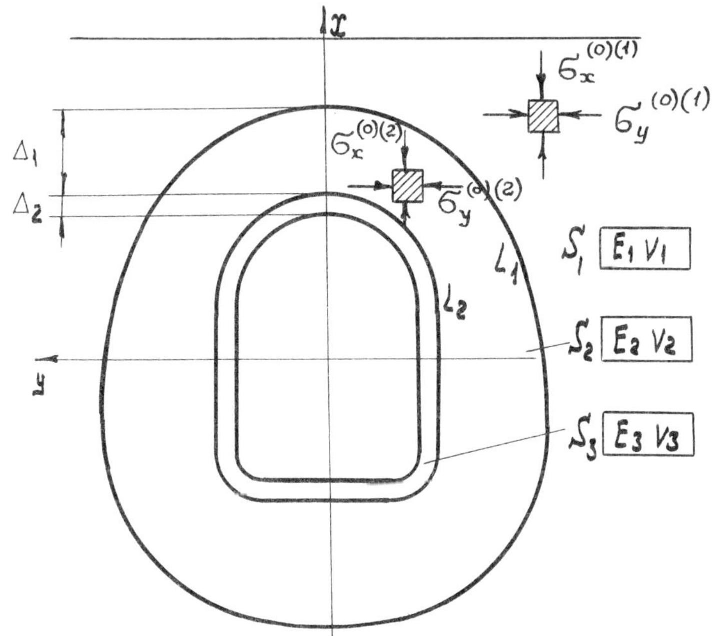

FIGURE 1. Design model

The massif, strengthened layer of rock and lining interact, as integrated deformable system, that is, conditions of contitinuity of vectors of displacements and total stresses are satisfied on the boundaries L_i (i=1,2). The internal boundary is not loaded. The initial distribution of stresses caused by gravitational forces in the ring S_2 and medium S_1 is given by formulae (1)

$$\sigma_x^{(o)(1)} = \sigma_x^{(o)(2)} = -\gamma H \alpha^*, \quad \sigma_y^{(o)(1)} = \sigma_y^{(o)(2)} = -\lambda \gamma H \alpha^*, \tag{1}$$

where γ is the unit weight of rock, H is the depth of the underground opening, λ is the coefficient of lateral earth pressure at rest, α^* is the correcting factor, included to take into consideration lagging of the lining behind the face of the underground opening.

The abovementioned method is generalized in the paper for a case when rock is subject to creep. Consideration of viscoelastic deformation of massif is carried out on the basis of theory of linear hereditary creep using method of variable moduli, according which deformation characteristics of rock in a solution of the theory of elasticity problem are presented as functions of time. The relations /2/ can be used for the majority of rocks:

$$E_1(t) = \frac{E_1}{1+\Phi(t)}, \quad \nu_1(t) = 0{,}5 - \frac{0{,}5-\nu_1}{1+\Phi(t)}, \tag{2}$$

in which $\Phi(t)$ is the creep function, determined as

$$\Phi(t) = \frac{\delta t^{1-\alpha}}{1-\alpha} \tag{3}$$

where δ, α are the creep parameters, t is time, counted out from the moment of putting the lining into operation.

The method of determination of the linear hereditary creep parameters from pressuremeter experiments has been developed recently in the Gersevanov Research Institute of Bases and Underground Structures (Moscow, USSR) /3/. Practice of the pressuremetric investigations shows that such inclined to rheological behaviour soils, as hard and semihard clays, display attenuating creep in many cases up to rather considerable pressure. A typical creep curve of such clay under step loading is shown on Fig.2.

An exponential core of creep was used to describe attenuating creep

$$L(t-\tau) = \theta \lambda^* \exp\left[-\lambda^*(t-\tau)\right], \tag{4}$$

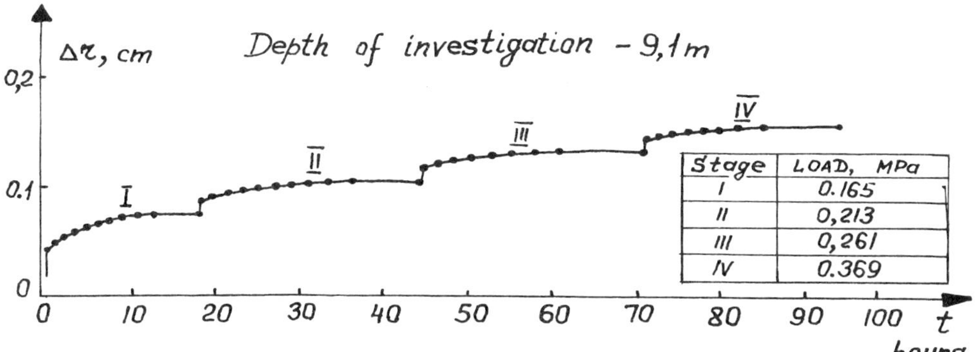

Stage	LOAD, MPa
I	0.165
II	0,213
III	0,261
IV	0.369

FIGURE 2. Typical creep curve of hard clay under step loading

using which the following expression could be obtained to characterize radial displacements $\mathcal{U}(t)$ of the pressuremetric borehole walls when pressure is constant (p=const) and $\tau=0$:

$$\mathcal{U}(t)=\frac{(1+\nu_1)r_0 p}{E_1}\left[1+E_1\theta\left(1-e^{-\lambda^* t}\right)\right]. \tag{5}$$

Bearing in mind, that

$$U_1=\frac{(1+\nu_1)r_0 p}{E_1}, \tag{6}$$

one can obtain

$$\mathcal{U}(t)=\mathcal{U}_1\left[1+E_1\theta\left(1-e^{-\lambda^* t}\right)\right], \tag{7}$$

where: p is the pressure in the cell of pressuremeter; E_1 is conventionally-instantaneous deformation modulus; θ and λ^* are parameters of creep; r_0 is the initial radius of the pressuremetric borehole.

The creep parameters θ and λ^* can be easily determined by the way an approximation of the experimental curve (Fig.2) with the function (7) using the method discribed in /4/. Time-dependent operator $E_1(t)$, being introduced into the solution of the theory of elasticity problem instead of modulus of elasticity E_1, when using the exponential core of creep to describe the pressuremetric loading will take the following form

$$E_1(t)=\frac{E_1}{1+\theta E_1\left(1-e^{-\lambda^* t}\right)}. \tag{8}$$

The expression (8) enables to compute the long-term modulus of deformation $E_{1\infty}$, when $t\rightarrow\infty$

$$\frac{1}{E_{1\infty}}=\frac{1}{E_1}+\theta. \tag{9}$$

Magnitudes of the creep parameters having been found with the pressuremetric experiments in hard clays are
$\lambda^* = (0,7 \pm 0,05) 10^{-4} s^{-1}$ and $\theta = 0,000419 \pm 0,000057$ MPa^{-1}.

Solution of the contact problem, as shown on Fig.1, when using the method of variable moduli (2) or (8), enables to evaluate stresses and forces in structure neglecting creep in the strengthened layer of rock at arbitrary moment of time either in case of preliminary strengthening or in case of grouting through completed lining. Nevertheless, technological features of the strengthening process should be taken into consideration when analysing stresses in lining.

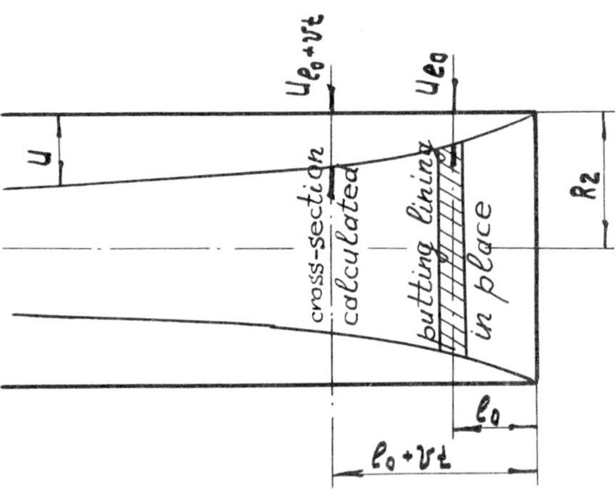

FIGURE 3. Development of displacements of walls of an underground opening.

If lining is being installed at the distance ℓ_0 from the face of the opening (Fig.3) a part of displacements u_{ℓ_0} has time to develop before the lining is put into operation (it is necessary to take into consideration that abovementioned displacements depend on not only the distance ℓ_0, but also on time interval between drifting of the part of the underground opening and installing of the lining), consequently during further advancement of the face as far as certain distance ℓ from lining which is function of the rate of advance $l=l_0+vt$ (v is the mean rate of advance, t is current time), the displacements are being transferred from the strengthened massif to the lining at the moment of time t_0+t /5/.

$$\mathcal{U}_{\ell_o+vt}(t_o+t) - \mathcal{U}_{\ell_o}(t_o) =$$

$$= \mathcal{U}(t_o+t)\left[\frac{\mathcal{U}_{\ell_o+vt}(t_o+t)}{\mathcal{U}(t_o+t)} - \frac{\mathcal{U}_{\ell_o}(t_o)}{\mathcal{U}(t_o)}\cdot\frac{\mathcal{U}(t_o)}{\mathcal{U}(t_o+t)}\right] =$$

$$= \mathcal{U}(t_o+t)\left[f(\ell_o+vt) - f(\ell_o)\frac{\mathcal{U}(t_o)}{\mathcal{U}(t_o+t)}\right]. \tag{10}$$

Here $\mathcal{U}_{\ell_o+vt}(t_o+t)$ and $\mathcal{U}_{\ell_o}(t_o)$ are the radial displacements at the distances ℓ_o+vt (at the moment of time t_o+t) and ℓ_o (at the moment of time t_o) from the face correspondingly; the displacements $\mathcal{U}(t_o)$, $\mathcal{U}(t_o+t)$ can be defined by the formula obtained from the solution /6/ of the plain problem of the theory of elasticity for a ring modelling strengthened layer in the medium which is modelling rock massif subjected to initial stresses caused by its weight. The formula is seen to be

$$\mathcal{U} = -\frac{(c_o-1)(1-2\nu_2+\beta)+2\beta(1-\nu_2)}{(c_o-1)(1-2\nu_2+\beta)+2(1-\nu_2)}\cdot\frac{1+\nu_2}{E_2}R_2\gamma H, \tag{11}$$

where

$c_o = \left(\frac{R_1}{R_2}\right)^2$, R_1 is the mean radius of the external boundary of the strengthened layer, R_2 is the mean radius of the opening, $\beta = \frac{E_2(1+\nu_1)}{E_1(1+\nu_2)}$ and magnitudes of the deformation modulus E_1 and Poisson's ratio ν_1 should be calculated at the moments of time t_o and t_o+t correspondingly in accordance with the formulae (2), (3) or (8). According to the theory of linear hereditary creep relations $f(\ell_o+vt) = \frac{\mathcal{U}_{\ell_o+vt}(t_o+t)}{\mathcal{U}(t_o+t)}$, $f(\ell_o) = \frac{\mathcal{U}_{\ell_o}(t_o)}{\mathcal{U}(t_o)}$ don't depend on time and can be calculated using the approximate solution by N.A.Davydova /7/ or the empirical formula

$$f(\ell) = 1 - e^{-1,3\frac{\ell}{R_2}}. \tag{12}$$

The displacements (10) can be defined, if the initial stresses are determined using formula (1), in which the correcting factor is defined from the following expression

$$\alpha^* = 1 - e^{-1,3\frac{\ell_o+vt}{R_2}} - \left(1 - e^{-1,3\frac{\ell_o}{R_2}}\right)\frac{\mathcal{U}(t_o)}{\mathcal{U}(t_o+t)}. \tag{13}$$

To calculate stresses in the lining when the face advanced on a considerable distance from the lining, one may assume

$$e^{-1.3\frac{\ell_o+vt}{R_2}} \to 0. \qquad (14)$$

In that case formula (13) will change to

$$\alpha^* = 1-\left(1-e^{-1.3\frac{\ell_o}{R_2}}\right)\frac{u(t_o)}{u(t_o+t)}. \qquad (15)$$

In case of strengthening by grouting of the massif through the lining at the distance $\ell_1 > \ell_o$ from the face the stresses in the lining are the sum of those caused by the advancement of the face up to the distance ℓ_1 (when there is no strengthened layer yet) and those caused by the advancement of the face after strengthening. That is why in case of grouting through the lining at the distance ℓ_1 from the face the calculation is carried out twice:

- the stresses and forces in the lining acting before strengthening are defined;

- the additional stresses and forces in the lining arising after creating of the strengthened layer.

Then, obtained results are summed up.

The stresses having acted in the lining before grouting carried out in time interval t after putting the lining into operation, are defined from the solution of the problem which idealization is indicated on Fig.1, when the layer S_2 is absent, that is when deformation characteristics $E_2=E_1=E_1(t_1)$, $\nu_2=\nu_1=\nu_1(t_1)$ are defined according to formulae (2), (3), (8) (or $E_2=E_1'(t_1)$, $\nu_2=\nu_1'(t_1)$, $E_1=E_1(t_1)$, $\nu_1=\nu_1(t_1)$, if there is a weakened layer of rock with characteristics E_1', ν_1' around the opening before grouting). The correcting factor is defined according to (13) when t_1 is substituted for t (substitution ℓ_1 for ℓ_o+vt is legitimate).

The additional stresses acting in the structure after strengthening are to be found from the sulution of the same problem (Fig.1) when deformation characteristics of massif are $E_1(t_1+t)$, $\nu_1(t_1+t)$. It is necessary to take into consideration presence of the layer S_2 with characteristics E_2, ν_2. The radial displacements being transferred to the lining by the strengthened massif are presented as

$$u_{\ell_1+vt}(t_o+t_1+t) - u_{\ell_1}(t_o+t_1) =$$

$$= u(t_0+t_1+t)\left[\frac{u_{\ell_1+vt}(t_0+t_1+t)}{u(t_0+t_1+t)} - \frac{u_{\ell_1}(t_0+t_1)}{u(t_0+t_1)}\frac{u(t_0+t_1)}{u(t_0+t_1+t)}\right] =$$

$$= u(t_0+t_1+t)\left[f(\ell_1+vt) - f(\ell_1)\frac{u(t_0+t_1)}{u(t_0+t_1+t)}\right], \tag{16}$$

where $u(t_0+t_1)$, $u(t_0+t_1+t)$ are defined according to (11) in which deformation characteristics are determined for the moments of time t_0+t_1 and t_0+t_1+t respectively.

Hence

$$\alpha^* = 1 - e^{-1.3\frac{\ell_1+vt}{R_2}} - \left(1 - e^{-1.3\frac{\ell_1}{R_2}}\right)\frac{u(t_0+t_1)}{u(t_0+t_1+t)}. \tag{17}$$

If it is necessary to determine maximum stresses in the lining when the distance between the face and cross-section calculated becomes considerable one, then one can assume in formula (17)

$$e^{-1.3\frac{\ell_1+vt}{R_2}} \longrightarrow 0. \tag{18}$$

RESULTS

Below there are results of stress analysis for single-track tunnel lining with 3m unsupported span and 2,8 m height. The mean radius of the opening R_2=1,88m. Inasmuch as calculation results depend on a number of dimensionless parameters, let us assume as initial data, ratios of the deformation moduli of the massif, the strengthened layer and material of the lining and all the geometric characteristics relate to the value of R_2.

It was assumed when calculating

$$\Delta_1/R_2 = 0{,}8;\ \Delta_2/R_2 = 0{,}16;\ E_1:E_2:E_3 = 4{,}8:9{,}6:24;$$
$$\nu_1 = \nu_2 = 0{,}3;\ \nu_3 = 0{,}15;\ \lambda = 0{,}43;\ \ell_0/R_2 = 0{,}5.$$

The cases of preliminary strengthening of massif and grouting through the lining (the presence of the weakened layer of rock before strengthening was not considered) are considered. The lining was calculated either without consideration of rock creep (in that case it was assumed ℓ_1/R_2 =1.5 when grouting was carried out through the lining), or with consideration of rock creep. In the last case there was an assumption of the parameters of linear hereditary creep α =0,7, δ =0,0047$s^{-0,3}$ and t_0=0,5 days; the acting forces in the structure were determined for the 60th day and was assumed that in case of grouting through the lining

$$t_1 = 15 \text{ days}, \quad \ell_1/R_2 = 15.5$$

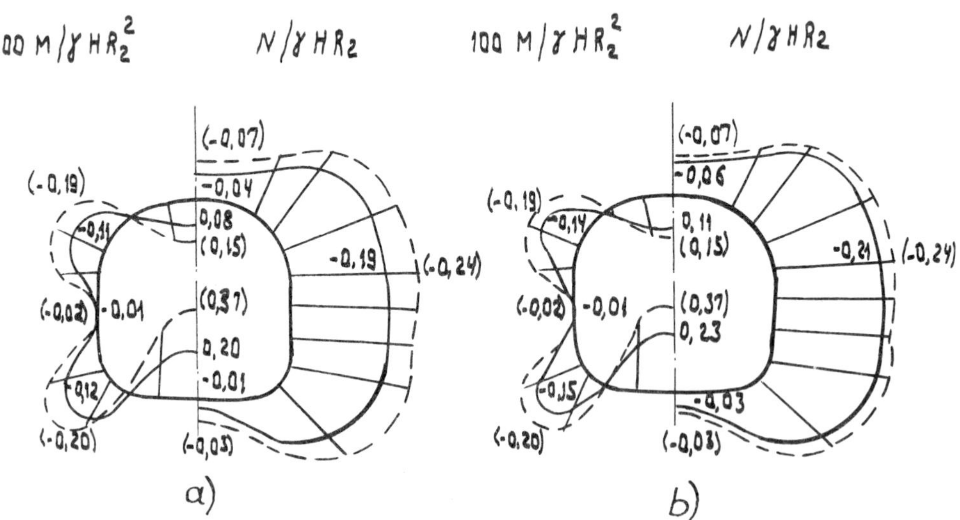

FIGURE 4. Distribution of bending moments $M/\gamma HR_2^2$ and longitudinal forces $N/\gamma HR_2$ in the lining after preliminary strengthening (a) and grouting through the lining (b) when rock is not subject to creep.

Fig.4a,b show distribution of bending moments $M/\gamma HR_2^2$ and longitudinal forces $N/\gamma HR_2$ correspondingly in case of the preliminary strengthening of rock not subject to creep and grouting through the lining (solid lines). For comparison there are distributions of the same forces (numerical values are given in brackets) in case of absence of any kind of strengthening (dash lines). One can see from Fig 4a,b that in considered case the preliminary strengthening gives on an average 20% reduction of forces in the lining, an effectiveness of grouting through the lining is less - the forces acting in lining are reduced approximately on 14%.

Fig.5 shows distribution of forces acting in the same structure on the 60th day when the preliminary strengthening (solid lines) or grouting through the lining (dash lines) are used in case of rock not subject to creep.

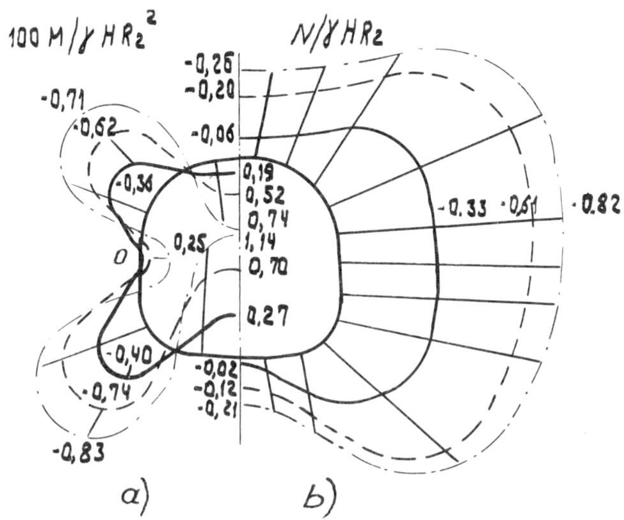

FIGURE 5. Distribution of bending moments and longitudinal forces in the lining when rock is subject to creep (solid lines - after preliminary strengthening; dash lines - after grouting through the lining; dot-and-dash lines - without any grouting).

One can see from Fig.5, that in rocks subject to creep the effectiveness of strengthening increases and it enables to reduce the forces in the structure on an everage on 50%. What is most important, as a result of strengthening the tensile stresses in the floor of the lining significantly decrease and there is no tension at all in the arch as calculations show.

Fig.6a,b show time dependent maximum compressive (Fig.6a) and maximum tensile normal tangential stresses on the internal boundary of the cross-section of the lining when the mean advance rate is $v=1,9$ m/day.

It can be seen from Fig.6, that in rock subject to creep increase of both compressive and tensile stresses with time

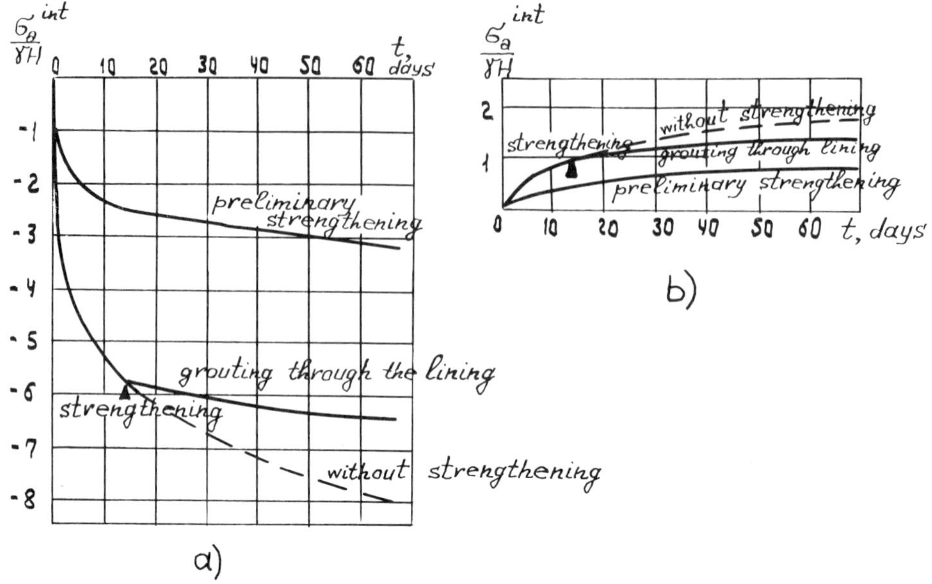

FIGURE 6. Changing of the maximum compressive and tensile normal stresses on the internal boundary of the lining cross-section in time after strengthening of rock subject to creep.

depends intrinsically on technique of strengthening. For instance, stresses reduce on the 40th day approximately in two times as a result of the preliminary strengthening; when grouting through the lining is used stresses in the same case reduce in 1,2 times on the 40th day. Effectiveness of the grouting through the lining is the higher the closer to face it is carried out.

To evaluate reliability of the results obtained using developed method of computation they were compared with the natural scale measurement data. The authors of the work /8/ having carried out large-scale studies of the influence of technique of strengthening on the displacements of arches of the metal frame support, kindly put necessary initial data at our disposal.

After determination of the displacements of points of the internal boundary of the equivalent ring S_3 the displacements of separate frames are computed, as it has been done in the N.S.Bulychev's work /9/. The computations were carried out with initial data: Δ_1 =1,5m; Δ_2=0,15m; E_1=13000 MPa; ν_1 =0,3; E_2 =8000 MPa; ν_2 =0,12; E_3=9611 MPa; ν_3 = 0,3; α=0,7; λ=1; δ = =0,0037 $s^{-0.3}$; γH =27 MPa; ℓ_0 =0,5m; ℓ_1 =60m; t_0 =0,5 day; t_1 =25 days.

The distribution of vertical displacements of the crown of the arch of the lining as function of time is shown on Fig.7 (solid line - measured, dash line - computed displacements).

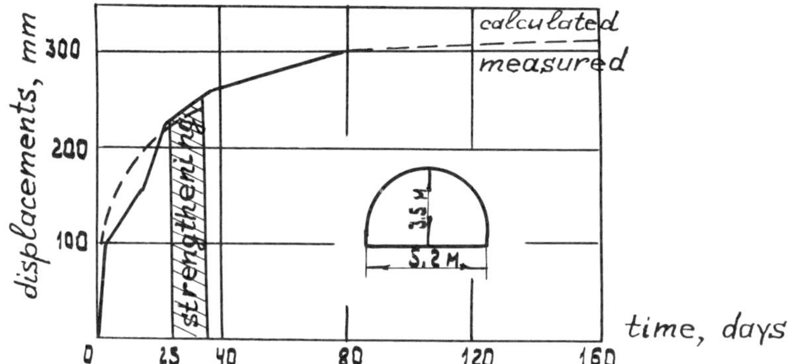

FIGURE 7. Dependence of vertical displacements of the arch of metal frame support from time.

One can see from Fig.7, that in spite of certain conventionality of the design model (substitution continuous closed ring for unclosed structure consisting of separate frames), magnitudes of the calculated displacements of the lining and character of their time-dependence after strengthening of the massif are in good agreement with the natural-scale measurements data (discrepancy is not more than 8%). The comparison confirms feasibility of using of the developed method for calculation and designing underground structures erected with strengthening of the surrounding massif.

REFERENCES

1. Fotieva N.N., Sammal A.S., Design of the closed Monolithic Lining with the Rock Strengthening Taken into Account. Proc. of the 9th Plenary scientific session of the International Bureau of Strata Mechanics. World Congress. Varna. 18-21 June 1985.- p.163-167.
2.* Amusin B.Z., Linkov A.M., On Using of the Variable Moduli Method for the Solution of the Class of Problems of the Linear Hereditary Creep. Izv. USSR Academy of Sciences. Mechanics of Solid Body, 1974. - No.6. - p.162-166.
3. Denisov V.N., Chetyrkin N.S., Golubev A.N., Long-term Investigation of Soil Deformability by Automatic Pressuremeter,

Proc. of the Symposium on the Pressuremeter and its Marine Applications, Paris, France, 1982.
4.* Vyalov S.S., Rheological Principles of Soil Mechanics, Moscow, "Vysshaya Shkola Publ. House", 1978.
5.* Fotiyeva N.N., Calculation of the Underground Structures Lining in Seismic-Active Regions. - Moscow: "Nedra Publ. House", 1980,- 270 p.
6.* Fotiyeva N.N., Savin N.I., Sammal A.S., Investigation of Influence of a Round Zone of Grouted Rock on Stress State of Mine Shaft Lining, Tula Polytechnical Institute, - Tula, USSR, - 11p. - Dep. in TsNIIEUgol, No.3686.
7.* Davydova N.A., Approximate Solution of the Problem of Displacements of the Surface of an Infinite Cylindrical Opening Loaded by Rigid Circular Test Cylinder of the Finite Length, "Fiziko-techn. probl. razrab. polezn. iskop.", 1968, - No.3, p. 111-117.
8.* Vlasenkov V.Ja, Chereslo I.Ja., Improvement of the Stability of Mining Openings at the Newly-Built Mine "Yuzhno-Donbasskaya" No.3, "Shahtnoye Stroitelstvo Magazin", 1986, No.10, p.28-29.
9.* Bulychev N.S., Mechanics of the Underground Structures, Textbook for College,- Moscow, "Nedra Publ.House", 1982,- 270 p.

---

* All references asterisked are published in Russian

STRENGTH AND CREEP OF SWELLING CLAYS

S.R.MESCHYAN
Professor, Doctor of Sciences (Engineering),
Academy of Sciences of the Armenian SSR,
Yerevan, USSR
and
S.G.HAIROYAN
Engineer, Institute "Gidroproyekt",
Yerevan, USSR

ABSTRACT

In order to check the possibility of expanding the generalized law of shearing creep (Meschyan, 1976) over the swelling soils the present paper is devoted to consideration of the results regarding determination of shearing resistance, free swelling pressure and shearing creep of the swelling bentonite-and-sand mixture in different states of its compactness and humidity. Experimental investigations show that the shearing creep law mentioned above, may be applied to the soils under consideration. According to this law the simple shearing creep deformations of these soils, independently of the state of their compactness and humidity and their standard shearing resistance $\tau_{f,st}$, are practically similar at equal levels of the tangential stress $\tau / \tau_{f,st}$ (τ is the tangential stress).

Determination of deformation properties of clayey soils at their shear, taking account of such factors as time (creep) alternation of the initial (natural) humidity and compactness, is of great interest in general, and particularly so in case of swelling soils. A special interest to determination of the shearing creep of swelling soils is caused by the phenomenon complexity, on the one hand, and by insufficient quantity of works in this field, on the other hand. Investigations in this field are devoted only to the shearing creep of swelling soils in one of their initial states of compactness and humidity [1]. The present paper is to fill in the blanks, i.e. to determine the shearing creep properties of swelling soils, varying their initial (natural) humidity and compactness in a wide range by both moistening and compacting them by different compacting pressures σ_z. The final aim of the paper is to find the possibility of expanding the shearing creep law discovered by one of the present authors [2,3] over the swelling soils:

$$\gamma_t = \omega(t)\, f(\tau / \tau_{f,st},\, t), \tag{1}$$

where $\omega(t)$ is the shearing creep measure, τ is the tangential stress and $\tau_{f,st}$ is the standard shearing resistance:

$$\tau_{f.st} = \sigma_z \operatorname{tg}\varphi + c \tag{2}$$

where $\operatorname{tg}\varphi$ and c are parameters.

A bentonite-and-sand swelling mixture containing 60 per cent (by the mass) of bentonite powder from the Saigyugh deposit in the Armenian SSR and 40 per cent of quartz sand has been tested for shearing resistance and creep in the torsion devices M-5 for solid samples [3] at two different values of the initial humidity w_o=0.150 and 0.315 (Table 1) and under the condition $w_o \gtrless w_P$ (w_P is the soil humidity at the plastic limit).

TABLE 1

Indeces of the Principal Physical Properties and Swelling Pressure $\sigma_{s,o}$ of Tested Samples

w_o	ρ_o, $\frac{g}{cm^3}$	ρ_s, $\frac{g}{cm^3}$	w_L	w_P	J_P	$\sigma_{s,o}$ MPa
0.150 0.315	1.825 1.844	2.68	0.859	0.260	0.690	0.3625 0.157
0.170 0.292	1.881 1.982	2.68	0.859	0.260	0.690	0.395 0.157

The free swelling pressure $\sigma_{s,o}$ (Table 1) and the standard shearing resistance $\tau_{f,st}$ for each initial state of compactness and humidity are determined when the initial humidity is preserved in the course of the sample compacting and shearing and when the samples are saturated $w=w_{sat}$. In the latter case the twin samples are saturated after being affected by the compacting pressure p_z. The data resulting from determination of the shearing resistance of the bentonite-and-sand twin samples at $w_o=0.150$ and 0.315 under two different conditions of their shearing and compacting are presented in Table 2 while their shearing resistance diagrams are given in Fig.1 [3].

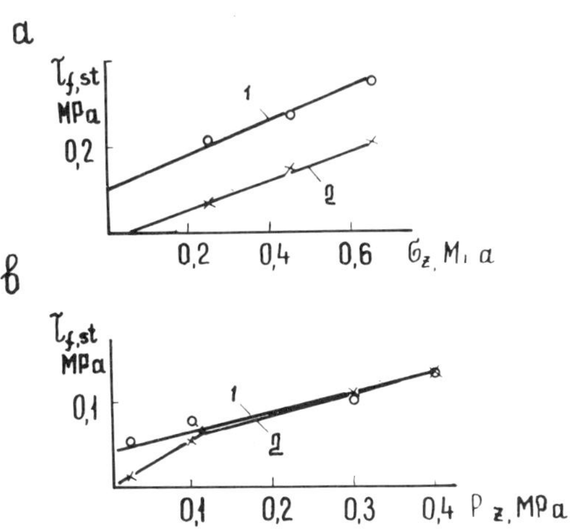

Figure 1. The shearing resistance diagrams of the bentonite-and-sand mixture 61-86.
a - $w_o=0.150$; b - $w_o=0.315$.
1 - sample test without moistening $w=w_o$;
2 - sample test after moistening at p_z

TABLE 2

Results of Determination of Bentonite-and-sand Mixture Shearing Resistance

Initial humidity and sample test condition		Standard Shearing Resistance $\tau_{f,st}$, MPa at p_z, MPa						
		0.025	0.10	0.25	0.30	0.40	0.45	0.6
w_0= =0.150	without moistening	-	-	(0.2081)	-	-	0.267	(0.345)
	with moistening	-	-	(0.0628)	-	-	0.143	(0.303)
w_0= =0.315	without moistening	0.0528	(0.0795)	-	(0.1004)	0.1250	-	-
	with moistening	0.0152	0.0603	-	(0.1064)	0.1266	-	-

The creep of the soil mixture under consideration is determined by testing seven sets of twin samples in seven different states of their initial compactness and humidity; their shearing resistance in Table 2 is cited within parentheses. Particularly, at w_0=0.150 the mixture shearing creep is determined before and after moistening the twin samples affected by two different compacting pressures p_z=0.25 and 0.65MPa, at w_0=0.315 it is found without moistening the samples affected by p_z=0.1 MPa, and at p_z=0.3 MPa it was determined both without moistening the samples and in their completely saturated state.

In each of the soil mixture states, mentioned above, its shearing creep is determined at three different tangential stress levels with their constant and step-by-step increasing values $\tau / \tau_{f,st}$=0.25; 0.5 and 0.75.

The double continuous lines in Fig.2 present the experimental shearing creep curves corresponding to the greatest and the least values of the creep deformation at the given level $\tau / \tau_{f,st}$ determined from the test of seven sets of the twin samples. Other creep curves, not indicated in Fig.2, are to be situated the curves in the Figure.

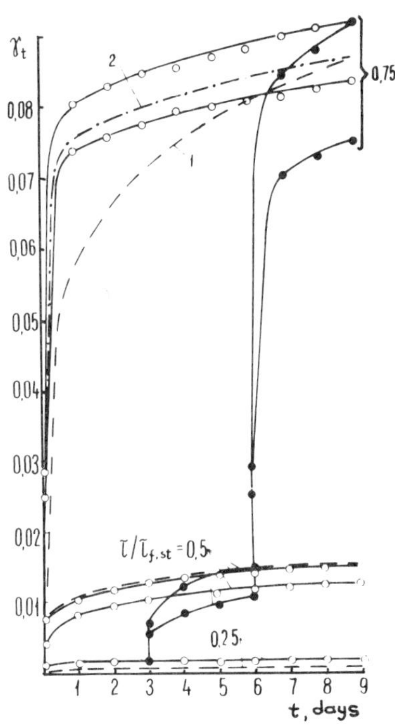

Figure 2. Composite diagrams of the experimental curve sets of the shearing creep of the bentonite-and-sand mixture 61-86 obtained from testing the samples in different states of their humidity and moisture, the samples being tested with and without moistening at p_z and at constant and step-by-step increasing levels of the tangential stress (continuous line) and their approximation without taking account of the creep curve insimilarity (1) and taking this insimilarity into account (2).

As it is seen from Fig.2, the scatter of the shearing creep deformations determined at equal levels of the tangential stress $\tau / \tau_{f,st}$ in seven different states of the swelling bentonite-and-sand mixture whose shearing resistance differs from each other more than five fold (see Fig.2), does not exceed ±10 per cent. This divergence of the experimental data does not exceed that of the experimental data obtained from testing one set of the twin samples.

What was stated above completely confirms the fact that the shearing creep law (1) defined for ordinary clayey soils [2,3] is also true for the shearing creep deformations of swelling soils; according to this law, at equal tangential stress levels $\tau / \tau_{f,st}$ the said deformations do not depend on the soil state of compactness and humidity, i.e on p_z and on the shearing resistance. It means that to obtain the equation of state for the swelling soils in case of their shearing (taking account of various factors) <u>it is sufficient to determine one set of the creep experimental curves</u> in one, arbitrary chosen, state of the soil compactness and humidity while the soil shearing resistance must be necessarily determined in all the states of the soil compactness and humidity in question, taking account of various affecting factors such as compacting pressure, moistening mode, etc.

To confirm the fact that expression (1) may be applied to the bentonite-and-sand swelling soil we have approximated, according to the known methods [3], a set of the shearing creep experimental curves of the studied soil mixture at $w_o =$ $=0.150$ when it was completely saturated after being affected by the compacting pressure $p_z=0.25$ MPa at the three levels of the constant tangential stress indicated above. The curve obtained at $\tau / \tau_{f,st}=0.5$ is assumed to be the curve of the single level of the tangential stress, and for the shearing creep measure the following expression is obtained:

$$\omega\,(t,\ w_o=0.15,\ \tau / \tau_{f,st}=0.5) = A\ t^m = 0.0099\ t^{0.174} \qquad (3)$$

and for the function of the tangential stress $f(\tau / \tau_{f,st})$ at $t=9$ days the following relation is found

$$f(\tau / \tau_{f,st},\ w_o=0.15) = B_1(\tau / \tau_{f,st})^n = 22.724(\tau/\tau_{f,st})^{4.503} \qquad (4)$$

satisfying the condition $f(\tau / \tau_{f,st} = 0.5) = 1$.

The creep curves built from expression (1) taking account of (3) and (4), in Fig.2 are shown by dash-lines. The considerable discrepancy between the curve according to expression (1) at $\tilde{\tau} / \tilde{\tau}_{f,st}=0.75$ and the experimental curve is caused by insimilarity of the shearing creep curves, i.e. by the dependence of the function of the tangential stress level (4) on the time factor. To take account of insimilarity of the shearing creep experimental curves in case of their approximation, the function of the tangential stress level is determined not only at t=9 days, but at other durations of the twin sample test, as well. Then expression (4) may be written in the following form [3]:

$$f(\tilde{\tau} / \tilde{\tau}_{f,st}) = B_1(t) \, (\tilde{\tau} / \tilde{\tau}_{f,st})^{n(t)} \tag{5}$$

where B_1 and n are functions depending on the duration of the sample test.

The dot-and-dash line in Fig.2 indicates the curve built according to relation (1) taking account of (3) and (5). As it is seen from Fig.2, taking account of insimilarity of the shearing creep experimental curves considerably improves the approximation.

Let us now consider results regarding determination of the shearing resistance and shearing creep of the bentonite-and-sand mixture in question in two other initial states of humidity w_o=0.170 and 0.293, i.e. preserving $w_o \gtrless w_P$ (table 1), and under two different conditions of the soil compacting and shearing.

The data on the shearing resistance determination as well as the data on the parameters $tg\varphi$ and c of the tested soil samples are presented in Table 3, and the shearing resistance diagrams are given in Fig.3.

The sample shearing resistance in each of the indicated states of the soil initial compactness and humidity has been determined when the samples were preliminarily compacted without moistening and when they were saturated in the arrester mode [4].

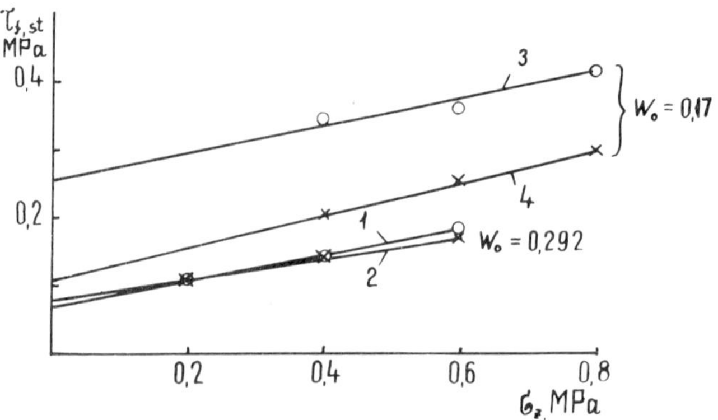

Figure 3. The shearing resistance diagrams of the bentonite-and-sand mixture 61-86 in two different states of its initial humidity w_o.
1,2 - w_o=0.292; the samples are compacted without moistening (1) and after moistening in the arrester mode (2);
3,4 - w_o=0.170; the samples are compacted without moistening (3) and after moistening in the arrester mode (4).

TABLE 3

Results of Determination of the Shearing Resistance of Bentonite-and-sand Twin Samples under Two Different Test Conditions

Initial moisture w_o and sample test condition		Standard Shearing Resistance $\tau_{f,st}$, MPa at p_z, MPa				tgφ	c, MPa
		0.2	0.4	0.6	0.8		
w_o=	without moistening	-	(0.335)	0.257	0.413	0.194	0.252
=0.170	with moistening	-	(0.202)	0.252	0.295	0.233	0.110
w_o=	without moistening	0.1079	(0.1355)	0.179	-	0.178	0.0697
=0.292	with moistening	0.1066	(0.1380)	0.1575	-	0.152	0.0765

As it is seen from Table 3, when the bentonite-and-sand samples with their humidity w_o w_P are compacted and sheared preserving their initial humidity w_o=const and after being saturated in the arrester mode $w=w_{sat}$, their shearing resistances considerably differ from one another because of the adsorptive decrease of strength at saturating. But when w_o=0.292 w_P=0.260, their shearing resistances coincide and confirm the results obtained by the authors earlier [4].

The shearing resistance is determined under two different conditions of compactness and shear of the twin samples:

a) at constant initial humidity $w=w_o$, i.e. without moistening;

b) after saturating the samples in the arrester mode $w=w_{sat}$.

In the first case the total outside load on the twin samples p_z was equal to the effective pressure $\sigma_z (p_z = \sigma_z)$ and in the second case $p_z = \sigma_{s,o} + \sigma_z$ where $\sigma_{s,o}$ is the pressure of the sample free swelling (see Table 1).

In all the four states indicated above the twin samples experienced the shearing creep, affected by one and the same effective compacting pressure σ_z=0.4 MPa at three different tangential stress levels with constant and step-bystep increasing values $\tau / \tau_{f,st}$=0.25, 0.50 and 0.75.

Results regarding the shearing creep deformations of two various bentonite-and-sand samples, considered above, under two different test conditions at three constant and step-by-step increasing levels of the tangential stress are presented in Fig.4. Like Fig.2, Fig.4 presents the limiting (of four) curves of the creep characterizing the greatest and the least values of the shearing creep deformations, i.e. the greatest divergence between the experimental data obtained at one and the same values of the tangential stress level $\tau / \tau_{f,st}$.

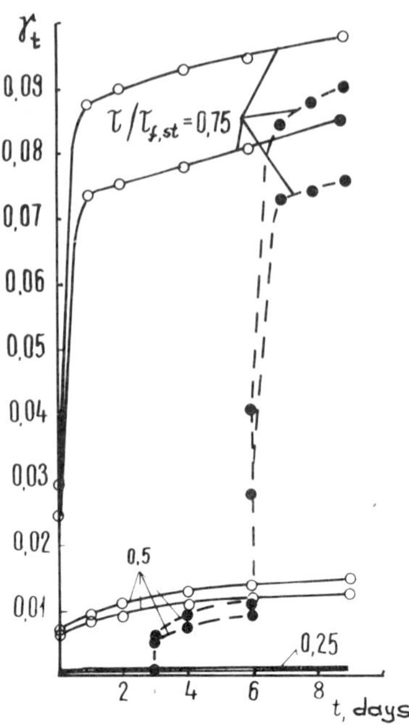

Figure 4. Two limiting curves of two experimental curve sets of the shearing creep of the soil 61-86 tested without the sample moistening $w=w_o$ and after the sample moistening in the arrester mode $w=w_{eq}$, affected by $\sigma_z=0.4$ MPa at constant (continuous lines) and step-by-step increasing (dash lines) of the tangential stress.

As it should be expected, the shearing creep deformations of the samples with similar shearing resistance values (see Table 3) and initial humidity $w_o=0.292 > w_P=0.260$, are practically equal at equal tangential stress levels. When the tangential stress levels are equal, absolutely similar results are also obtained when testing the samples with the initial humidity $w_o=0.170 < w_P=0.260$ whose shearing resitances considerably differ from each other in case of their compactness and shear occuring when their natural (initial) humidity is preserved (without moistening) and when they are saturated in the arrester mode (see Table 3). Hence, the shearing creep law (1) is true in this case, as well.

Finally, let us compare the results regarding the shearing creep determination of the bentonite-and-sand mixture presented in Fig.2 and 4. From this comparison it is easy to see that in testing the samples under eleven different conditions for their initial compactness and humidity and their shearing resistance with and without moistening, their shearing creep deformations are practically similar at equal tangential stress levels. It will be more correct to say that divergence of the data on the shearing creep deformation in testing samples, absolutely different in their properties, does not exceed divergence of the data obtained from testing one set of the twin samples. It is true both for the case of preliminary compacting the samples along the compacting branch of the compression curve and for the case of compacting after saturating the sample in the arrester mode.

Summarizing what was said above, we may confidently say that to determine the shearing creep properties of swelling soils (at considerable alternation of their properties affected by the most different factors) it is sufficient to determine from the experiment only one set of experimental curves in any state of the sample compactness and humidity. Besides, it is necessary to experimentally determine alternation of the soil shearing resistance depending on the factors of our interest (such as compacting pressure, test mode, moistening conditions, etc.). It means that alternation of the soil state affecting its shearing creep properties is taken into account through the alternation of the strength indeces.

REFERENCES

1. Meschyan, S.R. and Malakian, R.P., Zakonomernosti deformirovania nabukhyuschego grunta vo vremeni. Osnovania, fund. i mekh. gruntov, 1979, No1, s.21-24.
2. Meschyan, S.R., Ob opredelenii uravnenia polzuchesti glinistykh gruntov pri sdvige. Izv. vuzov. Str-vo i arkh-ra, 1976, No.2, s.172-176, il.
3. Meschyan, S.R., Eksperimentalnaya reologia glinistykh gruntov, M., Nedra, 1985, 342 s.
4. Meschyan, S.R. and Hairoyan, S.G., Vliyanie nachalnogo sostoyania na soprotivlenie sdvigu nabukhayuschego bentonitovogo grunta. Dokl. akad. nauk Arm. SSR, 1987, tom 84, No.3, s.119-1922, il.

EFFECTS OF LONG-TERM K_o-CONSOLIDATION ON UNDRAINED STRENGTH OF CLAY

Kazuya Yasuhara and Kazutoshi Hirao
Department of Civil Engineering,
Nishinippon Institute of Technology,
Kanda 1633, Fukuoka-ken, 800-03, Japan

Shunji Ue
Department of Civil Engineering and Architechture,
Tokuyama College of Technology,
3538 Takajo, Kume, Tokuyama, 745, Japan

ABSTRACT

The effects of long-term consolidation on undrained behaviour were investigated by triaxial tests and direct shear tests on a reconstituted marine clay. The results from both tests were considered from total stress basis. Therefore, the current paper focusses on the effect of secondary compression on undrained strength of clay. In this discussion, the importance of earth pressure at rest, K_o, during secondary compression was particularly emphasized. A method for predicting the variations of K_o with time during secondary compression was presented as well as a method for estimating the change in undrained strength due to secondary compression. Also the interrelation between K_o and undrained strength was discussed.

INTRODUCTION

Secondary compression, as a kind of creep in cohesive soils has been one of the objects of rheological studies in soil mechanics. It is widely accepted that long-term consolidation has an important influence on such fundamental behaviour of soils as compressibility and strength. Bjerrum and his coworkers (1958, 1963) made a pioneering contribution to this subject. Bjerrum, Simon and Torblaa (1958) reported that clays which exhibit secondary compression would gain in shear strength with time.

In a later paper Bjerrum and Lo (1963) stated that even for a clay that did not show an appreciable secondary time effect its shear characteristics were also dependent upon the age of the specimen, and with time the clay became more brittle. Mikasa et al. (1971) using a direct shear apparatus provided data which proved that shear strength was still increasing after 196 days in samples undergoing long-term consolidation .By investigating behaviour of pore pressure build-up due to arrested secondary compression of San Francisco Bay Mud, Shen et al. (1973) concluded that secondary compression caused an increase in undrained strength and at the same time yielded stiffer stress-strain characteristics for the Bay Mud. Recently, Mitachi et al. (1987) examined the influences of secondary compression on the stress-strain behaviour of isotropically and anisotropically consolidated clays and then proposed a constitutive model for these clays considering secondary compression. The authors (1983) proposed a method for estimating the change in undrained strength due to secondary compression in long-term direct shear and triaxial compression tests on two reconstituted clays. The extension of the proposed method is described in the current paper.

One of the recent topics attracting the attention of geotechnical engineers witch pertain to secondary or delayed compression of soft ground is the change in earth pressure at rest during long-term consolidation. Schmertmann (1983) posed the question of what happens to the variations of K_o during secondary compression. Although since then there have emerged a number of discussions and some evidence of K_o-variations during secondary compression at laboratory tests, this topic still remains the object open for discussion by geotechnical engineers. However, until the present time few powerful methods have been available for the explanation of change in K_o during secondary compression. The authors therefore attempt to supplement this feature of the research in the present paper.

PRECOMPRESSION DEVELOPED BY SECONDARY COMPRESSION

Of paticular importance in the studies of the behaviour of so-called "aged clay" which undergoes long-term consolidation sometimes followed by cementation is determining the pattern of the e-log p' relation for cohesive soils subjected to different stress and time histories. In general overconsolidated clay is classified into two categories : one is from the release of the overburden pressure (type-A) ; and the other is from factors other than the release of overburden pressure such as secondary compression, cermentation, dissication stress and cyclic loading (type-B).

Fig. 1 illustrates the void ratio, effective consolidation pressure and undrained strength relations corresponding to a geological history subjected to secondary compression. According to Hanzawa et al. (1980), the aged clay traces the e-log p' curve (PRQT path in Fig. 1(a)) in the case of $C_r = 0$ demonstrating the brittle behaviour. Besides this, they insisted that undrained strengths at points R and Q did not differ from each other. However, since the effective stress at point Q increases by $(p_i' - p_o')$, the strength at Q should increase more than the strength at R although both states at R and Q are of the almost same void ratio.

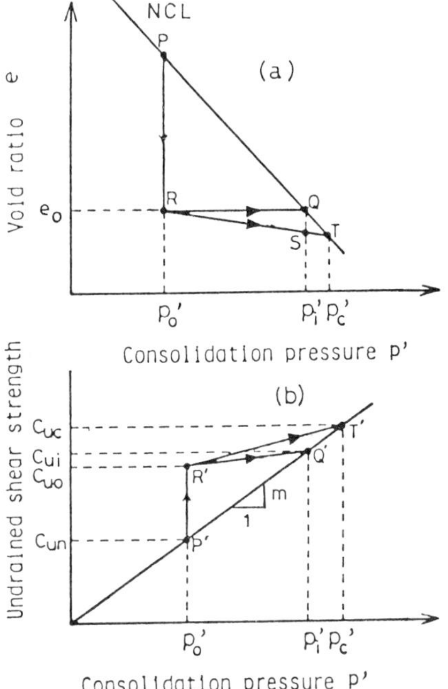

Fig. 1. Key sketch for e - log p' - c_u relations

Let us begin with the assumption that a soil element reaches point R in Fig. 1(a) after being subjected to secondary compression for the adequate time under a given overburden pressure. At this moment, a specimen is supposed to have a quasi-preconsolidation pressure, p_i' or p_c', rather than p_o'. The difference between p_c' and p_o' might be dependent upon the degree of secondary compression or cementation. This fact was pointed out by Leonards and Ramiah (1959).

By postulating linear loading and reloading branches of e-log p' curves shown in Fig. 1(a), for an aged clay Mesri and Choi (1979) and Murakami (1979) derived independently :

$$\frac{p_c'}{p_i'} = \left(\frac{t_1}{t_0}\right)^{C_\alpha/C_c/(1-C_r/C_c)} \qquad (1)$$

where t_0 is time required for natural deposition and primary consolidation, t_1 is age of deposit, C_c is compression index, C_α is coefficient of secondary compression, C_α/C_c = R, C_r is recompression index. In case of C_r = 0 for an aged clay, Eq.(1) becomes :

$$\frac{p_c'}{p_o'} = \left(\frac{t_1}{t_0}\right)^{C_\alpha/C_c} \qquad (2)$$

The coefficient and indices contained in Eq. (1) is defined by :

$$C_\alpha = d(\Delta e_s)/d(\log t) \tag{3-a}$$
$$C_c = d(\Delta e_p)/d(\log p) \tag{3-b}$$
$$C_r = d(\Delta e_r)/d(\log p) \tag{3-c}$$

where Δe_s, Δe_p, Δe_r : void ratio increments due to secondary compression, primary consolidation and release of overburden pressure, respectively.

As can be seen from Fig. 1(a) clays which potentially exhibit secondary compression show the behaviour similar to the overconsolidated soil. Therefore, quasi-overconsolidation ratio, n_q, for clay under secondary compression is equal to :

$$n_q = \frac{p_c'}{p_o'} = \left(\frac{t_1}{t_0}\right)^{C_\alpha/C_c/(1-C_r/C_c)}, \quad (Cr \neq 0) \tag{4-a}$$

$$n_q = \frac{p_c'}{p_o'} = \left(\frac{t_1}{t_0}\right)^{C_\alpha/C_c}, \quad (Cr = 0) \tag{4-b}$$

COEFFICIENT OF EARTH PRESSURE AT REST DURING SECONDARY COMPRESSION

Evaluation of K_0 during Secondary Compression

Since Schmertmann (1983) posed a question on the change in K_0 during secondary compression, some of the results from long-term triaxial consolidation tests on reconstituted and undisturbed clays (Akai , 1983; Yasuhara and Ue , 1983; Holtz and Jamikolowski , 1986) have been accumulated for discussion. Actually, however, few powerful or reasonably theoretical explanations of this matter have been available until the present time. Recently, Kavazanjian and Mitchell (1984) gave the following relation :

$$\frac{2.30\, C_\alpha}{(1 + e_o)t} = \frac{A}{2} \exp\left[\frac{\alpha\sigma_1(1 - K_o)}{D_f}\right]\left(\frac{t_1}{t}\right)^m \tag{5}$$

Very recently, based on the proposal by Mayne and Kulhawy (1983) Mesri and Castro (1985) obtained :

$$K_o = (1 - \sin\phi')\left(\frac{t_1}{t_0}\right)^{[C_\alpha/C_c/(1 - C_r/C_c)]\sin\phi'} \tag{6}$$

The authors have also been proceeding their discussion on the variation of K_o during secondary compression along the same lines as the research by Mesri and Castro. However, their assumption employed for obtaining Eq. (6) is different from the one used by the author (Yasuhara,1984). According to the authors' understanding, Eq. (6) is not applicable to the active K_o during loading. Rather, it is reasonable to adopt another

$$= u(t_0+t)\left[\frac{u_{\ell_0+vt}(t_0+t)}{u(t_0+t)} - \frac{u_{\ell_0}(t_0)}{u(t_0)}\cdot\frac{u(t_0)}{u(t_0+t)}\right] =$$

$$= u(t_0+t)\left[f(\ell_0+vt) - f(\ell_0)\frac{u(t_0)}{u(t_0+t)}\right]. \qquad (10)$$

$$u = -\frac{(c_0-1)(1-2\nu_2+\beta)+2\beta(1-\nu_2)}{(c_0-1)(1-2\nu_2+\beta)+2(1-\nu_2)}\cdot\frac{1+\nu_2}{E_2}R_2\gamma H, \qquad (11)$$

$c_0 = \left(\frac{R_1}{R_2}\right)^2$, R_1 is the mean radius of the external boundary of the strengthened layer, R_2 is the mean radius of the opening, $\beta = \frac{E_2(1+\nu_1)}{E_1(1+\nu_2)}$ and magnitudes of the deformation modulus E_1 and Poisson's ratio ν_1 should be calculated at the moments of time t_0 and t_0+t correspondingly in accordance with the formulae (2), (3) or (8). According to the theory of linear hereditary creep relations $f(\ell_0+vt) = \frac{u_{\ell_0+vt}(t_0+t)}{u(t_0+t)}$, $f(\ell_0) = \frac{u_{\ell_0}(t_0)}{u(t_0)}$ don't depend on time and can be calculated using the approximate solution by N.A.Davydova /7/ or the empirical formula

$$f(\ell) = 1 - e^{-1,3\frac{\ell}{R_2}}. \qquad (12)$$

$$e^{-1.3\frac{\ell_0+vt}{R_2}} \longrightarrow 0. \qquad (14)$$

$$\alpha^* = 1-\left(1-e^{-1.3\frac{\ell_0}{R_2}}\right)\frac{U(t_0)}{U(t_0+t)}. \qquad (15)$$

```
      WRITE(6,100) XM,Y
  100 FORMAT(/5X,"RESULTS OF CO-ORDINATE SEARCH"/
     *"ALFA=",F7.5,5X,"BETA=",F7.5,5X,"A=",F7.5/
     *"FM=",F10.5)
C  PREDICTED SETTLEMENT
      A=0
      SR=0
      NR=0
      WRITE(6,31)
   31 FORMAT("PREDICTED & EMPIRICAL SETTLEMENT
     *COMPARISION")
      DO 54 I=1,NP
      WRITE(6,32)P(I),SO(I)
   32 FORMAT("P=",F8.2,3X,"SO=",F8.3)
      NTR=NT(I)
      DO 55 J=1,NP
      K=NR+J
      B=TE(K)
      T=TE(K)
      CALL GAUSS(A,B)
      S=SO(I)*(TAN((0.002*P(I))**1.15))*
     *(1.+XM(3)*AINT)
      R=(S-SE(K))*([-SE(K))
      SR=SQRT(SR+R)
      WRITE(6,12) S,SE(K),TE(K)
   12 FORMAT("S=",F8.4,5X,
     *"SE=",F8.4,5X,"TE=",F8.4)
   55 CONTINUE
   54 NR=NR+NT(I)
      WRITE(6,51)SR
   51 FORMAT(5X,"MEAN QUADRATIC
     *DEVIATION=",F10.6)
      WRITE(1,61)
   61 FORMAT("ASSIGN PREDICTED LOADS AND TIME")
      READ(1,*)NP,(P(I),I=1,NP)
      READ(1,*)(SO(I),I=1,NP)
      READ(1,*)NK,(TR(I),I=1,NK)
      DO 24 K=9,NK
      B=TR(K)
      T=TR(K)
      A=0
      CALL GAUSS(A,B)
   24 GAUS(K)=AINT
      WRITE(6,30)
   30 FORMAT("DEVELOPMENT OF SETTLEMFNT IN TIME")
      DO 29 I=1,NP
      WRITE(6,27)P(I),SO(I)
   27 FORMAT(5X,"P=",F7,2,2X,"SO=",F10.5)
      SR=SO(I)*(TAN((0.002*P(I))**1.15))
      DO 29 K-1,NK
      S=SR*(1.+XM(3)*GAUS(K))
      WRITE(6,28)S,TR(K)
```

```
28    FORMAT("S=",F12.5,5X,"T(MONTH)=",F9.4)
29    CONTINUE
      END
C FORMATION OF OBJECTIVE FUNCTION
      FUNCTION FM(N)
      COMMON X,T XM(3),AINT,D(3),TM(3),SO(15),
     *NT(10),NP,P(150,TE(100),SE(100),KPR
      SR=0
      NR=0
      DO 104 I=1,NP
      NTR=NT(I)
      DO 105 J=1,NTR
      K=NR+J
      T+TE(K)
      A=0
      B=TE(K)
      T=TE(K)
      CALL GAUSS(A,B)
      S=SO(I)*(TAN((0.002*P(I))**1.15))*
     *(1.+XM(3)*AINT)
      SR=SR+(S-SE(K))*(S-SE(K))
      FM=SR
105   CONTINUE
104   NR=NR+NT(I)
      RETURN
      END
C INTEGRAL ON GAUSS
      SUBROUTINE GAUSS(A,B)
      DIMENSION AG(8),TG(8)
      COMMON X,T,XM(3),AINT
      DATA AG(1),AG(2),AG(3),AG(4),AG(5),AG(6),
     *AG(7),AG(8)/
     *0.10122854,0.22238104,
     *0.31370664,0.36278378,
     *0.36278378,0.31370664,
     *0.22238104,0.90122854/
      DATA TG(1),TG(2),TG(3),TG(4),TG(5),TG(6),
     *TG(7),TG(8)/
     *-0.96028986,-0.79666648
     *-0.52553242,-0.18343464
     *0.18343463,0.52553242
     *0.79666648,0.96028986/
      A1=(B+A)/2
      A2=(B-A)/2
      G=0
      DO 23 I=1,8
      X=A1+A2*TG(I)
23    G=G+AG(I)*EXP(-XM(2)*(T-X))/
     *((T-X)**(1.-XM(1)))
      AINT=G*A2
      RETURN
      END
```

```
C CO-ORDINATE SEARCH
        SUBROUTINE
        COMMON X,T,XM(3),AINT,D(3),TM(3),SO(15)
       *NT(10),NP,P(15),TE(100),SE(100),KPR
        Y=FM(N)
        WRITE(6,5)XM,Y,N
    5   FORMAT("CO-ORDINATE SEARCH"/4F10.4,
       *4X,"N=",I2)
        DO 3 I=1,N
   35   XM(I)=XM(I)+D(I)
        IF(XM(I)-TM(I))19,3,3
   19   Z=FM(N)
        IF(KPR)2,4,2
    2   WRITE(6,17) XM,Y,Z,I
   17   FORMAT(5F12.4,3X,I2)
    4   IF(Z-Y)33,33,1
   33   Y=Z
        GOTO 35
    1   XM(I)=XM(I)-D(I)
    3   CONTINUE
        RETURN
        END
        END
```

REFERENCES

1. Bartolomey, A.A., Omelchak, I.M., Permyakova, T.B., Omelchak,L.M. On stress-strain condition in Non-Linear Visco-Elastic Semispace. - Proceedings of the All- Union Conference "Actual Problems of Non-Linear Soil Mechanics". - Tchelyabinsk, 1985, pp.112-114. (In Russian).

2. Bartolomey, A.A., Dalmatov, B.J., Doroshkevitch, N.M., Sorohan, E.A., Fedorovsky, V.G. The work of pile foundations and the surrounding soil. Proc. of the IX Inter. conf. on Mech. and Found. End., V. 1., Okyo, Japan, 1977, pp.387-390.

TIME DEPENDENT BEHAVIOUR OF SAND

C.A. Mejia and Y.P. Vaid
Department of Civil Engineering
University of British Columbia
2324 Main Mall, Vancouver, B.C., Canada V6T 1W5

D. Negussey
Golder Associates
224 West 8th Avenue, Vancouver, B.C., Canada V5Y 1N5

ABSTRACT

An investigation of the time dependent behaviour of sands in oedometer and drained conventional triaxial loading is presented. Factors such as confining stress, angularity, relative density, stress ratio state and load increment magnitude are shown to influence time dependent deformation magnitudes. The results obtained suggest that the creep behaviour of sands closely resemble the creep behaviour of clays and metals.

INTRODUCTION

The stress strain behaviour of sand is generally regarded as time independent. For treatment of long-term deformation problems, this would be a satisfactory approach, as long as equilibrium time-independent soil parameters are used in the analysis. The time dependent response aspect of sand could become important in cases where loading frequencies or mobilized stress ratios are high. Typical problems encompassing such situations will be earthquake loading and expansion of a cylindrical cavity by pressuremeter.

Creep under constant pressure is the most vivid expression of time dependence of material behaviour. Reported fundamental laboratory studies of time dependent sand behaviour are few (1,2,3,4) and are mainly studies under one dimensional deformation conditions. This may be partly because of experimental difficulties associated with application of small load increments and direct measurement of small deformations in very short time span. The few reported investigations have not examined the influences of relative density, stress level and angularity of sand grains on creep behaviour systematically, even under the simple one-dimensional strain conditions.

Creep of sand in the oedometer represents deformation under essentially constant stress ratio R ($=\sigma_1'/\sigma_3'$) at stress states well below failure. Since deformation response of granular materials is intimately linked to mobilized R level, a systematic study of creep of sand under controlled increments of R would be of more interest than creep behaviour under constant R oedometer conditions. Such a study can be conveniently pursued in the conventional triaxial test and under drained conditions. Drained conventional triaxial conditions (constant confining pressure), are convenient because membrane compliance volume change errors do not occur in such stress paths. To the writers knowledge, only the work of Murayama et al. (5) constitutes research on some aspects of sand creep in the triaxial test. However, their investigation did not consider the influence of confining stress level, relative density and angularity of sand grains within the framework of a time dependent deformation study. Their test samples were subjected to several cycles of hydrostatic loading prior to shearing under constant mean normal stress conditions. As both axial and lateral stresses must vary to maintain a constant mean normal stress while shearing, such paths are subject to volume change measurement error due to membrane compliance. Both the shear and volumetric strain responses would therefore be subject to error because of the time dependent response of the rubber membrane to changing confining stress.

This paper presents a detailed study of the time dependent behaviour of sand. Drained behaviour was investigated under one-dimensional oedometer, constant R, as well as conventional triaxial, changing R, incremental compression loading. The effects of confining pressure, effective stress ratio, R, and relative density, D_r, on the magnitude of creep deformations in the triaxial test were examined. Two sands, one angular and the other rounded, but possessing identical gradations were tested to examine the possible influence of grain angularity on creep deformations.

EXPERIMENTATION

Sands Tested

Physical properties of the two sands used in this study are given in Table 1. Apart from differences in angularity, the two sands differ somewhat in mineralogy. Consequently, differences in the creep characteristics of the two sands may be partly due to different mineralogies.

Tests Performed

Oedometer tests were performed in a 7.5 cm diameter by 2.5 cm high instrumented polished stainless steel ring capable of measuring lateral stress. The vertical applied stress was measured both at the top and bottom to enable assessment of and correction for side friction. The side friction did not exceed 5 to 7 per cent of the applied load and stayed virtually constant during creep. K_o (the ratio of lateral to vertical stress under conditions of lateral restraint) values were determined from the measured lateral and vertical loadings. Tests were performed only on loose sand under various levels of vertical stress.

Triaxial tests were carried out on 6.3 cm diameter by 12.5 cm high specimens. Specimens at different densities and confining stress states were tested.

TABLE 1

Physical Properties of Sands Used in the Study

	Ottawa sand ASTM-C-109	Brenda Mine Tailings sand
Mean grain size, D_{50}	0.4mm	0.4mm
Uniformity coeff., C_u	1.5	1.6
Max void ratio, e_{max}	0.82	1.06
Min void ratio, e_{min}	0.50	0.69
Angularity	rounded	angular
Minerology	quartz	quartz (35%) feldspar (50%) others (15%)

Test Procedure

Test specimens were prepared loose by pluviation. The desired relative density was then achieved by controlled vibrations. Pluviation is considered to produce a sand fabric very similar to that of natural fluvial sands (6). The laboratory studies on pluviated sands should therefore correspond to creep behaviour of natural sands. Oedometer test specimens were air pluviated and tested dry. Triaxial specimens on the other hand were water pluviated and tested in a saturated state. Details of the specimen preparation technique are described elsewhere (7).

Creep loading was applied instantly by connecting the air loading piston to an air reservoir with a preset pressure. The computer interphased data aquisition system allowed high speed data scanning. This enabled capture of initial time-deformation data reliably to 1 sec elapsed times.

All specimens were loaded incrementally and creep under each increment was allowed for 20 min. In some tests creep was allowed at a larger load increment to assess the influence of load increment magnitude on creep response. In the oedometer tests, a ratio of load increment to current stress of one was used. Triaxial specimens were initially hydrostatically consolidated and shear stress increments were applied by increasing the axial load in amounts corresponding to increments of 0.1 in R under constant confining pressure. Small R increments were necessary to offset any transient undrained response in saturated triaxial specimens on sudden load application.

Creep under constant R was insured by making first order adjustments to axial loads to offset decreases in R due to area changes of triaxial specimens. R was maintained constant to within 0.05 per cent of the value under which creep was taking place.

Because of the generally small magnitude of deformations in sand, special care was taken to enhance the resolution of the measured strains. Both axial as well as volumetric deformations in all tests were measured to an accuracy of $1x10^{-5}$. Furthermore, tests were carried out in a constant temperature environment (maximum variation ±0.25°C) in order to eliminate the effect of temperature variations on creep deformations.

CREEP UNDER ONE-DIMENSIONAL DEFORMATION

Test results shown in Fig. 1a illustrate creep of tailings sand under various stress levels in one dimensional deformation. Volumetric creep deformations increase as the vertical stress level increases. This is shown more clearly in Fig. 1b, wherein volumetric strains after elapsed times of 1 sec and 20 min are presented. After the initial 1 sec, creep deformations to 20 min are shown to increase with stress level. The initial 1 sec deformations constitute approximately 80 percent of the total deformations that take place over a period of 20 min at all stress levels. Because succeeding stress increments are doubled, creep strain magnitudes per unit stress increment actually decrease with stress level. This tendency to stiffen with increasing stress level is a characteristic of non failure paths wherein lateral deformations are either restrained, as in an oedometer, or are contractive, as under hydrostatic loading.

The ratio, K_o, of horizontal to vertical stress was essentially constant at all stages of the tests. An average K_o of 0.55 was determined, and thus creep appears to occur at constant R in one-dimensional oedometer loading.

Figure 2a shows strain rates at small elapsed times are high and attenuate with time. The relationships are approximately bilinear and parallel at each stress level and initial strain rates increase for successive load increments. Separate linear segments are indicated for elapsed times below and above 8 sec. Linear relationships between log strain rate and log time have been observed by others (3,4) for sand creep under oedometer loading and elapsed times in excess of 1 min. However the bilinear type of creep response shown in Fig. 2a was not observed previously.

Behaviour of Rounded Ottawa Sand

Tests on loose Ottawa sand made under identical loading conditions show, Fig. 2b, creep behaviour similar to that for angular tailings sand. At identical stress levels and stress increments, creep deformation was smaller for the rounded Ottawa sand and the difference increased with stress level. K_o during creep of Ottawa sand was essentially equal to that for the tailings sand. The increased creep under identical R and stress level in the tailings sand is believed to be due to differences in angularity and to some extent differences in mineralogy.

CREEP UNDER TRIAXIAL LOADING

Characteristic Behaviour of Angular Sand

Typical results showing shear and volumetric creep of tailings sand under varying R levels are presented in Fig. 3. The tests were carried out by incrementing R by 0.1, starting from the hydrostatic R=1 state, so that the magnitude of volumetric deformations were small and transient undrained conditions did not develop. To enhance the presentation of the more salient creep response characteristics with increasing states of R,

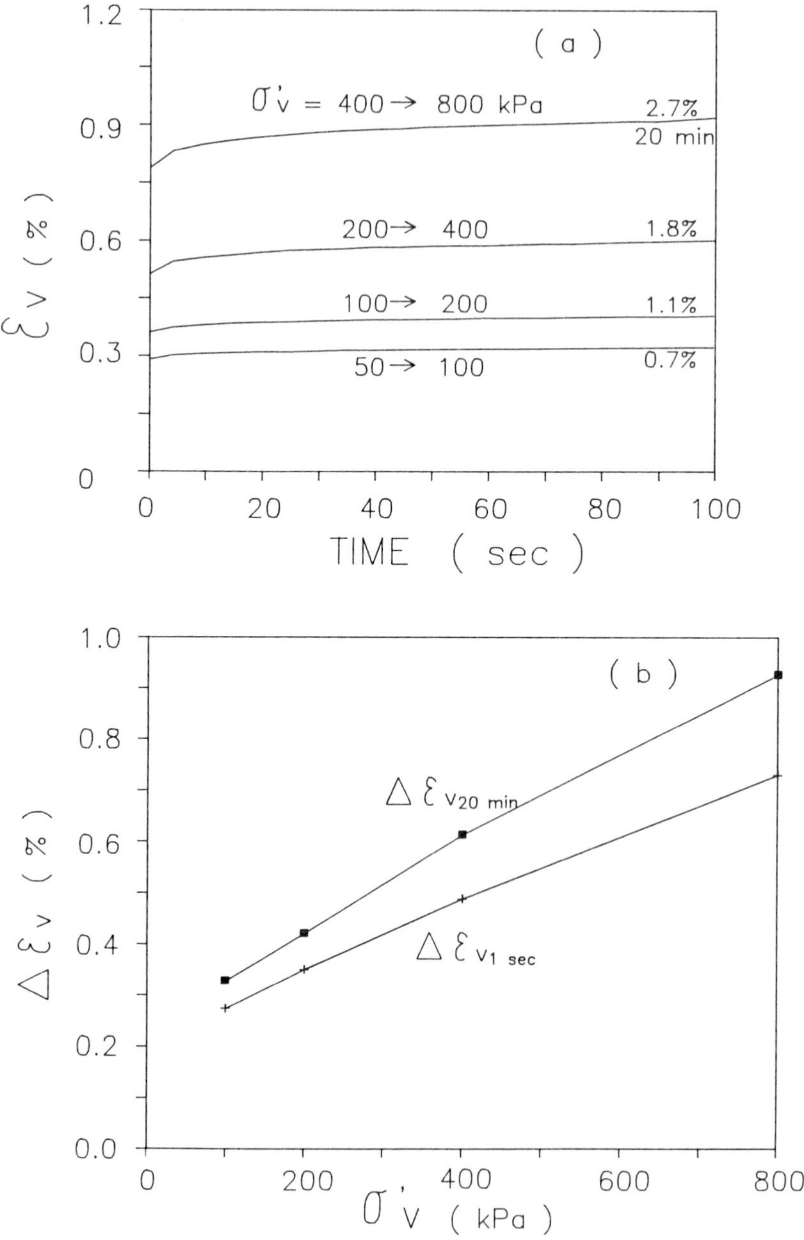

Figure 1. Creep of tailings sand under one-dimensional strain. (a) Strain time behaviour at several stress levels. (b) Instant and creep strains as functions of stress level.

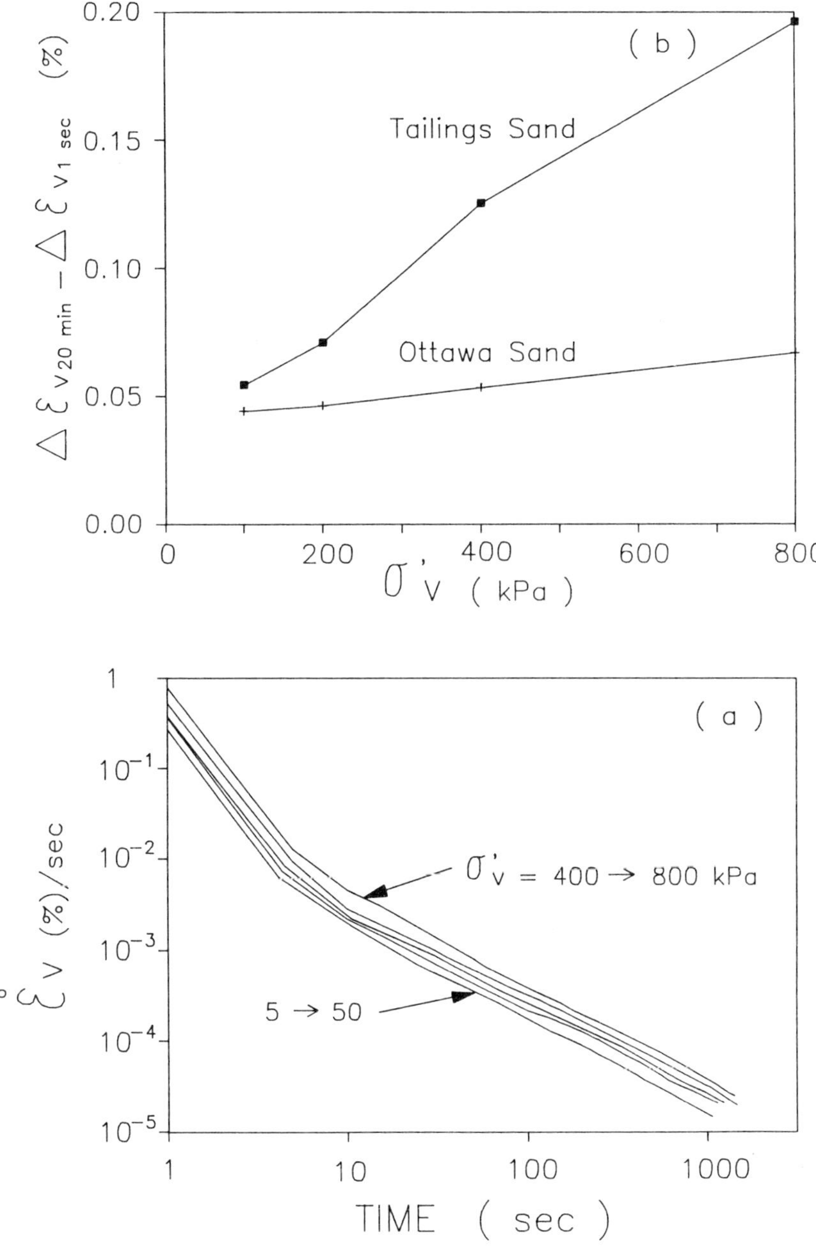

Figure 2. (a) Creep rate-time response of tailings sand. (b) Comparison of creep strains in tailings and Ottawa sands.

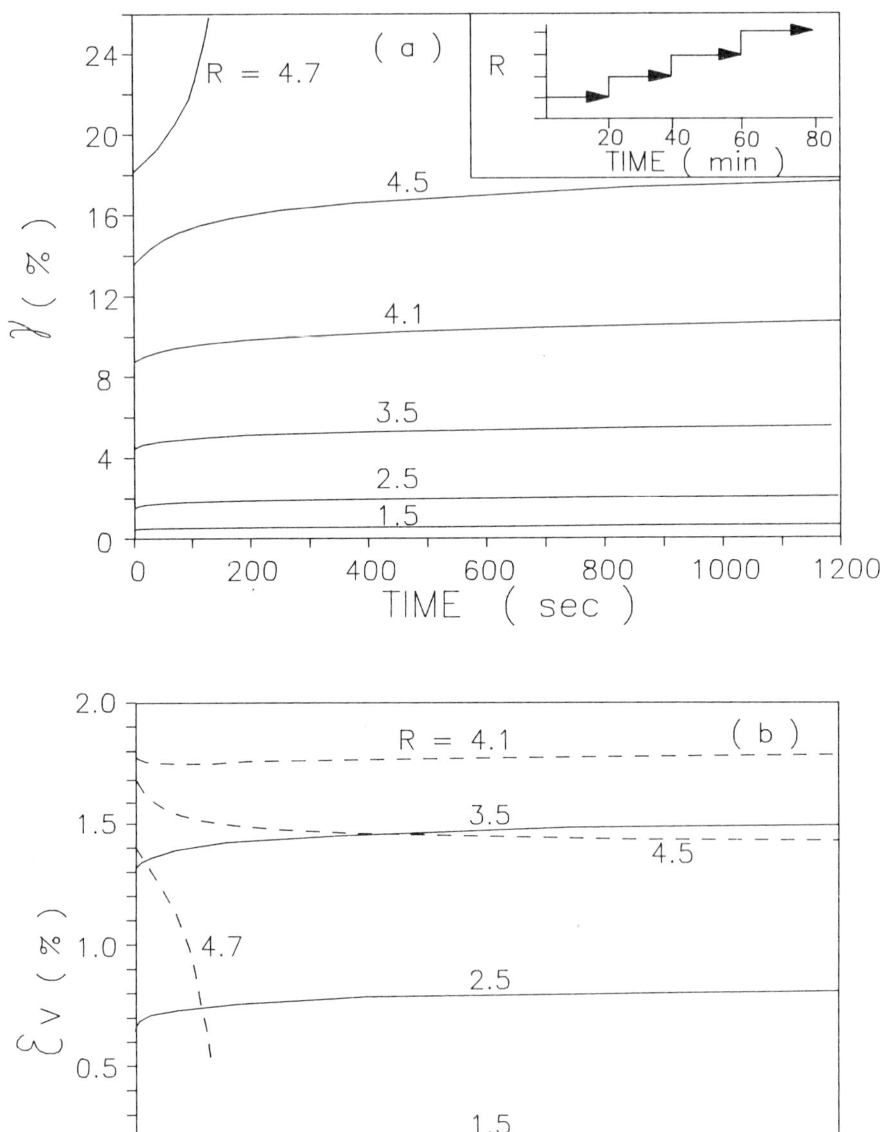

Figure 3. Creep of tailings sand a various R levels. (a) shear creep, (b) Volumetric creep.

fewer steps than were actually applied have been chosen for presentation. The results shown are for a relative density of 60 per cent and a confining pressure of 400 kPa. Both shear and volumetric creep strains magnitudes are small at low R values but increase rapidly with closer proximity of R states to failure. For R in the range of 4, volumetric creep strains begin to switch from contractive to dilative with time (Fig. 3b). This range of R corresponds approximately to the region of mobilized R in which maximum volume contraction occurs in static strain controlled drained tests. Volumetric creep for R in excess of 4.1 was entirely dilative. Creep under R = 4.7 resulted in rupture. This R level represents approximately the static failure value for the test relative density of 60 percent and confining stress of 400 kPa and rupture was therefore inevitable.

The initial shear and volumetric deformations to 1 sec elapsed time and under the applied shear stress increments corresponding to 0.1 increments in R were small and essentially independent of R state (Fig. 4). The proportion of creep strain to initial strain increases with R state. In both Fig. 4a and 4b, a distinct increase in initial and creep strain response may be noted at an R state of about 3.5 but when a stress ratio increment of 0.2 rather than 0.1 is applied. When application of the standard load increment magnitude of 0.1 in R is resumed the previous deformation pattern is re-established. Initial volumetric creep strain increments tend to be contractive at low R states but become dilative with increasing R.

Approximately parallel and linear shear and volumetric strain rate time relationships are indicated, Fig. 5, at low R states in logarithmic space. Such linear segments of shear and volumetric strain rates with time indicate the ratio of shear strain rate to volumetric strain rate remains fixed. This implies that creep strain increments follow an approximately fixed direction during creep deformation at R states of up to about 2.8. Hence, strain directions at small R stress states appear to follow paths that are characteristic to the applied stress increment direction. As the stress ratio states continue to increase and approach failure, a minimum creep rate and subsequent accelerating creep rate to rupture develop, as has also been observed previously (5). Thus, creep in sands consist of primary, secondary and tertiary creep stages and in the same way as for cohesive soils and other materials.

Effect of Relative Density and Confining Stress

The effect of relative density on creep deformations is shown in Fig. 6b. Initial deformations monitored after 1 sec of load increment application were small and relatively independent of density and R state and are not shown. However, subsequent creep deformations to 20 min elapsed time increase with R state but decrease with relative density. Application of a larger load increment resulted in a larger creep strain magnitude as was described previously. At equal relative density states, creep deformation magnitudes are also shown, Fig. 6a, to increase with confining stress level. Creep deformations are therefore dependent on relative density, the magnitude of the stress increment, confining stress and R level.

Peak stress ratio, R_{max}, values obtained from conventional triaxial, strain controlled, monotonic compression loading tests increase with relative density and decreasing confining stress level as shown in

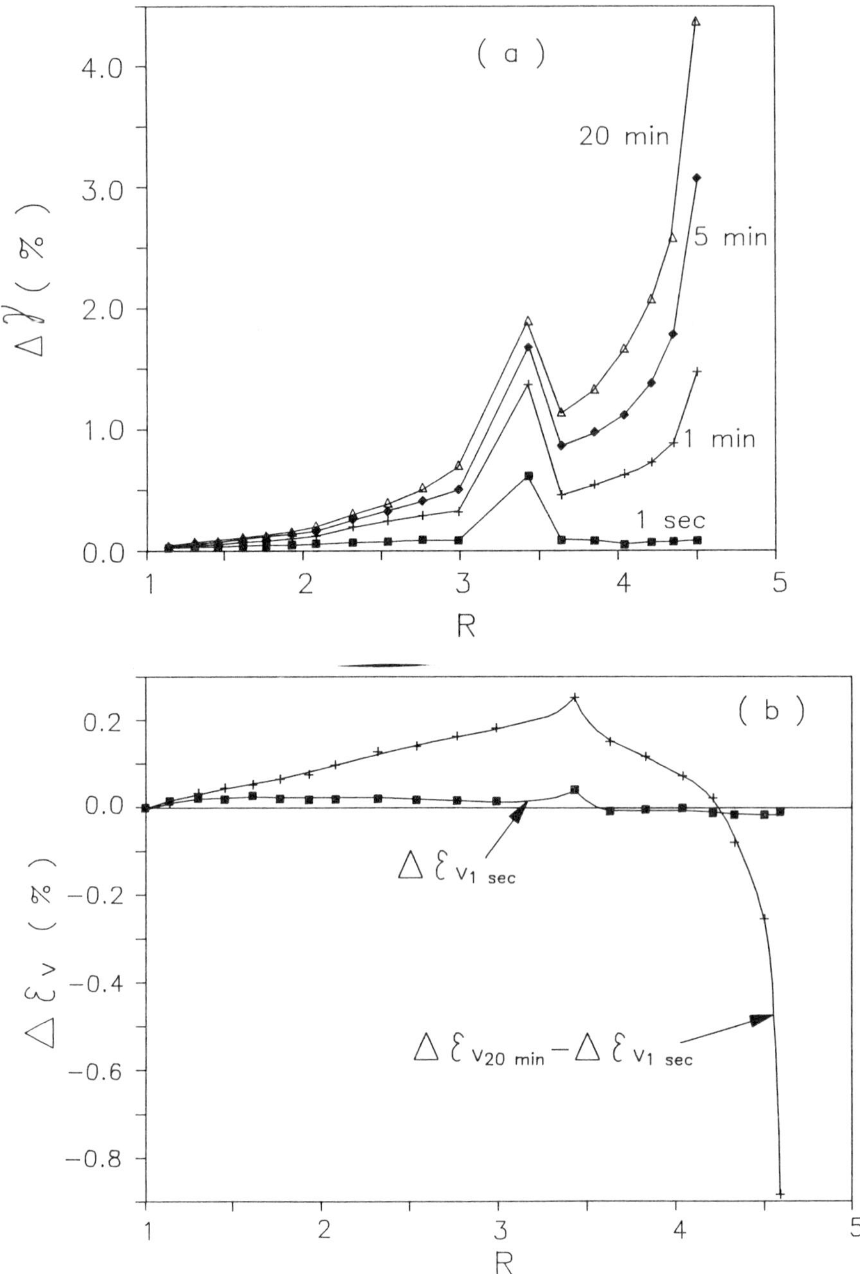

Figure 4. Instant and creep strains in tailings sand at various elapsed times. (a) Shear strains, (b) Volumetric strains.

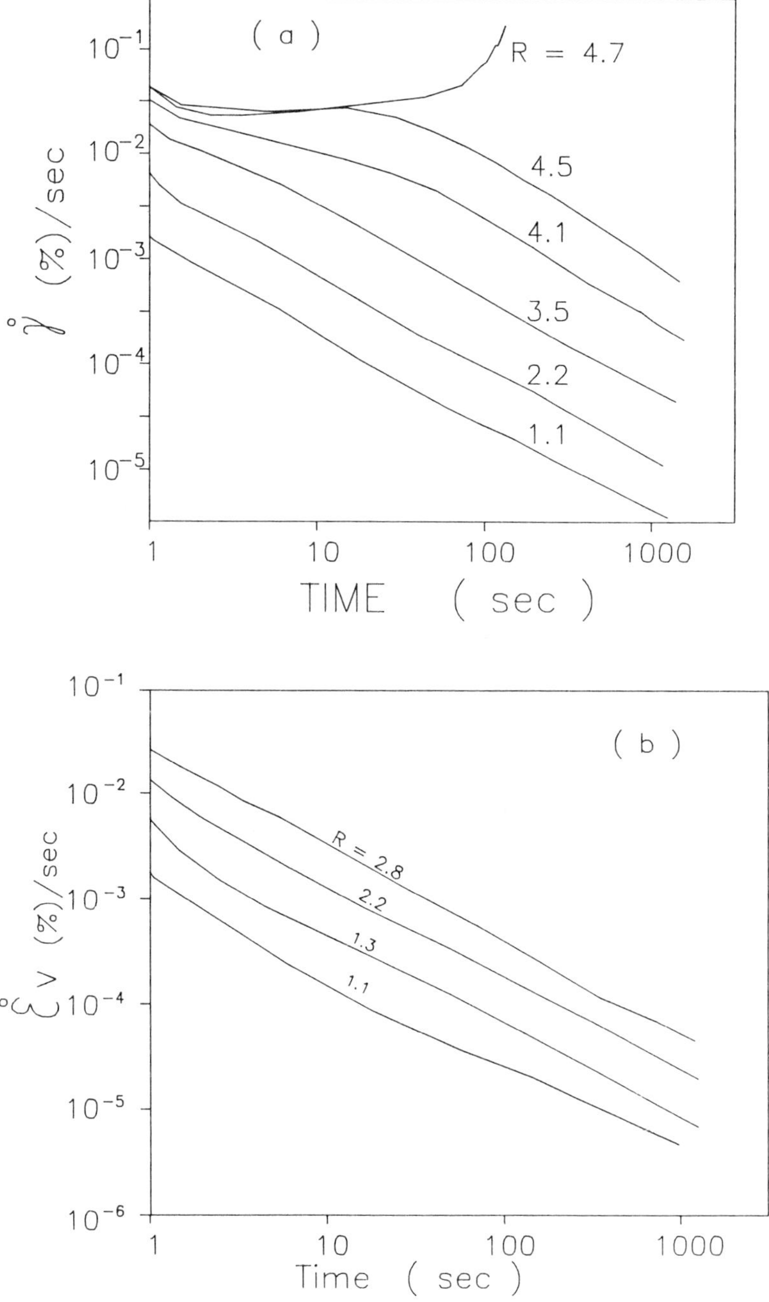

Figure 5. Creep rate-time response of tailings sand at various R levels. (a) Shear strain rates, (b) Volumetric strain rates.

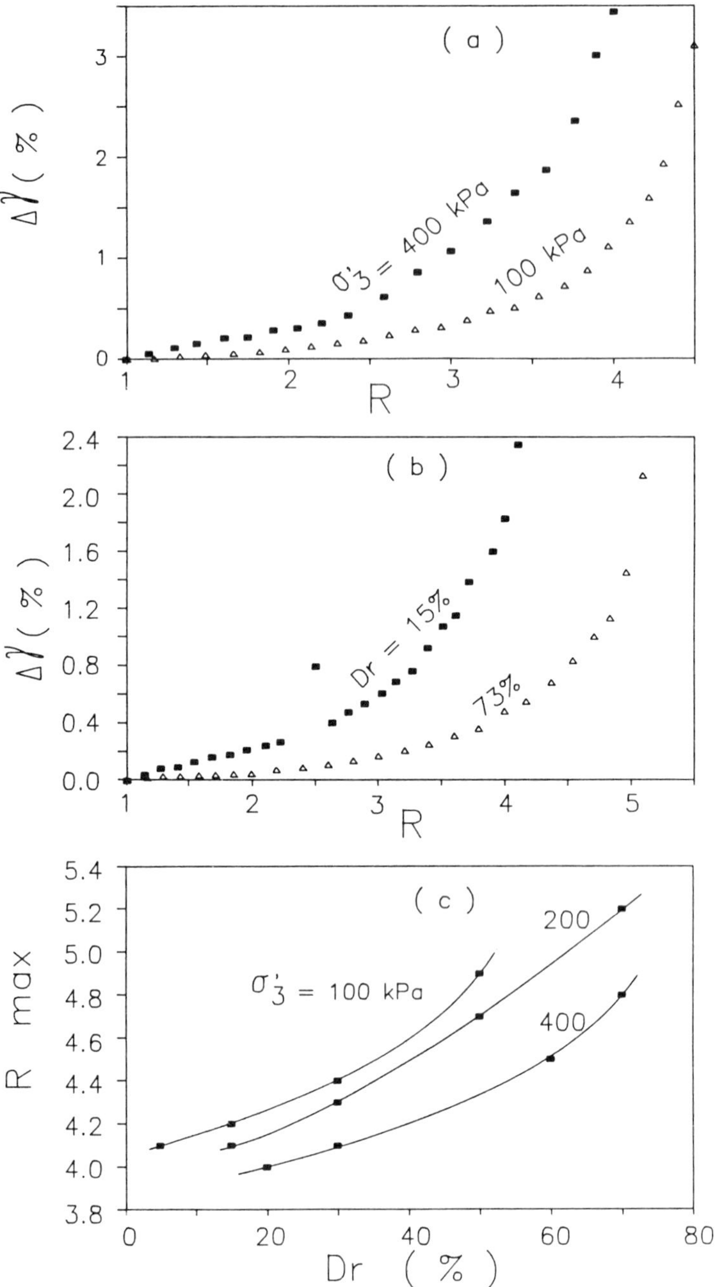

Figure 6. Effect of (a) confining pressure, (b) relative density on magnitude of creep strains, and (c) relative density and confining stress effects on failure R for tailings sand.

Fig. 6c. Creep strain magnitudes at equal elapsed time, stress ratio increment and R state increase with proximity of the stress ratio state to the respective peak stress ratio value. Normalization of R state by the corresponding R_{max} value would narrow the differences in creep strain and R relationships arising from changes in both relative density and confining stress.

Comparison of Angular and Rounded Sand Behaviour

Test results indicate that the time dependent deformation behaviour of rounded Ottawa sand is qualitatively similar to the test data and observations presented for the angular tailings sand. However, the magnitude of creep deformations and the influences of confining stress, relative density, R state and increment are less pronounced for the rounded sand in comparison to that for the angular sand.

Strain Hardening Under Creep

Test results shown in Fig. 7 represent shearing at a constant strain rate of 0.5 percent per min to a state R and switching to stress controlled mode to maintain R during creep. Results in terms of R state and shear strain for the angular tailings, and rounded Ottawa sand are presented in Fig. 7a and corresponding comparisons in terms of volumetric and shear strain state are shown in Fig. 7b. Both sands experience creep deformation but at comparable stress levels, stress increments and elapsed times, the angular sand develops more strain in creep. Creep straining tends to lead to hardening. On initiation of loading at a constant strain rate after a creep stage, the stress strain response is very steep and extends above the stress strain curve for the strain rate shown by dotted line in the insets. However, as the loading stage continues, the stress strain curve for the strain rate is regained. One difference between the two sands is however that the excursion above the stress strain curve and subsequent return to the stress strain curve for the rounded sand are more abrupt and brittle like.

Test data in Fig. 7a thus shows that the stress strain relationships that develop in response to shearing at constant axial strain rate are unique for each sand. Constant axial strain rate behaviour is very similar to behaviour at constant shear strain rate. Hence, the results presented suggest that a unique relationship between shear stress, shear strain and strain rate, as has been proposed for metals (8) and often called the mechanical equation of state, may also be valid for granular materials.

Figure 7b shows that both the angular and rounded sands experience volumetric creep deformation. During creep deformation dilatant and contractive volume change responses occur simultaneously or separately depending on R state. At R states corresponding to well below maximum contraction, the initial and creep stage volume changes tend to be contractant. In the intermediate stages of R and in the vicinity of maximum contraction, initial volumetric strains tend to be dilative and creep deformations contractive. On approaching failure states, both the initial and creep stage volume changes become dilative. These stages of volumetric deformation are shown more clearly in Fig. 8. For both sands, the strain paths resort to the monotonic loading response curve, without evidence of prior creep history, shortly after loading is initiated following a creep period.

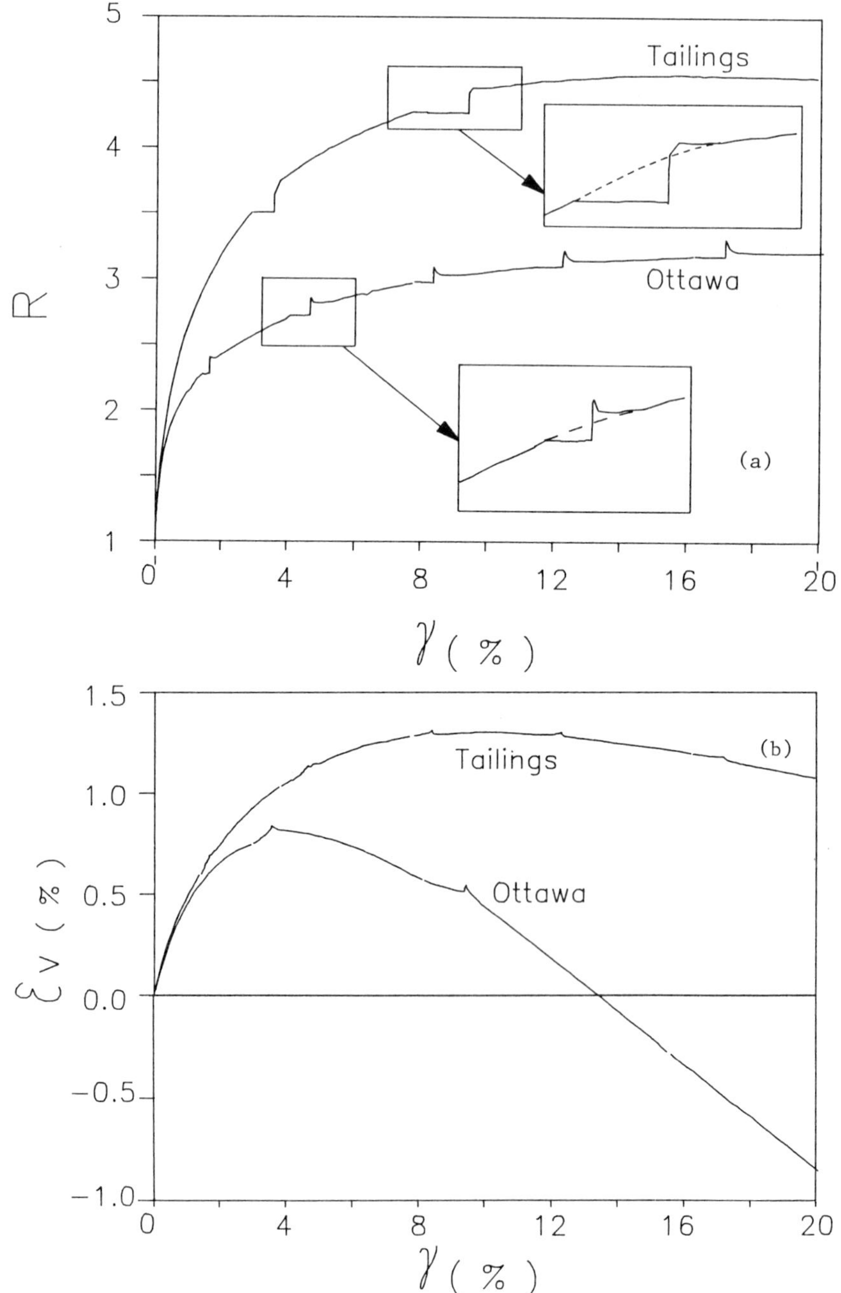

Figure 7. Creep history independence of constant rate of strain response of tailings and Ottawa sands.

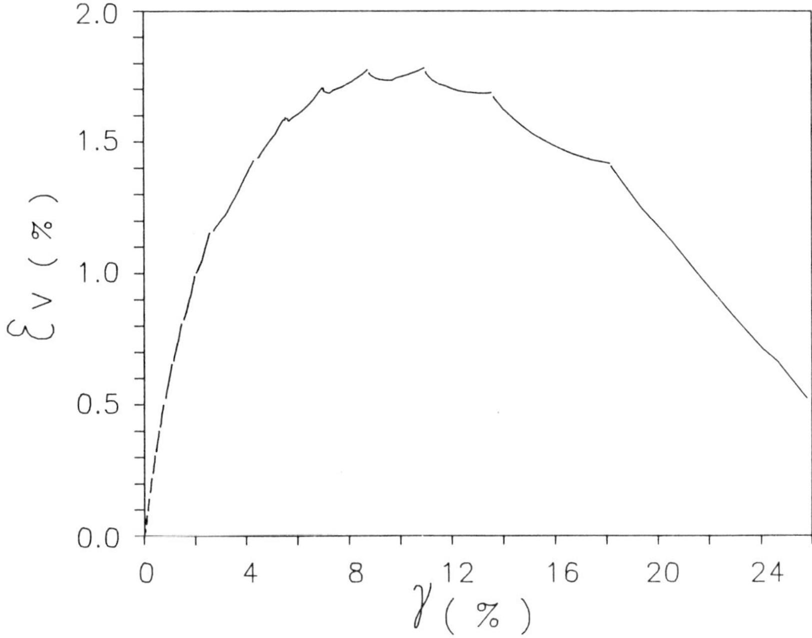

Figure 8. Development of contractive and dilative volumetric strains during creep of tailings sand.

CONCLUSIONS

Creep deformations of sand under one dimensional oedometer loading were found to increase with stress level and grain angularity. Parallel linear relationships were found between log creep rate and log time.

Under triaxial constant stress ratio conditions, both shear and volumetric creep deformations were found to increase with increase in stress ratio, confining pressure and grain angularity. Increase in relative density caused creep deformatoins to decrease. At low stress ratios, volumetric creep was contractive but changed to dilative with increasing stress ratio. At high stress ratios, creep rupture ensued.

Under constant rate of strain both angular and rounded sand showed behaviour corresponding to strain hardening creep law.

ACKNOWLEDGMENTS

This research was supported by a grant from the Natural Science and Engineering Research Council of Canada. Manuscript was prepared by Kelly Lamb and Janis Herchuk.

REFERENCES

1. Taylor, D.W., Fundamentals of Soil Mechanics, John Wiley & Sons, Inc., New York, 1948.

2. Terzaghi, K. and Peck, R.B., Soil Mechanics in Engineering Practice, John Wiley & Sons, Inc., New York, 1967.

3. Suklje, L., Rheological Aspects of Soil Mechanics, John Wiley & Sons, Inc., London, 1969.

4. Nonveiler, E., Settlement of a Grain Silo on Fine Sand, European Conference on Soil Mechanics and Foundation Engineering, Wiesbaden, 1963.

5. Murayama, S., Michihiro, K. and Sakaagami, T., Creep Characteristics of Sands, Soils and Foundations, **24**, No. 2, June ,1984.

6. Oda, M., Muramatsu, M. and Sasaki, T., Experimental Study of Anisotropic Shear Strength of Sand By Plane Strain Tests, Soils and Foundations, **18**, 1978.

7. Vaid, Y.P. and Negussey, D., Preparation of Reconstituted Sand Specimens, ASTM, STP No. 977, 1988.

8. Lubahn, J.D. and Felgar, R.P., Plasticity and Creep of Metals, John Wiley & Sons, Inc., New York, 1961.

FORCASTING OF LANDSLIDE PROCESSES ON THE BASIS OF THE ANALYSIS OF STRESSED STATE OF EXTRA-SCARP MASSIFS

D.M. AKHPATELOV
Moscow Institute of Civil Engineering (MICE)
Moscow, USSR

V.K. TSVETKOV
Volgograd Institute of Civil Engineering
Volgograd,USSR

ABSTRACT

The engineer method of analysis of slope and scarp stability which takes into account the initial stressed state of the soil mass is introduced in the study. The method is worked out on the basis of the analysis of solutions of many problems on stress-strained state (SSS) of soil masses in elastic and elasto-plastic position, and the form of breakdown surface is not taken as beforehand known, but is determined from the condition of minimum of the safety factor in every point of that surface. It is pointed out that the slope and scarp stability is greatly influenced by the coefficient of the initial stressed state of the soil massif. The work shows that it is possible to forcast the stability coefficient for the given period of time under the conditions of the known law of the cohesion changes in time.

Widely used in engineer practice, the analysis of the slope

and scarp stability is carried out, generally, with the account of, only, the vertical tension component equal to the soil mass's weight over the breakdown surface.

In other modern analysis methods, the characteristics of rocks, in view of difficulties in determination of factual tensions in extra-scarp area, are identified with the properties of two simplified models which submit to the boundary equilibrium theory or to the elasticity theory. The researches of many authors testify that the use of both theories is justified under some conditions. If the load on rock is such that, in every point of the extra-scarp zone, the resistance to shearing is not exceeded or exceeded on a very small area (which takes place, for example, at sufficiently small scarp heights), rocks practically behave themselves as a lineary strained medium. So, the elasticity theory is applicable in the given case. If the resistance to shearing is exceeded (the depth of working reached the boundary value), rocks turn into the state which is satisfactory described by the boundary equilibrium theory. In real conditions in the most important for tractice cases (at the stability coefficient proximate to I) there are, in the extra-scarp zone, elastic and plastic areas which predetermine the SSS of rocks and, finally - the stability of the extra-scarp mass.

The studies show that the results of forcasting of the processes which take place in soil mass, are influenced by its initial strained state. The coefficient of the initial stressed state of soil massif ξ should be chosen as parameter characterizing this state. The coefficient is equal to the ratio of horizontal normal tensions to vertical ones in an untapped, i.e. before the exploitation, soil mass (1). In case of natural slopes, this coefficient will translate the stressed state at some distance from the slope into the mass' depth. Should be noted the principle difference of this parameter from the coefficient of side-pressure which is a mechanical (strain) characteristic of soil. If the last one can be determined by means of mechanical soil experiments, the coefficient of the initial stressed state of soil massif must be measured immediately in the massif. Such a possibility was cited in work (2). In the absence of possibility to measure immediately this coefficient, it may be found through the analysis of the strength characteristics of soil and the visco-plasticity parameters (for example, the viscosity coefficient). The soil strength predetermines the possible values of the coefficient ξ . The visco-plasticity parameters allow to forcast the value of the ξ -coefficient with the account of time of the massif existance. Such a possibility is presented in work (3), according to which the ξ -coefficient changes in time. Undoubtedly, the forcasting of the ξ -coefficient supposes to take into account not only gravitational force, but other forces (seismic, glacial, etc.).

As show our researches (3), the ξ -coefficient plays an important role in stability of slopes and scarps. Such a conclusion is based on a comparison of isolines of the soil safety factor in point and dimentions of the areas of boundary equilibrium for uniform soil masses, but with different ξ -coefficients. It should be also noted that the account of this coefficient influences on the values of the determining strain and strength parameters of soil.

The present report outlines the possibility of taking into account of the ξ -coefficient of initial stressed state in the analysis of slope-scarp stability. We stand on the elaborated method of the slope-scarp stability analysis, in which, in contrast to the existing analysis methods, the form of the breakdown surface is not taken as beforehand known, but is found from the condition of minimum value of the safety factor in every surface point and depends on physico-mechanical characteristics of rock; should be taken into consideration all the components of tension under plane deformation, the influence of scarp base, the presence in the extra-scarp zone of elastic and plastic areas, and modification of physico-mechanical properties of rocks in depth and in time.

In the absence of plastic areas, the tensions in uniform scarp are determined through the precise solution of the elasticity theory's problems for a ponderable uniform half-plane with trapezoidal notches on its limit with the use of the theory of the complex variable functions (3,4,5). In case of bedding slopes, we use the final elements method (FEM) with the determination of the analysis model's dimentions, the way of its fixation, the number and dimentions of elements with the help of the precise solution obtained for uniform slopes (6).

In presence in the extra-scarp zones of plastic areas, the tensions are found by means of the approximative solution of the corresponding elasto-plastic problems (7,8).

The ξ -coefficient was taken into account in solution of the boundary-value problems. The way of its account is presented in work (1).

On the basis of proceeding of the results of a great number of analysis we got the dependences between the stability coefficient values, the physico-mechanical characteristics of rocks and geometric slope parameters:

under $\lambda \geqslant 0{,}1$

$$K = \frac{4}{7}(1 + \xi) \quad (a\lambda + b)\mathrm{tg}\,\varphi \qquad (1)$$

under $0 \leqslant \lambda < 0{,}1$

$$K = \frac{4}{7}(1 + \xi)\sqrt{10\lambda(d^2 - \mathrm{ctg}^2\beta) + \mathrm{ctg}^2\beta}\;\mathrm{tg}\,\varphi \qquad (2)$$

where: K - stability coefficient; ξ - coefficient of initial stressed state of soil massif; φ - internal friction angle; a,b,d - coefficients which depend on the slope angle β and which are determined through the plots in Fig.1; $\lambda = 2c\,\mathrm{ctg}\,\varphi/\gamma h$ - stability parameter (c - adhesion, γ - soil density, h - slope height). These formulas are just for uniform and bedding slopes when the breakdown surfaces cross the layers contacts. In the last case, the values of γ, c, ξ, tg φ are determined as weighted average.

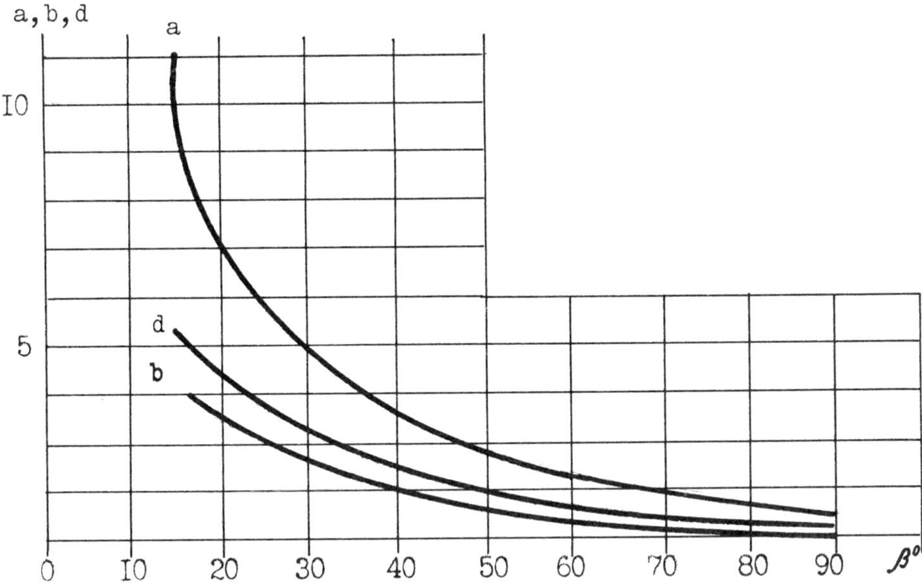

Figure 1. Diagrams of dependence of a-,b-,d-coefficients on β - angle.

Formulae (1) and (2) show the considerable influence that the parameter of the initial stressed state ξ exerts on the stability coefficient. Let's examine it on an example. Let's have some uniform massif with the foundation pit: h (depth) = 10 m and the slope angle $\beta = 40^\circ$. Soils which constitute the massif have the following characteristics: $\gamma = 18$ kN/m^3; $\varphi = 18^\circ$; C = 15 kPa.From the plots in Fig.1 we find: a = 3,7; b = 2,0; d = 2,5. Then, λ =(2.15.ctg 18^0/18.10) = 0,51. As $\lambda > 0{,}1$, we use formula (1) to determine the stability coefficient. We find: K = 0,72(1 + ξ). At $\xi = 1$, K = 1,44, and, at $\xi = 0{,}4$ K = 1,00, i.e.depending on the value of ξ , the slope may be in pre-boundary or boundary state.

If, revealing the dependence of the time factor on the slope and scarp stability, we use the creep linear theory, particularly, the Volterre principle, according to which, in solution of the similar classical problem on the elasticity theory, one should substitute the elastic constants of the material for the corresponding temporary operators, formulae (1), (2) will help to determine the K - value in every moment of time under condition that the adhesion value is the known function of time. Indeed, as is generally known, the angle of internal friction practically does not vary in time; besides, in case of uniform scarps, the ξ -coefficient value can be taken as constant, and the influence of the K-coefficient of negligible variation of the ratio of the adjacent layers' elasticity moduluses (under the variation of that ratio which does not exceed it two times) is not great, neither (8). Hence, formulae (1), (2) make it possible to determine the average value of the stability coefficient. When substituting the λ -values for these formulae, we have:

$$C = \frac{\gamma h}{2a}\left[\frac{7K}{4(1+\xi)} - b\cdot tg\,\varphi\right], \qquad (3)$$

$$C = \frac{\gamma h}{20(d^2 - ctg^2\beta)tg\,\varphi}\left[\frac{49K^2}{16(1+\xi)^2} - ctg^2\beta\cdot tg^2\varphi\right] \qquad (4)$$

If, in conformity with durable strength, the dependence of C on time t is represented graphically in Fig.2, we can determine the time span during which the K-value will fall to the given value, in particular, to K=1 (failure). The values of adhesion calculated with the formulae (3), (4) and taken from the plot in Fig.2, are compared. If $C > C_0$, the scarp is not stable. If $C < C_\infty$, the scarp failure is not possible.

The variation of adhesion in time can be written as:

$$C = C_0 - (C_0 - C_\infty)\, t/(t + T), \qquad (5)$$

where: T - parameter with dimentions of time.

Then, after the joined examen of (5) and (3) or (4), we can obtain formulae for determination of time t, during which the stability coefficient will drop to the given value of K:

$$t = \left\{\frac{8a\,(1+\xi)\,(C_0 - C_\infty)}{\gamma h\,[7K - 4b(1+\xi)tg\,\varphi] - 8aC_\infty\,(1+\xi)} - 1\right\} T, \qquad (6)$$

or

$$t = \left\{ \frac{320(1+\xi)^2(d^2-\mathrm{ctg}^2\beta)(C_0 - C_\infty)\cdot \mathrm{tg}\,\varphi}{\gamma h\left[49K^2-16(1+\xi)^2\cdot \mathrm{ctg}^2\beta \cdot \mathrm{tg}^2\varphi\right] - 320C_\infty(1+\xi)^2(d^2-\mathrm{ctg}^2\beta)\mathrm{tg}\,\varphi} - 1 \right\} T. \quad (7)$$

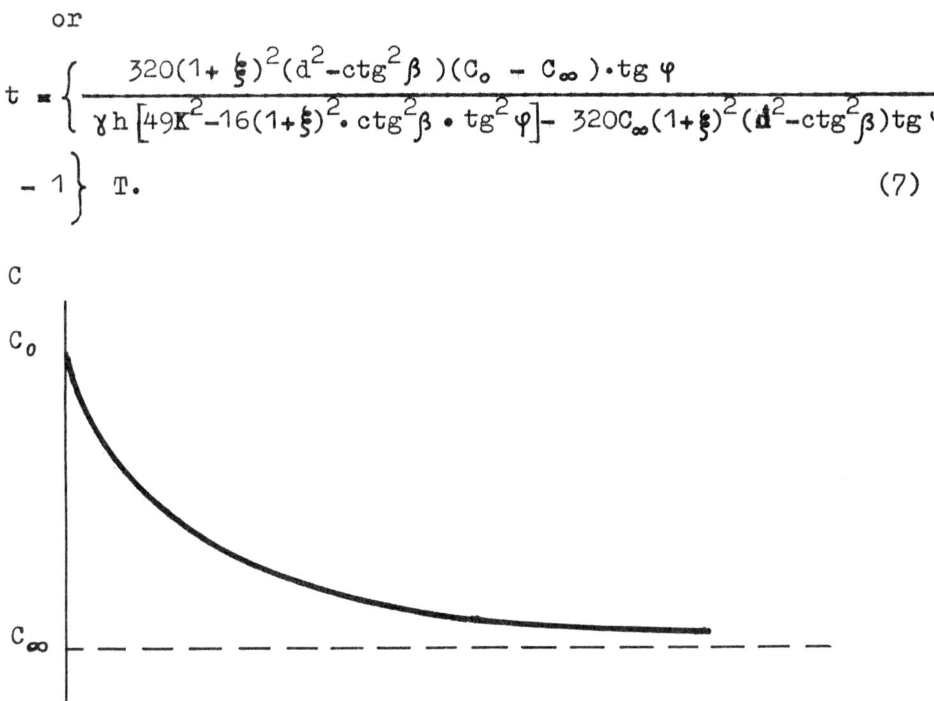

Figure 2. Variation of adhesion in time.

In case of natural landslide slopes being in the boundary state, the breakdown surface coincides with the contact layer. Studying their stability, we use the ratio:

$$K = (\Phi + \Psi \cdot \lambda)\cdot \mathrm{tg}\,\varphi , \quad (8)$$

where: $\Phi = \Sigma\,\sigma_n / \Sigma\,\tau_n$; $\Psi = S_1/2\Sigma\tau_n$; $\Sigma\sigma_n$ $\Sigma\tau_n$ - are the summums of normal and tangent forces (areas between the diagrams of these forces and the breakdown line); S_1 - area between the diagram of signle force and the breakdown line. Taking into consideration that such slopes are in the boundary state, the obtained relations allow, by reverse recalculations, to determine the ξ-coefficient value. Using the values of C and φ, which were determined in laboratory conditions along the breakdown line, and substituting them into formula (8), we find the values of coefficient of the landslide slope stability under two values of the initial stressed state. After this, the average quantity of the coefficient for the examined landslide slope, corresponding to K = 1, is computed from the formula:

$$\xi_{av} = \frac{4K' - 3K_{,} - 1}{4(K' - K_{,})} , \qquad (9)$$

where K' - stability coefficient under $\xi = 0{,}75$;

$K_{,}$ - under $\xi = 1$.

With the obtained value of ξ_{av} we can determine the Φ - and Ψ -values which, being equal with ξ_{av} as shown above, do not change in time.

Thus, in formula (8), there are only φ and λ as variables, and this formula is a stability chart of the examined landslide slope. Note, that C - and φ - values, obtained in samples, through differ from analogous quantities of the hole soil massif, in combination with the average value of ξ and the used analysis methods, they give, in the considered moment of time, the result corresponding to reality, i.e. K = 1. So, under variation of these values in time the results of calculations carried out with formula (5) must be reliable enough. The forcasting quantity of that formula consists in the fact that, by means of periodical determination of C - and φ - values in laboratory conditions it is possible to calculate the stability coefficient, and, by variation of its magnitude, to judge of the landslide slope's state (under $K < 1$ - landslide activation; under $K > 1$ - its stabilization). The average value of the ξ coefficient obtained theoretically, in combination with φ -, C -, γ - values, found in laboratory conditions, should be expediently used in calculations connected with the consolidation of the examined landslide slope by construction on it of different buildings, etc.

REFERENCES

1. Akhpatelov, D.M., Vorobyov, V.N., Account of the Initial Stressed State in Solution of Geometrical Problems by Numeric Methods. In Application of Numeric Methods to Geometrical Problems. MICE, Moscow, 166-174

2. Stefanoff, G., Akhpatelov, D.M., Determination of the initial Soil Stressed State. In Proceedings of the 11th International Conference on Soil Mechanics and Foundation Engineering. San Francisco/ 12-16 August, 1985.

3. Ter-Martirossyan, Z.G., Akhpatelov D.M., Analysis of Stress-Strained State of Multiphased Soil Massifs. - Manual Book, MICE, 1982.

4. Muskhelishvili, N.I., Some Basic Problems of Mathematical Theory of Elasticity. Ed. 4. Academy of Sciences of the USSR, Moscow, 1954, 647 p.

5. Tsvetkov, V.K., Analysis of Scarp and Slope Stability. Nizhne-Volzhskoe Edt., Volgograd, 1979, 238 p.

6. Tsvetkov, V.K., Study of Scarp and Slope Stability by Final Elements Method. In Application of Numeric Methods to Geometrical Problems. MICE, Moscow, 1986, 106-113.

7. Tsvetkov, V.K., Analysis of Uniform Slope Stability Under Elasto-Plastic Distribution of Tensions in Rock Massifs. Mountain Magazine, 1981, 5, 45-52.

8. Tsvetkov, V.K., Tensions in Non-Uniform Scarps and Slopes. Mountain Magazine, 1985, 7.

SOME OBSERVED EFFECTS OF TEMPERATURE VARIATION ON SOIL BEHAVIOUR

S.P.S. Virdi, BE, MSc, PhD
Lecturer at
Bilston Community College

and

M.J. Keedwell, BSc, MSc, PhD
Senior Lecturer at
Coventry (Lanchester) Polytechnic

ABSTRACT

The results of tests in which samples were subjected to variation of temperature and control tests carried out at constant temperature are described and discussed.

The temperature variations were imposed on samples of uniform sand and kaolin clay while undergoing drained and undrained creep, triaxial consolidation, and strain-controlled axial loading tests.

In the drained tests water was expelled from the samples during periods of temperature increase and absorbed by the samples during periods of temperature decrease. In undrained tests the effects of temperature increase and decrease were to cause a rise and fall respectively in the pore water pressure. It is concluded that in order to avoid disturbance due to temperature changes samples retrieved from a site investigation should be transported to the laboratory in insulated containers and stored and tested at their in situ temperature.

INTRODUCTION

It has been established by many research workers that the engineering properties of soils can be influenced significantly by temperature variations. Finn [1], Paaswell [2], Campanella and Mitchell [3], Plum and Esrig [4] and Laguros [5] have investigated the effects of temperature on the consolidation behaviour of soils. Temperature effects on the shear strength of soils have been studied by Lambe [6] and Sherif and Burrous [7] among others. Mitchell and Campanella [8], Campanella and Mitchell [3], Plum and Esrig [4] and Noble and Demirel [9] have investigated pore water pressure variations and volume change associated with temperature variations. The effect of temperature on the dry density and optimum moisture content of a compacted soil have been investigated by Youssef, Sabry and El Ramli [10].

Temperature variations can also cause a change in the strength of compacted subgrades and embankments by causing moisture migration. Results from Benkelman beam deflection test may vary largely with the temperature of the subgrade, as reported by Miura, Kawashima and Uchida [11]. It is also generally recognised now that close temperature control in a laboratory is essential in many types of soil testing.

There is however a lack of complete agreement on the effect of temperature on the engineering properties of soils,among previous researchers. For example, Lambe [6] suggested that the shear strength of soils increased due to an increase in temperature whereas several workers believe that an increase in temperature results in a decrease in shear strength. Therefore, it was decided to conduct additional studies at the Coventry (Lanchester) Polytechnic.

MATERIALS AND METHODS

Uniform sand (0.599/0.422 mm) and Speswhite kaolin were used in this investigation. Fully saturated specimens of sand were prepared by deposition under water, as described by Bishop and Henkel [12]. Samples of kaolin were prepared from slurry by one-dimensional consolidation, as described by Keedwell [13]. A summary of the index properties of the soils and sample preparation techniques used is given in Table 1.

Specially designed apparatus was used to achieve the desired sample temperature, consisting of a temperature control apparatus and modified triaxial cells as shown in Figs. 1 and 2.

Leakage through the rubber membranes, which usually occurs when water is used as the cell fluid, was minimised by using silicone oil instead of water. In preliminary tests the silicone oil was also used in the temperature control apparatus. However,its relatively high viscosity (50 centistokes) prevented the achievement of an adequate circulation rate.

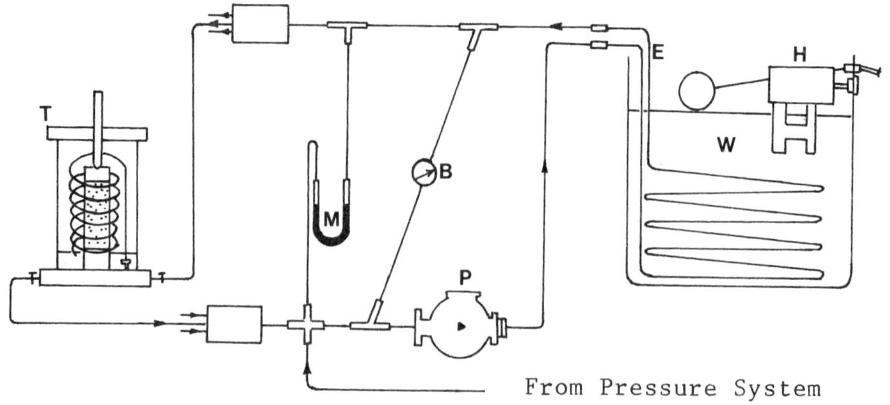

T - Modified Triaxial Cell
M - Mercury Manometer

P - Central Heating Pump
B - By-Pass

H - Water Heater
W - Water Bath

E - Heater Exchanger

Figure 1. The Temperature Control Apparatus

To improve the efficiency of the apparatus, standard 38 mm triaxial cells were modified by providing a heat exchanger made of small bore copper tube which allowed the use of water as the circulating medium and silicone oil as the cell fluid.

The temperature control apparatus was housed in the main section of the laboratory, which was maintained at a temperature of $20^\circ \pm 1^\circ$C. The triaxial cells were placed in a special section, the temperature of which was maintained at $9^\circ \pm 1^\circ$C. The temperature control apparatus was used to achieve soil temperature higher than 9°C and by switching it off the soil samples were allowed to cool down to $9^\circ \pm 1^\circ$C, i.e. the ambient temperature of the special section. A typical soil temperature versus time plot is shown in Fig.3. The time between start of a test and the commencement of temperature cycles varied from test to test, the average being 19 hours.

Calibrations

The components of the triaxial cells, and water present in the porous stones and the transmission line of the triaxial cells, expanded or contracted according to the temperature of the cell fluid. Pressure transducers, pipettes and triaxial cells were, therefore, calibrated so that accurate data could be obtained by suitable corrections. Details are given by Virdi [14].

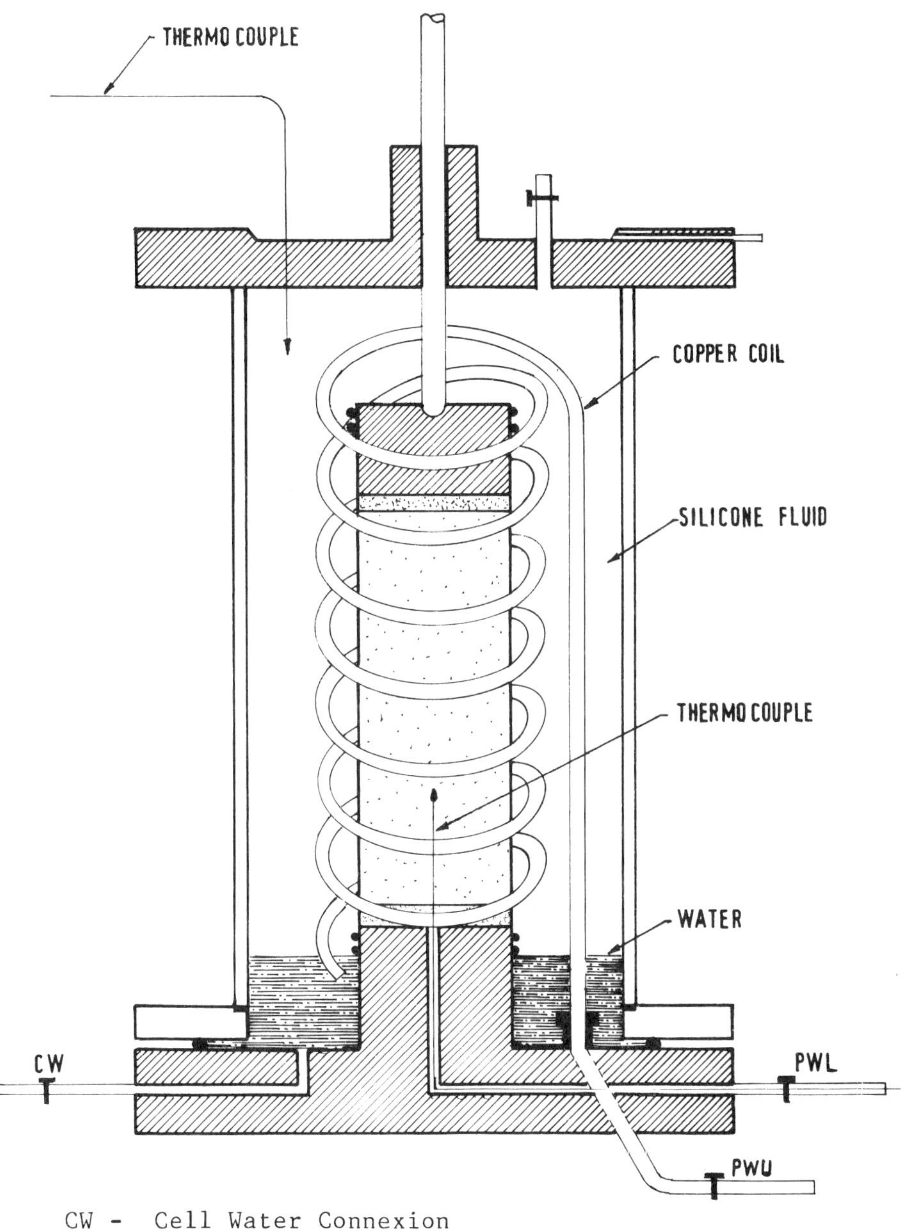

CW - Cell Water Connexion
PWL - Pore Water Lower Connexion
PWU - Pore Water Upper Connexion

Figure 2. Modified Triaxial Cell

Test Conditions

Drained creep, undrained creep and strain controlled tests were performed under constant and transient temperature conditions. The constant temperature tests were performed at 20°± 1°C and in the transient temperature tests the soil temperature was varied between 9°C and 50°C as shown in Fig. 3. Due to low thermal conductivity of soil grains the temperature adjustment period, i.e. the time required to heat a soil sample, was far greater than that required by the cell fluid. The temperature adjustment periods for heating and cooling modes were 3 hours and 9 hours respectively. Loading of kaolin samples was started after they had been consolidating for 24 hours at 20°C. The loads were added in small increments so that the development of positive pore water pressure could be kept to a minimum. A summary of test conditions is given in Table 1.

RESULTS

Drained Creep and Consolidation Tests (Figs. 4 to 9)

In every case tests were carried out on similar samples, one at constant temperature and one subjected to temperature changes. A comparison of the test results (e.g. samples 6 and 14, Fig. 4) shows that significant differences in behaviour were confined to the periods of temperature change. Once temperature equilibrium had been established, the sample which had been

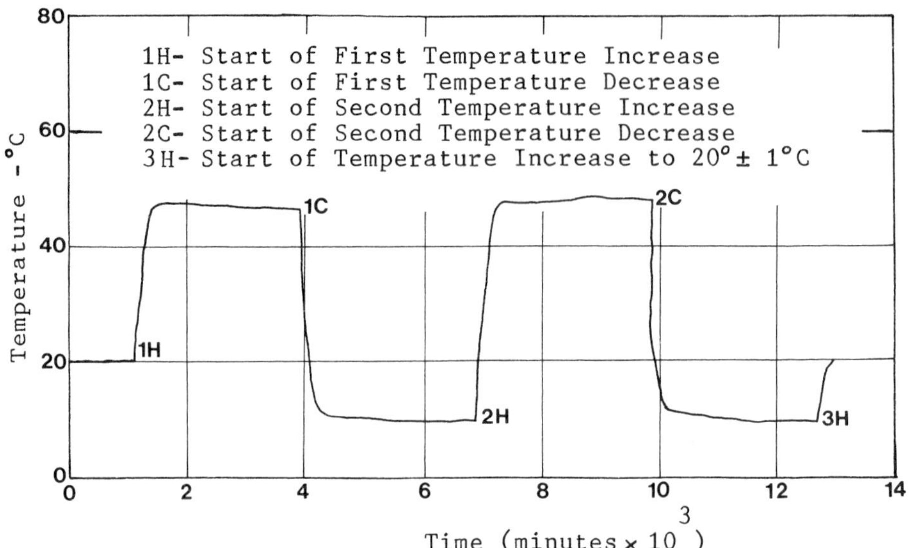

Figure 3. A Typical Plot: Sample Temperature versus Time

TABLE 1

Soil Type	Sample No.	Method of Preparation	Test Conditions
Remoulded Kaolin w_L = 66% w_p = 38% c'_{cu} = 0 ϕ'_{cu} = 24°	1 to 4 (undrained creep)	One dimensional consolidation from slurry. σ_1' =85 kN/m², $\sigma_2'=\sigma_3'$=0, then isotropically consolidated to 100 kN/m² at 20°C	Lateral stress held constant at 100 kN/m². Drainage prevented, deviator stress applied and temperature cycles started as shown in Fig. 3.
	6 to 9 (drained creep)	Same as described for undrained creep samples	Lateral stress held constant at 100 kN/m² Drainage allowed. Back Pressure=50 kN/m² Deviator stress applied and temperature cycles started as shown in Fig. 3.
	10 to 12 (undrained creep)	Same as described for undrained creep samples	Lateral stress held constant at 100 kN/m² Drainage prevented and deviator stress applied. Temperature =20° + 1°C(constant)
	13 (consolidation)	same as described for undrained creep samples	Lateral stress held constant at 150 kN/m² Drainage allowed. Back pressure=50 kN/m² Deviator stress = 0. Temperature cycles started as shown in Fig.3.
	14 to 16 (drained creep)	same as described for undrained creep samples	Lateral stress held constant at 150 kN/m² Drainage allowed. Back pressure=50 kN/m² Deviator stress applied. Temperature =20°+ 1°C(constant)
	20 (strain controlled)	Same as described for undrained creep samples	Lateral stress held constant at 150 kN/m² Drainage allowed. Back pressure=50 kN/m²

Table 1

Soil Type	Sample No.	Method of Preparation	Test Conditions
	20 (continued)		Rate of strain = 0.0007 mm/min. Temperature cycles started as shown in Fig. 3.
	22 (strain-controlled)	Same as described for undrained creep samples.	Lateral stress held constant at 150 kN/m^2. Drainage allowed. Back pressure=50 kN/m^2. Rate of strain = 0.000508 mm/min. Temperature = $20^\circ + 1^\circ C$ (constant).
(.599/ .422 mm) BSS uniform (Leighton Buzzard) sand. $e_{max.}$=0.779 $e_{min.}$=0.563 Initial porosity = 38.0% (average)	30 to 33 (drained creep)	Samples prepared by depositing sand under water. Compacted on a vibrating table then isotropically consolidated to 100 kN/m^2.	Lateral stress held constant at 150 kN/m^2. Drainage allowed. Back Pressure=50kN/m^2. Deviator stress applied and temperature cycles started as shown in in Fig. 3.
Initial porosity = 37.3% (average)	35 to 38 (drained creep)	Same as described for sample nos. 30 to 33.	Lateral stress held constant at 150 kN/m^2. Drainage allowed. Back pressure = 50 kN/m^2. Deviator stress applied. Temperature = $20^\circ + 1^\circ C$ (constant).
Initial porosity = 37.8%	41 (consolidation)	Same as described for sample nos. 30 to 33.	Lateral stress held constant at 150 kN/m^2. Drainage allowed. Back pressure = 50 kN/m^2. Deviator stress = 0. Temperature cycles started as shown in Fig. 3.

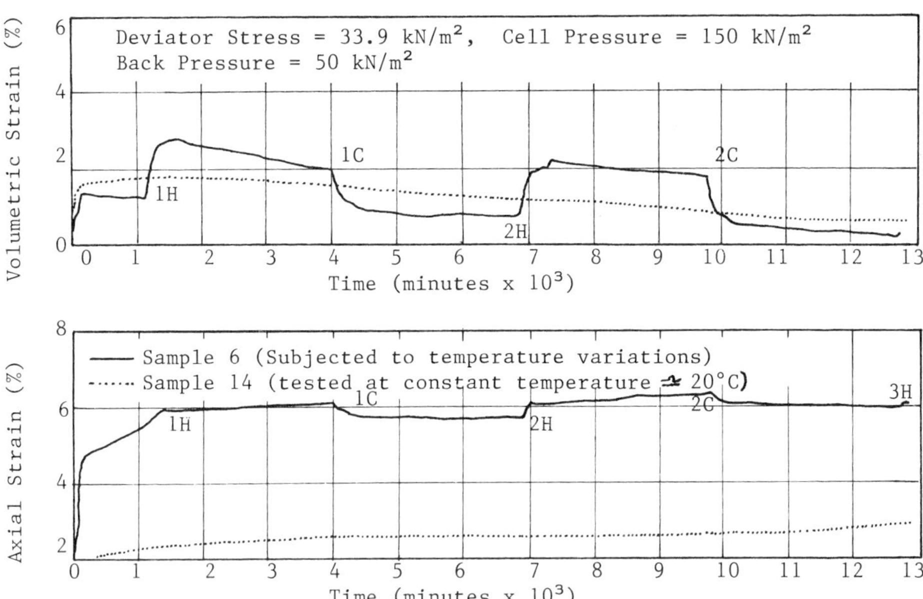

Figure 4. Remoulded Kaolin: Drained creep test; volumetric and axial strain versus time

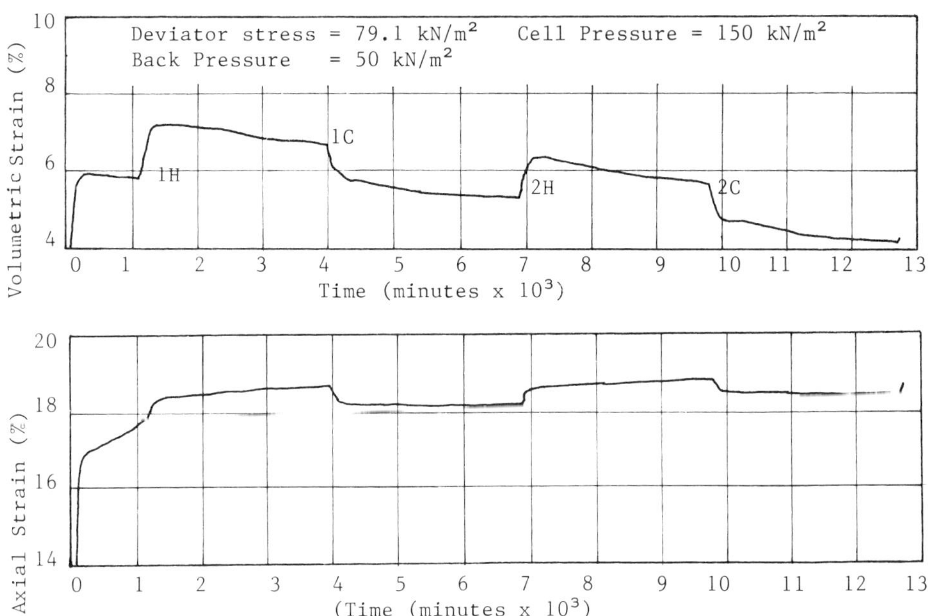

Figure 5 Remoulded Kaolin: Drained Creep Test, Sample 8, Volumetric and axial strain versus time

subjected to temperature change behaved in a similar manner to the sample tested at constant temperature.

Generally the effect of a temperature increase was to considerably reduce the volume of the sample and decrease its height and a temperature decrease had the reverse effect. Usually, the decrease in the volume of kaolin specimens, due to the temperature increases was greater than the volume increase due to the temperature decreases. For example, in the case of Sample 13, Fig.9, these figures were 0.52 ml. and 0.27 ml. respectively.

In all the tests the effects of temperature change on sample height and axial strain rate were greater at the higher levels of deviator stress. The trends of behaviour described above apply equally to the kaolin and sand samples.Some of the sand specimens, however, showed an increase in the height, as illustrated in Figs. 6 and 7.

There is evidence that the volume of water drained out or absorbed, due to temperature variations, is proportional to the moisture content of the soil. In the case of Sample 13 (kaolin) the volumes of water drained out and then absorbed, in the first temperature cycle were 1.645% and 0.796% of the sample volume respectively. In the case of Sample 41 (sand) these figures were 0.796% and 0.384%. The moisture contents of the kaolin and sand were 52% and 23% respectively. The ratio of the moisture contents i.e. 2.26, is similar to the ratio of volumes of water drained out and absorbed. The changes in volume of the soils during the second temperature cycle were proportional to their respective moisture contents.

Undrained Creep Tests on Kaolin

Undrained creep tests were performed under transient temperature conditions on Sample 1,2,3 and 4 using four levels of deviator stress,i.e. 30%, 50%, 70% and 90% of failure stress for a similar sample, respectively. In addition, two tests were performed at constant 20°C.

The pore water pressure in Sample 1 started to increase soon after the application of the load (see Fig. 10). After reaching the maximum value the pore pressure started to decrease. Results reported by Keedwell [13], also from undrained creep tests on kaolin, show a similar trend. During the first period of temperature increase the pore pressure increased until temperature equilibrium was achieved. The pore pressure reached a maximum value of 39.3 kN/m^2 and then started to decrease. The axial strain decreased by 0.46% during the temperature adjustment period. On lowering the sample temperature a reverse behaviour was observed. The axial strain increased by 1% during the temperature adjustment period,

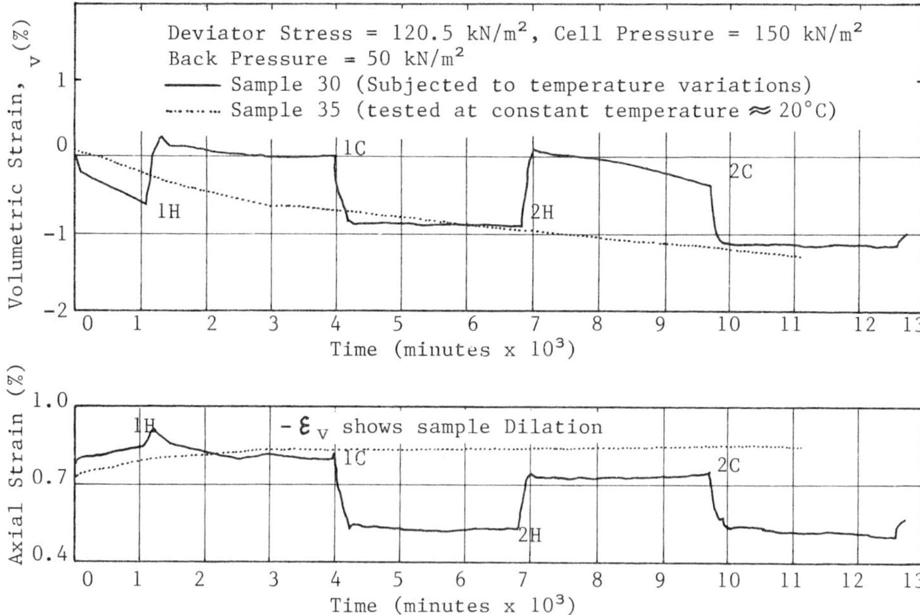

Figure 6. Uniform sand: Drained Creep Test, Volumetric and axial strain versus Time

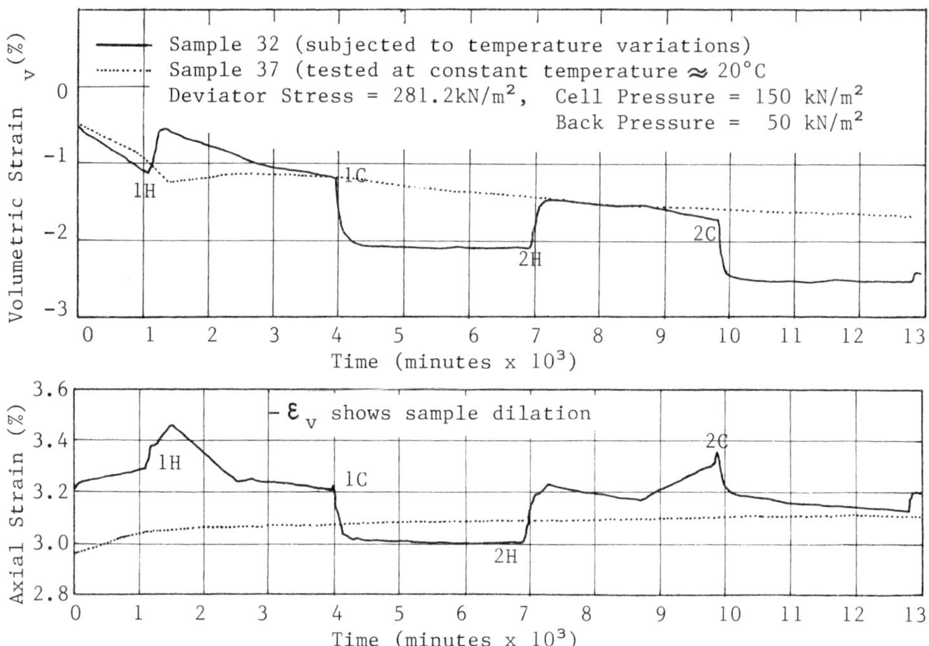

Figure 7 Uniform Sand: Drained creep Test, Volumetric and axial strain versus time.

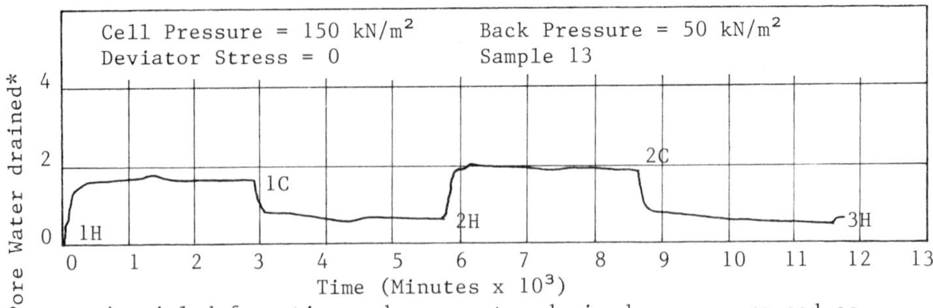

* axial deformation and pore water drained, are expressed as percentages of initial height and volume respectively

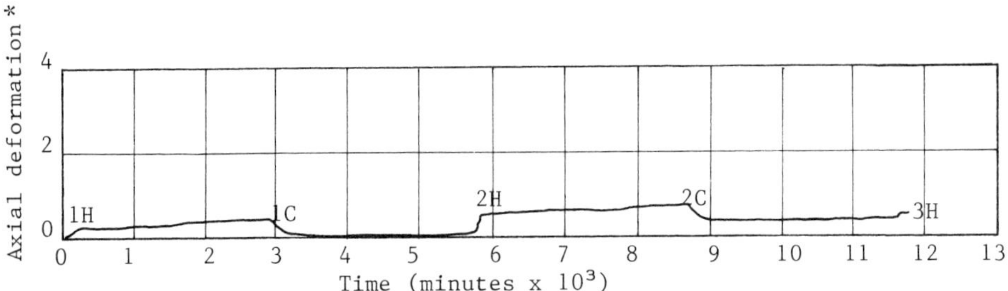

Figure 8. Remoulded Kaolin: Consolidation Test, Volume change and deformation versus time.

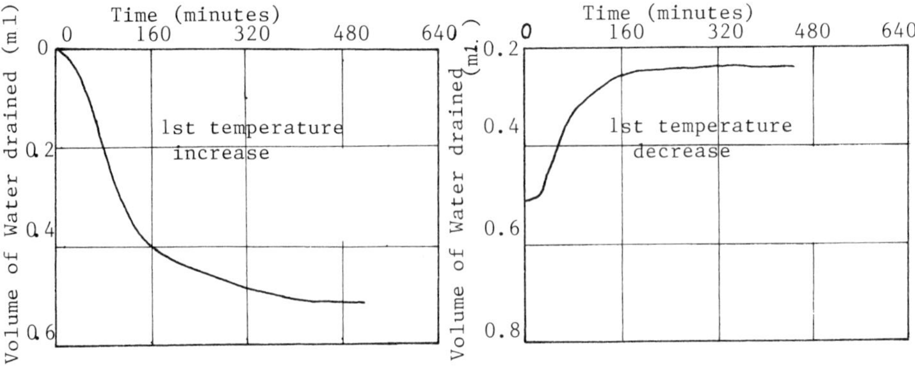

Figure 9. Remoulded Kaolin: Consolidation Test, sample 13 Volume change versus time during the first temperature cycle

but no further increase was observed after temperature equilibrium. The sample behaviour due to the application of the second temperature cycle was similar to that described for the first temperature cycle. Finally, when the sample temperature was brought to 20°C the pore pressure had decreased by 8 kN/m^2 and the axial strain increased by 1.6% as compared to their respective values just before the start of the first temperature cycle. To highlight the effects of the temperature changes, Fig.10 also includes results from a test performed at a constant 20°C. A similar behaviour was observed from samples tested at other stress levels.

Strain-Controlled Tests

Strain-controlled tests were performed under drained conditions on samples of normally consolidated kaolin, over-consolidated kaolin and uniform sand. Results of normally consolidated kaolin (Figs. 11 to 13) are described here.

During the period of axial loading the soil specimen was subjected to the temperature changes shown in Fig.3. The axial strain and the axial strain rate were only slightly affected during the first temperature adjustment period. The volumetric strain and the volumetric strain rate increased and the deviator stress decreased slightly. After the sample had attained temperature equilibrium, the axial strain, volumetric strain and deviator stress started to increase as in the case of constant temperature test. On reducing the sample temperature there was an increase in the volume of the soil, the sample length increased slightly, and the deviator stress increased by 17.5 kN/m^2.

During the second period of temperature increase the increase in the volumetric strain was similar to that due to the first temperature increase but the decrease in both the axial strain and the deviator stress (17 kN/m^2) was far greater. After temperature equilibrium had been achieved the shape of the stress-strain curve was virtually the same as if the sample were being tested at a constant temperature (see Fig.13). The volume of the sample, due to second temperature decrease, increased as mentioned earlier in the case of the first temperature decrease. The corresponding increase in deviator stress was 15.5 kN/m^2. The behaviour shown by over consolidated kaolin was similar to that of the normally consolidated kaolin. The behaviour shown by uniform sand was generally similar to that of the normally consolidated kaolin. However, 5500 minutes after starting the test, the sand specimen started to dilate.

DISCUSSION

Drained Creep Tests

Increase in temperature is likely to affect a soil in at least

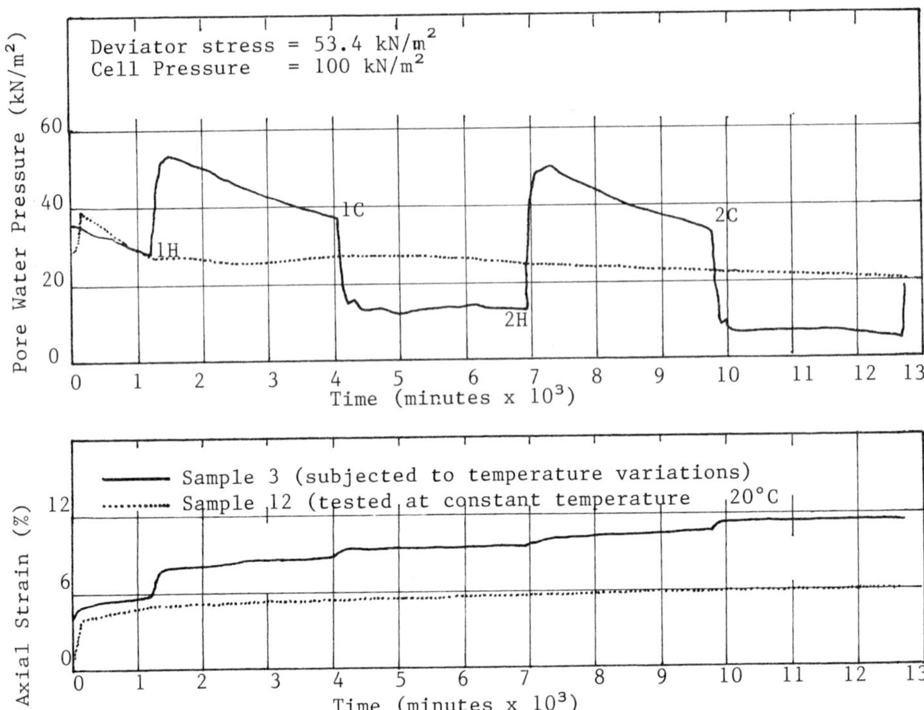

Figure 10. Remoulded Kaolin: Undrained Creep Test
Pore Water Pressure and Axial Strain versus Time

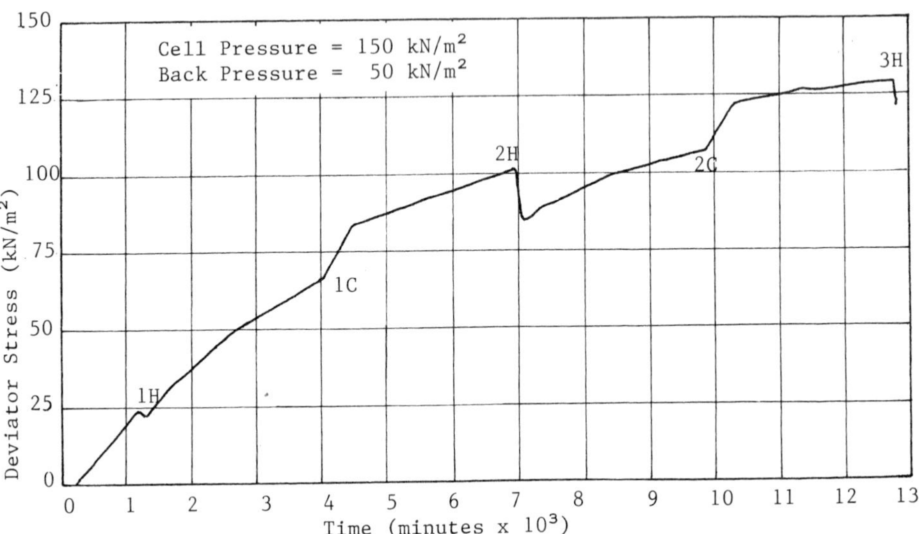

Figure 11. Remoulded Kaolin : Strain-controlled test, sample 20
Deviator Stress versus Time

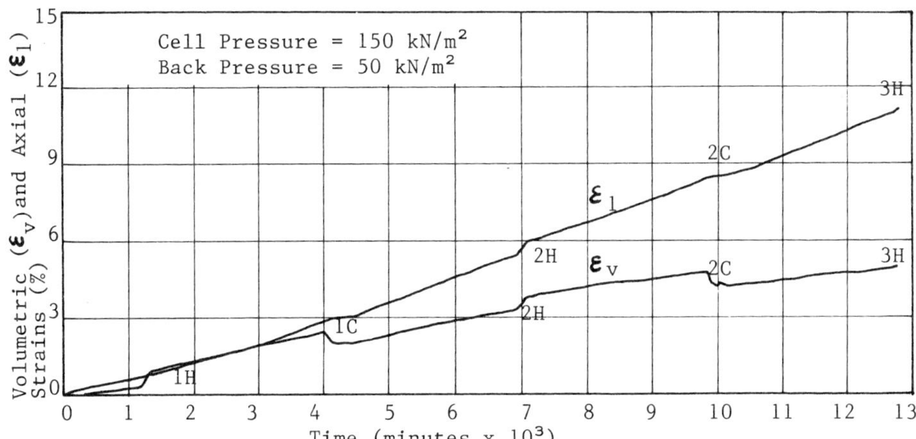

Figure 12. Remoulded kaolin: strain-controlled test, sample 20, Volumetric strain and axial strain versus time.

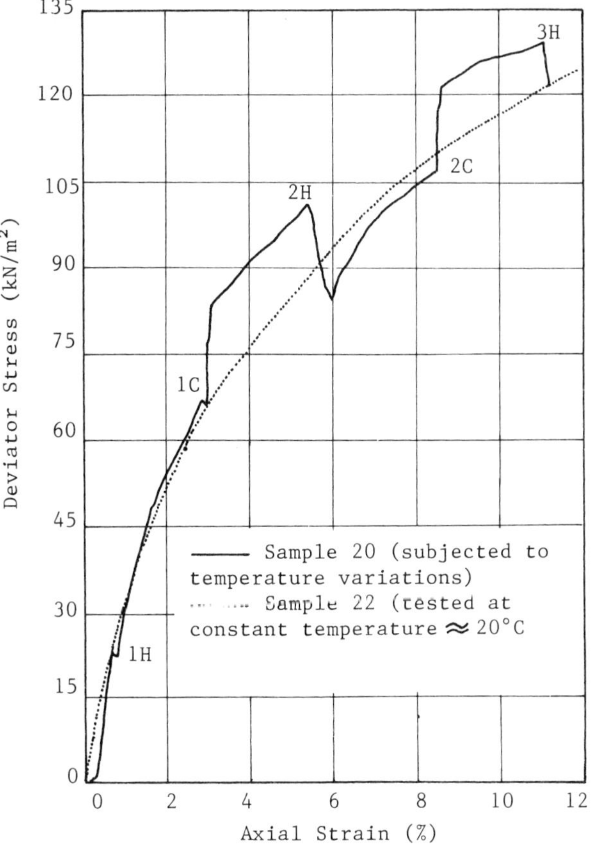

Figure 13. Remoulded kaolin: Strain-controlled Deviator Stress versus Axial Strain.

three ways. Firstly there is a change in the volumes of the pore water and soil particles, secondly an increase in the permeability of the sample due to the reduced viscosity of the pore water and thirdly a decrease in the viscosity of the contact zones. The third effect causes a reduction in the stiffness of the soil skeleton and hence a decrease in the void ratio. This happens while temperature change takes place. Once temperature equilibrium is achieved and more interparticle contacts have been developed due to the reduced void ratio, further significant changes in volume are unlikely, e.g. in the case of Sample 8 the orders of magnitude of the volumetric strain rate before starting the first temperature cycle and after the achievement of temperature equilibrium during the first and second temperature cycles are both -10^{-6} per minute. When the soil temperature is decreased then reverse phenomenon may be expected. Due to the greater volumetric shrinkage of the pore water as compared to the soil particles, a tension is produced in the pore water, which in turn causes the sample to absorb water. A similar view has been expressed by Campanella and Mitchell [3]. An interesting feature of the results, especially from the sand specimens, is that during the cooling periods many of the samples increased in height despite being subjected to axial load. Barden [15] has described tests on River Welland sand in which the samples were first axially loaded and then subjected to an increment of compressive isotropic stress. In some cases negative axial strain (increase in sample height) was observed. It is suggested, therefore, that induced anisotropy may explain the increase in sample height observed in the tests.

Undrained Creep Tests

The pore water pressure increased during periods of temperature increase and decreased when the temperature was decreased. This could be mainly due to the higher coefficient of expansion of the pore water as compared to that of the mineral solids. Variations in the axial strain appear to depend upon the level of stress used. From the observed behaviour it may be suggested that at lower stress levels the axial strain decreases due to temperature increase and increases due to temperature decrease.At higher stress levels (Fig. 10) increase in the axial strain is observed, whether the temperature change is an increase or decrease. The latter behaviour is probably due to the fact that in undrained tests the effect of temperature induced volume change on the height of the specimen is greatly reduced in comparison with the drained situation. Consequently at higher stress levels the axial load has the predominant effect on the observed axial strain. During a period of temperature increase the viscosity of the contact zones would be reduced, permitting an accelerated axial strain rate. Temperature decrease would reduce the volume of both pore water and mineral solids and hence produce the same effect on the axial strain rate as the temperature increase.

The effect of a temperature increase is to reduce the effective stresses, which is analogous to the unloading stage in over-consolidation. When the soil temperature is decreased the effective stresses increase; this is analogous to recompression of the soil. Plum and Esrig [4] have suggested that the new virgin portion of a consolidation curve, established by reloading after completing a temperature cycle, is displaced from the original curve toward higher pressures. This observation suggests that laboratory testing of natural soils, that have been subjected to a cycle of temperature change during the period of handling, could lead to an incorrect evaluation of the maximum previous pressure to which the soil had been subjected.

Strain Controlled Tests

Tests performed under transient temperature conditions, show little effect of the first temperature increase on either the axial strain or the deviator stress, (see Figs. 11, 12 and 13). The deviator stress decreased in the case of the normally consolidated kaolin, but the decrease was very small as compared to the subsequent changes. It appears that larger variations in the axial strain, volumetric strain and deviator stress are associated with higher stress ratios. A change in deviator stress also depends upon the change in the sample height in such tests. Due to the first temperature increase there were very small changes in the sample heights. Therefore, variation in the deviator stress was also very small. A change in the sample height, due to temperature variations, causes the compression of the proving ring to vary. An increase in sample temperature causes a decrease in the sample height, therefore, the compression of the proving ring decreases which in turn causes the deviator stress to decrease. When the sample temperature is lowered, an increase in the sample height results which causes the proving ring to compress more. Thus, an increase in the deviator stress results.

The decrease in deviator stress during the second temperature increase is shown by an almost vertical line. This could be due to a very short temperature adjustment period. The increase in deviator stress, due to a temperature decrease, takes place gradually because of the longer temperature adjustment period. Fig. 13 shows a comparison of tests performed under transient and constant temperature conditions. Due to an increase in the soil temperature the sample height decreased, which supplemented the compression of the sample by the test machine, thus, an increase in the axial strain is observed. In the case of a temperature decrease, the temperature change and the test machine have opposing effects on the sample height, and consequently no change in the axial strain is observed.

Overconsolidated kaolin and uniform sand when tested under

transient temperature conditions, produced higher maximum deviator stresses as compared to those from the constant temperature tests. This could be due to anisotropy induced by the temperature variations. The induced anisotropy, as described earlier, causes the soil to become stiffer in the axial direction. The soil, then, offers a higher resistance to axial stress. In the case of normally consolidated kaolin, a comparison of the results from the two types of test shows no difference in the maximum deviator stress.

CONCLUSIONS

The results indicate that variations in soil temperature produce changes in the soil behaviour in consolidation, creep and strain-controlled tests. In a consolidation test the observed effect of a temperature increase is analogous to an increase in the consolidation pressure and vice versa. The volume of a sample is decreased during a temperature increase due to the outflow of the pore water. Due to a decrease in the sample temperature, the reverse effect is observed. In addition to the volume change, the sample height decreases during a temperature increase and increases during a temperature decrease. In a drained creep test, the effect of temperature on the volume of a soil sample is the same as in a consolidation test. The temperature variation also has a significant effect on the axial and volumetric strain rates. All these changes take place only during the period of temperature adjustment. Once temperature equilibrium is achieved, the sample behaviour is similar to that of a nominally identical sample tested at constant temperature. The specimens of uniform sand increased in length after two cycles of temperature variation. It is suggested that the main cause is the anisotropy induced by the axial load.

The observed effect of temperature increase in the case of strain-controlled tests is to cause a decrease in the sample height, which in turn causes a decrease in the deviator stress due to the reduced compression of the proving ring. Similarly, a decrease in the soil temperature causes the deviator stress to increase.

The effect of a cycle of temperature increase and decrease may be assumed to be analogous to overconsolidation. During summer when the air temperature is 25°C - 30°C, a soil sample taken out of the ground is first subjected to a temperature increase, as the ground temperature in the UK, below the depth of 3m, is 6°C - 10°C. When the sample is stored and tested in a laboratory the sample temperature is reduced to the ambient temperature of the laboratory, which is generally 20°C. As overconsolidation changes the structure of the soil, it may be expected that soil properties determined in the laboratory in such circumstances will not be truly representative of the in situ soil.

In undrained creep tests on kaolin, the pore water pressure increases due to a rise in temperature and vice versa. Therefore, control of the laboratory temperature is of special importance if pore pressure measurement is involved.

Generally, it may be concluded that if laboratory tests are to yield properties representative of the in situ soil, not only should mechanical disturbances be avoided, but the samples should be transported to the laboratory in insulated containers and stored and tested at their in situ temperature.

REFERENCES

1. Finn, F.N., "The effect of temperature on the consolidation characteristics of remoulded clay". Special Tech. Publication No. 120, ASTM, Philadelphia,1951, pp. 65-71.

2. Paaswell, R.E., "Temperature effects on clay soil consolidation". Journal of the Soil Mech. and Foundations Div., Proc. ASCE, 1967, Vol. 93, No. SM3, pp. 9-22.

3. Campanella, R.G. and Mitchell, J.K., "Influence of temperature variations on soil behaviour". Journal of the Soil Mech. and Foundations Div.,Proc. ASCE, 1968, Vol. 94, No. SM1, pp. 271-290.

4. Plum, R.L. and Esrig, M.I., "Some temperature effects on soil compressibility and pore water pressure". Proc. Int. Conf. on Effects of Temperature and Heat on Engineering Behaviour of Soils, HRB Special Report 103, 1969, pp. 231-242.

5. Laguros, J.G., "Effect of temperature on some engineering properties of clay soils". Proc. Int. Conf. on Effects of Temperature and Heat on the Engineering Behaviour of Soils, HRB Special Report 103, 1969, pp. 186-193.

6. Lambe, T.W., "Compacted Clay: Structure". Transactions ASCE 1960, Vol. 125, pp. 682-706.

7. Sherif, M.A. and Burrous, C.M., "Temperature effects on the unconfined shear strength of saturated cohesive soil". Proc. Int. Conf. on Effects of Temperature and Heat on Engineering Behaviour of soils, HRB Special Report 103, 1969, pp. 267-272.

8. Mitchell, J.K. and Campanella, R.G., "Creep studies on saturated clays". Symposium on Laboratory Shear Testing of Soils, ASTM-NRC, Ottawa, Canada, ASTM Special Tech. Publication No. 361, 1963, pp. 90-103.

9. Noble, C.A. and Demirel, T., "Effect of temperature on strength behaviour of cohesive soil". Proc. Int. Conf. on Effects of Temperature and Heat on Engineering Behaviour of Soils, HRB Special Report 103, 1969, pp. 204-217.

10. Youssef, M.S., Sabry, A. and El Ramli, A.H., "Temperature changes and their effects on some physical properties of soils". Proc. 5th Int. Conf. Soil Mech. and F.E., 1961, Vol. 1, pp. 419-421.

11. Miura, Y., Kawashima, K. and Uchida, H., "Influence of structure and temperature on deflection of asphalt pavement - An approach to temperature correction". Proc. Int. Sym. on Bearing Capacity of Roads and Airfields, Trondheim (Norway), 1982, pp. 384-393.

12. Bishop, A.W. and Henkel, D.J., "The measurement of soil properties in Triaxial Test". E. Arnold, 1962, London.

13. Keedwell, M.J., "The rheology of clay". Thesis submitted to the Leicester Univ., Leicester, for the degree of Master of Science, 1971.

14. Virdi, S.P.S., "Rheology of soils with special reference to temperature effects". Thesis submitted to the CNAA for the award of degree of Doctor of Philosophy, 1984.

15. Barden, L., "A quantitative treatment of the deformation behaviour of granular material in terms of particulate mechanics". Proc. Int. Conf. on Struct. Solid Mech. and Eng. Des., Univ. of Southampton, 1969, pp. 599-612.

AN INTERPRETATION OF SOME OBSERVED EFFECTS OF TEMPERATURE VARIATION ON SOIL BEHAVIOUR

S P S VIRDI, Bilston Community College
M J KEEDWELL, Coventry Polytechnic

SYNOPSIS

A rheological equation has been developed to interpret some of the effects of temperature variation on soil behaviour reported in Virdi and Keedwell [1].

It is demonstrated that subject to the acceptance of some simplifying assumptions regarding the nature and structural arrangement of the particles in the tested soils, the proposed rheological equations can provide a plausible explanation of the observed behaviour.

INTRODUCTION

The theory of reaction rates has been applied to chemical reactions, diffusion and viscous movement [2] and a common feature is that the relative movement of the atoms occurs in a time dependent manner. Since soils exhibit creep, it is likely that soil deformation is a rate process. A number of workers, Murayama and Shibata [3]; Mitchell [4] ; Christensen and Wu [5]; Andersland and Akili [6]; Mitchell, Campanella and Singh [7]; Andersland and Douglas [8]; Erol, Demirel and Lohnes [9]; Keedwell [10]; Virdi [11] among others, have applied the theory of absolute reaction rates to predict the creep and consolidation behaviour of soils. Atomic theory assumes that every atom is in oscillatory motion due to thermal energy possessed by it and that this motion is about an equilibrium position. To induce shear flow extra energy is needed to surmount the energy barrier, which may either be supplied by increased stress or increased temperature. The rate process equation has provisions for incorporating the above mentioned factors and can be used to predict the dependence of soil behaviour on temperature and stress level.

The main objective of this paper is to provide feasible explanations of the observed effects of stress level and temperature variations on the time-deformation behaviour of kaolin and uniform sand using a rheological equation which combines the rate process theory and the particulate mechanics approach.

THEORY

Volume change due to Temperature Variation

Temperature change may be expected to cause change in volume of a soil element for three reasons (Campanella and Mitchell [12])

(a) Thermal expansion or contraction of the void water.

(b) Thermal expansion or contraction of the soil particles

(c) Relative movement of particles caused by temperature induced changes in contact zone viscosity and interparticle electrical and Van der Waal forces.

The rheological equation developed in the following paragraphs is intended to predict the "structural viscosity" effect on temperature induced volume change listed as (c) above.

During periods of temperature change volumetric strain rate will be affected by all three of the effects (a) (b) and (c). It is reasonable to assume, however, that only structural viscosity effects would control volumetric strain rate when the temperature was maintained at a constant level. Consequently the rheological equation is only applicable to the latter periods.

Development of the Rheological Equation

According to the theory of reaction rates, a certain minimum amount of energy, called the activation energy, ΔE, is required to achieve a bond rupture. The relationship between energy and displacement of an atom is shown in Fig 1.

To surmount the energy barrier, the relative movement of atoms must be equal to $\lambda_3/2$, where λ_3 is the mean distance between equilibrium positions. It has been shown that the net frequency of jump in the direction of force, f, is

$$\nu_f = (2kT/h) \exp(-\Delta E/kT) \sinh(f.\lambda_3/2kT) \qquad (1)$$

where k is the Boltzmann Constant
T is the absolute temperature
h is the Planck's constant

If λ_1 is the distance between atoms in the direction normal to the plane of shear and to the direction of flow, and λ_2 is the distance between atoms in the plane of shear and normal to the direction of flow, then each time an atom moves a distance λ_3 in the direction of flow, the shear strain is λ_3/λ_1 . The shear stress causing flow is $f/\lambda_3 . \lambda_2$, hence the rate of shear strain,

$$\dot{\gamma} = (2\lambda_3/\lambda_1)(kT/h) \exp(-\Delta F/RT) \sinh(\tau . \lambda_3^2 . \lambda_2/2kT) \qquad (2)$$

where ΔF is the free energy of activation.
R is the Gas Constant

Assuming $\lambda_3 = \lambda_2 = \lambda_1$ Herrin and Jones [13]
then

$$\dot{\gamma} = (2kT/h)\exp(-\Delta F/RT)\sinh(\tau . vf/2kT) \quad (3)$$

where $vf = \lambda_2 . \lambda_3^2$ is the volume of a flow unit.

Keedwell [10] combined the rate process theory with particulate mechanics approach and obtained the following relationship:

$$\dot{\varepsilon}_1 = 2\lambda . \dot{\gamma}\cos\beta . s \quad (4)$$

where $\dot{\varepsilon}_1$ is the rate of axial strain
s is the average number of contacts/unit length in axial direction
β is the inclination to the vertical of the direction of shear at a typical particle contact.

The shear strain rate, $\dot{\gamma}$, is obtained from the rate process equation and the other variables are the same as used in the stress dilatancy theory of Rowe [14]. Fig 2 represents an assembly of spherical particles within a soil element. Rowe [14] assumed that an increment of relative movement of particles, $\dot{\delta}$ takes place in a direction inclined at an angle β to the vertical and that the average spacings of the interparticle contacts in vertical and horizontal directions are L_1 and L_2 respectively. Rowe [14] has defined an angle here denoted by η, as:

$$\tan\eta = 2L_1/L_2 \quad (5)$$

If the soil is assumed to be isotropic or cross anisotropic with major principal strain direction being along the axis of symmetry (the vertical direction in Fig.2), then using the convention that compressive strains are positive.

The increment of axial strain rate,

$$\dot{\varepsilon}_1 = 2\dot{\delta}\cos\beta/L_1 \text{ (See Rowe [14])}$$

or

$$= 2\dot{\delta}\cos\beta . s \quad (6)$$

in which $s = 1/L_1$

and the increment of Lateral strain, $\dot{\varepsilon}_2 = \dot{\varepsilon}_3 = -\dot{\delta}\sin\beta/L_1 . \cot\eta$ (7)

or

$$\dot{\varepsilon}_2 = \dot{\varepsilon}_3 = -\dot{\delta}\sin\beta\tan\eta . s. \quad (8)$$

where s is the number of interparticle contacts per unit length along the axis of symmetry.

If the thickness of contact zone in the direction A-A is λ then

$$\dot{\delta} = \lambda . \dot{\gamma} \quad (9)$$

where $\dot{\gamma}$ is an increment of contact zone shear strain.

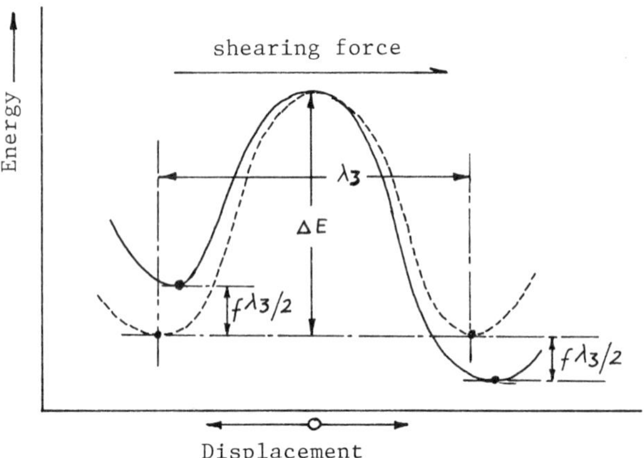

Fig 1. Influence of Shear Force on Energy Barriers opposing Particle Movement.

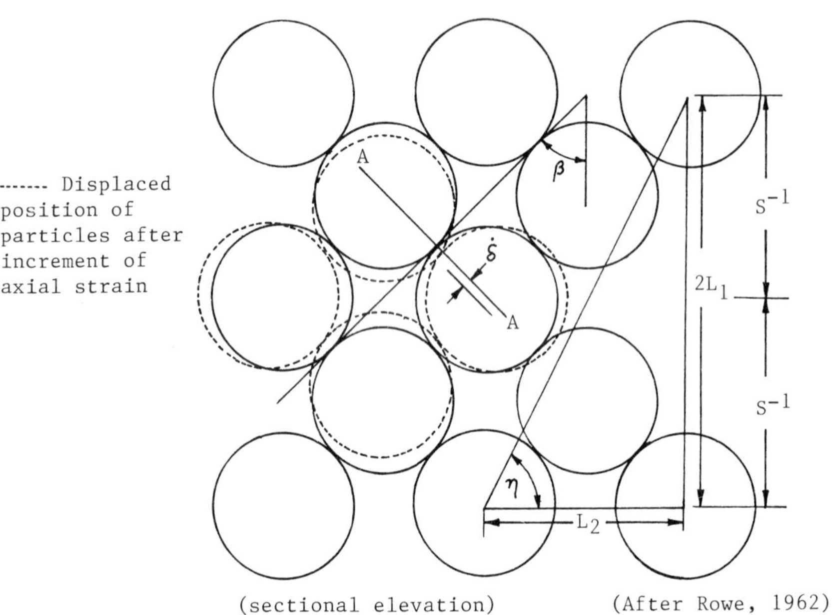

Fig 2. An Assembly of Spherical Particles (face centred cubic Packing)

From equations 6 and 9

$$\dot{\varepsilon}_1 = 2\lambda.\dot{\gamma}\cos\beta.s \tag{10}$$

$$\dot{\varepsilon}_2 = \dot{\varepsilon}_3 = -\lambda.\dot{\gamma}\sin\beta.\tan\eta.s \tag{11}$$

The increment of volumetric strain $\dot{\varepsilon}_v$ corresponding to $\dot{\gamma}$ is :

$$\dot{\varepsilon}_v = \dot{\varepsilon}_1 + \dot{\varepsilon}_2 + \dot{\varepsilon}_3$$

i.e.

$$\begin{aligned}\dot{\varepsilon}_v &= 2\lambda.\dot{\gamma}\cos\beta.s-2\lambda.\dot{\gamma}\sin\beta.\tan\eta.s \\ &= 2\lambda.\dot{\gamma}s(\cos\beta - \sin\beta\tan\eta) \\ &= \dot{\varepsilon}_1(1-\tan\beta\tan\eta)\end{aligned} \tag{12}$$

Combining equation 3 and 10

$$\dot{\varepsilon}_1 = 2\lambda.s.\cos\beta(2kT/h)\exp(-\Delta F/RT)\sinh(\tau.vf/2kT) \tag{13}$$

and from equations 12 and 13

$$\dot{\varepsilon}_v = (1-\tan\beta.\tan\eta)\,2\lambda.s.\cos\beta\,(2kT/h)\exp(-\Delta F/RT)\sinh(\tau vf/2kT) \tag{14}$$

Referring to Fig 3

$$\frac{y}{d} = \sin\beta \quad \text{or} \quad y = d\sin\beta \tag{15}$$

and

$$x = d\cos\beta \tag{16}$$

where y = vertical distance (c/c) between particles.
d = average diameter of particles
x = horizontal distance (c/c) between particles

From Rowe [14]

$$\tan\eta = 2y/x \tag{17}$$

From equations 15 and 17

$$\tan\eta = 2\tan\beta$$

Replacing $\tan\eta$ by $2\tan\beta$ in equation (14) (18)

then

$$\dot{\varepsilon}_v = (1-2\tan^2\beta)\,2\lambda.s.\cos\beta\,(2kT/h)\,(\exp(-\Delta F/RT)\,\sinh(\tau.vf/2kT) \tag{19}$$

Determination of the Value of Parameter β by Measurement of Sample Height

Rowe and Barden [15]; Kirkpatrick and Belshaw [16]; Lee [17]; Deman [18] and Drescher and Vardoulakis [19] reported that the use of non-lubricated end platens in triaxial specimens is responsible for non-uniformity of stress and deformation.

In the case of the tests reported in Virdi and Keedwell [1] it was nevertheless decided not to use lubricated ends because of the unquantifiable effect of temperature variation on the thickness of the rubber discs needed to reduce the friction between the specimen and the platens.

The effect of using non-lubricated platens is that the effective height of the sample is reduced to that of an active element sandwiched between two "rigid" cones as illustrated in Fig 4.

Deman [18] suggested that the value of angle of rigid cone, θ, (Fig 4) varies between 46° at low strain and 33° at peak strain for medium sand. Kirkpatrick and Belshaw [16] suggested the value of angle θ to be close to 60°. The following values of angles of rigid cones, θ, have been assumed in this investigation:

(a) Leighton Buzzard sand - 50°

(b) Kaolin Clay - 47°

The height and volume of the active element located between the apexes of the rigid cones, have been defined here as effective height, H_e, and effective volume, V_e (see Fig 4). It appears from the work of Drescher and Vardoulakis [19] that the applied stress is resisted only by this active element. In the case of uniform sand, the four particles shown in Fig 3 are defined as a deforming unit. For a given value of parameter β, the vertical distance (Y) between the centres of particles of a unit is determined and hence the number of units within the effective height H_e participating in the deformation process is estimated.

The observed values of parameter β can be determined at different stages of the test as follows:

The number of particle units, Np, involved in the deformation process is H_e/Y

From Fig 3. $Y = 2.d.\sin\beta_i$ (20)

where d = average diameter of sand particles
β_i = initial value of 'β', i.e. after consolidation but before loading.

Therefore $Np = H_e/2d\ \sin\beta_i$ (21)

After the soil has deformed by H_l (mm)
the deformation per particle unit is

$$H_l/Np \qquad (22)$$

From (21) and (22)
Deformation/particle unit $= H_l.2d\ \sin\beta_i/H_e$ (23)

d = average diameter of particles

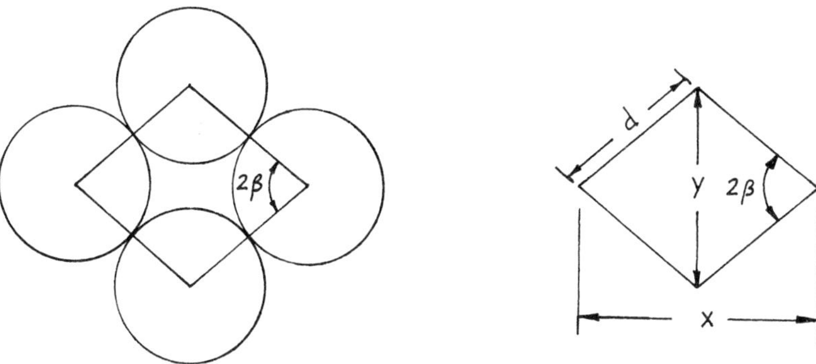

Fig 3. An Assumed Particle unit in a Uniform Sand Specimen

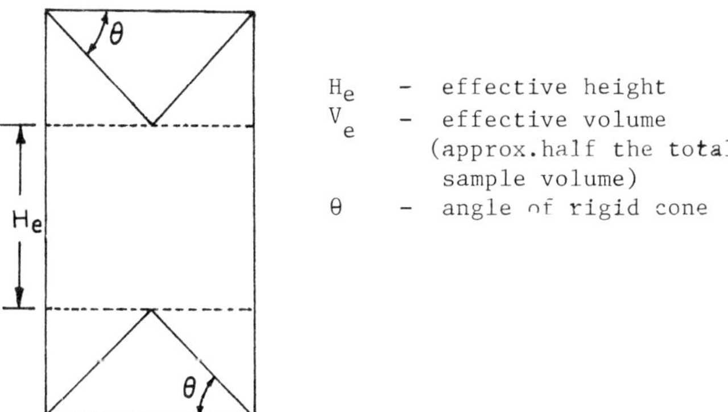

Fig 4. Development of rigid cones due to the use of fixed end platens

After deformation, $Y = (2d \sin\beta_i - H_1 .2d \sin\beta_i)/H_e$

$$= 2d \sin \quad (1- \frac{H_1}{H_e}) \qquad (24)$$

If β_1 denotes the value of parameter β after deformation, then

$$Y = 2d \sin\beta_1 \qquad (25)$$

From equations 24 and 25

$$\beta_1 = \sin^{-1} (\sin\beta_i(1 - \frac{H_1}{H_e})) \qquad (26)$$

Similarly at other stages of deformation, values of 'β' can be calculated

> In deriving equations 20 and 27 the assumption was made that the soil particles can roughly be represented by uniform spheres. In the case of clay soils, which have plate-like particles, the use of parameters β and η does not seem to be appropriate. However to test the application of equation (19), use is made of the approach described earlier.

A scanning electron micrograph revealed that the contacts in a specimen of kaolin, prepared by one-dimensional consolidation of slurry, are edge to face and end to face type. To simplify the calculations a triangular arrangement of particles, as shown in Fig 5(a) has been assumed.

Fig 5(b) shows a unit of kaolin particles assuming that the average length of kaolin particles is 2μm.

The effective height, H_e, can be determined by assuming the angle of rigid cone, θ, to be 47°.

Referring to Fig 5 (b)

$$Y = 2 \sin\beta_i/1000 \text{ mm} \qquad (27)$$

If the sample deformation is H_1 mm, then

$$\text{Deformation/particle unit} = H_1 .2\sin\beta_i/H_e .1000 \qquad (28)$$

After deformation, $Y = 2\sin\beta_i/1000 - H_1 .2 \sin\beta_i /H_e .1000$

$$= 2\sin\beta_i (1- \frac{H_1}{H_e})/1000 \qquad (29)$$

If β_1 is the value of parameter β after deformation, then

$$Y = 2\sin\beta_1/1000 \qquad (30)$$

From equations (29 and 30)

$$\beta_1 = \sin^{-1} (\sin\beta_i(1- \frac{H_1}{H_e})) \qquad (31)$$

similarly the values of β at other stages of the test can be determined.

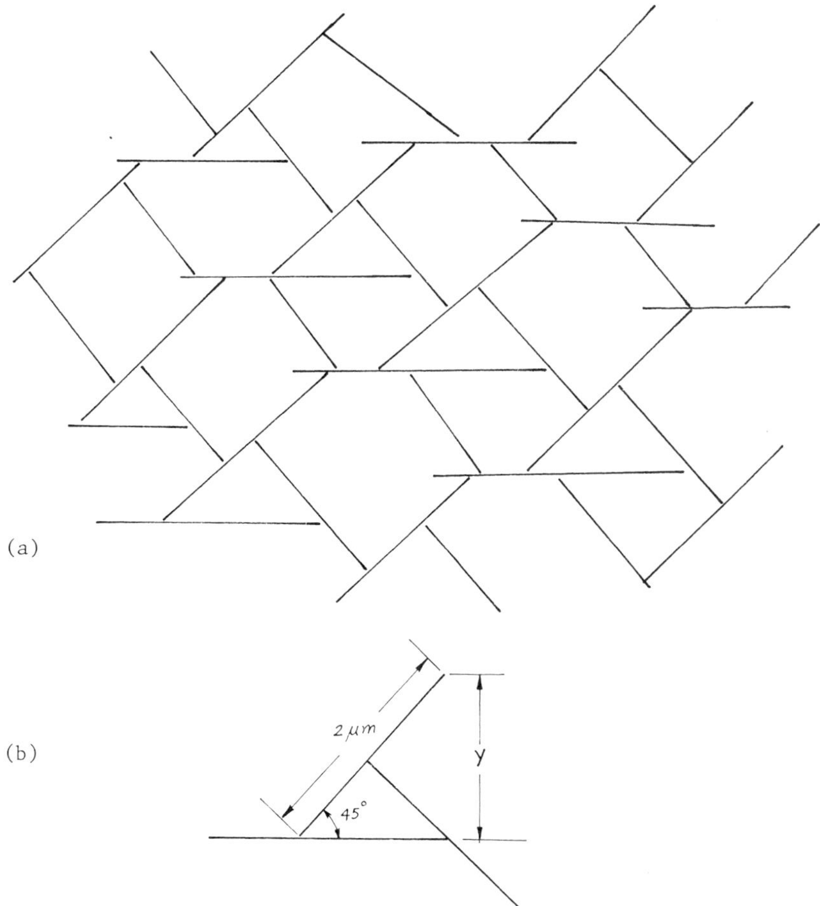

Fig 5. Assumed Structural Arrangement of Kaolin Particles

RESULTS AND DISCUSSION

Drained creep tests, at four stress levels and strain controlled tests were performed in a modified triaxial cell using specimens of uniform sand and kaolin clay. The first series of tests was performed at a constant temperature of 20° ± 1°C and the second under transient temperature conditions. In the second series, the samples were subjected to two cycles of temperature increase and two cycles of temperature decrease within a range of 9°C and 49°C (approximately). For full details of sample preparation, loading conditions, test equipment etc. see Virdi and Keedwell [1].

The creep tests were performed under stress levels ranging from 27% to 85%. Figs 6 & 7 show the data plotted as log $\dot{\varepsilon}_v$ versus time for both types of soils and log $\dot{\varepsilon}_l$ versus time for uniform sand. The strain rates used in equation (19) have been derived from these plots and it is quite obvious that change in volumetric or axial strain rate takes place while the temperature of the specimen is changing. Once the soil achieves equilibrium between temperature, stress and structure, there is very small further change. Similar findings are reported by Campanella [20] and Keedwell [10]

Strain-controlled tests were performed on uniform sand and kaolin clay. It was observed that the change in sample height due to variation in sample temperature caused the compression of the proving ring to vary and hence the deviator stress.

Comparison of β Values Calculated by Two Methods

Values of parameter β are listed in Table 1, that have been calculated by using:

(i) the rheological equation (equation 19)
(ii) the measured sample heights (equations 20 & 26)

As regards the parameters in equation (19), the following values were used:

$$
\begin{aligned}
k &= 1.3803 \times 10^{-22} && \text{Joules/mole - °K} \\
h &= 1.104 \times 10^{-35} && \text{Joules - min.} \\
R &= 8.31 && \text{Joules/mole - °K} \\
\Delta F &= 8.7885 \times 10^{4} && \text{Joules/mole}
\end{aligned}
$$

In accordance with a suggestion by Keedwell [10] it was assumed that for the creep samples analysed:

$$\tau.vf/2kT = 0.1 \text{ (approx.)}$$

In the case of strain-controlled tests $\tau.vf/2kT$ varies with the stress level as shown in Table 1.

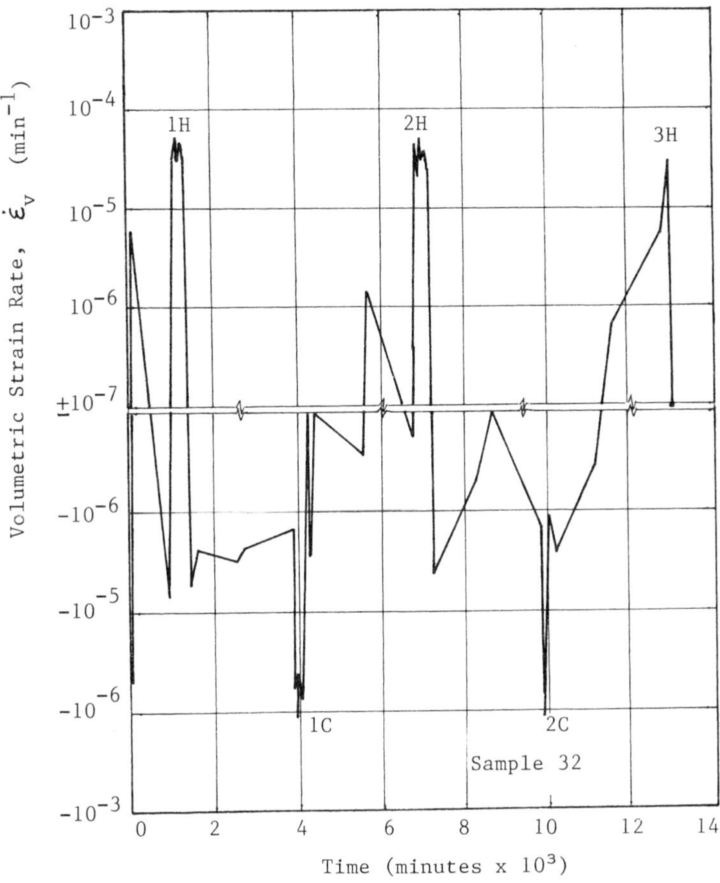

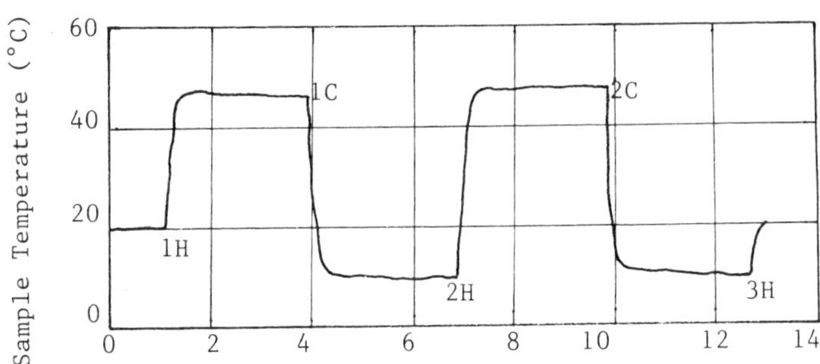

Fig 6. Uniform Sand, Drained Creep:
(a) Volumetric Strain Rate versus Time
(b) Sample Temperature versus Time

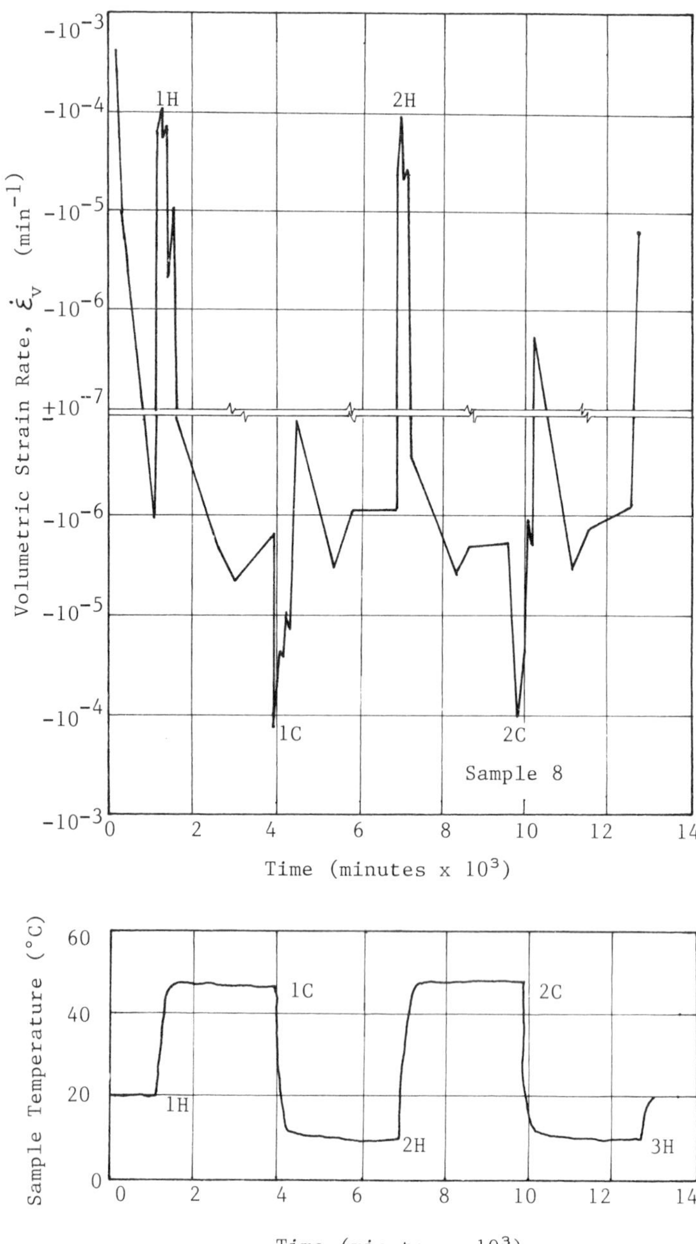

Fig 7. Remoulded Kaolin, Drained Creep Test:

(a) Volumetric Strain rate versus time
(b) Sample Temperature versus time

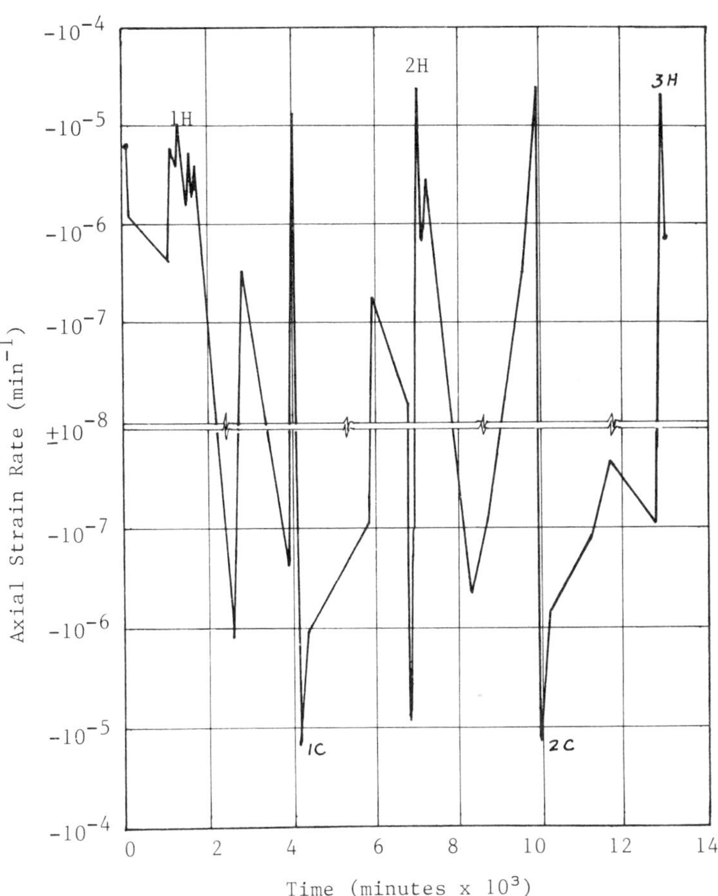

Fig 8. Uniform Sand, Drained creep test, Sample 32: Axial strain rate versus time

It was estimated that:

for uniform sand: $\lambda = 10^{-2}$ cm (approx) $s = 20$ cm^{-1} (approx)
for Kaolin clay : $\lambda = 10^{-6}$ cm (Approx) $s = 10^{5}$ cm^{-1} (approx)

In the case of calculations of β from sample heights it was assumed that after consolidation but before axial loading:

for uniform sand: $H_e = 30.845$ mm ; $\beta_i = 37^o$
for kaolin clay : $H_e = 20.228$ mm ; $\beta_i = 45^o$

Table 1

Comparison of the values of Parameter β obtained by using the Rate Process Theory and Observed Deformation

Time (min)	Temp (°C)	Vol.strain rate (min^{-1})	Axial Deformation (mm)	τ.vf/2kT	β-using rate process theory	β-using observed deformation
			Drained Creep - Uniform Sand			
1068	21	-10^{-6}	1.010	0.1	35.3	35.5
1518	49	-10^{-6}	1.066	0.1	35.3	35.3
5718	10.5	-10^{-7}	0.924	0.1	35.3	35.4
			Drained Creep - kaolin			
600	21	-10^{-6}	3.470	0.1	35.3	35.7
1378	49	-10^{-6}	3.692	0.1	35.3	35.2
5778	10.5	-10^{-7}	3.655	0.1	35.3	35.4
			Strain-Controlled Test - Uniform Sand			
260	20	-10^{-7}	0.027	0.1	35.3	36.9
1680	44.7	-10^{-7}	0.121	0.6	35.3	36.8
5730	11.75	-10^{-6}	0.401	2.4	35.3	36.4

Axial Strain Rate Data

Fig.8 shows the axial strain rate plotted against time for a specimen of uniform sand tested under drained creep conditions. The strain rates derived from this plot are much less than the strain rates predicted by equation (13). It is considered that these results may be due to temperature induced changes in the height of the "rigid cones", which of course cannot be predicted by equation (13), as it relates to the "structural viscosity" effects occuring in the active element of the samples.

CONCLUSIONS

1. A rheological equation has been developed which combines the rate process theory and the particulate mechanics approach.

2. This equation appears to offer a plausible explanation of the effects of temperature variation on the volumetric strain rates measured in creep and strain controlled tests carried out on specimens of uniform sand and kaolin.

3. Measurements of axial strain may have been affected by the absence of lubricated ends, as the axial strain rates were much less than those predicted by equation (13).

4. Ideally lubricated ends should be used and the axial strain rate of the specimen measured by an instrument attached directly to the specimen inside the triaxial cell. A careful calibration for the effect of temperature on any such instruments would then be required.

REFERENCES

1. Virdi S P S and Keedwell M J, "Some observed effects of temperature variation on soil behaviour,"

2. Glasstone S, Laidler K and Eyring H, "The theory of rate process", McGraw Hill Book Company, New York, 1941.

3. Murayama S. and Shibata T "Rheological properties of clays" procl 5th Int.Conf.Soil Mech. and F.E., 1961, pp 269-273.

4. Mitchell J K, "Shearing resistance of soils as a rate of process," Journal of the Soil Mech. and Foundations Div., Proc. ASCE, 1964, Vol 90, No.SMI, pp 29-61.

5. Christensen R W and Wu T H., "Analysis of clay deformation as a rate process" Journal of the Soil Mech and Foundations Div., Proc. ASCE, 1964, Vol 90, No SM6, pp 125-157.

6. Andersland O B, and Akili W "Stress effect on creep rates of a frozen clay soil", Geotechnique, 1967, Vol 17, pp 27-39.

7. Mitchell J K, Campanella R G, and Singh A "Soil creep as a rate process", Journal of the Soil Mech. and Foundations Div., Proc. ASCE, 1968, vol 94, SMI, pp 231-253.

8. Andersland O B and Douglas A G "Soil deformation rates and activation energies", Geotechnique, 1970, Vol 20, pp 1-16.

9. Erol O., Demirel T and Lohnes R A "Rate process theory applied to soft clays", Int. sym.on soft clays, Bangkok, Thailand, 1977, pp 117-132.

10. Keedwell M J "Rheology and the anlaysis of in-situ soil deformations", thesis submitted to C N A A for the award of degree of Doctor of Philosophy, 1978.

11 Virdi, S P S "Rheology of soils with special reference to temperature effects", thesis submitted to C N AA for the award of degree of Doctor of Philosophy, 1984.

12. Campanella R G and Mitchell J K, "Influence of temperature variations on soil behaviour" Journal of the Soil Mech. and Foundations Div., Proc.ASCE, Vol 94, No SM3, pp 709-734.

13. Herrin M and Jones G "Behaviour of bituminous materials from the view point of absolute rate theory," Proceedings Association of Asphalt Paving Technologists. vol 32, Ann Arbor, Mich.1963.

14. Rowe P W "The stress dilatancy relation for static equilibrium of an assembly of particles in contact." Proc. Royal Society, 1962, A269, pp 500-527.

15. Rowe P W and Barden L., "Importance of free ends in triaxial testing", Journal of the Soil Mech. and Foundations Div., Proc.ASCE, 1964, Vol 90, SMI, pp 1-27.

16. Kirkpatrick W M and Belshaw D J, " On the Interpretation of the triaxial test," Geotechnique, 1968, Vol 18, pp 336-350.

17. Lee K L "End restraint effects on undrained static triaxial strength of sand," Journal of the Geotech. Eng.Div., Proc.ASCE, 1978, Vol 104, No GT6, pp 687-704.

18. Deman F, "Achsesymtrische spannungs-und verformungsfelder in trockenem sand", Dissertation, Universitat Karlsruhe, Veroffentlichungen IBF, No 62, 1975.

19. Drescher A and Vardoulakis I, "Geometric softening in triaxial tests on granular material," Geotechnique 1982, Vol 32, No 4, pp 291-303.

20. Campanella R G "Effect of temperature and stress on the time deformation behaviour of saturated clay.", Thesis presented to University of California at Berkeley, for the award of degree of Doctor of Philosophy.

21. Barden L "A quantitative treatment of the deformation behaviour of granular material in terms of particulate mechanics", Proc. Int.Conf on Struct. Solid Mech. and Eng.Des., Univ. of Southampton 1969.